The Schelling–Eschenmayer Controversy, 1801

New Perspectives in Ontology
Series Editors: Peter Gratton, Southeastern Louisiana University, and Sean J. McGrath, Memorial University of Newfoundland, Canada

Publishes the best new work on the question of being and the history of metaphysics

After the linguistic and structuralist turn of the twentieth century, a renaissance in metaphysics and ontology is occurring. Following in the wake of speculative realism and new materialism, this series aims to build on this renewed interest in perennial metaphysical questions, while opening up avenues of investigation long assumed to be closed. Working within the Continental tradition without being confined by it, the books in this series will move beyond the linguistic turn and rethink the oldest questions in a contemporary context. They will challenge old prejudices while drawing upon the speculative turn in post-Heideggerian ontology, the philosophy of nature and the philosophy of religion.

Editorial Advisory Board
Thomas J. J. Altizer, Maurizio Farraris, Paul Franks, Iain Hamilton Grant, Garth Green, Adrian Johnston, Catherine Malabou, Jeff Malpas, Marie-Eve Morin, Jeffrey Reid, Susan Ruddick, Michael Schulz, Hasana Sharp, Alison Stone, Peter Trawny, Uwe Voigt, Jason Wirth, Günter Zöller

Books available
The Political Theology of Schelling, Saitya Brata Das
Continental Realism and its Discontents, edited by Marie-Eve Morin
The Contingency of Necessity: Reason and God as Matters of Fact, Tyler Tritten
The Problem of Nature in Hegel's Final System, Wes Furlotte
Schelling's Naturalism: Motion, Space and the Volition of Thought, Ben Woodard
Thinking Nature: An Essay in Negative Ecology, Sean J. McGrath
Heidegger's Ontology of Events, James Bahoh
The Political Theology of Kierkegaard, Saitya Brata Das
The Schelling–Eschenmayer Controversy, 1801: Nature and Identity, Benjamin Berger and Daniel Whistler

Books forthcoming
The Late Schelling and the End of Christianity, Sean J. McGrath
Schelling's Ontology of Powers, Charlotte Alderwick
Hölderlin's Philosophy of Nature, edited by Rochelle Tobias
Affect and Attention After Deleuze and Whitehead: Ecological Attunement, Russell J. Duvernoy

www.edinburghuniversitypress.com/series/epnpio

The Schelling–Eschenmayer Controversy, 1801

Nature and Identity

BENJAMIN BERGER AND
DANIEL WHISTLER

Translations by Judith Kahl and Daniel Whistler

EDINBURGH
University Press

Edinburgh University Press is one of the leading university presses in the UK. We publish academic books and journals in our selected subject areas across the humanities and social sciences, combining cutting-edge scholarship with high editorial and production values to produce academic works of lasting importance. For more information visit our website: edinburghuniversitypress.com

© Benjamin Berger and Daniel Whistler, 2020, 2022
English translations © Judith Kahl and Daniel Whistler, 2020, 2022

Edinburgh University Press Ltd
The Tun – Holyrood Road
12(2f) Jackson's Entry
Edinburgh EH8 8PJ

First published in hardback by Edinburgh University Press 2020

Typeset in 11/13 Adobe Garamond by
Servis Filmsetting Ltd, Stockport, Cheshire

A CIP record for this book is available from the British Library

ISBN 978 1 4744 3439 3 (hardback)
ISBN 978 1 4744 3440 9 (paperback)
ISBN 978 1 4744 3441 6 (webready PDF)
ISBN 978 1 4744 3442 3 (epub)

The right of Benjamin Berger and Daniel Whistler to be identified as the author of this work has been asserted in accordance with the Copyright, Designs and Patents Act 1988, and the Copyright and Related Rights Regulations 2003 (SI No. 2498).

Contents

Preface vii
Translators' Note xii
Abbreviations xv

Introduction: Schelling and Eschenmayer in 1801 1

Part I Texts

A. C. A. Eschenmayer, *Spontaneity = World Soul, or the Highest Principle of Philosophy of Nature* 17
F. W. J. Schelling, *On the True Concept of Philosophy of Nature and the Correct Way of Solving its Problems* 46

Part II Commentaries

1 Quality 65
2 Potency 94
3 Identity 117
4 Drive 139
5 Abstraction 162

Part III Appendices

1 A. C. A. Eschenmayer and F. W. J. Schelling, *Correspondence, 1799–1801* 187
2 A. C. A. Eschenmayer, *Principles of Nature-Metaphysics Applied to Chemical and Medical Subjects* [Extracts] 199

3 A. C. A. Eschenmayer, *Deduction of the Living Organism* [Extracts] 205
4 A. C. A. Eschenmayer, *Review of F. W. J. Schelling's* First Outline of a System of Philosophy of Nature *and* Introduction to his Outline 215

Notes 225
Bibliography 261
Index 268

Preface

Adam Carl August von Eschenmayer is not a well-known figure in the history of philosophy. Even among scholars working on the German Idealist tradition, he tends not to be valued as a major philosopher in his own right; indeed, it would take a serious stretch of the imagination to suggest that Eschenmayer was one of the great post-Kantian thinkers, on a par with J. G. Fichte, F. W. J. Schelling, and G. W. F. Hegel. He was, however, one of Schelling's most perceptive and provocative critics during the first decade of the nineteenth century. From 1797 to (at least) 1812, Eschenmayer and Schelling repeatedly influenced and contested one another's work. Hence, Marquet describes Eschenmayer as a 'curious interlocutor who reappears at each important turn in [Schelling's] thought',[1] and Roux remarks that Eschenmayer was both Schelling's 'opponent' and 'companion of choice'.[2] Even the anglophone literature has come to acknowledge in passing the importance of Eschenmayer's provocations: Vater names him as a key 'collaborator' of Schelling's;[3] Grant devotes several pages to him in *Philosophies of Nature after Schelling*;[4] Zammito has recently written of his 'crucial contribution to the emergence of philosophy of nature';[5] Förster's critique of Schelling in *The Twenty-Five Years of Philosophy* acknowledges his importance;[6] and Lauer and Wirth chart his role in the genesis of Schelling's account of reason and personality.[7]

It is customary to speak of three major controversies between Eschenmayer and Schelling:[8]

1. An exchange in January 1801 to be located in the pages of Schelling's own *Journal of Speculative Physics*, comprising Eschenmayer's first critical review of Schelling's early philosophy of nature, *Spontaneity = World Soul*, and Schelling's editorial response, *On the True Concept of Philosophy*

of Nature. Appearing together, these texts contain Eschenmayer's extensive critique of Schelling's early work and Schelling's own defence that ambivalently appropriates many of Eschenmayer's central concepts and concerns, while also announcing the advent of his new form of metaphysics that was to be published in the May 1801 issue of the same journal as the *Presentation of my System of Philosophy*.
2. A fierce debate in 1803–4 over the respective capacities of philosophy and faith to explain the emergence of difference from identity, undertaken not just in their correspondence but also in Eschenmayer's *Philosophy in its Transition to Non-Philosophy* and Schelling's notorious response, *Philosophy and Religion*.
3. A series of letters published in the wake of Schelling's 1809 *Investigations into the Essence of Human Freedom*, in which the two argue over the place of humanity in nature, the limits of reason, and how to properly conceive God's personality.

Until recently, discussions of the Eschenmayer–Schelling relationship have focused upon the latter two controversies; this volume, by contrast, aims to introduce Eschenmayer's earlier work to an anglophone audience by means of his *1801* debate with Schelling. What follows, then, is the first volume in any language devoted exclusively to the 1801 controversy, and it includes the first English translations of any of Eschenmayer's work. We seek to demonstrate the significance of this controversy both for the evolution of the discipline of philosophy of nature and for the development of absolute idealism more generally in the early years of the nineteenth century.

However, as will become clear in the following, we do not think that the 1801 controversy with Eschenmayer is of merely historical interest. For the stakes of this debate concern profoundly important questions about the aims, importance and proper method of speculative thought itself. Can we philosophise about nature *as such*, or must the philosophy of nature always be derived from prior reflections upon the nature of mind and knowledge? How might one philosophise from the perspective of anything other than one's own consciousness? Are the natural qualities we perceive in ordinary experience merely *apparent*, or do they have an irreducible reality? Are the most general categories of reality – matter, life, mind – essentially *different* from one another? Or are they 'identical' in some way? These are some of the questions raised in the debate between Eschenmayer and Schelling – questions that we believe continue to be central to any philosophy of nature worthy of the name. Thus, in addition to making the case that the 1801 controversy with Eschenmayer is important for an understanding of the history of German Idealism, this volume also seeks to contribute to contemporary discussions about speculation and the philosophy of nature.

In order to achieve these ends, the volume is structured as follows. After a historical introduction contextualising the controversy, Part I consists of complete English translations of the two central texts of the 1801 controversy: Eschenmayer's *Spontaneity = World Soul* and Schelling's response, *On the True Concept of Philosophy of Nature*. Both of these texts are explicitly presented as commentaries on Schelling's earlier 1799 *First Outline of the System of Philosophy of Nature*, but in fact quickly proceed to exhibit the essential, twofold difference between Eschenmayer's and Schelling's views in January of 1801: while Eschenmayer develops a broadly Fichtean conception of nature's determinacy as produced by the I and understands that determinacy to be rationally comprehensible in terms of various proportions of two forces, Schelling refuses to collapse the philosophy of nature into transcendental idealism and criticises the reduction of qualities to proportions of nature's forces.

Part II then contains five commentaries on central themes, problems and arguments that emerge from the 1801 controversy as they impact German Idealist metaphysics. The five commentaries concern, in turn, the philosophical construction of material qualities in nature; the algebraic concepts of 'potency' and 'potentiation'; the metaphysical model of identity and difference at stake in Schelling's thought of 1801, in contrast to competing Fichtean and Hegelian models; Eschenmayer's Fichtean concept of drive and its implications for the philosophy of nature; and, finally, Schelling's conception of abstraction and its methodological role in speculative thinking. January 1801 was a significant moment in Schelling's development, standing, as it does, on the precipice of his entry into his system of identity, inaugurated by the publication a few months later of his *Presentation of my System of Philosophy*, and much of the commentary will be spent unfolding the significance of the controversy for the evolution of Schelling's own philosophy within this extraordinarily brief period. By focusing on the concepts of quality, potency, identity, drive and abstraction, our commentary seeks to delineate 'the nature-philosophical roots of [Schelling's] identity philosophy'.[9]

In the final part of the volume, four appendices are provided to aid the reader in understanding Eschenmayer's early philosophy in particular: the first reproduces Eschenmayer and Schelling's extant correspondence between 1799 and 1801, including Eschenmayer's substantial and important response to the *Presentation of my System of Philosophy* in summer 1801, which the editors of the ongoing critical edition to Schelling's works have labelled 'the most philosophically significant letter' either sent or received by Schelling during those years.[10] The second and third appendices contain extracts from some of Eschenmayer's other early treatises in philosophy of nature: the 1797 *Principles of Nature-Metaphysics* and the 1799 *Deduction of the Living Organism*. The fourth and final appendix reproduces in full Eschenmayer's anonymous April 1801 review of Schelling's *First Outline* and *Introduction to the Outline*, and it should be read as his final word on the debate with Schelling over the proper status, method and content of philosophy of nature.

*

As is often remarked, English-language Schelling scholarship is currently enjoying a time of plenty: not only has Schelling never had it so good in English, but it is highly unlikely he ever will again. We have evidently benefited enormously from the fruits of this work; indeed, it was Iain Grant's remark a few years ago that a robust account of Schellingian metaphysics rests on the conversion of quantities into qualities that set in chain the reflections that follow.

Yet one limitation to some recent anglophone Schelling scholarship has been its obsession with telling stories – stories of Schelling's development over the decades as well as stories of his influence on and applicability to later philosophies and problems. Narrative is a very Schellingian device, of course, and one that illuminates a great deal about what philosophy in fact is, but we do not believe that diachronic questions – that is, questions of change and continuity – are the only interesting questions to ask of Schelling. Indeed, the telling of stories can, at times, obscure sustained reconstructions of particular texts or sets of texts in Schelling's corpus. Synchronic analyses are needed as well, and we hope the focus we strive to achieve in parts of this volume constitutes a very small gesture towards this end.

This volume was made possible by the support of Sean McGrath, Peter Gratton and Carol Macdonald. Graham Weatherall's and Matic Kastelec's suggestions on draft translations were invaluable, and Richard Gaskin improved the translation of the Latin in *Spontaneity = World Soul* no end. The University of Liverpool workshop on *Philosophies of Nature*, funded by the British Academy, provided us with the occasion to begin our sustained discussion of Eschenmayer, and the conversations that took place at that workshop – with more people than we can name here – proved to be enormously helpful. Subsequent discussions with Danielle Macbeth, who read and commented on a draft of Chapter 2, were also indispensable. Funding from the Alexander von Humboldt Foundation and the EURIAS scheme, via the Collegium de Lyon, provided an opportunity to develop the work in the first place. Most of all, any virtue in what follows is owing to Grace Whistler and Carmen De Schryver.

An earlier version of the translation of Schelling's *On the True Concept of Philosophy of Nature*, along with an early variant of Chapter 5, appeared in *Pli* 26 (2014). We are grateful to the editors for permission to reuse them here.

Translators' Note

The texts translated in this volume are taken from the following German editions:

Spontaneity = World Soul
 A. C. A. Eschenmayer. 'Spontaneität = Weltseele, oder das höchste Prinzip der Naturphilosophie'. *Zeitschrift für speculative Physik* 2.1 (January 1801), ed. F. W. J. Schelling: 3–68.

On the True Concept of Philosophy of Nature
 F. W. J. Schelling. 'Anhang zu dem Aufsatz der Herrn Eschenmayer betreffend den wahren Begriff der Naturphilosophie, und die richtige Art ihre Probleme aufzulösen'. In *Historisch-Kritische Ausgabe*, volume I/10: *Schriften 1801*, ed. Manfred Durner. Stuttgart: Frommann-Holzboog, 2009. 85–106.

Schelling–Eschenmayer Correspondence, 1799–1801
 From F. W. J. Schelling, *Historisch-Kritische Ausgabe*, volume III/1: *Briefwechsel 1786–1799*, ed. Irmgard Möller and Walter Schieche. Stuttgart: Frommann-Holzboog, 2001, and volume III/2: *Briefwechsel 1800–1802*, ed. Thomas Kissner, Walter Schieche and Alois Wieshuber, Stuttgart: Frommann-Holzboog, 2010.

Principles of Nature-Metaphysics Applied to Chemical and Medical Subjects
 A. C. A. Eschenmayer. *Sätze aus der Natur-Metaphysik, auf chemische und medicinische Gegenstände angewendt*. Tübingen, 1797.

Deduction of the Living Organism
 A. C. A. Eschenmayer. 'Dedukzion des lebenden Organism'. In A. Röschlaub (ed.), *Magazin zur Vervollkommnung der theoretischen und praktischen Heilkunde* 2.3 (Frankfurt, 1799): 327–90.

Review of Schelling's First Outline *and* Introduction to the Outline
A. C. A. Eschenmayer (unattributed). 'Rezension: F. W. J. Schelling, *Erster Entwurf eines Systems der Naturphilosophie* und *Einleitung zu seinem Entwurf eines Systems der Naturphilosophie*'. *Litteratur-Zeitung* 67/68 (Erlangen, 7/8 April 1801): 529–40.

Numbers in square brackets inserted into the translations indicate corresponding page numbers in the above German editions. Notes by the author or (on one occasion) by the original editor of the text are denoted by an asterisk (*) and are placed at the bottom of the page; our own notes are indicated by an Arabic numeral and follow at the end of the volume. Where possible, we have made use of the helpful and informative notes provided by the editors in the corresponding volumes of the *Historisch-Kritische Ausgabe*.

Since many of these texts are framed as critical readings and partial defences of Schelling's *First Outline of the System of the Philosophy of Nature*, we have, as far as possible, followed Keith R. Peterson's translation choices. Whenever these texts are quoted by Eschenmayer or Schelling, we follow Peterson's translation. Quotations from Schelling's *System of Transcendental Idealism* are taken from Heath's translation; and we are grateful to Iain Hamilton Grant for making available to us his soon-to-be published translation of Schelling's *Universal Deduction of the Dynamic Process*.

Following Peterson, we translate the German *die Aktion* (or *Akzion*, as Eschenmayer occasionally spells it) by the non-standard 'actant'. Here is Peterson's justification for this choice: 'Schelling uses the latinate term *Aktion*. In an attempt to mirror the foreignness of the term in German, in most cases I have chosen to translate "actant" rather than "actor" or "action" ... The "dynamic atom" that Schelling designates by *Aktion* is best understood as an individual "actant", a "natural monad" or "simple productivity"' (p. 244). Also following Peterson, we translate *hemmen* as 'to inhibit' and *der Kunsttrieb* as 'technical drive'. One major departure from Peterson is in our translation of *die spezifische Beschaffenheit* as 'specific composition', rather than 'specific constitution', to emphasise to today's ears its provenance from the study of chemistry, which Eschenmayer insists upon.

A unique translation issue in respect to this set of texts concerns the word *das Verhältnis*. Usually translated as 'relation', it also has the more precise meanings of 'proportion' and 'ratio', which are particularly important in Eschenmayer's attempted mathematicisation of the philosophy of nature. Often in Eschenmayer's text, the reader can trace a lexical evolution in the argument from vaguer 'qualitative' uses of *Verhältnis*, when repeating the language of the scientific inquiry under explanation (such as, in chemistry, the relation of two compounds), to more precise employments that designate the specific quantitative ratio to which such initially posited relations are ultimately reducible. To reflect this dialectic, we have translated *das Verhältnis* as 'relation', 'proportion' or 'ratio', depending on context. On the other hand, *das Gleichgewicht* and *das Übergewicht* are always translated according to their scientific senses of 'equilibrium' and 'preponderance'. *Die Grade* (degree) poses another problem: Eschenmayer and, subsequently, Schelling place much emphasis on this concept and often use the abstract noun *die Gradation* and the adverb *gradual*. Unfortunately, no parallel constructions are available for 'degree' in common English usage; hence, we have often used phrases such as 'a matter of degree' and 'by degrees' as substitutes.

Otherwise, any translation difficulties are consistent with other philosophical texts of the time. For example, while neither Eschenmayer nor Schelling use *aufheben* in anything like a Hegelian manner, both employ it distinctively – Eschenmayer to mean 'to overcome' and Schelling to mean 'to cancel out' or 'to annul'.

Abbreviations

The following abbreviations will be used in citations:

FG J. G. Fichte. *Gesamtausgabe*, ed. the Bayerischen Akademie der Wissenschaften. Stuttgart: Frommann-Holboog, 1971–.

Foundations J. G. Fichte. 'Foundations of the Entire Science of Knowledge'. In *The Science of Knowledge*, ed. and trans. Peter Heath and John Lachs. Cambridge: Cambridge University Press, 1982. 89–287.

FSW J. G. Fichte. *Sämmtliche Werke*, 11 vols, ed. I. H. Fichte. Berlin: Veit, 1845–6.

Harris and Heath F. W. J. Schelling. *Ideas for a Philosophy of Nature*, trans. Errol E. Harris and Peter Heath. Cambridge: Cambridge University Press, 1988.

Heath F. W. J. Schelling. *System of Transcendental Idealism*, trans. Peter Heath. Charlottesville: University of Virginia Press, 1978.

HKA F. W. J. Schelling. *Historisch-Kritische Ausgabe*, 3 series, currently 24 vols, ed. the Schelling-Kommission of the Bayerischen Akademie der Wissenschaften. Stuttgart: Frommann-Holzboog, 1976–.

HW G. W. F. Hegel. *Werke in 20 Bänden*. Frankfurt am Main: Suhrkamp Verlag, 1970.

KGS Immanuel Kant. *Gesammelte Schriften*, 29 vols, ed. the Königlich Preußische Akademie der Wissenschaften. Berlin: de Gruyter, 1900–.

MF Immanuel Kant. *Metaphysical Foundations of Natural Science*. In Kant, *Philosophy of Material Nature*, trans.

	James W. Ellington. Indianapolis: Hackett Publishing Company, 1985. 3–134.
Peterson	F. W. J. Schelling. *First Outline of the System of the Philosophy of Nature* and *Introduction to the Outline of the Philosophy of Nature*, trans. Keith R. Peterson. Albany: SUNY Press, 2004.
Rupture	J. G. Fichte and F. W. J. Schelling. *The Philosophical Rupture between Fichte and Schelling*, ed. and trans. Michael G. Vater and David W. Wood. Albany: SUNY Press, 2012.
SSW	F. W. J. Schelling. *Sämmtliche Werke*, 14 vols, ed. K. F. A. Schelling. Stuttgart: Cotta, 1856–61. [Cited when *HKA* volumes are not currently available – that is, for writings from around 1802 onwards.]

All translations are our own when the citation is solely to a non-English-language source.

Introduction: Schelling and Eschenmayer in 1801

A. C. A. Eschenmayer (1768–1852) and F. W. J. Schelling (1775–1854) were born fairly close to one another in neighbouring towns west of Stuttgart (Neuenbürg and Leonberg), and, during the mid-1790s, both attended the University of Tübingen (although in different faculties); yet, the first recorded contact between them dates from 1797, in a now-lost letter in which Eschenmayer sent Schelling a copy of his newly completed dissertation on the philosophy of nature. It is to this dissertation that Schelling refers in his first published reference to Eschenmayer at the end of the 1797 *Ideas for a Philosophy of Nature*. Over the subsequent two years, Eschenmayer's and Schelling's thought evolved considerably, and, in 1799, Schelling took up correspondence with Eschenmayer once more to request an essay for publication in his planned *Journal for Speculative Physics*. In September 1800, Schelling did finally receive something from Eschenmayer: a sixty-eight-page critique of Schelling's own *First Outline of a System of the Philosophy of Nature*. It appeared in January 1801 and was immediately followed by a substantial 'appendix' by the editor – that is, Schelling – under the title *Appendix to Eschenmayer's Essay concerning the True Concept of Philosophy of Nature and the Correct Way of Solving its Problems*.[1] Schelling himself presented this appendix to Eschenmayer in correspondence as a means 'to come to a complete understanding' with him, although there is little reason to believe that Schelling was in fact optimistic about their coming to any substantive philosophical agreement. Indeed, despite Schelling's positive allusions to Eschenmayer in the 1801 *Presentation of my System of Philosophy* and the 1802 dialogue, *On the Absolute System of Identity*, the controversy of 1801 only led the two philosophers to commit more fully to their fundamental disagreements, as evidenced by Eschenmayer's subsequent review of both the *First Outline* and the *Introduction to the Outline*, as well as his biting refutation of the *Presentation* in a letter sent to Schelling in summer 1801 – a letter that put an end to their correspondence for three years.

These are the basic historical details that gave rise to one of the more important intellectual disputes in German Idealism and the philosophy of nature. The task of this introduction is to explain the philosophical significance of these critical reviews, treatises and letters – that is, to explain why the 1801 controversy ought to intrigue anyone interested in the philosophy of nature, the development of post-Kantian Idealism, and the very possibility of speculative thinking. To begin, it is helpful to briefly consider Eschenmayer's place in the Idealist tradition.

Eschenmayer's early philosophy of nature

Even when Eschenmayer is portrayed as 'a minor figure', he is rightly understood, by some interpreters, to have decisively 'influenced the speculative thought of the time'.[2] This impression of his relative importance on German philosophical developments after Kant has recently been furthered by the surge of interest in the nature-philosophical strands of German Idealism: Zammito, for example, writes of Eschenmayer's role in 'building' philosophy of nature 'into a movement'.[3] And Eschenmayer's significance was not lost on his contemporaries: as we shall see, Schelling himself praises him as 'after Kant . . . the first to secure the grounds for a dynamic physics'[4] – that is, the first philosopher to have appreciated the significance of the Dynamics section of Kant's *Metaphysical Foundations of Natural Science* for a general metaphysical description of nature, or 'nature-metaphysics' as Eschenmayer calls this discipline in his first German work. Moreover, this assessment was not unique to Schelling. In a letter to Goethe, A. W. Schlegel writes of Eschenmayer that 'there is perhaps no other physician in Germany at the moment who combines so much physics and philosophy with his own science';[5] Novalis and Ritter read and annotated his early writings on nature;[6] and Fichte praised his critical reviews of Schelling.[7]

Eschenmayer's formative years were spent in the Karlsschule in Stuttgart between 1784 and 1790, where he received his training in medicine.[8] Among his teachers was Carl Friedrich Kielmeyer, the influential biologist and philosopher of nature. Alongside Kant and Fichte – and even more so than Platner and Brown, whose theories of medicine he studied carefully at that period – Kielmeyer stands as one of the more considerable influences on the early Eschenmayer. In 1832, looking back on his intellectual development, he writes:

> The first lasting sense for natural science I derived from the penetrating lectures of State Counsellor Kielmeyer ... From him I derived the fundamental idea of the continually varying proportions of the three fundamental life-forces in living nature, from plants to man ... His lectures caught me at an age that was most receptive for the ingenious formulation of analogies and of induction.[9]

Nevertheless, Eschenmayer did not devote his life to the 'pure theory' of philosophy of nature, but – until 1811 – maintained a medical practice in Kirchheim. The relation between medicine and philosophy becomes increasingly important for his nature-philosophical project, as can be seen in the Preface to the 1799 *Deduction of the Living Organism* (translated in Appendix 3 below), which he addresses to physicians who lack any theoretical understanding of the very subject of their professional activity – the organism. As Eschenmayer himself puts it, 'My intention is merely to make medicine philosophical' by 'secur[ing] the physician's object a priori'.[10] The task of the essay, then, is 'to provide a foundation for medicine through a transcendental deduction' of life itself.[11] The aim of aiding medical practitioners with a theoretical supplement provides one central motivation for Eschenmayer's attempts at philosophy of nature. It is in this way that, as Jantzen has argued,[12] 'philosophy and medicine come together' in his writings.

Given his attempt to provide medicine with a transcendental grounding, it is no wonder that Kant's *Metaphysical Foundations of Natural Science* plays a particularly influential role for the early Eschenmayer. His first three works of philosophy of nature or 'nature-metaphysics' – the 1796 Tübingen dissertation, the 1797 German adaptation of the dissertation, *Principles of Nature-Metaphysics Applied to Chemical and Medical Subjects*, and the 1798 treatise, *An Attempt to Develop the Laws of Magnetic Phenomena A Priori from the Principles of Nature-Metaphysics* – seek to illuminate the magnetic, electrical, chemical and biological properties of natural objects by grounding them upon a Kantian account of the dynamic construction of matter. Ziche summarises Kant's influence as follows:

> Eschenmayer attempted to generalise the construction of matter from two opposed forces – that is, attraction and repulsion – as Kant had developed in his *Metaphysical Foundations*, drawing on the significance this force-dualism had for Kant, to turn it into a programme for a general metaphysics of nature, and to use this model to solve concrete individual problems in the philosophy of nature and natural science.[13]

Fichte is the third great influence on Eschenmayerian philosophy of nature, and – while he may well be referred to in Eschenmayer's first treatises – it is in 1799, with the publication of his *Deduction of the Living*

Organism, 'the highpoint of Eschenmayer's transcendental-philosophical engagement',[14] that Eschenmayer's Fichtean commitments become most explicit. Whereas the *Principles* seeks to rationally ground the empirical sciences of chemistry and medicine on the basis of Kant's dynamic construction of matter, the *Deduction of the Living Organism* seeks to derive the existence of the human organism from the sheer fact of the mental activity of the I. Thus, as Marchetto argues, the development from the *Principles* to the *Deduction* constitutes a shift in Eschenmayer's attention from the a priori *concepts* required for an empirical understanding of qualitative determinacy to the 'necessary conditions of *self-consciousness*' which ground the investigation of the living organism.[15] Wiesing is therefore entirely correct in describing Eschenmayer during these years as 'a Fichtean among physicians'.[16] Moreover, it is, broadly speaking, this approach to the philosophy of nature that continues to motivate Eschenmayer's work in 1801 with the publication of the text at the centre of his controversy with Schelling, *Spontaneity = World Soul*; indeed, this text draws expressly on Eschenmayer's Fichtean derivation of life in order to criticise Schelling's turn away from transcendental philosophy.

Eschenmayer's philosophical development does not stop there. Far from it, in fact. Jantzen discerns four major periods in Eschenmayer's thought: an initial period of 'transcendental philosophy provoked by Kant and in dialogue with Schelling' from 1796 to 1801; a second period of 'critique of philosophy and "transition to non-philosophy"' from 1803 to 1806 – the period which corresponds to Eschenmayer and Schelling's second great controversy; a third period of 'university teaching' from 1811 to 1816; and a final period in which Eschenmayer's interests turn to 'animal magnetism and parapsychology' from 1816 to 1838.[17] Hence, just like Schelling, Eschenmayer continues to evolve and experiment with new viewpoints throughout his life; just like Schelling, these changes are often split into a series of different phases or systems; and, just like Schelling, he is criticised for this mutability. For example, the Left Hegelian David Friedrich Strauss, who had been a student of Eschenmayer's in the 1840s, speaks of him as an 'old fantasist and dilettante, lacking critical sense and having a mania for systems'.[18]

Our concern in this volume, however, is with the first stage of Eschenmayer's thought, his philosophy of nature, especially as presented in 1801. It is worth stressing that Schelling was a privileged dialogue-partner for Eschenmayer throughout this early period. Looking back at his earliest work from the vantage point of 1852, Eschenmayer wrote that it was 'as contemporary, admirer and friend of Schelling, [that] I began my research into philosophy of nature'.[19] Schelling, moreover, was equally admiring of Eschenmayer: prior to the controversy of 1801, he writes of

Eschenmayer's dissertation as 'an excellent academic work, which deserves to become better known than such writings normally are',[20] and he refers the reader of his *On the World Soul* to Eschenmayer's proof 'derived from first principles' that 'establishes a priori a law of the relationship between electrical currents'.[21] After the controversy of January 1801, Schelling is even more explicit in stating how much Eschenmayer's early work had influenced him, particularly regarding the use of algebraic notation in the philosophy of nature: the Preface to the 1801 *Presentation* makes much of its formal dependence on Eschenmayerian terminology,[22] as does the 1802 dialogue on Reinhold's philosophy.[23]

That Schelling and Eschenmayer drew philosophical inspiration from one another should not suggest, however, that they were in agreement about either the goals or methodology of the philosophy of nature. The origins of their dispute in January 1801 are to be found in Schelling's *First Outline* of 1799, which takes aim at Eschenmayer's philosophy of nature as exemplary of the failings of dynamical explanation in the field. These criticisms will be treated at length in Chapter 1, but generally Schelling dubs Eschenmayer's early work – naming the *Principles* in particular – an 'ill-conceived attempt' at philosophy of nature,[24] precisely in so far as it seeks to reduce all difference in nature to the play between repulsive and attractive force. It is on the basis of such remarks that, in 1801, Eschenmayer launches a defence of his own early philosophy of nature and a thoroughgoing critique of Schelling's *First Outline*. One of our aims in this volume is to demonstrate the manner in which this disagreement between Schelling and Eschenmayer about the nature of quality has far-reaching consequences for Schelling's own philosophical project of the period, in what has typically been understood as the transition from the early philosophy of nature (1797–1800) to the system of identity (1801–4).

At the threshold of the identity philosophy

In 1801, Schelling stood at the beginning of a new venture in idealist metaphysics. The publication of the *Presentation of my System of Philosophy* in May of that year commenced an innovative direction in his thought – emphasised by the possessive 'my' in the title, which testifies to Schelling's own sense that this text was to exhibit a new degree of intellectual maturity and originality. It set forth the core positions of the identity philosophy and, indeed, is the text to which Schelling returns throughout much of his later developments as the basis for his metaphysical perspective. It is this text, moreover, to which Schelling refers a few years later in a letter to

Eschenmayer, writing of an epiphanic moment 'when the light burst upon me in philosophy in 1801'.[25]

What has been less often acknowledged is that fundamental aspects of the *Presentation*'s metaphysics were first announced in *On the True Concept of Philosophy of Nature*, in the midst of the controversy with Eschenmayer. It is in *On the True Concept* that Schelling writes, 'In the following issue [of the *Journal of Speculative Physics*], I hope to begin the new presentation of my system ... and to show how in the end one is forced to solely affirm that view which I have characterised above, namely that in which all dualism is forever annihilated and everything becomes absolutely one.'[26] As this passage suggests, the Schelling–Eschenmayer controversy of 1801 was one of the major causes of Schelling's turn to identity philosophy: the announcement of a new (or, at least, renewed) metaphysics is motivated by, among other things, Eschenmayer's challenge to and provocation of Schelling in *Spontaneity = World Soul*.

The novelty of Schelling's metaphysics of 1801 is not, however, as obvious as the above might imply. The Preface to the *Presentation*, for example, plays it down:

> No one should think that I have altered my system of philosophy. For the system that appears here for the first time in its fully characteristic shape is the same one that I always had in view in the different earlier presentations, which I constantly used as my personal guiding star in both transcendental and natural philosophy.[27]

According to this passage, the identity philosophy does not present some absolutely new metaphysical vision, but rather makes explicit the 'foundation'[28] always underlying his work in both transcendental philosophy and the philosophy of nature. Thus, while there is novelty in that Schelling's 'first principles' are 'here expressed for the first time', these principles are, according to the Preface, employed to maintain a status quo in which the two branches of philosophical activity are understood to be two parallel fields of inquiry.[29]

Many commentators have noted this ambivalence in the Preface between innovation and continuity. Vater, for instance, points out that 'the Preface has a double, if not contradictory, burden: to convince the reader that Identity Philosophy is not new ... and that it is new.'[30] Tilliette similarly speaks of 'a certain contradiction' that holds between the competing claims to novelty and to continuity in the *Presentation*.[31] The ambiguities and even inconsistencies of the Preface to the *Presentation* have led, more generally, to a scholarly problem that has long surrounded Schelling's development in early 1801: does the *Presentation of my System of Philosophy* mark *a point of rupture* in Schelling's trajectory or not?

Braeckman's interest in this question of the origins of the identity philosophy is representative:

> One of the most intriguing episodes in Schelling's philosophical development is the transition from the *System des transzendentalen Idealismus* (1800) to the *Darstellung meines Systems der Philosophie* (1801), the starting point of the identity system . . . The question inevitably arises: what happened in the transition from the *System des transzendentalen Idealismus* to the *Darstellung*, and above all, what made this transition possible? What, in other words, caused the constitution of absolute idealism?[32]

The scholarly debate over the genesis of the identity philosophy has come to be framed around those, on the one side, who maintain that the *Presentation* basically repeats the model of philosophical science proposed in the *Introduction to the Outline* and the *System of Transcendental Idealism*, in which transcendental philosophy and philosophy of nature are understood as parallel sciences grounded by the more fundamental metaphysical discourse of the identity philosophy; and those, on the other side, who insist that, between the *System of Transcendental Idealism* and the *Presentation*, something fundamental changes, and the philosophy of nature is given pride of place (destroying any supposed parallelism). Those who hold the second view often highlight the importance of the essays Schelling published in his *Journal for Speculative Physics*, such as the *Universal Deduction* and *On the True Concept*, both of which declare in no uncertain terms the systematic priority of the philosophy of nature. On this latter interpretation of Schelling's intellectual development, then, there emerges some preliminary evidence for the vital significance of the 1801 controversy with Eschenmayer, if it can indeed be shown that these texts – and *On the True Concept* in particular – play a role in Schelling's subsequent development of the identity philosophy.

Traditionally, the anglophone scholarship has almost universally subscribed to the 'parallelism interpretation' that emphasises the continuity with the writings of 1799 and early 1800. For example, Nassar, who propounds one of the more sophisticated versions of this model, claims, 'It is in the *System [of Transcendental Idealism]* that Schelling seeks to establish the identity of the productivity of nature and the productivity of mind, which becomes the founding idea of his philosophy of identity.'[33] She continues, 'the *System* should be perceived as the point of transition . . . to the philosophy of identity – with *transition* here not implying a break or rupture'.[34] In the *System of Transcendental Idealism*, Schelling himself is clear that 'neither transcendental philosophy nor the philosophy of nature is adequate by itself';[35] rather, they move in opposite directions, both of which are necessary components of an absolute philosophical system. From this perspective, transcendental philosophy and philosophy of nature are parallel sciences, and if there is to be an *absolute* science, it will ground both of these philosophically activities in one ultimate reality – a reality that Schelling comes to call 'identity' in 1801.

This is a compelling interpretation. The problem with such a reading, however, is that it fails to take into account the significance of texts such as *On the True Concept*, which explicitly demonstrate Schelling's newfound commitment to the systematic priority of the philosophy of nature and therefore imply his abandonment of transcendental philosophy altogether. Indeed, beginning in 1801, Schelling no longer shows an interest in elucidating the transcendental conditions which make knowledge of the natural world possible; he is now unabashedly concerned with *what nature is* and how the mind can be cut from the same cloth as it.

The 'nature-philosophical interpretation' of the origins of the identity philosophy thus refuses the parallelism between transcendental philosophy and philosophy of nature and, instead, insists that Schellingian identity philosophy is forged out of the prioritisation of the philosophy of nature. In this regard, with the publication of the *Universal Deduction* in November 1800, a significant shift occurs. Comparing his *Universal Deduction* to his *System of Transcendental Idealism*, Schelling writes, 'We have reached this point from completely contrary directions – going from nature to us [in the *Deduction*] and from ourselves to nature [in the *System*] – but the *true* direction for he who values *knowledge* above all else, is that which *nature itself* has taken'.[36] He continues:

> Philosophy of nature gives both a *physical explanation of idealism* and proves that the latter *must* erupt at the limits of nature, exactly as we see erupt out in the person of man ... The philosopher himself simply overlooks this, since with his first act, he already receives his object in the highest power, as the I, as endowed with consciousness, and only the physicist gets beneath this illusion. One would like therefore to call out to all men who now doubt philosophy and do not see the ground: come to physics, and learn the truth![37]

According to Schelling, modern philosophy has perennially overlooked the natural origin of consciousness; hence, the task of absolute idealism is to discover this natural ground and, in so doing, expose the supposed self-sufficiency of *transcendental* idealism as an illusion. It is this perspective of absolute idealism which is ultimately presented in Schelling's system of identity in 1801.

This entire debate about how to interpret the *Presentation* can be summed up by the following question: is the *System of Transcendental Idealism* or are the essays written for the *Journal of Speculative Physics* to be considered normative for Schelling's further development? The latter option has gained some recent support, even among English-language scholars. Grant is most forthright on this issue, arguing that 'Schellingianism' – including the philosophy of identity – '*is* naturephilosophy throughout'.[38] Beiser is another proponent of this interpretation: in 'renouncing' the earlier parallelist model, the *Presentation* becomes 'the final triumph of *Naturphilosophie*, which had now become identical to the standpoint of reason itself'.[39] He continues:

> Absolute idealism is not a synthesis of the idealism of the *Wissenschaftslehre* with the realism of *Naturphilosophie*, a combination of both standpoints where each has equal legitimacy. Rather, it is nothing less than the inversion of the *Wissenschaftslehre*.[40]

We believe that attending to the details of the 1801 controversy with Eschenmayer will further substantiate this nature-philosophical interpretation of Schelling's identity philosophy. Indeed, one might go so far as to suggest that the only reason that this debate rages on is owing to a failure in the scholarship to acknowledge the significance of the confrontation with Eschenmayer for the subsequent trajectory of Schelling's thought.

The stakes of the 1801 Schelling–Eschenmayer controversy

No less than in the *Universal Deduction*, Schelling is explicit in *On the True Concept* about the systematic priority of the philosophy of nature:

> Because philosophy of nature and transcendental philosophy have been spoken of as opposed yet equally possible orientations of philosophy, many have asked which of the two is accorded priority? – Without doubt, philosophy of nature, because it lets the standpoint of idealism itself first come into being, and thereby provides for it a secure, purely theoretical foundation.[41]

There are two reasons that Schelling accords the philosophy of nature systematic priority. First, this is the aspect of science which attends to what is, metaphysically speaking, more fundamental. While transcendental idealism attends to the structure of the mind and its unity with nature via the mental activity of the I (what Schelling calls the 'subjective subject-object'), the philosophy of nature attends to the physical reality that raises itself to I-hood, 'uniting' with the mind by *generating* it in the first place through a strictly natural process (what Schelling calls the 'objective subject-object'). This is why, throughout *On the True Concept*, Schelling insists that transcendental idealism only ever treats that which is ontologically derivative: there is 'one unbroken series, which proceeds from the simplest in nature to the highest and most complex'[42], and the transcendental philosopher only has resources to understand part of this series, that is, the 'highest and most complex' or the manner in which nature appears to consciousness. Only a philosopher of nature can sink beneath this complexity and illuminate the initial terms of this series, including 'the simplest in nature'. Without further explanation, of course, this is vague; more needs to be spelled out when it comes to the ontology of these 'simples' and how the philosopher of nature accesses them in thought. These issues are explored in Chapters 2, 3 and 5 of this volume. At this stage, it need simply be emphasised that one reason Schelling accords priority to the philosophy of nature from late 1800 onwards is that – unlike philosophies of mind – the philosophy of nature concerns itself with that which is more basic in reality.[43]

The second reason that Schelling accords philosophy of nature priority is related to the first, and it can be understood in terms of nature's self-determining and self-sufficient character. This had been a core component of Schelling's writings in the philosophy of nature since at least 1799. The opening of the *First Outline*, for example, is absolutely clear that any successful philosophy of nature needs to abide by two principles: the principle of nature's *autonomy* and the principle of nature's *autarchy*.[44] For Schelling, nature is autonomous, that is, self-determining or self-legislating, in so far as the process through which nature transforms itself into life and, ultimately, mind is an *independent* process; no intervention is necessary in order to motivate nature's diversification. And nature is autarchic or self-sufficient in so far as this physical process can be fully explained with reference to nature's structure alone; no alien principles of explanation are required. *On the True Concept* goes on, then, to explicate the consequences of this view: once the autonomy and autarchy of nature are acknowledged, the philosophy of nature proves to be first philosophy and 'idealism' or the philosophy of mind 'will [now] be derived from first principles'.[45] Thus, whereas the *First Outline* embeds the principles of nature's autonomy and autarchy within a system of parallel sciences, Schelling commences a new metaphysical system in 1801 by radicalising his earlier idea that nature is autonomous and autarchic. From this point forward, all conceptions of mind and its relationship to nature must be grounded upon a 'secure, purely theoretical foundation', that is, a philosophy of nature that simply does not begin with the I and its practical engagement in the natural world.

Many sources influenced features of Schelling's 1801 position on the philosophy of nature, from Kant's third *Critique* and Goethe's writing on natural science to Kielmeyer's lecture on organic forces and Baader's *On the Pythagorean Square in Nature*. And while we certainly do not wish to downplay their role in the formation of Schellingian philosophy in general, the systematic view outlined in *On the True Concept* emerges directly from conversations with Eschenmayer. For instance, it was Eschenmayer's *Spontaneity = World Soul*, first read by Schelling in 1800, that most virulently challenged the assumptions of nature's autonomy and autarchy in the *First Outline* and thereby provoked Schelling not just to defend this position, but to radicalise it as described above. In so doing, he was explicitly rejecting Eschenmayer's broadly Fichtean insistence that nature is *not* self-determining and that the natural world is *not* explicable on the basis of nature's activity alone.

It is therefore important to understand the Eschenmayerian view that motivates Schelling to turn away from the parallelism of his earlier thought, in which the philosophy of nature and transcendental philosophy were set on a par with one another. From Eschenmayer's perspective, the reason we conceive nature as the self-determining ground of life and the mind is only because *we posit* nature as being productive of our organic existence. That is, since 'nature in itself' for Eschenmayer 'is nothing other than simple being, mere passivity',[46] nature's apparent activity of self-determination is a *projection* of our own self-determining activity. On this account, the original source of activity is not nature, but the mind which posits nature *as* self-determining.[47] This is why, in *Spontaneity = World Soul*, Eschenmayer claims that Schelling's fundamental error is to conceive 'the principle of becoming' as immanent to nature itself.[48] According to Eschenmayer, 'We know ... no other principle of becoming ... than *spontaneity*'.[49] To be sure, Eschenmayer recognises that we can – and naturally do – *represent* this principle as immanent to nature: through a living subject's act, nature does appear to be motivated by an autonomous development leading to its differentiation as a complex material world. But the ultimate source of this activity must be the spontaneity of the I.[50]

Eschenmayer is explicitly following Fichte in identifying the I as the source of nature's determinacy. And, given his commitment to a transcendental perspective, this is understandable: if one insists upon beginning from transcendental premises, it is unclear how one might become convinced of speculative metaphysics. Just as the Freudian can always appeal to analytic theory to account for the resistance of the analysand, so too can the transcendental philosopher refer to the transcendental illusions of reason in order to explain the dogmatist's attempt to understand nature as it is in itself. From Schelling's perspective, however, the transcendental idealist simply presupposes the limits of our knowledge and thereby fixes rational thought as finite. Against this view, he argues that philosophical reason is fully rational only when it transcends the finite perspective of consciousness and enters into the rational structure of nature.

One way to grasp the difference between Eschenmayer and Schelling on the source of nature's determinacy, then, is to interpret their dispute in light of their respective conceptions of reason. While they agree that all self-determination is rational, Eschenmayer cannot fathom how rational self-determination could have any source other than the mind. Consequently, for Eschenmayer, any self-determination – and therefore any rationality – glimpsed in natural processes must be capable of being traced back to the activity of consciousness. Schelling, by contrast, is able to argue that nature is autonomous because he understands it as intrinsically rational; and he believes that a speculative physics is possible because he thinks that philosophical reason can immerse itself in the rational structure of nature. The conflict over locating the original source of activity in nature, therefore, is partly bound up with an epistemological dispute regarding the nature of reason.

Given the above, the metaphysics and epistemology of Schelling's 1801 *Presentation* can be understood as emergent from the debate with Eschenmayer. And these points by no means exhaust the ways in which this debate influenced Schelling. In addition to the fact that it was Eschenmayer's critique that led Schelling to dig in his heels about the principles of nature's autonomy and autarchy, it further led him to adopt a whole range of key nature-philosophical positions: the idea that the most general forms in nature constitute a series of *potencies*; the idea that each of these potencies or stages of nature is an expression of an original *identity*, and not some original duplicity; the idea that the philosopher of nature must trace this series of potencies by first abstracting from consciousness (the highest potency) and subsequently becoming identical with inorganic nature (the lowest potency); the idea that philosophy proper concerns itself with the potencies of nature in their eternal being, rather than in their temporal or historical manifestation – these ideas, which are essential to Schelling's system of 1801, are some of the fruits borne by the controversy with Eschenmayer.[51]

Thus, the starting point of this volume is the contention that Schelling's disagreement with Eschenmayer over the status of philosophy of nature and its relation to transcendental philosophy matters: it matters for our understanding of Schelling's philosophy of nature; it matters for the story we tell of Schelling's philosophical development, particularly as regards the emergence of his identity philosophy; and it matters for a full awareness of the conceptual debates taking place in German Idealism in 1801.[52]

Structure of the commentary

In what follows, translations of *Spontaneity = World Soul* and *On the True Concept* are supplemented by five chapters of commentary on the

Schelling–Eschenmayer debate and its importance for understanding Schelling's philosophy of nature. Because the 1801 controversy originates in a debate about how a philosophy of nature might account for qualitative determinacy in the natural world, this topic is the focus of Chapter 1. Although the problem of accounting for qualitative determinacy has a long philosophical history, Kant's 1786 *Metaphysical Foundations of Natural Science* gave the issue a new surge of life with its influential 'dynamic construction of matter', which became normative for both Eschenmayer and Schelling. But the two quickly began to argue over precisely how the dynamic character of matter could explain the phenomena of magnetic polarity, electrical charge and chemical interaction. The first chapter of commentary therefore analyses Eschenmayer's and Schelling's respective accounts of qualitative difference by tracing their arguments from 1797 to the texts of 1801.

Building upon this discussion of quality and quantity, the second chapter of commentary focuses on the concept of 'potency', a concept which first appears in Eschenmayer's *Principles* and is quickly incorporated into Schelling's own philosophy of nature. We attempt to explain how Schelling transforms this Eschenmayerian concept in order to explain each general feature of reality as an expression of identity (A = A). Interestingly, although Schelling refuses the notion that the philosophy of nature can be reduced to mathematics, he nevertheless adopts mathematical notation in his attempt to move beyond Eschenmayer's mathematicisation of nature. The chapter thus goes on to distinguish this uniquely *idealist* conception of potency – with its origins in geometry – from the more traditional, Aristotelian conception of potency, and it concludes with a defence of its apparent formalism.

Chapter 3 draws upon the discussions of quality and potency in Chapters 1 and 2 in order to consider how identity and difference are ultimately understood in Schelling's metaphysics of the period. We argue that the Eschenmayer controversy decisively influences Schelling's conception of 'the identity of identity' in the *Presentation of my System of Philosophy*, and we contrast this model of identity with the dialectical model of the 'identity of identity and difference' first put forward by Hegel in his 1801 *Differenzschrift*, as well as with the reflexive model for identity that Fichte had been developing in the *Wissenschaftslehre*. In doing so, we aim to show that Schelling develops a cogent model for understanding the production of identity that does not depend upon a dialectical notion of difference.

Chapters 4 and 5 focus on the fundamental difference between subjectivist and absolutist philosophies of nature, represented by Eschenmayer and Schelling respectively. Eschenmayer's subjectivism is most apparent in the significant role played by 'drive' in *Spontaneity = World Soul*, as this

Fichtean term is meant to unite nature and consciousness in an essentially subjective activity. Central to Schelling's critique of Eschenmayer is that this subjectivism prevents him from seeing that nature itself – prior to any subjective drive – is self-determining, and it is this disagreement with Eschenmayer that finally forces Schelling to fully embrace, in no uncertain terms, the ontological priority of nature in *On the True Concept*. Following our reconstruction of this debate in the fourth chapter of commentary, Chapter 5 explores the methodological implications of the Schellingian turn to nature. What must the philosopher *do* in order to understand nature's determinacy, if the source of this determinacy is utterly natural? How, in other words, does Schelling think he can describe the structure of nature *in itself*, without any reference to consciousness and the way nature *appears* to consciousness? In this final chapter of commentary, therefore, we make use of a number of the concepts Schelling develops in the Eschenmayer controversy – most notably, 'abstraction' and 'depotentiation' – in order to expound Schelling's methodology in 1801.

Part I
Texts

Spontaneity = World Soul, or The Highest Principle of Philosophy of Nature

A. C. A. Eschenmayer

[3] 'What is matter other than *extinguished* spirit? All duplicity is cancelled in it; its state is a state of absolute identity and of rest. In the transition from homogeneity to duplicity a world already dawns, and with the restoration of duplicity the world itself opens up, and what is this world other than *visible* spirit?'[1]

These are the profound words of *Schelling* in his master work: *First Outline of a System of Philosophy of Nature*. In them lies that ultimate problem which, instead of being solved, is so often merely put off for future work – that problem which, instead of finally resulting in an inalterable axiom, has been treated only in intermediate and provisional propositions. At the heart of [this problem] is the question of [4] the bond between *nature* and *concept*, between *law* and *freedom*, between *dead mechanism* and *living dynamism*. We are able to divine the meaning of these words from the author's work, yet for us to grasp their fully significance, we lack the master's finishing touches.

Schelling expresses the *problem* itself at the end of his conclusions on p. 254:

'What is the universal source of activity in Nature? What cause brought forth the first dynamic juxtaposition in Nature (of which the mechanical is a mere consequence)? Or what cause first cast the seed of motion into the universal rest of Nature, duplicity into universal identity, the first spark of heterogeneity into the universal homogeneity of Nature?'[2]

The author found himself driven to this problem after grasping the concept of nature in its highest universality and charting its descent through its essential stages – and it is at precisely the point where the author breaks off that the problem surfaces. All the conclusions of this acute work press towards the articulation of this problem – and so they must, [for] *Schelling* works from an *unconditioned empiricism*.³ That is, there should be no question of the first *movens* of nature within [5] empiricism, for the philosopher of nature, as he encounters nature, finds it already posited in *becoming*,⁴ and he can do nothing more than develop the already-active principles of nature in their activity. Empiricism is therefore unconditioned only for the philosopher of nature – unconditioned, that is, only under the condition of excluding that *principle* of *becoming* implied in Schelling's questions above, questions that can only be answered in transcendental philosophy. This explains how, having worked from an *unconditioned empiricism* and pursued this [principle of becoming] through its separation into successive inorganic and organic branches before it finally returned into itself by means of their union, *Schelling* must ultimately conclude precisely with the above problem.

That *originary principle* which, to speak with Franz Baader,⁵ wafts the breath from above into the dead columns of Prometheus, sets the pulse of nature in motion (i.e. the reciprocal play of its dualism), but [itself] remains unknown. Here is precisely the point at which the *unconditionality* of *empiricism* must be overcome and a place be admitted for a higher creative self: the tomb of *empiricism* is the resurrection of *rationalism*. The aim of what follows is to demonstrate this point.

[6] What then is this *originary principle*?

It is so close to us but we search for it out in the immeasurable; – it becomes sensible before our very gaze but we assign it to a non-sensible substrate; – it is reflected everywhere from the crystal to the leaf, from the leaf to the noble shape of the animal, but only in us does it conceal itself; – it is, as Baader says, an *ascension*, – the sun which illuminates the sunken night in a new dawn. Through it, spirit becomes visible in the awakening of nature and, when it is lacking, spirit is extinguished in the sleep of matter.

This principle = World soul
and
World soul = Spontaneity

Detailed Proof.

My *spirit* and *nature* stand opposed to one another; in me is *freedom*, in nature *law*. In so far as I glimpse myself, I am spontaneity, pure activity, principle of becoming; nature, on the contrary, [is] dead mechanism, passivity, mere being. *However, nature forces the products of its lawfulness onto me and I force the products of my freedom onto it.*

[7] In this reciprocal play my freedom is evidently restricted, while the force of nature is diminished.

Concerning the first claim: in so far as I perceive and intuit, I stand under the power of nature; my faculty of representation is completely directed by it, such that I am not merely pure activity, mere principle of becoming; rather, there is also within me a being-affected-by-the-outside, i.e. I am also nature. Conversely, there is not merely passivity within outward nature, for I must at the very least ascribe to it a drive which can no longer be inwardly deduced and which seeks [to effect] its causality in me.

Concerning the second claim: even in free acts I am still restricted. I can neither obliterate existing matter nor newly create any; all my power is limited solely to forming and modifying it; nature strives against me through matter and such striving-against is, at the very least, conditioned activity (that is, activity mediated by striving).

In both cases, activity and passivity are found on both sides. According to the first claim alone, however, consciousness of constraint and of necessity [8] is in me and I predicate the opposite of nature, while, according to the second claim alone, consciousness of freedom and of independence is in me and the opposite is in nature.

Evidently, in this whole deduction it is a matter of one absolute quantum of activity alone that is attributed to two opposed potencies (spirit and nature); the more activity in me, the more negation in nature, and vice versa; the two exhibit a perfect reciprocity. Therefore, there is, in general, no passivity but only activity, but this activity is attributed to *opposed potencies*: what is *positive* in me is *negative* in what is opposed to me (a mathematical truth). And thus we have obtained a clear view: if the philosopher were to succeed in undertaking the unification of these opposed potencies in the I, then this reciprocal play would be merely one product of the I.

Spirit and nature, subjectivity and objectivity, being and becoming, would then form the very synthetic unities in which the I consists. The absolute quantum of activity would merely be the measure by which reason calculates individual states as more or less active – a series could be constructed: on its positive side, activity and free action are preponderant, while, on its negative side, natural necessity and [9] necessary action. And at both extremes – that is, on the positive [side], pure spontaneity and, on the negative, pure natural necessity – there are infinite potencies, i.e. the preponderance of one factor would be infinitely large, thus making the other disappear completely.

I have tried to deal with the majority of this material in an issue of Röschlaub's Journal under the title *Deduction of the Living Organism*.[6] I point the reader there for the details, and here repeat only what is relevant:

If one picks out the competing parts which bring about the world in all of its manifold existence, then one encounters two hierarchies, as *Schelling* has shown very nicely in the work cited above: one for *inorganic* nature, which runs from light to electricity and from electricity to magnetism, and another for *organic* nature, which runs from the formative drive to irritability and from irritability to sensibility.[7] If empiricism goes this far, then it goes far enough, at least as far as higher physics requires it to go. However, *empiricism* as such should be overcome, for it ends precisely at the point where the subordination of lower principles under one all-encompassing sphere becomes a problem. It does not raise itself to the originary principle, which produces itself and (according to determinate laws) [10] causes the external world, i.e. to the *original drive* of nature.*

As realising itself into the external world, as attempting to set the causal chain in motion without possessing causality through itself, the original drive evidently bears the character of both spontaneity and nature in itself. This self-realising, which, in striving outward, never exhausts itself and, like an infinite factor, reproduces itself always anew, recognises only spontaneity as its creator. And yet this self-realising tries to act as a cause without ever being able to do so – and here one recognises the imprisoning chains of nature. Spontaneity [11], *bound* through the medium of nature, *expires* in a drive; nature, *raised* through the medium of spontaneity, is *kindled* into a drive. The drive takes up the middle point between spontaneity and nature; it is, as it were, the unity, the *punctum saliens*,[8] of the inorganic and organic world, constituting itself between two opposed potencies. Accordingly, it is by virtue of spontaneity that nature awakens before our eyes, and by virtue of nature that spontaneity submits to the laws of finitude. The original drive, the point of unity between the two, is therefore the genuine basis (the originary principle) from which the philosopher of nature can tie together the development of his lower principles.

More evidence for these conclusions can be found in the following:

The philosopher, in so far as he finds man typically engaged, is obliged to ascribe to him *free reflection* and *free production*. These are two faculties which, when expressed, encounter each other from opposite directions: one seeks that which annihilates the other, and so the gains of one are the losses of the other, in perfect reciprocity. However, both are infinite, thus

---

* The awkward position in which physics finds itself when it ascends to the original drive is so very ancient and its trace is so unmistakeable in antiquity that it can only be explained from the way in which our ancestors undertook an imaginary game, climbing from one concept of nature to another – as it were, getting to the end in one fell swoop and presupposing in physics the idea of a *world soul*. This was a hypothesis that the higher physics made in the gloom of antiquity: and now, in how many shapes does this hypothesis return to us! – Our philosophy overcomes *empiricism*: spirit and nature should be united in one original drive, and while the lower states of this drive hurry from term to term mechanically, the other, higher state is seen to ascend above law through reciprocal play.

equal to each other. In virtue of this equality, they must touch [12] in the middle free from external disturbance, posited in an absolute equilibrium and persisting in this condition of death-like rest eternally. Hence, one cannot really speak of either one or the other side winning or losing. – However, it is not [actually] so, for man is himself conscious every moment of a free reflection and a free production – this is an undeniable fact – and, as a result, the two functions cannot meet each other in the *middle*, because otherwise that consciousness would thereby be immediately annulled.

As certain as this fact is, it is just as certain that the two functions must be *kept apart from each other*, and this is the work of spontaneity. *In the infinite keeping-apart of opposed activities spirit is revealed*, as *Schelling* has already pointed out so accurately. Through this keeping-apart, each function becomes independent of the other and each can follow its tendency without restriction. How otherwise would free reflection and free production be possible? How would a concept be possible if not in that moment when I abstract, analyse, restrain from synthesis? How would a product be possible if not in that very moment when I connect together, proceed synthetically and restrain from analysis?*

[13] Spontaneity, thought in its highest aspect, consists in the infinite keeping-apart of the functions of these two faculties: mediated through reflection it proceeds to *annihilation*; mediated through production it proceeds to *creation*; but [actually] it is every time limited by *matter*, and, in place of annihilation, there arises a separation or abstraction (concept), and, in place of creation, a binding together or modification (intentional product) – and this is as far as the causality of spontaneity goes.

Through the *keeping-apart* of the two faculties an act becomes possible – an act tied to *consciousness* of *freedom*. (Concept and intentional product).

As much as this is certain, so too is the other side – that the tendency to absolute equilibrium, to absolute coming-together dwells indelibly in both opposed faculties and in this tendency lies the opposite of spontaneity – *nature*.

Just as spontaneity refuses for itself alone all lawfulness, so too does nature strive [14] to produce for itself an absolute law (of equilibrium) – and just as spontaneity would lose itself in absolute infinity, so too does nature try to cancel itself in absolute finitude. Neither of the two is valid: neither the tendency to absolute equilibrium nor the keeping-apart of both functions to infinity occurs; instead, a *third* [does], which

---

* The faculty to choose is predicated of spontaneity only in its lower aspects; the higher [viewpoint] is [13] that the binding of both faculties is overcome over the course of a finite period and then choice emerges.

simultaneously bears in itself the character of spontaneity and of nature. This third is the *drive*: through it absolute finitude is overcome. – *Nature awakens*; but also in it spontaneity is quietened – *spirit expires*. And thus there emerges a series: between its infinite endpoints lies the sum-total of the finite and at its midpoint there falls the idealist limit which separates objectivity from subjectivity.

Through the *tendency* to *absolute equilibrium* of both faculties an act becomes possible – an act tied to consciousness of *necessity*. (Sensation and intuition).

Therefore, just as the drive obtrudes from active causality, so too the necessary act obtrudes from the free. But both activities belong to one and the same I, in which these opposed potencies, spirit and nature, are bound.

[15] Against this and all similar claims, experience protests almost gleefully, since, on the one hand, it does not consider it necessary to follow the philosopher in his speculative circle, while, on the other hand, [experience] finds it impossible to recognise its own footprint a priori. It is indeed true that if we are not capable of setting down our conclusions in a way in which experience can comfortably take them up, then their mistrust is fully justified.

We want to give experience itself a speaking role:

'It is strange, it says, how from such a high vantage point the philosopher leads us to such deep truths, e.g. that it is our I itself that projects nature or a universe in general out of itself – and of this the subject knows not a word.'

I claim that it is only natural that from no conceivable principle of nature could the highest link in the chain ever be derived, but that it can only be in virtue of spontaneity that nature awakens before our eyes – albeit in the original drive, which awakens nature and extinguishes itself [as spontaneity]. Such an extinguished spontaneity can presumably not be accompanied by consciousness of freedom, by the [16] conviction that it is our work, but rather, it is by means of the feeling of this original drive that consciousness and the awareness of natural necessity appear to us (in sensation and intuition).

Experience raises the objection: granted for the general case, but go into the particulars and answer the following questions for me:

'Is it the case that the new-born child, whose diffident and unsteady eyes for the first time encounter the rays of the sun, has herself projected that bright disc – is she affected by her own product, does she close her eyes? Considering the novelty of this child's sensation – sometimes sweet, sometimes sour – and how she gazes on each object, does she also project her own mother? What more remains for her to learn, what is she still to experience?'

I answer that all this follows from the correct antecedents. In fact, these are the ultimate questions of the greatest significance and to answer them is the most difficult task for those who insist that experience can be submitted to an a priori construction – a procedure which from a certain standpoint [17] of philosophy has much plausibility for us. Let us see how the philosopher proceeds to answer these questions . . .

Our spontaneity must have some material on which it can act as cause, for it itself cannot create anything; but where does the material come from? I answer: through the necessary activity, mediated by drive, which separates sensation and intuition from each other. Sensation and intuition, however, are not functions that run into the infinite *all at once*, but, mediated by a counter-striving which is stimulated in them [i.e. in sensation and intuition] by the original drive, they are *inhibited at each point of the infinite line*. It is this manifold *inhibition* that produces in us a multiplicity of material. There arises a reciprocal relation between sensation and intuition in which all reality, on the one side, and all magnitude, on the other, emerge. Thus, in virtue of the original drive, consciousness of an external world becomes possible – *but just merely possible*, for to attain reality it still lacks a second condition. It is claimed that, as soon as this drive becomes active, the new-born child produces all reality and all quantity within and outside herself, that through her necessary activity material emerges, and, in this way, such a *possible* consciousness of an external world is secured. However, there is no consciousness of external things without *self-consciousness*, [18] and this is the missing condition which transforms possible consciousness into something actual. The child only gradually develops self-consciousness, individuality. It is only through her own self that an external world breaks out, since how could she be *herself* conscious of something, if her *self* still lay asleep? Man grows into self-consciousness; all education is nothing but a modification of our self-consciousness, nothing but a limitation of our individuality. The individuality of the child breaks forth initially upon the reflection of her mother – homogenous to homogenous; it breaks forth upon the similar eyes acting as a mirror for her own, and only now does her self break free from the external world. And what is this but the beginnings of future experience, what is education but an experience presented from multiple viewpoints? Accordingly, I cannot say that each sensation of the sweet or of the sour is new to the child, [for] the child is new to herself, she is only just finding herself and, indeed, for the first time in this sensation she marvels not at the object, but she marvels at herself. And likewise not at the sensation of brightness: the first *transmission* of this sensation from the object (the shining disc) is foreign to her, and how could it be so transmitted, if her self had not itself first broken free from the external world?

[19] This *confrontation* [*Gegenverhältnis*][9] *between what is homogenous* is therefore that through which man is summoned to self-consciousness and restricted to individuality, and (here the emphasis really rests) this reciprocal relation [*Wechselverhältnis*] kindled by the drive first nourishes life and existence. However, this *confrontation* [*Gegenverhältnis*] is no longer my work: *I* and *you* are – in regard to *our emergence* – quite independent of each other; we are the means and cause of ourselves, but we are dependent on each other in respect to *reflections on our own activities*. How must such an encounter now appear to man? Evidently – as something *contingent*, as a *blind chance* which meets him. When this chance occurs, his self-consciousness alters, such that the different possible limitations of the individual depend on different reflections. Nevertheless, *as self-consciousness alters, so too does the external world*. Thus, despite all the a-priority that the philosopher demands, when it comes to the child's individual life, the series of experience is still always secured as *contingent*.

To the original I stands opposed the individual [I]. The former is present independently of all experience; the latter is first brought up into producing experience. – The former contains the original form of the law of representation; the latter gives it content and application. – In the former, possible future developments [20] are only there in design; in the latter, they are brought to implementation. Everything held in [the original I] is *simultaneously* present: future and past are one. Everything held in [the individual I] emerges for it over a temporal series: future and past are separated, and it encompasses the present not as the forms of the external world, the separate series of sensations and intuitions which the [original I] produces, but as the emergence of appearances from the midst of it – that is, the passage of sensation to intuition which first comes about in the [individual I] is *contingent*. On this point rests the history of the human race.

I pass on to another investigation. It is a beautiful thought that the universe is equivalent to *one* organism.[10] An initial implication of this thought is that the whole visible universe, even if it were depicted in terms of a higher relation, connected to yet another higher sphere, should be treated as one individual factor alone; thus, further constructions would be immensely simplified. The second implication of this thought is that the universe can be conceived as a self-enclosed whole whose parts and laws must be explored within their own sphere alone. Therefore, as far as our eyes penetrate, thus far extends the universe; and as far as the universe extends, thus far extends our concept: as far as the light [21] can communicate between me and our outer limits, then, if it sends back a glimmering spark from beyond a myriad of worlds, it is all ours; and so too the possibility of constructing with other mediating terms cannot be denied. What lies beyond the border (that is, a second factor) remains obscure to us; it is, however, not merely obscure to our sensory horizon, but also to our concept; its laws [are] an eternal mystery to us.

I say it is a *beautiful* thought to describe the universe as an enclosed sphere (organism), whose manifold rays never roam beyond the periphery, but always touch on the centre and the pole. However, whether such a thought is also *true* has not yet been proven. If one extends empiricism to the unconditioned, as *Schelling* has done in some of his works, then the principle of the universal organism must be taken as a fundamental ground. But it is thereby in no way absolved from suspicions that it is just a hypothesis, for – if the consistent empiricist should claim to prove this principle, then it can only be done in a non-philosophical way, i.e. proceeding backwards from experience. That is, he must argue something like this: because everything which we observe and can be submitted to our inquiries is ultimately harmoniously related, because [22] a relative equilibrium persists across the manifold disturbances of its parts, because everything within [the universe] is in discord with itself and yet the whole is at one with itself, so must the universe be equivalent to an organism. The rationalism which overcomes the unconditionality of empiricism raises this question to a much more distinct level: it asks what are the conditions under which organism as such emerges, and it thus points us back to transcendental philosophy, i.e. it assigns us the task of discovering the roots of the organism in ourselves.

In unconditioned empiricism the *principle* of *becoming* is already presupposed. This is nowhere illuminated more clearly than in the following principles from which *Schelling* begins in the cited work: '*Nature is its own legislator (autonomy of nature).*' '*Nature suffices for itself (autarchy of nature).*' Bringing them together: '*Nature has unconditioned reality (principle of philosophy of nature).*'[11] Evidently, the *principle of becoming*, which is completely foreign to the concept of nature in itself, is already incorporated in [nature]. We know, however, no other principle of becoming (beginning a series absolutely) than *spontaneity*. When bound [23] with nature, it is extinguished in a drive and is represented *immanently* to nature as *world soul*.

What unconditioned empiricism here claims about nature, rationalism claims precisely the opposite – for *spirit*. *Only spirit is its own legislator, only spirit suffices for itself* (autonomy and autarchy of the will). *Only spirit has unconditioned reality* (principle of transcendental philosophy).

This above semblance of dialectics is resolved in the author's remarkable words: *When matter is at rest spirit dies, and in the awakening of nature spirit is visible*. In the original drive two factors are united. In so far as the lower factor (nature) becomes preponderant, the drive strives for absolute finitude; in so far as the higher factor (spontaneity) is preponderant, the drive strives to produce an absolutely infinite product. Neither of the two [actually] occur, [for] the determinate finite [product] fills in the space between the two extremes, or as Schelling expresses it: *the absolute activity of nature is inhibited at all points on the infinite line.*[12]

I come now to the specific proof of one of *Schelling's* major claims, and this is for no other reason than because much in philosophy of nature comes down to this important undertaking.[13]

[24] I do not comprehend the ease with which the author (p. 14f) assumes an *infinite multiplicity of tendencies to be originally united in one product*.[14] I do understand that a capacity for infinite development lies in each natural product, for – if a product of an actant [*Aktion*][15] is of a determinate degree, then the point of inhibition ought to fall away and the positive factor of that stage be expressed in its tendency to the infinite. And to the extent that this tendency (of universal natural activity) can be inhibited again at all other points, so an infinite multiplicity of tendencies obviously appears to be united in that product – except that there are always only *two* tendencies which inhibit through each other at different points. The capacity for infinite development therefore lies not in the *composite union of infinitely many tendencies*, but merely in the *infinite succession of two original tendencies*. This difference is in fact more significant than it first appears, for – I want to insist that [Schelling's] error in constructing a *complex actant* (of the individuality of a product) rests on this unexamined assumption. In order to specify this error with precision, a bit of preparation is required, and I will lay down some claims with which the author himself ought to agree.

[25] Originally the philosopher of nature knows merely two tendencies opposed to each other (a third which has newly come to be talked of will be discussed later in the essay). They come from deductions whose highest parts are borrowed from transcendental philosophy. These tendencies are normally known as *attractive* and *repulsive* force. Since these forces are opposed to each other, infinitely many points of inhibition can be thought in them, and these points consist in the gradually increasing or decreasing preponderance of one or the other force. These points of inhibition can be nicely presented in a mathematical formula which has many analogies with a numerical series: I have established these very formulae elsewhere under the name of a series of degree.[16] If one now wants to label every *unequal* coming-together of these forces an *actant of a determinate degree*, then it cannot be denied that they must give rise to an infinite mix of actants. But no actant is distinguished

from another in respect to its *simplicity* or *complexity*. They all emerge in the same way; their difference lies merely in the level of degree, and from this ground alone is the philosopher of nature compelled to posit qualities = degrees. Yet where, according to the author, does the difference between *simple* and *complex* actants lie?¹⁷ There are only three possibilities:

1. [26] Either there are more than the two opposed tendencies (e.g. three). In which case, I can call that actant complex which consists in three tendencies, and simple that which only consists in two.
2. Or one can specify determinate points of inhibition in the series of degree and so, for example, that [actant] is called simple which corresponds to the geometrical progression of parts. In which case, the complex would be that which arises through the interpolation of two such parts.
3. Or one can take a determinate number of simple actants together and call the point at which they converge a complex actant.

If I now also accept that [establishing] the *complexity* of an *actant* is a necessary requirement for the philosopher of nature, [then] in order to secure, both separately and in every case, the abiding individuality of actants as well as their multiplicity (thereby overcoming their continuity as mere differences of degree), then I do not see how this requirement can be satisfactorily met by the author. In order to show this more clearly, I will go through each of the three possibilities in turn:

[27] Concerning the first case – If there are three original tendencies, where is the deduction of the third?

Where the author assumes a complex actant, a third tendency is not introduced at all. Only at the end of the work does he remark*,¹⁸ prompted by *Franz Baader's* writing, *On the Pythagorean Square*, that gravity is a fundamental force different from the attractive force. However, since the remark on gravity is independent of the claim now under discussion, I lay it aside. For me, gravity is no fundamental force, but a fundamental relation [*Verhältnis*]¹⁹ which, like any other relation, must have several terms, and thus cannot merely be attained by means of the attractive force alone. I return to this point in more detail below.

Concerning the second case – The author puts forward the following

---

* *Editor's [i.e. Schelling's] Remark.* Equally in the beginning of [the section] where the construction of an inorganic world in general is spoken of, a reason is mentioned (p. 110) for treating gravity as something different from an attractive force. However, this alters nothing in the author's argumentation above.

proposition: *the originary points of inhibition of universal* [28] *natural activity are to be found in original qualities.*[20]

In this proposition the author draws attention to a *number* of originary points of inhibition, or what is the same thing, simple actants. However, whence do they come, or more generally, what is original and what is not? In a continuous series of development, we find no such determinate interruptions that, in respect to their originality or simplicity, have some kind of distinguishing feature that the others (even the first point of inhibition) do not share – unless we locate determinate points in the series and, for instance, call simple or original those which are geometrically-progressively proportionate to each other. In fact, this idea seems to have much truth to it, and to get at a cryptic intimation of nature. *Baader* has already remarked how matter at rest is only captured in a dead arithmetic, as it were, in addition and subtraction, whereas animated nature is elevated to a living dynamic through exponentiation and logarithms. – Perhaps the major characteristic of nature in its stages of development lies in some such progressive proportion [*Verhältnis*]. In this case, that actant is called complex which emerges through the interpolation of terms in a series. Nevertheless, it is clear that the author does not mean anything of this kind, for nothing like it is mentioned.

[29] There is still the third case: 'That a union of many simple actants is equal to a complex actant.' However, mathematically, this construction is the most impermissible of all. This is seen most clearly in the doctrine of the composition of forces, which shows that, no matter how large the number of assumed forces may be, what results from reduction by parallelogram is the same as if it only originated from two forces. What [holds for] directions in the composition of forces [holds also for] degrees in the composition of one actant. The result in the former case is always the diagonal, which is one and the same no matter whether I split the active force into three or four directions or let it act as one. In the case of the actant, [the result] is always the middle degree, which is one and the same no matter whether I separate the simple actant into three or four different degrees or let it act as one. The sum of the ratios [*Verhältnisse*] is always the same. For example, if I combine the simple actants = 4 and = 10, then the middle actant 7 results, and this is the same as what results if I posit, instead of the actant = 4, the still-simpler actants = 1 and 3 and, instead of = 10, = 5, 3 and 2. The middle degree is still always = 7 and in the second case it is no more complex than before, and in general [no more complex] than any other actant.

[30] From this argument it follows that if actants are posited = degrees, no composition occurs which would differ in nature to that of simple [actants]. Perhaps though the author took a completely different view of

the matter? Later, such [a view] will be shown to consist in the idea of an absolute involution of the organism; however, for the moment this is laid aside, since [it is] independent of his claims about complex actants.

The author's claim, 'Each quality is an actant of a determinate *degree*, for which there is no other measure than its product',[21] is erroneous owing to a complete misunderstanding of mathematics. The mathematician does not want to bring about the product as it is in nature through his calculations, but rather he only wants to show how numerical ratios parallel such products. If the author differentiates actants by differences of degree, then he is thereby laying claim to their measurability. Thus, the claim obviously possesses the following contradiction: *For the measurability of degree there is no measure*. All things considered, the concept of a complex actant remains incomprehensible to us, and in fact, the author himself acutely remarks that it is complete nonsense 'to want to explain the infinite multiplicity of material in the world through various degrees of one and the same actant'.[22] [31] That is, in light of the above, the author has yet to elevate himself above simple actants and their differences of degree by means of any comprehensible construction. It is true, as S.[chelling] objects on p. 20,[23] that the idea that specific differences in density should hold step with differences in quality does not accord with experience (an apparently insolvable knot for the philosopher of nature, on which I have already remarked in an earlier piece[24]). However, is experience the adjudicator between the product, which is to be constructed, and reason, which constructs? If I call nature its own legislator, letting it be sufficient to itself, then experience is the highest to which we can elevate ourselves – what does not lie in our intuition and sensation is an eternal puzzle for us, and I do not understand why anyone would undertake the thankless trouble of specifying a method of constructing nature for a nature which constructs itself. However, such a claim is not meant so seriously: unconditioned empiricism begins from a universal organism, and must begin from it, since that creative principle which originally dwells in us is only brought into nature by this means. Rationalism overcomes empiricism, and thus reason becomes the legislator of both itself and nature; the principle of becoming (spontaneity) is the original impulse which [32] first awakens nature itself; experience itself lies in our outline (but how can what is outlined master the outline?). The roots of the organism lie within ourselves, and the philosopher of nature has merely to develop its sequences and collisions. Therefore, I would rather say to those appealing to experience in this specific case: *construct until you achieve the individuality of the natural product and thereupon you will see for yourself why specific differences in density differ so much from differences in quality.*

For I hold such a construction to be one of the most important tasks in philosophy of nature, to the extent that it contains the requirement to make experience agree with the a-priority of our principles. Then, as I have said, one will not look for a solution to this task, but rather just for an approximation of a solution!

It was apparently the atomist who introduced into the philosophy of nature an expression which our dynamics has not yet got rid of – I mean the concept: *specific composition*.[25] This term belongs primarily to chemistry and physiology; however, it appears to do the work of prohibiting us from all further constructions or, at the very least, it substitutes itself for the lack of further constructions. [33] In a purified dynamics concerned solely with proportions of degree, such an expression should no longer be incorporated.

Schelling still appears to favour this concept due to his assumption of a *multiplicity* of original actants. However, I ask: how can one simple actant be distinguished from others, if not by a mere difference of degree? Obviously, I must assume that this simple actant emerges from different fundamental forces than the others do, if the word *specific* is to mean anything else but difference of degree. A multiplicity of fundamental forces is, however, something completely indemonstrable for the dynamist. As was shown with respect to the doctrine of the composition of forces, I can indeed split the fundamental forces into infinitely many directions, dividing them, as it were, into infinitely many derivative forces. However, when I undertake the reduction of them, reducing their plurality by means of subordination to an ever-narrower sphere, with the aim of discovering their fundamental expression (a task that belongs primarily to kinematics), then in the end there still remain *two fundamental forces*. They cannot be derived from each other, but are instead opposed to one another. Assuming a multiplicity of fundamental forces irreducible to one another is therefore a genuine absurdity in dynamics.

[34] However, Schelling clearly says on p. 106:

> For the original construction of matter one requires original basic forces. – I assert, however, that one can succeed with this construction from original basic forces only in mechanics (in the broad sense of the word, i.e. in so far as one views matter merely as occupation of space in general). However, it does not make the *formation* of a *single* material conceivable because, in this case, one abstracts from all specific difference of matter and does not brings any other difference into view than the various degrees of its *density* (i.e. its occupation of space), as is also the case in Kant's metaphysics of nature.[26]

In the above claims, the *specific composition* of matter is clearly differentiated from specific densities, with the addendum that both cannot depend on the same construction. However, I ask: in what then do specific differences of matter originally consist? If there are only two fundamental forces from which matter can be originally constructed, multiplicity in the forces can only be [a matter of] degree, and so empirical determinations of matter must only be [a matter of] degrees. Seen *from this point of view*, all specific compositions of matter disappear and are resolved into a matter of degree [*Gradation*]. Has the author taken *another viewpoint*? [35] Indeed. – He proceeds from a *universal organism* which, however, is grasped undeveloped and in an *original involution*. Here the question arises: are a multiplicity of future developments – that is, the differentiation of future directions – supposed to be already implicit within this *involution*, or are only those two original simple tendencies supposed to reside within [it]: an original evolving and an original retarding (expansion and contraction)? In the first case, it just requires an evolution for the numerous directions, the individual forms of bodies, to come to appearance precisely as they are in nature – *fiat miraculum*. That is, all the limits of pure productivity would already be grasped in the involution. In the second case, things progress naturally, but we thereby lose the multiplicity of directions, the definiteness of figure, which *S.[chelling]* assumes without further ado. In the first case, no original retarding [tendency] is needed; in the second case, however, the original retarding [tendency], the ultimately multiple law, would have to either completely abandon itself or be abandoned in order to produce the difference in figure. It must soon tend towards either a gradated line or a bent one: either [it] strives towards the regular hexagon of the crystal or to produce the elliptical form of a leaf. Where does this plurality of tendencies now come from? I can easily understand that the original retarding as such [36] gives limits, but that it gives this or that limit (direction) is incomprehensible to me without further proof. For this to make reasonable sense, one must assume that *pure productivity*, grasped in infinite evolution – when inhibited at different stages of its infinite tendency – will immediately be exhibited by the definiteness of a figure. However, if this does actually happen, what then is such becoming-inhibited at different stages and evolving with determinate, finite velocities, other than a *difference of degree*? Are the original evolving and retarding [tendencies] not merely a different way of expressing the forces of repulsion and attraction from which, as I have already shown, all specific differences in matter are transformed into differences of degree? How can *Schelling* say that this retarding [tendency] only appears as a force of attraction from the lowest standpoint? Where then is the higher standpoint, if it is to be comprehensible? What is more, I must assume of the repulsive force what the author predicates of his original evolving [tendency] – that it strives outwards from one point (original involution) and from the centre towards an infinite periphery. Thus, the attractive force and original repulsion stand parallel to each other. Besides, the analysis of this type of idea also shows that the conditions of a universal organism are not to be discovered here at all, and that [37] the formation of only *one* matter is just as little grasped from it as if one merely constructed with both the fundamental forces. As a minor point, I add, as an objection to the above claim, that mechanics has nothing to do with density in respect to *its emergence*, but merely with density as *mass* (in reference to other masses), whereas the actualisation of conditions (which are also purely productive) under which a density comes about and its different degrees are matters for dynamics alone.

The above does not enlighten us at all as to the question of why the claim 'that the empirical qualities of matter with their specific densities are variable'[27] is contradicted so frequently by experience. Although the loud echo of experience, which continually pursues the philosopher of nature, is silenced through universal proofs – as it were, through a dictate of reason – yet still it is appropriate here to attempt [to consider] the following: whether some reasons that hold good for lower levels of reflection [too] will show that the concept, *specific composition*, which hinders all our progress here, is a mere semblance and ultimately reducible to a ratio of degree.

[38] Experience (I mean here, specifically, in chemistry), when it speaks concisely, says the following: sulphur and alkalis, for example, are substances with specific compositions; the qualities which I perceive in one are highly differentiated from the qualities of the other, and still more so are its relations with other chemical bodies, such that in some relations their differences appear to pass into a genuine opposition: the sulphur, for example, is fluid, the alkali fixed; the sulphur tasteless, the alkali possesses a burning taste; the sulphur [is] easily combustible, the alkali already burned, etc. Their specific densities, however, are basically the same. Now, if the claim that qualities change with densities were correct, how could their properties be so different? Should there be merely a difference of degree between capacity to be burnt and having been burnt? And if so, could this be so narrowly explained as the difference between the specific weights of the two substances? If, furthermore, the binding of the sulphur with the alkali results, according to the above claims, in a mere middle-degree, how could the construction of such a middle-degree produce a mixture, such as liver of sulphur?[28] And why is the specific weight of the mixture so seldom (and really, never) the midpoint between the specific weights of the constituents?

[39] Experience counters such a priori claims with these specific questions, and if no complete answer to them can be forthcoming here, then their basic character can at least be sketched in the following:

Qualities are relations to an individual being with senses (sensation). As many types of sensation as there are, there are that many different relations. These relations, however, are so heterogeneous that they do not allow for any parallelism at all, indeed not even oppositions. For – what does a colour have in common with a sound, or a sound with a taste or scent, etc.? However, not only are the types of sense different, but each sense has specifically different sensations: the multiplicity of colours, sounds, sensations of smell, taste and touch are proof enough. Now are these differences merely ones of degree [*gradual*]? – Although this question seems in appearance to have a negative answer, there remains one important factor on the other side. The sensations of one genre, e.g. colours, are completely different, but they belong to the same kind of sense, and so could well belong to one family. Furthermore, the types of sense, which appear to admit of no analogy at all between each other, end up in one and the same consciousness and thus must be reconcilable with each other at their root. Therefore, the following problem is set. [40] *Consciousness appears homogenous (identical) with itself and yet all the seemingly irreconcilable types of sense appear to converge in it; furthermore, each type of sense appears homogenous in itself while retaining a multiplicity of sensations within it.* The main part of this task, which I have touched upon in more detail in my essay Deduction of the Living Organism[29] is solved through the assumption that: *two factors opposed to one another are united in consciousness; this becoming-one is universal homogeneity, absolute unity of consciousness, in which state nothing is to be differentiated. If this homogeneity were now to come apart into heterogeneity, then an ideal limit must be fixed, outside of which, on one side, the positive factor is predominant and, on the other side, the negative factor.* In this way relations emerge which are completely opposed to one another and yet can touch up against each other at the ideal limit, and so thereby leave the unity (identity) of consciousness undamaged. – [They are] relations which therefore perfectly solve the above problem. The binding of the specified features is now resolved precisely into a construction of a *series of degrees*, and so specific difference, both in the types of sense and in the sensations of *one* sense, is transformed into one of degree. Yet, one may still ask how these relations are to be further explicated [41] and how experience can thereby be reconciled with them.

If a cluster of parallel rays of sunlight is refracted through a prism, there arises an image of the sun composed of seven colours: red, yellow, green, etc. One might now give a *Newtonian* or *Eulerian* hypothesis, such that the difference is merely one of degree – for *Newton* different degrees of refractivity, for *Euler* different degrees of the speed of the shocks on the aether. All other colours are, then, mere compositions of the seven fundamental colours and so also stand to each other in a proportion of degree.

If a string is altered proportionally in terms of size, length and tension, then the whole series of tones from the lowest to the highest can be emitted. Therefore again, [this is] a mere difference of degree. Moreover, there are again seven fundamental tones which, in configuration with their five secondary tones, make up all tonal combinations.

Here occurs an important objection:

Granted that the seven fundamental colours and seven fundamental tones together with their composites are differentiated merely in terms of degree, a *specific difference* still inheres within them, e.g. the [42] colour blue with which sulphur burns is specifically different from every other colour blue, and cannot be produced by means of any mixture – likewise the blue of the sky. Sunlight is specifically different from every other white light, just like the light of the moon. The colour red on a fabric is specifically different if it is applied onto bright, shiny paper or matt, dull paper, etc.

It is just the same with sounds:

The sound of a violin is specifically different from the same note [played] on a flute; the sound of the horn just as [different] from the same note on the piano, the human voice from the voice of animals, the sound of a waterfall from the firing of a cannon, etc.

This objection is, in fact, not superficial; it has broad and real significance. To say that this difference depends on the structure of the body onto which the colours and sounds are applied – is *to say nothing*. We would then need to explain this, for the body itself does not reach our eyes and our ears, but only its colour, its sound; only in the sound which strikes against my ear can I recognise *specifically* whether it was caused by a flute [43] or a violin, if I have not otherwise glimpsed the instrument itself. The C-sharp on the piano and the C-sharp on the flute maintain one and the same note, but still in the sound itself there lies something *specifically* different. The body from which the sound comes may impress this difference upon it, but then I would still want to know how the sound *as mere sound* is capable of including *another difference*, in addition to its proportions *of degree*.

I do not know whether what I have said makes clear the whole import of the matter. On the one hand, the unrelenting demand for identity within each type of sense must [also] allow for an explanation of its abiding heterogeneity, [and this] – as we have proven above – can only be done through proportions of degree. And on the other hand, experience shows us that proportions of degree are pushed aside for yet another difference. How is this to be reconciled?

The point of reconciliation lies in the assumption that: *There are two kinds of degree – one which progresses arithmetically and another which progresses geometrically. The multiplicity of sounds from the same sound-producing body maintain among themselves merely an arithmetical proportion; the multiplicity of sound-producing bodies, on the other hand, maintain among themselves a geometric proportion. I take this latter proportion* [44] *for the energy or geometric intensity of the sound.* Each sound-producing body therefore has its own energy or intensity, whereas the arithmetical series of its tones can agree precisely with the series of tones of another sound-producing body. Energy or geometric intensity is therefore the specific difference between sound-producing bodies.

With this result, we have at least shown that the problem is capable of mathematical solution – a conclusion which is usually an extremely desirable one for philosophy of nature. The following analysis contains the main components of such a solution.

Our sense of hearing is limited by two extremes, between the lowest and highest audible sounds. We assume that a sound consists in transmitted vibrations that are mediated by the air or at least through a medium of which air is the vehicle. Furthermore, [we assume] that the lowest pitch must make at the very least 10 vibrations per second and the highest pitch at the very least 1,000 vibrations per second. Vibrations are movements which can be seen as iterations of *one and the same* space. If the vibration, instead of repeating within *one and the same* space, were thought of as a continuous line, then the law of velocity ($C = S / T^{30}$) [45] would also be applicable to sounds. Now, the question is: how does this law behave with respect to higher and lower tone? This is obvious. If 1 vibration of a low tone passes in a given time through just as large a space as 100 vibrations of a high tone, then the velocity would be equal between all audible tones. For – when it comes to a lower tone – the quantity of the successions is compensated for by the size of the individual vibratory movements. And vice versa: what the high tone loses in the size of individual vibratory movements is compensated for by the quantity of successions of smaller vibrations. Therefore, the difference between high and low consists in the quantity of successions of vibrations in general. We would therefore call that tone *the lowest* which had *exactly the same* velocity as the *highest*, but which, in a given time, only consisted in 1 vibration, while the highest made 100 vibrations. Such a ratio, in which the velocity is the same but the quantity of vibrations differ, I call an *arithmetical proportion* – such that these quantities of vibrations in high and low tones are obviously proportionate to each other, and thus, through continual interpolating, the two terms of the geometrical progression can be produced – but this is not [46] the place to show it and it is also quite independent of our hypothesis. My aim here is merely to show how the concept of a *specific composition* is to be entirely discarded from dynamics, and replaced by some kind of magnitude, even if what I say here ought to be initially granted only the status of a hypothesis.

I hypothetically assume this arithmetical ratio between variable sounds from the same body, and now move on to what is far more significant.

In the series of tones, the quantity of vibrations proportionately increases in a given time towards a *maximum*. Above [this maximum] there lies no higher tone and on the other side of it the quantity decreases towards a *minimum*, beneath which there is no lower tone. Evidently, however, this quantity can still increase or decrease further – at the very least, the dynamist sees no obstacle to the composition of his construction from the fact that a numerical increase or decrease could always be taken further. Since [such endless increase or decrease] does not happen, there must *dwell some kind of law in ourselves which absolutely limits the series of sounds for us*. In virtue of the finitude of our nature in general, [47] no *division into infinity* occurs for our power of sensation, even if the mathematician can postulate it. If one posits that the highest audible pitch makes 1,000 vibrations in 1 second, then 1/1,000 of a second is the *fixed unit of time, the indivisible instant,* for our sense of hearing, during which our power of sensation's highest analysis is carried out. Now, in nature, the most remarkable law that exists (the proof of which I cannot provide here) runs: *the maximum of a lower force passes over into the minimum of a higher*. If we apply this law to our sense of hearing, then the maximum of a lower-sound-producing body must pass into the minimum of a higher one: the 1,000 vibrations of A is driven still higher, and dissolved into the 10 vibrations of B, and the difference between the two can therefore be expressed in a *permanent, fixed sound-energy*, i.e. *one* vibration of sound from B must, in a given time, pass through the potency of the space of one vibration from A. That is, the velocity of B is greater than that of A, whereas the quantity of vibrations in the series of sounds from A is exactly the same as B. The difference between the *two* sound-producing bodies is therefore precisely the inverse of the difference between different sounds in *one* sound-producing body. In the first case, the velocity was the same but the quantity of vibrations differed; in the present case, on the contrary, [48] the velocity is different but the quantity of vibrations the same.

We observe such a proportion in the sound of the piano and the flute. The sound of the latter is more energetic than the sound of the former. The quantity of vibratory movements, their arithmetical ratio with each other, is the same, i.e. they maintain equal pitch (an equal series of notes as each other), but the energy, the geometrical intensity of their sounds, is different, i.e. the *specific composition* of the sounds differs – and this solves the problem of showing how sound could possess another difference in addition to its proportion of degree. If we think up a series of terms according to these presuppositions, and draw a limit for all audible objects at the extreme [of the series], then the specifically different sounds are merely different intensities, with respect to which the maximum of one series of sounds always passes over into the minimum of another. The terms themselves can maintain a geometrically-progressive ratio among themselves, whereas the sphere between two terms is occupied by the arithmetical ratio of *one* series of sounds. All specific difference is transformed into a matter of degree.

We observe similar behaviour daily in the arbitrary use of coins, only with the difference that [49] the unity constituted in this case is arbitrary, whereas that constituted in the above case proceeds from a natural law of our power of sensation. All kinds of silver, for example, maintain among themselves an arithmetical ratio, but the maximum of silver passes into the minimum of gold, and the maximum of gold passes over yet further into the minimum of gemstone. Silver, gold, gemstone are unities on which we bestow an imaginary value, but gold is a higher unity than silver: it is, as it were, more energetic and intensive than silver.

These claims, stated above in terms of our sense of hearing, are equally valid when applied to all the other types of sense – only the analysis of the other senses has not yet gone deep enough to set out such clear analogies. The specifically different sensations of light, of smell, of taste and of touch are merely different intensities of the same fundamental proportion, whereas each individual type of smell or taste can pass through an arithmetical series of degrees. It would be worth investigating whether the sevenfold division revealed in the fundamental colours and sounds is not also present in the other types of sense. Perhaps we merely lack a prism for smell and taste. Each sense is, on this view, a mere measurer of degree; without being affected from outside, [50] it is neutral, homogenous, but, when affected, it becomes heterogeneous, thereby displaying – inhibited at different stages – the multiplicity in sensation.

I come now to an even *higher relation*, which, when corroborated by others in the future, *will complete the whole, and indubitably give rise to the permanent form of the one system.*

It has been shown that each type of sense has for itself many different relations which are resolved into a series of degrees. However, the question now arises: *what relation do the different types of sense have to each other, since they seem to have absolutely no point in common?* It was already mentioned above that there must be a relation to the extent that they are united in the same consciousness and pullulate from the same root – what, then, is this relation? Here I assert that there is, once more, just a different energy between them, and their incompatibility, which experience appears to reveal to us, could have its ground in the degree of the potencies through which they are separated from one another. It is in this way that, we believe, their continuity, their interlocking, is overcome.

[51] The following features help draw us closer to the solution to this problem, and also confirm our hypothesis:

When we consider the intensity of the senses from our eyes down to touch (in so far as intensity, like velocity, generates an inverse proportion of time to space), *then we observe that they stand to one another in a descending ratio.*

The eye searches for images in the immeasurable distance and needs only a moment to penetrate this distance, such is the tremendous sphere of its activity!

The ear, by contrast, receives its sound from only a few miles away, and the time of transmission is here already a perceptible one.

Smell stands only a few steps from its object, and although here precise observation may fail, the time of transmission is certainly greater than that of sound.

Taste is very close to contact, distinguishable from it solely by the presence of a moisture adhering to the surface [of the tongue].*

[52] And finally *touch* passes over into an inner assimilation with the object. In both the latter cases, the time is immeasurable. *What a changing ratio from immeasurable distance to contact! Thus, while in the first case time almost disappears through space becoming immeasurable, in the last case space disappears through time becoming immeasurable.*

Both extremes of intensity can be more popularly expressed as follows: my eye needs only a few moments to contact its object off in the immeasurable distance, whereas my touch would have to take an immeasurable time to annul the space between it and this object and so come into contact with it. In between the two extremes lie the other senses, as median intensities.

Another aspect which determines our view of the types of sense as merely higher or lower energies [53] is the following: *the smaller the space in which the sense organs are compressed, the more intensive is their effectiveness.*

The eye, the most spiritual of all, refracts its rays through a small lens, and collects them on a membrane (the retina) of insignificant area –

The organ of hearing already has observable holes and spirals –

The organ of smell extends over a surface increased by means of a lamellar spatial structure –

---

* One could claim that, with respect to taste, the object has already come into immediate contact with the organ. [52] I am asserting, though, that immediate contact belongs solely to the sense of touch, which the tongue has in common with all the other senses, when it comes to tasteless bodies. But what stimulates taste must always possess dissolved or dissolving parts, thus it is effective only by virtue of the medium of a liquid.

And [the surface] which, with respect to the *organ of taste*, is already stretched out considerably is, with respect to *touch*, fully extended over the whole surface of the individual.

Therefore, there is also an inverse proportion of intensity here. What for the *eye* is a living intussusception, a concentrated force, is already lost in *feeling* in mechanical *coexistence* and *separation*, in *spiritless extension*.

Let us now say without qualification that it follows from all of the above that when the energy of light-perception decreases into a minimum, the maximum of sound-energy increases, and where this decreases, the sphere of smelling begins, etc. – i.e., more popularly expressed: [54] *Over that distance, which for the sense of smell is a maximum, the time of transmission is an indivisible unit of time, a minimum, for perception by the sense of hearing. And over that distance, which is the maximum for the sense of hearing, the time of transmission is merely a minimum for the eye, i.e. infinitely small, thus imperceptible.*

What, then, is the material object causing our representations?

If each of our senses extracts a number of qualities from [the purported object], what then remains other than a dissolved nothing? But, as qualities are merely different proportions of degree, so what is the object other than the collective expression of such?

If the question were now to arise how this collective expression could be brought under the form of a law – regarding this I would say: assume in general that in nature (or transferred from your own nature) two forces stand opposed to one another, then one will strive to infinity, the other to a point. Where they meet one another, outside of their common middle, there the negative endeavours to inhibit what the positive endeavours to achieve. However, the tendency of the positive goes to infinity; its expansion therefore meets resistance, [55] and this gives us the phenomenon of a filling of space = matter. Evidently, this expansion is greater, the nearer the positive force lies to that middle, and so the more intensive it remains. [It is] less, the further it is from that middle and so the more extensive it becomes. The different stages of this filling give us the phenomenon of degrees of *elasticity*. Moreover, what happens with the preponderance of the positive factor also happens conversely with the preponderance of the negative factor. Instead of striving outward, as in elasticity, there is here a tendency into itself, around its own centre (one should not make the mistake here of thinking of gravity). This gives us the phenomenon of *mass*, and, indeed, at different stages a different mass. For now in both cases, space stands in an inverse proportion to its mass, thus giving us the phenomenon of a series of *specific densities*.

The collective expression of an object is therefore its *specific density*, and the description of its qualities, as they are ascribed to this or that sense, is only a specific expression of this.

We now stand once more at the very point from which we departed, but the empirical-dialectical puzzle of why differences in specific densities [56] conform so little to the whole host of differences in quality still remains unsolved. I am asserting, however, that the series of propositions set out above is capable of disclosing to us something concerning this problem. There is no space here to get much closer to [a solution] and I leave this gap open for future investigations.

In what follows, I will make a few remarks that can serve as an illustration of the kind of viewpoint made available by this kind of construction:

The qualities of different types of sense, whose union is the material object, stand in some ratio of intensity to one another, and indeed, because the object is, under certain circumstances, something permanent in the sensory world, [they also stand] in a relation of equilibrium. The equilibrium alone is permanent while the qualities, which constitute the factors of this equilibrium, are infinitely changeable. For example, what the eye gains in energy during changes in the intensity of light-sensations is to be subtracted from the energy of the other senses – for instance, through a diminished energy of taste- or smell-sensation, etc. What, for example, the sulphur initially possesses in capacity for light-development can be extracted from it through a loss of taste-development, whereas what the alkali initially possesses [57] in taste-development can be extracted from it through a loss in its capacity for light-development, etc. In such a relation, there obviously exists a mix of unknown laws, and chemistry is thereby extended over an almost illimitable field, even if, on the other hand, there is the consolation of attaining a finite construction.

By means of the above hypothesis we have now at least demonstrated that the obscure concept, *specific composition*, can be transformed into the constructible concept, *energy*, as is appropriate for a dynamics that hopes for universal comprehension.

Many of the preceding remarks are indeed directed against *Schelling's nature-philosophical outline*, but they are not meant to break with the *whole*. Since it contains so many new and radical ideas, it seems entirely appropriate that this work only proves to us that our future writings will remain shackled to it. If here and there its novelty and energy – features unparalleled among our most sublime reformers – might obtrude at the expense of consistency, then novelty and energy are the most secure means to enthral and fascinate us from the first, and to kindle that frugal brightness which [58] philosophy spreads into our field with a vivid surge of light. The most serious [criticism] with which this work is to be burdened, after the above elucidations, consists in its abandonment of the demand regarding the first principle of a system – even if, in my opinion, there is an even higher demand than this. Unconditioned empiricism cannot, I am all but certain, fully ground the form of a nature-philosophical system. In general, it seems still too early to speak of a system of philosophy of nature, before a propaedeutic for it is available. For precisely this propaedeutic would undertake the transition from transcendental philosophy to philosophy of nature; it would be concerned with the proofs that all laws of nature are *transferred* from our spirit alone, that the first impulse of nature dwells in ourselves – *spontaneity = world soul*.

* * *

Baader's remarkable essay: *On the Pythagorean Square or the Four World-Regions in Nature*,[31] as well as some of *Schelling's* remarks on *gravity*, which are appended to his outline,[32] prompt me to express a few thoughts on the subject.

[59] When one begins to construct in philosophy of nature, one assumes – in order to awaken nature from its dead slumber – two tendencies, which meet each other from opposite directions. For – as *Schelling* aptly puts it – one cannot philosophise at all about an inactive object. These tendencies are usually referred to by the expressions: repulsive and attractive forces. However, it still leaves the question: whence [comes] the impulse – the striving in these forces? In the finite world, forces are only transmissions from term to term. Nature does not know of a self-producing force. Tendency – striving is a characteristic of spontaneity alone, and is quite foreign to the concept of nature. Yet, we can take no further step in nature without presupposing those fundamental forces. What first follows from this assumption are two remarkable proportions:

1. *Each force, independently of the other, has a tendency to infinity: for where there is no contradiction, there is absolute infinity.*
2. *When dependent on the other, they cancel each other out and all tendency disappears, for – where there is nothing but contradiction, there is absolute finitude.*

[60] In the first proposition, the character of our *spirit* is evidently expressed: *striving to infinity*.

In the second proposition, the character of its opposite – *nature* is expressed: *striving to the absolutely finite*.

Therefore, these forces have no tendency in and for themselves. They are, on the one hand, only distinguished in so far as spirit separates them and, on the other hand, only connected in so far as nature unites them. Nature and spirit enter into conflict with each other: when spirit is victorious in this struggle, the *original drive* arises, and it is this which separates these forces and awakens their tendency to infinity. – When nature become preponderant in this struggle, a *drive opposed to the previous one* (a negative drive) emerges – one which unites these forces and endeavours to prioritise and advance their tendency to absolute finitude. And what do we call this negative drive? – *Gravity*. The original *positive drive* and *gravity* are opposed to one another: gravity is the unifying mediator of these forces and the original drive the disrupter of their rest. *Separation* and *unification* of these forces is the reciprocal play out of which arise the infinitely many middle-terms that lie between the absolutely finite and the infinite – that is, the world in its manifoldness. [61] This is the deduction of gravity, and thus, instead of two principles, the two fundamental forces introduce *four* principles into philosophy of nature.

A happy and apt analogy is contained in *Franz Baader's* idea that these four principles in nature are comparable to the four world-regions. *The two fundamental forces are midday and midnight, the ascent separates them and the decline unites them again* – (the daily cycle of nature). When the original drive, whose phenomenon is the rising sun, begins to gain a preponderance over gravity, then dawn breaks and the fundamental forces sunk in rest approach their point of separation. When in the preponderance of the drive (that is, the mean velocity of the drive) gravity becomes imperceptible, then the sun rises, nature awakes, the polarities of the earth are posited in activity and the horizon expands. – When the drive hastens to its zenith and approaches its maximum, then the brilliance of nature is at its highest and these forces reach the highest stage of their separation. – When, however, the drive has actually reached its maximum, – its phenomenon is the passage of the sun through its midday-sphere – then the minimum of the preponderance of its adversary, gravity, begins. Henceforth, nature runs the reverse course – the day declines, [62] the sun again approaches its setting. – When gravity hastens to its mean velocity, then the evening draws on, the horizon contracts. And when [gravity] actually reaches [its mean velocity] and the drive is completely extinguished through the preponderance of gravity, then the sun sets, these forces move into their point of unity and the polarities come to rest. – When gravity attains its nadir, its maximum, then it is midnight, the deepest stillness of nature. – However, to the maximum of gravity the minimum of the ascending drive is bound and so nature reverses, following its earlier course. Hence, the changing of the day is merely the prototype of higher relations.

The same analogy can also be extended to the changing of the seasons: here gravity is, as *Baader* remarks, the positive principle of cold which produces winter (if it is, in fact, helpful to positively name that which inhibits everything positive).

If we think of the cycle of the sun as only apparent, thereby fixing it in rest, then this provides all the conditions needed to bring about the turning of the axis of our planet. If the sun is fixed, then so too is gravity – like two unchangeable foci of an ellipse.

[63] Through an eternal, self-enclosed cycle, nature becomes a unity, an individual. However, this immeasurable sphere has an indeterminate quantity of subordinated spheres within it: the multiplicity of individuality and its polarities proceed to infinity – and, considered as forces, all these fundamental laws recognise that the maximum of the lower force passes into the higher of the encompassing force until at last the highest of all-encompassing forces turns back into the lowest. Many more aspects of this investigation are treated with uncommon perspicacity in *Schelling's nature-philosophical outline* under the rubric: *The task of deducing the dynamic series of stages*.[33] The basic aspect of such an investigation is contained in the following principles: I am an individual and have become one through the reflection of mankind, [for] the homogenous breaks forth at the homogenous; therefore, where there is individuality, a reflection must occur. I first raise myself to self-consciousness as an individual, but self-consciousness in a spirit is precisely what a centre of gravity is in nature; how I attain self-consciousness is then how the natural product attains its centre of gravity. To develop this, a new chain of reasoning is required, and here is not the place to begin it.

By means of this entire investigation these results [have been attained]. [64] There are four principles:

1. and 2. *Two opposed fundamental forces* – (midday and midnight, which are two sides of the triangle according to *Baader*).
3. *Gravity* (the descent, the unifying basis of the triangle).
4. *The original drive* (the ascent, the pulsating central point of the triangle) *spontaneity = world soul*.

In the following passage (§ XXXIII) from my earliest piece, my *Dissertation*,[34] I already differentiated these four principles precisely:

> On matter § IV. The forces of *attraction* and *repulsion*, which emerge in tandem, (hence 1. and 2. two fundamental forces opposed to each other) arise with no internal principle of motion; [instead] causes of change in degree should be sought in what is posited externally to them. If we attended to matter retarded in absolute rest, we would attribute absolute equilibrium to it and no intuitable quality. But since we can trace the level of degree of prime matter only from an external cause – which, when it ceases, the effect will also cease – it is necessary to insist that *matter tends by its own constant inclination to a state of absolute equilibrium*, (gravity, tendency to absolute equilibrium, negative drive), just like reciprocal electrical charges, which

forever strive to rush into an embrace that is destructive of both. The sun (4. phenomenon of the expanding drive) seems to serve as *the cause which prevents absolute equilibrium* on our planet.

In conclusion, I want to call attention to some requirements which become manifest to the philosopher of nature as he proceeds further.

One of these requirements is for a detailed phyto-zoology: while the philosopher of nature [already] possesses the form, he must also get hold of the content and, indeed, an ordered and collated content. For the observing class of the learned is apparently separated from the reasoning [class] by some law of energy in the human mechanism.

Under this rubric, I do not merely mean an *anatomia comparata* but also, at the very least, the first lines of a *physiologia comparata* of both plants and animals. Perhaps Prof. *Kielmayer** in Tübingen might [66] make known to us his results in these fields.[35]

Another neglected requirement [for the philosopher of nature] is mathematics. As long as we stay within the hypothetical part, within the principles of experience of natural science, then we see nothing but qualities, which appear to admit no numerical value or construction from geometrical analysis. However, if we intend to find a lasting viewpoint, then the mathematical part of natural science is unavoidable, and thus it is a somewhat unfair objection of *Schelling's* that the construction of the two fundamental forces expressed in formulae concerning degrees of density alone is a real lead-weight in natural science.[36] If one remains with such relations and attempts no further deductions, then all does indeed appear futile – for they teach [67] experience nothing. – The foregoing can, however, serve as an example that it is possible to go further. The lead-weight of natural science rests rather on the assumption of specific composition, which pure dynamics understands very unwillingly. And what is pure dynamics other than mathematics? Is its aim not to state formulae through which we should discover appearances in nature? Obviously, it requires from us a higher knowledge than this of arithmetic, algebra, pure geometry and mechanics, and the very soul of mathematics, analytic geometry and higher analysis, belong particularly to it. Philosophy of nature takes its subsidies from all parts of mathematics, but its results occur only in its

---

* Unfortunately, this wealthy property owner provides so little assistance to our poor public funds. [66] I mean here his invaluable *zoology*, a work in which he has equally invested his power and his time, two aspects which – in other minds not capable of subduing the natural law of inertia – stand typically in an inverse proportion. Furthermore, [this is] a work in which felicitous analogies and inductions and frequent intellectual insight (divination, as it were) have long been developed from the highest principles of philosophy of nature.

highest regions. – Is not the difference between a *straight* and a *curved* line precisely the point of distinction between inorganic and organic nature? For where the straight line wanders off irregularly in edges and angles, there is the lowest stage of inorganic nature (aggregation of masses). Where the straight line becomes regular and expresses itself in determinate forms (crystallisation), there approaches the passage from the inorganic to the organic. Where the first stage of organisation begins, there the *curved line* becomes dominant: from sprouting leaves to the noble shape of animals, nothing but elliptical and parabolic forms – the hallmark of individuality and proof that mechanics, which can only operate in straight [68] lines, here curves back into a circle. However, no such cycle arises when the four deduced principles do not intertwine with one another in steady obedience to [their] law – in them lie the pulse and breath of nature.

On the True Concept of Philosophy of Nature and the Correct Way of Solving its Problems[1]

F. W. J. Schelling

[85] The concept I have of the science that I name 'philosophy of nature' has been quite clearly explained in many passages in the second issue of the first volume [of this journal],[2] and the relation I believe I can establish between it and transcendental philosophy is ascertainable from those same texts by anyone who is fairly accurately informed about the state of contemporary philosophy.

Already in the *Introduction* to my *Outline of the System of Philosophy of Nature*, there is the following passage on p. 15:

> Up to this point the idea of speculative physics has been deduced and developed; it is another business to show how this idea must be realised and actually carried out. The author, for this purpose, would at once refer to his *Outline of a System of the Philosophy of Nature*, if he had no reason to suspect many even of those who might consider that *Outline* worthy of their attention would come to it with certain preconceived ideas, which he has not presupposed, and which he does not desire to have presupposed by them.[3]

And the following are given as such presuppositions:

1. That many people misled by the term 'philosophy of nature' expect transcendental deductions of natural phenomena, the same as exist in various fragments [of the transcendental system] elsewhere; [86] for me, however, philosophy of nature is a self-sufficient whole and is a science fully differentiated from transcendental philosophy.
2. That many will find in my *Outline* their own concept of dynamic physics – namely, where I cite the [theory] that all specific changes and differences in matter are merely changes or differences of the degree of density – but this is not my opinion.[4]

It is precisely on these points that Eschenmayer disagrees with me in the above critique of my *Outline of Philosophy of Nature*. As important to me as the judgement of this sharp-witted philosopher on my work must be, for, after Kant, he was the first to secure the grounds for a dynamic physics, I do so wish that he had not so happily left unread that *Introduction*. For, to judge from a number of passages, he was not acquainted with it while composing his critique, as I refer to it explicitly in the Preface to the *Outline* in relation to the very concept of this science [of philosophy of nature], which I had everywhere only presupposed [in the *Outline* itself]. Otherwise, Eschenmayer would have seen that his objections to me were not completely unexpected. He would have not only adduced arguments against my treatment of this science, but would also have begun to find answers to them on the basis of my presuppositions – and so we would have been one step further on than we are now.

After Eschenmayer saw that he had been deceived in expecting to find transcendental philosophy or a part of it (I know not which) in my *Outline*, there were only two possible hypotheses: *either* that I did not know at all that point of view which Eschenmayer holds as true – the idealist – which is of course difficult to believe, since instead of being sketched at the beginning of the work as is usual, this viewpoint is rather hidden in the middle of it, and without doubt banished there on purpose.[5] For the author says clearly enough in one passage: philosophy of nature is for him a result of an unconditioned empiricism[6] (this word, as one can deduce from the *Introduction*,[7] being used instead of *realism* [87], which would have been a very awkward expression). *Or* [the second hypothesis is] that the author had taken fright before the imposing mass being put in place by the cranks of idealism and perhaps still more before certain captious questions which emerge out of the collision of idealism with experience. For example:

> Is it the case that the new-born child who first gazes upon his mother has projected this mother and with her the sun, whose rays now illuminate his eyes for the first time?

And other such questions, like those set out in *Clavis Fichtiana seu Leibgeberiana*,[8] from which I will only take a few more as examples:

> For example: the man whom I encounter means to leave home by a free decision, but how is it now possible that he is simultaneously located on the street by means of my necessary act of producing?

Or:

> Here is a tree which someone planted fifty years ago for posterity, how is it that I now produce it as it is through productive intuition?

Or:

> How happy is the idealist that he can consider the divine works of Plato, Sophocles and all other great minds as his own?

In regard to the last of these questions, the author ought not to forget the extent to which such happiness is tempered by certain other works (e.g. his own).

[88] These are only examples of the sorts of questions that could easily lead to embarrassment; however, they are not [embarrassing] for me, and anyway, both before and after the appearance of my *Outline*, I have provided proof from which one can conclude that an idealist point of view on nature is not alien to me.[9] Without doubt, there is a reason for the *fact* that I separate philosophy of nature and transcendental philosophy from one another and have tried to generate the latter in a quite different direction than the former. If the reason for this fact has not been extensively dealt with in this journal before now, then this is merely because, for the time being, the journal is devoted more to the internal culture of this science than to investigating and proving its possibility (of which I am personally certain), and also because this proof can be achieved successfully only in a general presentation of philosophy. The next issue of this journal, however, is to be dedicated entirely to the new working through and development of my system from its first grounds;[10] I will thus use this opportunity to very briefly sketch it and make only the following remarks.

If it were just a matter of an idealist type of explanation, or rather construction, then this is not to be found in philosophy of nature as I have established it. – But then was it just a matter of that? – I have expressly proposed the opposite. – If therefore the idealist construction of nature as I establish it is to be judged, then it must be judged according to my *System of Transcendental Idealism*, but not my *Outline of Philosophy of Nature*.

But why then should it not be idealist? And is there even (and the author agrees with this) any type of philosophising other than the idealist? Above all, I hope that this expression is to be further determined [in what follows] than it has been up until now. There is an idealism of nature and an idealism of the I. For me, the former is original, *the latter* is derived.

[89] I wish that, above all things, philosophy on philosophising would be distinguished from philosophy itself.[11] To be able to philosophise, I must already have philosophised, for how else would I know what philosophising is? If I now emerge from this to find out what philosophising itself is, then I see myself merely as something known in myself – and during this entire investigation I never get out of myself. – There is no question that this philosophy on philosophising is subjectively (in relation to the philosophising subject) the *first*, but there is just as little doubt that

in the question 'how is philosophy possible?' I assume *myself* already in the highest potency, and therefore the question is likewise only answered for this potency. – The derivation of this potency itself cannot in turn be provided by the response, for the *question* itself already presupposes it. As long as I maintain myself in this potency while philosophising, I can behold nothing objective other than in the moment of its entry into consciousness (for the latter is precisely the highest potency, to which I have raised my object once and for all through freedom) and no longer in its *original* coming-into-being at the moment of its *first* emergence (in *nonconscious* [*bewußtlosen*] activity). As it comes into my hands, it has already run through all the metamorphoses which are necessary for it to rise up into consciousness. – To see the objective in its first coming-into-being is only possible by *depotentiating* the *object* of all philosophising, which in the highest potency is = I, and then constructing, from the beginning, with this object reduced to the first potency.

This is only possible through abstraction, which must now be determined more precisely – and with this abstraction one moves from the realm of the doctrine of science [*Wissenschaftslehre*] into *pure-theoretical* philosophy. The doctrine of science [*Wissenschaftslehre*] is not philosophy itself, but philosophy about philosophy. In it, the equality posited by consciousness between the object – *about* which one philosophises and which in philosophising is that which produces and *acts* [*Handelnde*] – and the subject – *which* philosophises, and which in the self-same act [*Akt*] is that which reflects and intuits – is never annulled – and must never be annulled if it is to be claimed that that object = [90] I. For consciousness, when it is once attained, consists precisely in the perpetual identity of that which acts and that which intuits this activity [*Handeln*]; that which acts is not *in itself* = I, it is = I only *in* this identity of that which acts and that which reflects on this act [*des auf dieses Handelnde reflectirenden*]. And since the doctrine of science [*Wissenschaftslehre*] takes its object into that very potency where it is already raised into identity with that which reflects, as = I, it can never construct this identity, thereby never escaping the circle of consciousness. As such, it can only construct what immediately appears to consciousness – that is, *everything* [*Alles*] only in its highest potency.

Although the doctrine of science [*Wissenschaftslehre*] initially attempts to derive *consciousness*, owing to an inescapable circle it ends up employing all those *means* which this already *completed* consciousness (in the philosophising subject) presents to it to exhibit everything in that potency in which it is already raised into consciousness. It therefore takes its object (that which acts and produces) already to be I, although it has only first become I at that moment when reflection posits it as identical with it. [This moment], however, first occurs in *free* and *conscious activity*. In free activity, that which acts is still the same objective [element] which acted in non-conscious intuition; it is now a *free* act solely because it is posited as identical with that which intuits.

If I now abstract from what is first posited in the philosopher's object by this free act, there remains something *purely objective*. By means of this self-same abstraction, I move to the standpoint of *purely theoretical* philosophising (exempt from all subjective and practical interference): this pure-theoretical philosophising results in *philosophy of nature*; for, by means of that abstraction, I reach the concept of the pure subject-object (= nature), from which I then rise to the subject-object of consciousness (= I). The latter becomes the principle of the idealist or, what means the same thing to me, the practical part of philosophy; the former is the principle of the pure-theoretical part; both in their union give the system of ideal-realism which has become *objective* (the system of art). With [this system of art,] philosophy, which in the doctrine of science [*Wissenschaftslehre*] [91] must proceed from a merely subjective ideal-realism (contained in the consciousness of the philosopher), produces itself out of itself, as it were, and so is completed.

Through the gradual but *complete* becoming objective of the pure subject-object, the (intuiting) activity, which in *principle* is limitlessly ideal, raises itself to the I, i.e. to the subject for which that subject-object (that ideal-real) is itself object. From the standpoint of consciousness, nature appears to me as objective and the I as subjective; from this standpoint I cannot otherwise express the problem of philosophy of nature than as it is expressed in the Introduction to my System of Idealism – that is, *to let the subjective emerge from the objective.*[12] Expressed in higher philosophical language, this means the same as:

> '*to let the subject-object* OF CONSCIOUSNESS *emerge from the* PURE *subject-object.*'

Many philosophical writers (among them one of late who has undertaken to judge something grounded in idealism, something that has only been made possible through him, although he ought to be convinced that he has yet to obtain sufficient knowledge of it) appear to have taken this *objective* [element], from which philosophy of nature should proceed, I don't quite know for what, but certainly for something objective in itself. So, it is no wonder if the confusion in their representations proliferates substantially on the back of this. I presuppose that I am speaking to those [readers] who are well aware of what philosophy understands by the objective.

For them, 'objective' signifies the same as '*real*'. – *For me*, as they could have seen from the System of Idealism,[13] the objective is itself *simultane-*

ously the real and the ideal; the two are never separate, but exist together originally (even in nature). This ideal-real becomes objective only through [92] the emerging consciousness in which the subjective raises itself to the highest (theoretical) potency.

With nature-philosophy [*Natur-Philosophie*] I never emerge from that identity of the ideal-real; I continually preserve both in this original connection, and the pure subject-object from which I proceed is precisely that which is simultaneously the ideal and the real in the potency 0. From this comes into being for me the ideal-real of the higher potency, the *I*, in relation to which the *pure* subject-object is already objective.

The reason that those who have grasped idealism well have not understood philosophy of nature is because it is difficult or impossible for them to detach themselves from the subjective [element] of intellectual intuition. – For the purpose of philosophy of nature, I demand intellectual intuition as it is demanded in the doctrine of science [*Wissenschaftslehre*];[14] however, I demand, in addition, abstraction from the *intuiting* in this intuition, an abstraction which leaves behind for me the purely objective [element] of this act, which in itself is merely subject-object, but in no way = I, for the reasons provided above.

Even in the System of Idealism, in order to devise the theoretical part, I had to take the I out of its own intuition, to abstract from the subjective in intellectual intuition – in a word, to posit it as *non-conscious*. – However, in so far as the I is non-conscious, it is not = I; for the I is only the subject-object in so far as it cognises itself as such. The acts, which are there established as acts of the I and so in the highest potency, are genuinely acts of the pure subject-object, and are *as* such not yet *sensation, intuition*, etc. They only become them by being raised into consciousness.

I do not expect anyone to understand me at this level of generality. It is against my will that I here speak of what I intend; for what one intends is best spoken about by doing it. Anyway, those who do not agree with me on the principle can still [93] participate in the investigations, since they are free to translate all the principles which are necessary for their own understanding into the idealist potency. For *within* science, it initially matters little in what way nature is constructed, if it is only constructed. For a start, [the above] is not a matter of natural science, but an altered point of view on philosophy as a whole and idealism itself which the latter will sooner or later be forced to accept. – Idealism will remain; it will only be derived from first principles, and in its first beginnings from nature itself, which until now appeared to be in the starkest contradiction with it. Moreover, as I have already remarked, the *doctrine of science* [*Wissenschaftslehre*] will never get to this point. – To be subjectively possible, all philosophising, even the purely theoretical by which nature-philosophy comes into being, presupposes the doctrine of science [*Wissenschaftslehre*] and grounds itself on it. – *The latter*, precisely because it is the doctrine of *knowing* [*Wissens-Lehre*], can take everything only in the highest potency and must not abandon this. – It is, however, a question not of the doctrine of science [*Wissenschaftslehre*] (a closed and complete science) but the system of knowing itself. – This system can come into being only by abstracting from the doctrine of science [*Wissenschaftslehre*], and if the latter is ideal-realism, it [the former] has only two major parts – a purely theoretical or realist part and a practical or idealist part. Through the union of these two, ideal-realism cannot again come into being, but rather real-idealism must come into being (what I have called above ideal-realism become objective and) by which I understand nothing other than the system of art. Only it must not be imagined as if these parts are separate within the system itself, as I here represent them. – In it, there is absolute continuity; it is *One* unbroken series, which proceeds from the simplest in nature to the highest and most complex, the artwork. – Is it bold to want to establish the first, truly universal system which ties together the opposed ends of knowing? – Those who understood the System of Idealism and followed my investigations in philosophy of nature with some interest will at the very least not take it to be [94] something absolutely impossible. He will have seen how gradually from all sides everything approaches the One, how already very distant phenomena, which have been sought in quite different worlds, shake hands and as it were impatiently await the final binding word to be spoken about them. If, at the very least, an initial plan is successfully executed, one will thereupon find comprehensible and thus acceptable the idea that it is to be made from completely different sides and that one first tries to correct individual investigations before one unites them as parts of one and the same whole. – No one will find it unnatural for me to consider everything which can now occur as means to this end. For, not before it is both necessary and useful will I try to agree with others on *what is first*, and then it will appear, anyway, of its own accord and free of contradiction. For those for whom the preceding is still not clear, I shall say nothing further than I do not proceed in this manner without reason. I know that it leads to the goal and I will pursue it undisturbed, without taking notice of objections which are made against it and which will be answered by the future results themselves.

As soon as I began to proclaim philosophy of nature, the following objection was frequently made to me: I *presuppose* nature without asking the critical question of how we thus come to suppose a nature. Eschenmayer seems to have something like this in mind.[15] I answered that whoever raises himself by abstraction to the pure concept of nature will see how I presuppose nothing for the construction but what the transcendental-philosopher likewise presupposes. For what I call *nature* IS for me nothing but the purely-objective [element] of intellectual intuition, the pure subject-object, what the transcendental philosopher posits as = I, because he does not make the abstraction – from the intuiting – which is necessary if a purely objective, i.e. a genuinely theoretical, philosophy is to come about. – That pure subject-object [95] is already determined by its nature (the contradiction which lies within it) to activity and indeed to determinate activity. This determinate activity gives rise, passing through all its potencies, to a series of determinate products, while it potentiates itself both with what is unlimited in it (the ideal) and with its products. – Whether these products are those which are presented in experience or not does not initially concern me; I look merely to the self-construction of the subject-object. If from this [self-construction] arise products and potencies of ideal activity that can be shown in nature, then I clearly see that my attempt was genuinely a deduction of nature, i.e. a philosophy of nature. I have therefore not presupposed what *you* think of as nature, but rather derived it (although you will permit me, after I have performed the experiment for myself, to announce my philosophy in advance as a philosophy of nature). In general, I have presupposed nothing but what can immediately be taken from the conditions of knowing itself as a first principle, something originally and simultaneously subjective and objective, through the activity of which a consciousness is also posited, alongside the objective world as such. For this consciousness [the objective world] becomes object and vice versa. With this concept we have reached back further than Spinoza managed with his concepts of *natura naturans* and *natura naturata*,[16] which are merely relatively opposed, and *both* are only the subject-object regarded from different points of view.

Philosophy of nature has this advantage over idealism, that it proves its principles purely theoretically, and has to make no particular, practical demands, unlike the latter which precisely for this reason possesses no purely theoretical reality, as I have already observed in the Preface to my System of Idealism.[17]

By means of the fact that I abstract from the intuiting activity in intellectual intuition, I take the subject-object only from its own intuition (I make it non-conscious), but not from mine. It is constantly conceived in my intuition as *my* construction, and I know that throughout I only have to do with my own construction. The task is: to make the subject-object in this way objective, and to generate it from itself to the point where it [96] coincides as one with nature (as product). The point where it becomes nature is also that where the unlimitable in it raises itself to the I and where the opposition between I and nature, which is made in ordinary consciousness, completely disappears, so that nature = I and I = nature. At this point where everything which is still activity (not product) in nature is transferred into the I, nature endures and lives only in this I which henceforth is one and all and in it everything is contained. And it is at precisely this point that idealism begins.

What has therefore been established in the System of Idealism under the names of theoretical and practical philosophy[18] is already to be regarded as the idealist part of the complete system of philosophy. The acts which are derived in the theoretical part of idealism are acts whose simple potencies exist in nature and are established in philosophy of nature.[19] – The coming-into-being of these higher potencies fall into the transition from the realist to the idealist part; *as* consciousness comes into being, all earlier acts raise themselves into sensation, intuition, etc. – Because philosophy of nature and transcendental philosophy have been spoken of as opposed yet equally possible orientations of philosophy, many have asked which of the two is accorded priority? – Without doubt, philosophy of nature, because it lets the *standpoint* of idealism itself first come into being, and thereby provides for it a secure, *purely* theoretical foundation. However, the opposition between philosophy of nature and idealism has the same worth as the traditional opposition between theoretical and practical philosophy. – Therefore, philosophy returns to the ancient (Greek) division into physics and ethics, both of which are united through a third part (poetics, or philosophy of art).

Eschenmayer, it is true, feels that it is not yet time to speak of a system of philosophy of nature.[20] I would be anxious to know how long we will have to wait and how we shall know in the future that the time for this science has come? – Perhaps when experience has progressed further? – But *how far* [97] are we really with experience? – This can only be judged from philosophy of nature. Experience is blind and must first learn to see its own richness or lack through science. Moreover, a completely a priori science cannot be dependent on contingent conditions like that of the progress of experience; rather, on the contrary, the latter must be accelerated onwards by the former, which presents ideas that lead to invention. One can never say of a self-sufficient science: it is not yet time to invent it, for it is always time for it to be invented. – Therefore, one will always only be able to say: this specific attempt to establish science has not yet succeeded. – That what I have established in my Outline of Philosophy of Nature is not even taken by myself to be *the system itself* is already explained in the title of the work and very specifically in its Preface, where I write: 'The author has too lofty a notion of the magnitude of his undertaking to announce in the present treatise anything more than the first outline, let alone to erect the system itself.'[21] – I also explained that this piece was not primarily meant for the general public, but for my students.

The academic teacher who has to proffer a completely new science cannot hope to make it sufficiently understandable without a manual; and to the extent that he does not wish to waste time with dictation, there remains no other option but the press. It is unfair to demand the same perfection of a work which appears for such a specific and expressly stated purpose, and which has been published piecemeal according to circumstance,[22] as one would demand of a piece worked out for a general purpose and with the necessary leisure. – However, taking into account these contingent conditions, it was still impossible to think of a *system* of philosophy of nature, as long as one could not yet presuppose the standpoint for it. There remained nothing else but to lead the science to the point from which it could *begin* to become system. This was effectively achieved through that piece. The germs of the system, as I will establish it in the future, all lie scattered therein, and the theory of dynamic process, which is the foundation of all speculative physics and even of the doctrine of organic nature, is expressed quite determinately there in outline and introduction.[23] – In such a presentation [98] all possible levels of reflection [*Reflexionspuncte*] on which the philosophy of nature can rest must necessary be run through and noted, and the highest which grasps all others under itself and which must be the principle in any effective system could here rather only be the *result*.

Of these levels of reflection, that of the atomist is without doubt the first; it was thus natural to use it to find a way into the system. However, I do not consider the customary form of atomism a viewpoint that could play a role in any true philosophy of nature, even at an inferior level of reflection; and this is clearly shown by the fact that I have transformed the atoms of the physicist into something completely different.[24] – So I willingly surrender this whole atomist viewpoint to Eschenmayer and to anyone else who wishes to busy themselves with it. By means of the construction, which is still to appear in full but has already begun to be presented and justified [in the *Outline*], all those principles attacked by Eschenmayer, together with the system from which they spring, annul themselves. For example, take the principle so objectionable to Eschenmayer: every quality is an actant [*Aktion*][25] at a determinate degree, for which one has no other measure than its product.[26] – Who speaks here? The atomist. And for him, whence does the measure of a degree come? No degree is possible except by an inverse proportion [*Verhältnis*][27] of opposed factors; for example, a determinate degree of velocity [is constituted] by the inverse proportion of the space passed through and the time taken to do so. However, the atomist lacks such a measure, since for him actant does not refer to a determinate proportion of opposed forces, but to something *absolutely* simple.[28] The difference between my viewpoint and Eschenmayer's does not lie in *these* principles, but rather in the fact that, in the proportion of original forces to each other, he has claimed that solely a quantitative difference, determinable by the relative excess or deficit of one or the other force, is possible, and as can be seen from the first part of his treatise, he claims this still. Moreover, by these different quantitative proportions, as well as the formulae through which they are expressed, he believes that he has derived *all* specific differences of matter, although they will never give him anything except differences in specific degrees of density, and so a host of other determinations [of matter] remain entirely indeterminate.

[99] *I* try to construct the qualitative determinations of matter from a relation [*Verhältnis*] of two forces other than [this quantitative ratio] which determines specific weights [*Schwere*]. Since Eschenmayer believes he has determined these qualitative determinations by means of such a quantitative proportion, to which they are in fact never reducible, he therefore neglects them *as* specific properties. For what is understood by the specific but the unconstructible, or rather that which cannot be constructed?

Since, for *Eschenmayer*, in matter there is nothing but this same proportion of forces which determines the degree to which it fills space, something else *positive*, something containing the ground of another determination, cannot be posited for him even by a change in degree. Therefore, the properties of a body must for him always stand in direct proportion to the degree to which they fill space. – Now, I would like to know how the specific weight of iron, for example, could be directly proportional to the considerable coherence of this metal, or how the specific weight of mercury could be directly proportional to the weak coherence of this metal? – Even through endless changes to specific weight – and he knows nothing of matter but this – nothing would ever change but the specific weight. Now I desire to know how, from this change in the specific weight, any other determination of matter that did not stand in a precise proportion to it could emerge? – *Eschenmayer* himself admitted a long time ago that the series of qualitative determinations of matter is in no way parallel to the series of specific weights, and he admits it again now. – And how does he answer this difficulty? With the question: can *experience* arbitrate between the product that is to be constructed and reason which constructs?[29] – However, the product which one is charged with constructing is known – prior to achieving this task – only through experience, so the question actually runs: is experience to arbitrate *between* experience and constructing reason? – Put like this, an affirmative answer is clearly absurd. – For myself, I ask, on the contrary: should not the coincidence of the product found in experience [100] with the one which has been constructed be the most certain mathematical proof of the *correctness* of the construction? – What is under discussion here is not whether construction should occur at all (this goes without saying); rather, it is a question of whether this construction is carried out *correctly*. – Such an occurrence can surely not be proven with the general saying: the human spirit is the legislator of nature. This saying is quite good: there is no doubt that reason gives laws to nature, even that reason always constructs correctly – however, the question is WHETHER, in an individual case, *reason* itself has actually constructed. – From the fact that reason gives laws to experience it does not follow that it has the right to contradict experience; rather, just because it is its legislator, [reason] must be in the most perfect agreement with it, and where this is not the case, it can be rightly inferred that it is not legislating reason that has constructed, but some empirical [form of] reason. – In the philosophy of nature, I claim: nature is its own legislator.[30] Eschenmayer cannot grasp how, having presupposed this, one could still take the trouble to construct nature. – If *Eschenmayer* had the same concept of nature as me, that claim would be no more strange to him than that which he opposes to it as the basic principle of rationalism: the human spirit is its own legislator.[31] If this were true, one could ask, how could the philosopher make that vain effort to construct the I with all its determinations? – human spirit is human enough to have got on with it, or rather it has already got on with it.

It is certainly true that in the philosophy of nature I consider that subject-object which I call nature in its self-construction. One must have raised oneself to the intellectual intuition of nature to conceive it. – The empiricist fails to so raise himself, and for this precise reason *he* is always the one constructing in all his claims. It is therefore not astonishing to find what has been constructed and what should have been constructed so seldom coincide. – Because the philosopher of nature raises nature to self-sufficiency and lets it construct itself, he never has cause to oppose it to constructed nature (i.e. experience) nor to correct it according to [constructed nature]. The constructing [nature] cannot [101] err, and the philosopher of nature just requires a secure method to prevent it from erring through his interference. Such a method is possible and the next task is to make it known in detail. However, [the question of] whether he has correctly applied this method, which in itself must be infallible, can ultimately be resolved for the philosopher only by its success – that is, by the coincidence of that nature constructing itself before our eyes with that nature that has been constructed. Therefore, for him experience is in fact not the principle but the task of construction, not the *terminus a quo* but the *terminus ad quem* of construction. – Where this *terminus ad quem* is not attained, one can rightly infer that either the correct method was not applied or it was applied incorrectly or in an incomplete manner.

I return to the question of the basis for the specific properties of matter.

— Eschenmayer himself has tried to move the investigation forward in the preceding treatise. He now takes into account relations which he elsewhere has not; that is, the relations of bodies to the different senses, whose differences he once more tries to present as merely a matter of degree [*graduale*]. I find the whole thing very astute with individual claims of compelling truth; however, the fundamental question, for the sake of which this whole apparatus is assembled, still remains unanswered; that is, *how* by mere differences in degrees of density are these different relations of bodies to the senses posited? — The author does not link the above result that was discovered in a different way, as if through anticipation, back to his basic principle: the common expression of an object is its specific density. Therefore, as he himself states (p. 56[32]), the entire investigation decides nothing with respect to the principal point. Rather, it appears that this new way has led the author into new difficulties, for he now must claim that the senses, which have been put into play, are differentiated merely by degree [*gradual*]. Instead, a more helpful way would be to have previously determined *what* is actually raised by varying degrees into the senses? It cannot be the same as that which lies at the ground of the gradation of matter (i.e. that which affects the senses). This leaves unanswered [102] the following questions. What gradation of matter is required for it to be e.g. an odour or a ray of light, i.e. to be the gradation of sense corresponding to the sense of smell or the sense of sight? And how do these gradations of matter that acquire a determinate relation to a specific sense relate to those which acquire a determinate relation to the electrical or chemical process? — Without doubt, each determinate gradation of the latter kind corresponds to a determinate relation of bodies to the senses, and vice versa — but what is entirely lacking here is a binding concept, and this leaves a wholly unresolved antithesis.

I do not want to speak at the moment of the gaps in the theory proposed by *Eschenmayer* (which he may well fill in through future investigations), but rather focus on the first principle, namely that the differences between all the senses are *merely differences of degree*,[33] which he — as far as I understand it — has neither proven nor even made reasonably comprehensible. It seems to me that it all comes back to the following main claims.

1. There are different senses (which he postulates provisionally).
2. Each of these senses has its own distinctive sensation (which he again postulates).
3. Between the different sensations of one and the same sense there is merely a difference of degree; for example, the different sounds which one and the same body emits.
4. Within the general sphere of each sensation [*Sinnesempfindung*], and

even in the absence of the determinate differences of degree in (3), there are further differences which appear specific (for example, the specific sounds of a violin and a flute even when playing the same high or low notes).

5. Therefore different gradations appear in (3) and (4): the former grounded on an arithmetic proportion, the latter on a geometric proportion. – 'It is [103] thus explained how in addition to its (inner) proportion between degrees, the sound can take on still another (external) proportion. Specifically different sounds are merely different intensities: the maximum of one tonal series always passes over into the minimum of another.'[34] The same is applicable to all the other senses, only the analysis for them is not pursued in sufficient depth. For example, specifically different olfactory sensations are only different intensities of one and the same (geometric?) basic proportion, whereas each specific type of odour contains an arithmetic series.

6. Yet precisely such a proportion as between specifically different sensations of one and the same sense (4) is repeated between the different senses themselves, so that here too the minimum of one (for example, sensation of light) immediately passes over into the maximum of another (for example, acoustic sensation?).

We will abstain entirely from remarking on this cleverly devised theory – in part because such remarks are easy to make, in part because we can always refrain from doing so until, by sustained construction, the author has derived his theory *from his first principle*, on which we do not agree.

Its main principles have simply been extracted in order to facilitate comparison with our own point of view on this matter.

It appears to us that we are no longer so far from Eschenmayer, now that he allows for the validity of another proportion than the merely arithmetic (through which specific weight alone is determined). After admitting to a geometric proportion – perhaps of forces? – he will also admit that the possibility of different dimensions of matter (which can never be perceived from the merely arithmetic) depends on their various relations to each other in space. Therefore, he will admit that, as there are only three dimensions of matter, only *three* different relations of forces to each other are possible in reference to space. We will agree with each other that in the *first* construction plainly only the third dimension (over which gravity [*Schwere*] [104] alone has power and in which – when it is perfectly produced – the first two [dimensions] are effaced) arises. Therefore, we will also agree that in the *first* construction nothing but an arithmetic relation of the two forces to each other is given; hence, the production of different dimensions *as such* is only possible by a *reconstruction* of the product.

We will thus raise the product above the first potency, at which Kant, for example, constructed, and into a second, where the construction no longer depends on the simple opposition of two forces, but on the opposition between the ideal activity of the higher potency (light) and the constructing [activity] of the first [potency]. Where the product is suspended at different levels of reconstruction, it first receives *qualities*. These qualities refer to nothing but the different relations of bodies to the different moments of reconstruction. What is more, far from being dependent on a specific weight, they are 'posited in matter by means of the tendency of ideal natural activity to annul weight. After we wrest the product away from the first construction, we will have forever given it life and made it capable of all the higher potencies. We will find that uniform nature, which forever repeats itself, once again repeats, albeit in higher potencies, *all* the functions of the preceding potency in the organism, namely in the single function of sensibility. It will have to be accepted that the difference between the senses is as little a matter *of mere degree* as the difference between two forces or two poles of a magnet, and that for us the sense of sight represents an *idealist* pole and the sense of touch a *realist* one (from which it will in turn become clear that, because its external condition is an ideal activity that works at a *distance*, the former is not at all limited by spatial conditions as the latter is). We will glimpse in the other three senses only a repetition of the three moments of the reconstruction (magnetism, electricity and the chemical process) occurring at a higher potency (from which it can be immediately explained once again why in respect to the first an arrangement of rigid bodies has been exquisitely made, while the organ of the second spreads out on a surface and the third ultimately appears bound to a half-fluid organ). For us, then, nature will no longer be a dead, merely extended whole, but rather [105] a living whole which increasingly reveals the spirit incarnated in it and which, by means of the highest spiritualisation, will in the end return into itself and complete itself.[35]

The difference which prevails between *Eschenmayer* and myself in respect to the *whole* treatment of nature ultimately rests merely on the fact that *he* retains the opposition between spirit and nature that occurs in *consciousness*, and requires the former as the single factor for constructing the latter. On the other hand, *for me*, in transcendental philosophy what he ascribes to nature is in the I and in philosophy of nature what he ascribes to the I is in nature. I am compelled to infer such a fundamental difference between our viewpoints from statements like the following, 'An absolute quantum of activity is distributed between two opposed potencies (spirit and nature), so the more activity in me, the more negation in nature, and vice versa'[36] (which is true from a lower level of reflection, but false from a higher one). 'The original principle which according to *Baader* wafted down from the breath on high into the statue of Prometheus and brings to life the first throb in the pulse of nature (the interplay of its duality) – is *spontaneity*,[37] which *he* posits in spirit, whereas *for me* what does all this is *in nature itself* – the active *soul* of nature. For I do not admit two different worlds, but without reservation only *one and the same*, inclusive of everything, even what in ordinary consciousness is opposed as nature and spirit.

If *Eschenmayer* would care to clarify this point, science could only gain by it.

It is gradually becoming clear that even idealism has its spirit and its letter – and is to be understood in different ways. In the following issue, I hope to begin the new presentation of my system with an enumeration of these different ways, and to show how in the end one is forced to solely affirm that view which I have characterised above, namely that in which all dualism is forever annihilated and everything becomes absolutely one. Since I must hope [106] that Eschenmayer has become more familiar with my viewpoint both through my System of Idealism and through the present debate (in this journal) than was possible for him through a mere reading of the *Outline*, we might now be able to be informed of each other's viewpoints very quickly and find out whether we actually proceed from the same principles or only appear to do so.

Having spoken up until now only of those points on which Eschenmayer and I are, at least apparently, in disagreement, I would love to now speak of those which unite us, or at least those ingenious statements of his to which I must accede. However, space does not allow this at present. In conclusion, I only ask Eschenmayer to compare what he writes on p. 58 about the *fourth* principle, spontaneity, as indwelling *in us* with what he cites on p. 65 of his dissertation: '*The sun* seems to serve as the cause which prevents absolute indifference'[38] – so that he can enter into agreement with me on that point which is still in doubt. This impulse of spontaneity falls within the sphere of nature itself; it is *light*, the sense of nature, by means of which nature sees into its own limited interior. It is that which seeks to wrest the ideal activity imprisoned in the product away from the constructing activity. As spontaneity is day, so the constructing activity is night; the former is the *I* of nature itself, the latter its not-I. And just as this pure activity [i.e. spontaneity], simple in itself, becomes *empirical* (colour) through conflict with the constructing activity, so this latter, in conflict with the former, is forced, along with its product, to become *ideal*, reconstructing its product under different forms in order to bring it back under its rule – first through magnetism, in which both factors of indifference remain within it; then through electricity, in which it must look for one factor of indifference outside of itself, in a different product; and finally as chemical force, in which the attainment of one or both of the factors of indifference requires a third. Until finally, this immortal activity, which is unlimited according to its principle, weds itself *as* ideal activity entirely to the product, laying the foundation of life in nature, and life is in turn raised *by degrees* [*Stufe zu Stufe*] into the *highest* indifference by an ever-higher potentiation.[39]

Part II
Commentaries

Chapter 1

Quality

Schelling's *On the True Concept* gives a somewhat misleading picture of what is at stake in his disagreement with Eschenmayer:[1] it relegates to the end of the essay many of the specific problems within philosophy of nature that propelled their dialogue, so as to, instead, foreground the more global problem of the relation between the philosophy of nature and transcendental idealism. This is not to downplay the conclusions Schelling reaches concerning the priority of philosophy of nature; rather, our point is that *On the True Concept* obscures both the importance of the specific problems in the philosophy of nature and their connection to Schelling's views regarding the nature of reality and the philosopher's access to it. In this chapter, we provide a summary of the longstanding disagreements within the philosophy of nature that led to *On the True Concept* (and ultimately to the identity philosophy), focusing on the specific problem that ignites the controversy in 1799: the problem of constructing material qualities. Indeed, for Jantzen, everything '*turns on*' this problem of quality.[2] By charting Eschenmayer and Schelling's interactions on material quality from 1797 to early 1801, we hope to provide some of the intellectual context to their arguments in *Spontaneity = World Soul* and *On the True Concept*.

We also hope thereby to indicate more broadly how much of the subsequent development of German Idealism arises out of these debates on quality. The various nature-philosophical attempts devised to best explain the diversity of material qualities in the natural world become, from 1801 onwards, part of the theoretical apparatus of the metaphysics of absolute idealism. For example, we attempt to show in Chapter 3 that, in Leistner's words, 'the question of the extent to which the mathematical construction of matter can construct or derive the specific quality of matter from quantitative proportions of two fundamental forces [is not] just an exotic problem in philosophy of nature', but also concerns 'the basic theoretical question of the original genesis of difference from identity'.³ From this perspective, it becomes plausible that the philosophy of nature ought – at least, on occasion – to have systematic priority for contemporary readers of the idealist tradition. It would not, then, be an abstruse, marginal supplement to idealist philosophy, of interest only to those scholars of German Idealism working on the concept of nature. Understanding the details of debates over the construction of material qualities, for example, might help to elucidate the genesis of absolute idealism as a whole. As Beiser argues,

> Above the portals of the academy of absolute idealism there is written the inscription, 'Let no one enter who has not studied *Naturphilosophie*.' Without an understanding of at least the central doctrines, basic arguments and fundamental problems of *Naturphilosophie*, the absolute idealism of Schelling and Hegel is all but incomprehensible.⁴

To understand such developments, then, we must attend to the various solutions to the problem of how to 'naturalistically reconstruct qualities from quantities'⁵ – a problem bequeathed to the later generation of idealists by Kant's *Metaphysical Foundations of Natural Science*. Of course, the question of whether the vast array of specific qualities of matter can be constructed on the basis of mathematical reasoning alone is not merely a post-Kantian one, but dates at least as far back as the early seventeenth century. Yet Kant had renewed it in particularly acute form by arguing that the only appropriate explanation of material quality was a dynamical one – that is, one that saw reality in terms of the relation between intensive magnitudes of different forces. What gave Kant pause for thought was – as we shall see – whether specific material qualities were accordingly to be understood on the model of quantitative proportions. That is, for Kant and, after him, Eschenmayer and Schelling, a major question for philosophy of nature was whether such dynamical explanations (i.e. explanations in terms of the ratios that hold between forces considered as intensive magnitudes) could ever be sufficient to account for the very specific differences found in the natural world. As Eschenmayer wonders as late as *Spontaneity = World Soul*: even if these ratios were able to explain the difference between blue and red, could they also explain the difference between our perception of the blue of the sky and the blue of a sapphire? Could they explain how different an F-sharp played on a piano sounds compared to one played on a flute?

Kant's dynamics

In the 1786 *Metaphysical Foundations of Natural Science*, Kant seeks to provide a transcendental grounding for Newtonian science in a more detailed manner than is laid out in the first *Critique*.[6] It is within this context that he presents his account of the fundamental forces of matter, seeking by these means to ground Newtonian mechanics while arguing, *pace* Newton, that matter is constituted by the forces of repulsion and attraction, and not merely the force of inertia.[7]

Kant is interested in the most basic way in which natural objects can be sensed (since nature is precisely that which is sensible), and he argues that this capacity to be sensed is made possible, at the most basic level, through the *motion* of objects. As part of his overall survey of the different features of matter and its motion, in the second chapter on dynamics 'motion is regarded as belonging to the quality of the matter under the name of an original moving force'.[8] More specifically, according to 'the first proposition of dynamics', 'matter fills space . . . by a special moving force'.[9] That is, matter actively *resists* other material from occupying its space, and in so doing, it *fills* the space it appears to simply occupy. A material body – and every part of that material body – repels all other matter from it; and yet, no material body is immune from being compressed by *another* body's activity of repulsion. In other words, because the repulsive force of body A can be weaker than the repulsive force of body B (and the force of B weaker than C, and so on *ad infinitum*), no material body is absolutely impenetrable: 'Absolute impenetrability is indeed nothing more or less than a *qualitas occulta*.'[10] The concept of repulsive force, then, replaces the mechanistic concept of the absolute impenetrability of matter and grounds an understanding of matter as infinitely divisible: matter is not solid but elastic, precisely because it is constituted by a force of repulsion.[11]

However, were repulsive force the only force in nature, then matter would not, in fact, fill space, for it would come to no determinate *limit* (the force of repulsion would expand indefinitely). Kant therefore goes on to argue that the force of repulsion must be limited by a second force, a force of attraction, if matter is to actually exist and not dissipate into non-existence by expanding infinitely outward via its repulsive force.[12] A second force is therefore necessary, because (1) the repulsive force itself cannot be self-limiting, as it is simply expansive and thus, by definition, incapable of compression; and (2) despite the fact that the repulsive force can be weakened and, so one might think, ultimately come to a halt, this force can be actually weakened only *ad infinitum*, which means it will continue to expand indefinitely.[13] Finally, (3) the spatial limitation of matter cannot be understood with respect to the compression resulting from the repulsive force of a second material body, precisely because this second body must itself have determinate spatial limits. Kant argues, then, that there must be a compressive force at work throughout the material universe, a force belonging to all matter everywhere as a universal force of *attraction*:[14]

> Attractive force is that moving force of matter whereby it compels another to approach it; consequently, when such force is found among all parts of matter, then it endeavours by means of this force to diminish the distance of its parts from one another, and hence the space which they together occupy.[15]

Kant thus argues that repulsion and attraction are both necessary if matter is to be encountered in experience. With only *one* of these forces, 'no matter is possible'.[16] Indeed, both forces belong to 'the essence of matter . . . and one cannot be separated from the other in the concept of matter'.[17] Moreover, it is absolutely essential, to Kant, that these forces cannot be reduced to any further force: 'For they are called *fundamental* forces precisely because they cannot be derived from any *other* force.'[18] As will become clear below, these ideas prove inspirational to Eschenmayer in his attempt to develop a system of nature based upon the two irreducible forces of repulsion and attraction. For Kant, elucidating the nature of these fundamental forces is one of the essential tasks of critical philosophy, because it demonstrates 'the only a priori comprehensible universal characteristics of matter', namely, its original elasticity and its heaviness through which it 'endeavours to move in the direction of the [material body with the] greater gravitation'.[19]

On this basis, Kant's main objective in the chapter on dynamics is to associate the dynamic construction of matter with the categories of quality, and he achieves this in a number of ways. First, the elasticity and weight of a specific material body simply distinguishes it as the distinct body it is. Secondly, since matter just *is* repulsive and attractive – that is, since these are not forces acting upon matter from without or from within, but forces constitutive of matter as such – repulsion will account for the *reality* of matter, attraction for its *negation* (since it negates the positive force of repulsion), and the consequent filling of space to a specific degree for its determinate *limitation*.[20] In this way, the three moments of dynamic construction correspond to the three categories of quality. There is, moreover, a third way to understand Kant's association of quality with dynamics, and this concerns the potential connection between dynamics, on the one hand, and empirical knowledge about specific qualities in nature, on the other. Indeed, the metaphysical construction of matter in the chapter on dynamics aims to ground all *empirical* investigation into the sensible qualities of matter – that is, the chemical constitution of material bodies. This argument rests, in turn, on a distinction Kant makes in the Preface to *Metaphysical Foundations* between proper and improper science: 'The first would treat its object wholly according to a priori principles, and the second, according to laws of experience.'[21] Chemistry is paradigmatic of the latter, according to Kant, and thus 'should be called systematic art' or 'experimental doctrine' (since it is not science proper).[22] Kant's intention is not to denigrate chemistry, but to simply point out the fact that our knowledge of chemical properties cannot be achieved by a priori reasoning and instead depends upon empirical investigation. Central to this claim is the idea that chemical phenomena 'are incapable of the application of mathematics'.[23] What is crucial for our purposes is that it is precisely Kant's argument about the gap between, on the one hand, proper science based upon a priori, mathematical reasoning, and, on the other, improper science based upon empirical discovery that Eschenmayer challenges in his derivation of specific chemical phenomena from the basic forces of nature.

Although Kant does not think that one can know, a priori, whether specific chemical processes in fact exist, this does not mean that there is no connection between a priori knowledge of natural forces and empirical knowledge of chemical phenomena. Indeed, from the perspective of transcendental philosophy, one can determine whether it is possible to even *think* of chemical processes given the necessary features of matter.[24] Thus, Kant argues, the *Metaphysical Foundations* 'is not the place to point out hypotheses for *particular* phenomena', but it *is* the place to point out 'the *principle* according to which such phenomena are all to be judged'.[25] As Friedman argues, this suggests that chemistry 'represents the true subject matter and goal of Kant's preferred dynamical natural philosophy':[26] 'The specific variety of matter ... is not resolved by theoretical explanatory hypotheses, for Kant, but by a progressive and open-ended experimental program guided throughout by the regulative use of reason.'[27] The chapter on dynamics, then, grounds not only Newtonian mechanics, but research in chemistry as well. This is the point at which Eschenmayer intervenes to argue that a priori dynamical explanation can in fact tell us a great deal about material qualities such as chemical properties. But in order to make such a claim, he must bite the bullet regarding the *fundamental* nature of the forces: for Eschenmayer, *everything* in nature – including all sensible quality – is reducible to a proportion between repulsive and attractive force; all quality is mere appearance which can be derived from the irreducible forces of nature.

Eschenmayer in 1797

Eschenmayer's three early works on philosophy of nature – his 1796 dissertation, the 1797 *Principles of Nature-Metaphysics* (extracted in Appendix 2) and the 1798 *Investigations* – all present themselves as extensions of Kant's chapter on dynamics in the *Metaphysical Foundations*. While other influences, such as Kielmeyer, Platner and Kant's pre-critical writings are evident, it is from Kant's *Metaphysical Foundations* that Eschenmayer begins.

Nevertheless, as extensions of Kant's dynamics, these early works of philosophy of nature do not merely repeat Kantian dogma; like so many German Idealists, Eschenmayer is interested in radicalising Kantian conclusions, often far beyond the limits of what Kant himself explicitly allowed. If Eschenmayer is a Kantian, he is often a Kantian dynamist *in spirit*. This is nowhere clearer than in the very title of the 1797 *Principles of Nature-Metaphysics Applied to Chemistry and Medicine*. The application of Kantian principles to medicine certainly goes beyond the letter of Kant, and speaks to Eschenmayer's own concern – as summarised in the Introduction – to exhibit 'the possibility of a medicine as an absolutely certain and mathematizable science'.[28] However, more important for the study of quality in nature is Eschenmayer's concentration on the domain of chemistry: he contests Kant's commitment to the strictly experimental character of chemistry by extending the a priori principles of dynamics into this domain; indeed, he even claims, 'Among the natural sciences it is pre-eminently chemistry that makes a claim to the principles that set out the metaphysics of nature.'[29]

By 1799, Eschenmayer had become 'discontented' with the details of his project as presented in the *Principles*,[30] yet it remained central to his general nature-philosophical perspective; after 1797, he continued to promote a vision of dynamics as providing the principles necessary to unify all domains of scientific inquiry, thereby collapsing the Kantian distinction between proper and improper sciences. This is the vision that Eschenmayer is seeking to describe with the term 'nature-metaphysics' in the *Principles* of 1797: a universal description of the dynamic structure which underlies all natural phenomena.[31] Eschenmayer's aim then, as Marks puts it, is to show that 'all natural sciences, no matter how very different their objects, should be reducible to [two] real fundamental forces'.[32] Thus, Eschenmayer begins the section on chemistry of the *Principles* by speaking of 'establishing a priori principles suitable for providing unity to the systematic treatment of natural science, such that all its parts converged in one idea, as it were'.[33]

To discover these a priori principles, Eschenmayer continues, the philosopher of nature must cast off 'the particular empirical determinations of external objects' until 'the concept of matter in general' is attained, and, from this point, a mere 'analysis of this concept' will reveal such principles.[34] The philosopher of nature thus undertakes a reduction of the empirical concerns of the natural sciences in order to discover that which is common across all scientific domains. And the concepts that result provide a philosophical framework that holds good for any scientific endeavour, whether in the field of physics, chemistry or medicine. Moreover, Eschenmayer continues, such an endeavour will finally justify the many theories which, until now, held merely hypothetical status in the sciences: 'What is merely theoretical dualism for the natural sciences is genuinely postulated by dynamics.'[35] Dynamical explanation – indeed, philosophy of nature in general – is therefore necessary for *certainty* in the sciences: nature-metaphysics provides the transcendental warrant for securing such certainty in all domains.

Eschenmayer's Kantianism is clearest in identifying these a priori principles of nature-metaphysics. He writes, 'Dynamics teaches us that the existence of matter can be thought only under the assumption of the concurrence of two original forces – these forces are the force of attraction and the force of repulsion.'[36] The conditions of the possibility of matter are thus specified as the two forces of Kant's *Metaphysical Foundations*. He also broadly follows Kant's argumentation: if matter is defined as 'an empirical filling of space within determinate limits', then, he claims, the only way to make sense of it is through postulating as its sole necessary conditions a force that is a 'cause of empirical filling' – that is, the repulsive force – and a force that is a 'cause of the determination of the limits of empirical filling' – that is, the attractive force 'that attempts to limit the force of repulsion'.[37]

It is the next step Eschenmayer makes that moves decisively beyond Kant: he uses the above force-dualism to explain specific material qualities and the differences that hold between them. He writes:

> According to the dynamic [viewpoint], differences in matter can be just as great as the host of ratios that hold between the forces of attraction and repulsion. In accordance with the various specific densities of matter, differences in other sensible proportions occur.[38]

For Eschenmayer, one material quality is to be distinguished from another only on the basis of the underlying difference in the ratio holding between the forces of repulsion and attraction. Thus, unlike Kant, Eschenmayer is adamant that all specific qualities in the natural world are reducible to the interrelation of these two dynamic principles, and that such reduction is possible without any reference to experience. On this view, mathematics alone can account for the qualitative determinacy in nature.

Chemical properties function as a limit case in this regard: if dynamical explanation is sufficient to make sense of even specific *chemical* qualities and their various changes through the chemical process, then Kant must be wrong: *all* qualities can be explained in this manner. Eschenmayer's argument proceeds to this conclusion as follows: (1) since the fact of 'the empirical filling of space' is reducible to the two fundamental forces of repulsion and attraction; (2) 'since the empirical filling of space is given in infinitely different ways to our intuition'; and (3) since differences in the relation between the two forces 'consist merely in a matter of degree';[39] it follows that all differences in material qualities – as they appear to us in intuition – should be understood as differences in degrees – that is, differences in the ratio that holds between the two forces. From this, Eschenmayer concludes, '*Qualities* are thus degrees, and a degree of matter is some specific ratio of the forces of attraction and repulsion.'[40] With respect to chemistry in particular, this means that 'chemical processes are changes in the ratios of degree in matter'.[41] Even chemicals qualities can be reduced to quantitative relations.

One corollary of this argument is that every qualitative difference in matter is reducible to a difference in density. That is, since the repulsive force fills space and the attractive force restricts this filling, then the different ratios between them result in different densities of matter. Moreover, if all qualities are to be explained by precisely this ratio, then all qualitative difference should correspond to difference in density. Eschenmayer recognises this: 'If now the qualities are given with the degrees, then they must also change with the different densities. This proposition might not appear to be fully in agreement with experience, but it follows immediately from the above.'[42] The last sentence expresses a worry that is quickly suppressed: if, according to the a priori reasoning of nature-metaphysics, differences in material quality correspond to differences in density, why is this not the case empirically? Why, that is, do all other changes in quality appear irreducible to changes in density? Eschenmayer skates over this concern here so as to privilege the results of his a priori speculation;[43] however, Schelling will later exploit this worry and cause the Eschenmayer of 1801 to return in more detail to the question of the correspondence between density, on the one hand, and quality as it is experienced, on the other.

In 1797 – despite his incipient anxiety over the density–quality correspondence – Eschenmayer is fully committed to explaining all material qualities as the product of the two forces. And it is on this basis that he develops a mathematics of the dynamics of quality. Two features of this mathematical model are noteworthy. First of all – and here Eschenmayer is once again radicalising a Kantian insight, this time from *On an Attempt to Introduce the Concept of Negative Magnitude into Philosophy* – he understands the relation between the two fundamental forces as the equilibrium of two tendencies to infinity. The attractive force is defined as 'a tendency to bring matter back to a point' and the repulsive force as 'a tendency to expand matter into the immeasurable', such that 'if we designate the force of attraction with the letter A and the force of repulsion with B, then $A = \frac{1}{\infty}$, $B = \infty$'.[44] What is distinctive here is both the concept of infinity and the resultant concept of the finite. The former 'refer[s] not so much to completed infinities but rather to tendencies, or motions towards infinity';[45] and in regard to the latter, Eschenmayer 'explains the tentative and always changeable nature of the finite as the union of two contrasting infinities'.[46] Finitude is a synthesis of a tendency to the infinitely large and a tendency to the infinitely small.

The second noteworthy feature of Eschenmayer's mathematical model is his deployment of a potentiated series – that is, an infinite series of quantities related to one another exponentially. We consider the origins and significance of this series in the next chapter; at this stage, what is of interest is the way he uses the potentiated series to articulate his radicalised Kantian dynamics. Eschenmayer claims that finitude (or, more accurately, every quality pertaining to every finite object) is to be defined as the product of two opposed infinite tendencies (the repulsive force = $\frac{1}{\infty}$ and the attractive force = ∞). An unlimited series of terms between $\frac{1}{\infty}$ and ∞ describes the possible forms of the finite: 'Finitude is no degree, but an indeterminable host of degrees can be thought within the finite.'[47] That is, finitude is itself quantitatively infinite, and it is this infinite series that Eschenmayer formulates as follows, representing the forces of attraction and repulsion by 'A' and 'B' respectively:

$$A.B^{+n}, \ldots A.B^{+3}, A.B^{+2}, A.B^{+1}, M^0, A.B^{-1}, A.B^{-2}, A.B^{-3}, \ldots A.B^{-n}$$

The series represents 'a geometric procession'[48] of possible proportions resulting from the interplay of the two fundamental forces. Because the forces are infinite tendencies, the series 'can be extended indeterminately on both sides',[49] generating an infinite number of possible material qualities – each quality relating to the others as a higher or lower proportion of the very same dynamic interaction. The series ought to be read, therefore, as a diagram, rather than a mathematical equation.

The zero potency (M^0) at the centre of the series plays a significant role, one that Schelling will seize on in his discussion of philosophical methodology in *On the True Concept*. If, according to Eschenmayer – in language that will also become central to Schelling's identity philosophy – each term in the series is a 'relative equilibrium', then the zero potency marks the point of 'absolute equilibrium'.[50] This is, in Châtelet's words, the point of a 'strange compression of *two infinites*';[51] in Eschenmayer's own words, 'M is to be considered as a zero, since it presents no determinate qualities itself.'[52] The zero potency is degree-less; the point at which nothing is posited. As Jantzen summarises (indicating the connection to Schelling's identity philosophy), 'Matter in the 0 potency signifies *indifference*'.[53] It is only when there is relative difference between the two dynamic magnitudes – that is, only when either of the forces increases or decreases – that quality – or anything, for that matter – appears.

In the 1797 *Principles*, Eschenmayer is quick to apply this series to various natural phenomena, such as the mechanics of the lever. Here, the point of absolute indifference is the fulcrum around which the various increases and decreases in the series are balanced. In 1817, Eschenmayer will call the mechanics of the lever the phenomenon that 'objectively expresses' the mathematics of his potentiated series.[54] Even more significant, though, is the application of Eschenmayer's mathematical series to the polar phenomena of magnetism and electricity. Châtelet presents the most robust account of Eschenmayer's innovation in this area: his model for magnetic and electrical qualities marks a moment when 'the infinity point of the classical age gives way to the neutral indifference points which mark degrees of equilibrium and from which polarities continuously spring'.[55] More specifically, on the Eschenmayerian series, each pole is rearticulated as an extreme point on the series ($A^{+n}.B$ or $A^{-n}.B$) and the magnetic or electrical indifference point is understood as $A^0.B$. Accordingly, 'the signs "+" and "−" serve to mark the opposition of two magnitudes which, *put together*, suppress one another reciprocally.'[56] More prosaically, the achievement of Eschenmayer's serialisation of polarity is that it enacts 'a "return" of quality into quantity'.[57] This will be crucial for Schelling's identity philosophy and one of the major reasons why his 'formal schema for the system' is a magnetic line strongly indebted to Eschenmayer's potentiated series. On Eschenmayer's model, the opposition that holds between positive and negative charges – between the two polarities – is not a matter of some irreducible difference in kind, but is reducible to difference in degree.

Schelling in 1797

As noted in the Introduction above, in Schelling's first book on the philosophy of nature, he praises Eschenmayer's *Principles* for its attempt to apply Kant's dynamics to the field of chemistry.[58] There is, moreover, much – superficially at least – in the way of overlap between Eschenmayer's

1797 work and Schelling's *Ideas for a Philosophy of Nature* published later that year: both attempt to position themselves as the true heirs to Kant's *Metaphysical Foundations*, both stake the possibility of a successful post-Kantian philosophy of nature on the rehabilitation of chemistry, and both make much of the notion of degree in the construction of quality.[59] While the closeness in publication dates might lead one to believe that Schelling is merely praising a contemporary who has happened to reach a position similar to his own, some scholars go further: Marquet, for instance, posits substantial influence of Eschenmayerian thought on Schellingian philosophy of nature at even this early stage.[60]

Nevertheless, Schelling's praise in the *Ideas* should not, we submit, lead anyone to presume that he is in fact in agreement with Eschenmayer when it comes to the details of the relationship between dynamics and chemistry. Although he is no doubt enthusiastic about Eschenmayer's early writings, the *Ideas* provides a more traditionally Kantian account of the relationship between the fundamental forces of nature and chemical phenomena. According to Schelling, chemical phenomena cannot be known through a priori reasoning, precisely because they are *phenomena* to be sensibly intuited. The fundamental forces, by contrast, are not phenomenal objects of possible experience, but are, rather, conditions for the possibility of objective experience.[61] Consequently, 'the universal forces [i.e., repulsion and attraction] are considered *absolutely necessary*, while the chemical forces are viewed as *contingent*.[62] Following Kant, then, Schelling develops a 'transcendental discussion of the concept of matter in general',[63] a discussion which seeks to demonstrate that any coherent understanding of matter must presuppose the principles of repulsion and attraction. In this Kantian mode, Schelling asks: why must objects that we intuit as external to the mind be conceived in terms of repulsive and attractive force? Yet, unlike Kant, Schelling's derivation of the forces begins with the structure of intuition, which Schelling takes to be 'the highest element in our knowledge' in so far as it grants the mind access to a reality beyond itself.[64]

Intuition, according to Schelling, is the unity of the mind's 'positive', 'unlimited activity outwards' and the 'negative' relation of the mind to itself which restricts the first activity.[65] The latter tendency – in making the mind aware of its world-oriented activity – limits the mind's indeterminate interest in the objective world and thereby secures the possibility of finite (i.e. actual) knowledge of some determinate object. Schelling claims that, in intuition, these 'absolutely opposite, mutually restricting activities are united'.[66] Once the mind seeks to *understand* the object, however, it takes its own original and opposed activities to be at work *in nature* as repulsive and attractive force: the positive, infinite activity of the mind that extends outward becomes the repulsion of matter; and the negative, self-directed activity of the mind becomes the universal force of attraction.[67]

That knowledge of the natural world presupposes the forces as the foundational principles of natural science has significant implications for the relationship between dynamics and more specialised sciences. First and foremost, it means that the natural sciences must be grounded upon philosophical knowledge regarding the forces of nature: mechanics, for example, is grounded upon dynamics, since any consideration of the collision of material bodies and the movement that follows collision will be intelligible only if one understands those bodies as filling a determinate space.[68] Chemical motion too is only fully intelligible on the basis of a more original dynamic motion.[69] Nevertheless, precisely because these principles are *presupposed* in scientific inquiry, the phenomena understood by the natural scientist cannot be reduced to those foundational principles. In other words, something in addition to the fundamental forces must be at work in nature.

It is at this point that the Schelling of the *Ideas* reveals himself a more traditional Kantian than Eschenmayer. According to Schelling, our knowledge of chemical processes is achieved on the basis of sensation. Although such processes may be dependent upon the fundamental forces of nature, experience is also required in order for us to know them. This is why he identifies chemistry as 'applied dynamics, or dynamics considered in its contingency'.[70] For Schelling, chemistry aims to 'investigate the *qualitative* diversity of matter' in so far as this diversity is related to the non-mechanical attractions, repulsions, combinations and separations of material bodies.[71] And because the qualitative specificity of matter is 'given to us in sensation', a science of quality will necessarily be empirical.[72]

Significantly, however, the mind does not sense sheer qualities such as heat or brightness, but qualities *of a specific degree*: 'We feel . . . the *more* or the *less* of elasticity, heat, brightness, and so on.'[73] Thus, Schelling writes, 'Every quality, in so far as it is to affect us, must have a *degree*, and that a *specific* degree, a degree which *could* have been higher or lower, but is now (at *this moment*) precisely of this *particular* degree.'[74] And this leads Schelling to emphasise the importance of dynamics: If (1) quality must be sensed; (2) sensation is only possible when something is given at a determinate degree; and (3) 'no degree is conceivable save that of the forces [of repulsion and attraction]'; it follows that 'all quality rests on forces in so far as they have a specific quantity (degree)'.[75] Schelling therefore argues that 'all quality in bodies rests on the quantitative . . . relationship of their basic forces'.[76]

This does not mean, however, that Schelling promotes an a priori deduction of the qualities that can be encountered in experience. Although clearly inspired by Eschenmayer's application of dynamics to chemistry, the *Ideas* remains closer to the letter of Kant's text in its insistence that knowledge of chemical processes must be based upon experience.[77] But Schelling does not remain a Kantian for long. Over the subsequent four years, he will go on to radically revise his conception of quality. The next major stage in this development appears in the *First Outline*.

Schelling in 1799

Eschenmayer is not named in the published text of the 1799 *First Outline of a System of the Philosophy of Nature*. However, in a remark added to his teaching copy, Schelling writes,

> *Quality* is originally absolutely *inconstructible*, and it must be, because it is the *limit* of all construction by virtue of which every construction is a determinate one. All previous attempts to construct qualities have been incapable of leading to anything real for this reason. With so-called dynamic philosophy the attempt is made to reduce qualities to analytical formulas, and to express them by means of the variable relations of repulsive and attractive force. Indeed, Kant has nowhere genuinely ventured to construct the specific (qualitative) diversity of matter out of his two basic forces. A few who wished to apply his dynamic principles have gone further. I will name only *Eschenmayer* here . . . One ill-conceived attempt to construct the qualities and series of degrees of qualities according to Kantian principles is to be found in his 'Principles from the Metaphysics of Nature' and his 'Investigations'.[78]

As Jantzen summarises, this passage launches a 'scathing critique of Eschenmayer's mathematical construction of specific matter (i.e. qualities)'.[79]

Eschenmayer himself never read these remarks. Yet, even if he is never elsewhere named in the published text, he could not – and did not – fail to perceive anticipations and repetitions of the above critique. In various passages of the *First Outline*, it becomes clear that Schelling no longer holds the Kantian optimism, expressed in the *Ideas*, for conceiving qualities as – in some sense – related to the forces of repulsion and attraction. And this turn away from the constructability of quality is motivated in a number of ways:

1. The construction of quality, he argues, relies on 'strange manners of thinking concerning the concept of dynamical philosophy'[80] – that is, that two forces are sufficient to explain all material diversity. Such a conception of dynamism is ultimately only pre-Kantian mechanical

philosophy – with its traditional armoury of mathematical tools – transposed into the fashionable language of dynamics.
2. The reduction of qualities to forces can only be undertaken from 'the standpoint where nature is viewed only as *product* and not as *productivity*'.[81] Consequently, dynamical physics lacks a genetic account of how the fundamental forces themselves came to be. Just as the atomist presupposes the existence of atoms, so too the dynamist presupposes the existence of the two forces.
3. Eschenmayer's construction of matter follows Kant in its failure to differentiate gravity from attraction, as a third principle that ultimately unites repulsive and attractive force. Of course, Schelling himself made the same error prior to the *First Outline*, and it was only upon encountering Franz Baader's 1798 *On the Pythagorean Square in Nature* that he came to insist upon the distinction between attraction and gravity.
4. Differentiating material bodies in terms of the various proportions of repulsive and attractive force constituting those bodies will only ever yield quantitative differences between the bodies. Density ≠ qualitative determinacy. Rather, qualitative determinacy must be understood in terms of 'original qualities' which are irreducible to proportions of the fundamental forces.

In the rest of this section, we expand on the above reasons for Schelling's rejection of the construction of qualities in 1799.

Schelling's feud with the mathematicians

In November 1798, Novalis writes to Friedrich Schlegel of Schelling's incipient feud with the mathematicians,[82] and nowhere is this feud more evident than in Schelling's attack on dynamical explanation in the *First Outline*. During this period, Schelling is far from Eschenmayer when it comes to appreciating the foundational role of mathematics in the philosophy of nature: whereas, for Eschenmayer, mathematics supplies the fundamental principles required in order to comprehend the material universe, for Schelling, such mathematical principles are not fundamental, but derived *from* the philosophy of nature. Thus, he writes to Fichte, 'In my opinion, philosophy of mathematics is an abstraction from philosophy of nature.'[83] And, in a letter to Eschenmayer, he explains, 'It seems to me that the mathematician, just as much as the logician, has until now asserted his exceptionality by establishing his propositions – *the principles of which really emerge in another science.*'[84] Schelling's attack on Eschenmayer's dynamic reductionism in the *First Outline* is at the heart of this more general dispute regarding mathematical explanation: to reduce all qualities to mathematical proportions is to get things the wrong way around – that is, to accord priority to conceptual abstractions over natural processes. In other words, Schelling accuses Eschenmayer of failing to respect the basic principles of any good philosophy of nature – the self-sufficiency or autarchy of nature, according to which the explanation of nature must employ categories from nature itself, rather than abstractions of the mind.[85]

As is already becoming apparent, this debate about the construction of qualities is intimately connected to a broader debate between Schelling and Eschenmayer about the relationship between the philosophy of nature and transcendental philosophy (or the priority of nature or mind). We explore these broader issues in Chapters 4 and 5; the central point at this stage is that Schelling is fundamentally sceptical of Eschenmayer's overuse of mathematics in the philosophy of nature. Mathematics *alone* will never exhibit the qualitative determinacy of matter.

Product and productivity

Eschenmayer's failure to discern the derivativeness of mathematics is symptomatic of another failure of the post-Kantian dynamist enterprise, according to Schelling: its tendency to focus on the natural product rather than nature's fundamental productivity. That is, the dynamist's excessive use of mathematics illustrates her failure to attain the original productivity of nature (*natura naturans*), through which alone natural products (*natura naturata*) are philosophically intelligible. Although the dynamic construction of matter may *appear* to draw the philosopher nearer to the creativity at the heart of nature, it remains at the superficial level of what *is*: everything has already come to be. That is, although the proportions between repulsion and attraction may explain quantitative features of material bodies such as specific density, they tell us nothing about the *genesis* of such bodies. According to the *First Outline*, the dynamic construction will only ever demonstrate *that* products are quantitatively distinct on account of the different proportion of the fundamental forces; it will never explain *how* these differences arise.

A particularly damning instance of the Kantian–Eschenmayerian failure to consider nature's productivity concerns the status of the basic forces themselves. No account of their genesis is given. In order to properly explain the existence of these forces, the philosopher of nature must attend to nature's essential productivity to chart how it expresses itself as *various* forms of duplicity – including, but not limited to, the forces of repulsion and attraction. Thus, for Schelling, the forces – which are fundamental for Kant and Eschenmayer – are derivative of a more fundamental process in nature. This is 'the deeper meaning in Kant's construction of matter out of two opposing forces'.[86] Schelling's philosophy of nature is, in other words, intended to be far more thoroughgoing than Eschenmayer's, and it is why he claims that 'the point from which Kant begins the dynamical philosophy [is] the same point at which our theory stops'.[87]

Gravity

The key example of the incompleteness of the Kantian–Eschenmayerian construction of matter is gravity. Influenced by Baader, Schelling argues that the fundamental force of attraction cannot be conflated with gravity, since this force would serve *two* essential functions: it would *limit* the repulsive force and thereby allow matter to fill a determinate space (attraction) *and* it would individualise a material body and put it in relation to *other* material bodies through its heaviness (gravity proper). Thus, following Baader, Schelling argues that gravity must be an independent third force 'which binds the individual to a determinate system of things and assigns it its position in the universe'.[88] Kant's attractive force may limit the continual expansion and ultimate dissolution of matter, but it does so only with respect to velocity – that is, it slows down the speed of matter's repulsion. And this simply does not account for the fact that a material body is – *as matter* – intrinsically related to other material bodies in the universe. Such relationships can only be accounted for by a third activity in nature, namely, gravitation. Thus, Kantian attractive force 'is as little identical with gravity as time is identical with space'.[89] In the *Universal Deduction*, Schelling helpfully concludes: 'All of this suffices to show the incompleteness of the attempt to construct matter from the mere conflict of the two opposing forces without the mediation of a third.'[90]

'Qualities = Actants'[91]

In the *Ideas*, Schelling had argued that, although specific chemical qualities cannot be derived from pure reason, the forces of repulsion and attraction can be applied to empirical phenomena in order to explain the appearance of quality. In the *First Outline*, Schelling revises his view and argues that *any* account of chemical qualities in terms of the fundamental forces – whether this account issues from pure reason or refers to experience – will necessarily fail to elucidate the nature of quality. Simply put, Schelling now argues that all attempts to conceive qualities in terms of proportions of forces will reduce quality to quantity and thereby evacuate the phenomena of its qualitative reality. Schelling therefore develops a new approach to thinking about quality in the philosophy of nature, an approach that finds as much inspiration in the atomism of mechanistic natural philosophy as the dynamism of Kant's transcendental philosophy of nature.

According to Schelling, the dynamist is correct to criticise the mechanist for conceiving matter as devoid of force, but incorrect to reject all forms of atomism. Although one should not fall back into the view that the natural world is comprised of absolutely impenetrable corpuscles, one can appeal to *dynamic* atoms to explain the qualities that we sense in experience. Schelling labels these dynamic atoms 'actants' (*Aktionen*) and identifies them as the 'original qualities' in nature – qualities which cannot be reduced to some more basic relationship between the fundamental forces of matter but are themselves the most fundamental elements of reality. 'Every original actant is just like the atom for the corpuscular philosopher; truly *singular*, each is in itself whole and sealed-off, and represents, as it were, a *natural monad*.'[92] However, if such original qualities are to be *indivisible*, they cannot be spatially extended; they must be 'pure intensities', 'pure actions',[93] or – as Schelling somewhat misleadingly puts it – the strictly '*ideal* ground of the explanation of quality'.[94]

Since the actants themselves are non-extended, pure intensities, they can only be sensed if expressed within the world. And since the actants are clearly supposed to explain sensible qualities, it follows that there is no original actant without a material object or natural 'product' which expresses its intensity: 'The actant itself, abstracted from its product, is nothing.'[95] Actants *are* only in so far as there exist real products in nature which express them – or: 'Quality is action, for which one has no measure other than its own product.'[96] This leads Schelling to argue, once again, that Eschenmayer is insufficiently empiricist in his philosophy of nature: since qualities are only measurable through the material objects that express those qualities to various degrees, all knowledge of qualities is necessarily empirical knowledge.

> One cannot expect to be able to take a look into the interior of that actant itself and determine the magnitude (the degree) of the action, as if by means of mathematical formulas. All attempts to do this have until now led to nothing real. Our knowledge does not reach *beyond* the product, and no other expression for the magnitude of the action can be given than the *product itself*.[97]

As Schelling puts it in the *Introduction to the Outline*, 'that which is known, not in itself, but only in its product, is known altogether *empirically*'.[98] Actants are thus 'ideal' in so far as they are 'originary productivities' which can be known exclusively through their effects.[99]

To complicate matters, Schelling claims that an actant cannot, on its own, generate material products, but that all products result from some combination of actants.[100] Schelling's idea is that, on the one hand, actants strive for the same ultimate goal: the collective filling-up of space, 'such that in every part of a given material, no matter how small, all tendencies would still be met with'.[101] On the other hand, as 'originary productivities', actants differ from one another in terms of the forms they seek to produce in nature, and through their 'continual striving . . . towards the production of a determinate form', actants will inhibit one another.[102] The material products encountered in experience, then, express 'various degrees of intensity of every actant'.[103] In other words, 'Every product . . . is = to a determinate *synthesis* of actants.'[104] In all material things, each and every actant is expressed; it is only their proportions that differ.[105]

As described below, in *Spontaneity = World Soul*, Eschenmayer develops a persuasive critique of Schelling's account of simple and complex actants. He also points out that Schelling's identification of actants with various degrees of the inhibition of nature's productivity appears extraordinarily similar to his own dynamic construction of quality. However, before considering these issues, it is important to recognise the uniqueness of Schelling's philosophical vision in 1799, even if he is ultimately closer to Eschenmayer than he acknowledges. Schelling's conception of material qualities, as presented in the *First Outline*, has more in common with Leibniz than it does with the critical Kant.[106] Indeed, according to the Schelling of 1799, in order to understand qualitative determinacy in nature, one must appeal to the strictly ideal, non-extended points which determine the sensible qualities of material bodies. He still has a story to tell about the fundamental forces of nature, but he now argues that the play between them can only ever yield quantitative specificity, namely, specific density. Schelling does not therefore criticise Eschenmayer for making the conflict between repulsion and attraction determinative, but for making this conflict explanatory of too much.[107]

Eschenmayer in 1801

Spontaneity = World Soul forms Eschenmayer's response to the Schelling of 1799. Here, he both attacks Schelling's theory of actants and defends his own construction of specific material qualities. The problem of quality is, in fact, the guiding thread running through the whole essay, from the section on drive to that on sensation, from the world soul to the series of sounds – it is all an attempt to demonstrate that the dynamic model is broadly sufficient to construct all qualitative differences in the natural world.

Eschenmayer's critique of the discussion of quality in the *First Outline* is twofold. It begins with the problematic of complex actants – that is, the manner in which, according to Schelling, actants can be joined in order to constitute natural diversity. Eschenmayer aims to show, *pace* Schelling, that complexity in nature 'lies not in the *composite union of infinitely many tendencies*, but merely in the *infinite succession of two original tendencies*'.[108] All qualities are syntheses of the two fundamental forces of repulsion and attraction; therefore, qualities cannot be distinguished in terms of complexity, but only in terms of the quantitative proportion that holds between the two forces. Assuming, then, that the basic tenets of dynamism hold and that material quality should always be understood as the product of a dualism of tendencies, it follows that there is no difference *in kind* between apparently complex and apparently simple material qualities: they are all various degrees of the interplay of forces. Hence, Eschenmayer concludes, 'The concept of a complex actant remains incomprehensible to us.'[109] Of course, this merely assumes that the dynamic construction of quality is in fact justified, and that Schelling's criticisms of dynamism are misguided – even though this is precisely what is under debate. Eschenmayer does, nevertheless, go on to make some provisional arguments for dynamism, the most successful of which are based on a principle of parsimony appropriated from kinetics: whenever a complex force is postulated, it can always be reduced to two tendencies. Yet this still assumes too much: for Schelling, complex actants are precisely not forces that can be reduced to simpler forces; they are '*productivities*'.

The second front of attack Eschenmayer opens up on the *First Outline*'s account of quality concerns the phrase 'specific composition', which occurs occasionally in Schelling's text. Eschenmayer selects this phrase as representative of Schelling's broader refusal to reduce qualities to more original principles. The second half of Eschenmayer's essay – considered in more detail below – is therefore devoted to a refutation of the idea that there are irreducibly specific qualities: even where we experience qualitative specificity, Eschenmayer argues, dynamical explanation functions successfully. That is, he endeavours to demonstrate that the kind of claim to the irreducibility of quality, of which Schelling's phrase 'specific composition' is illustrative, has no place in a genuine philosophy of nature, and, indeed, hinders proper nature-philosophical reasoning.

However, Eschenmayer's most interesting argument in *Spontaneity =*

World Soul concerns the way that Schelling's own account of actants can – in fact – lead one to the precise mathematical philosophy of nature championed by Eschenmayer himself. Indeed, according to Eschenmayer, it turns out that much of what Schelling says in the *First Outline* is fairly reconcilable with his own potentiated series of ratios. That is, Schelling's conception of actants as points of inhibition generated out of the gradual retardation of productivity is, for Eschenmayer, another way of depicting qualities *in a potentiated series*. From this perspective, Schelling is not so far away from the dynamist position as he thinks. This is especially true if one considers the similarity between repulsion and attraction, on the one hand, and the *First Outline*'s discourse on nature's tendencies of production and inhibition, on the other. If one recasts Schelling's conception of the original duplicity in nature (i.e. production and inhibition) in terms of the interplay of repulsive and attractive force, then the following plausibly results:

> Originally the philosopher of nature knows merely two tendencies opposed to each other . . . Since these forces are opposed to each other, infinitely many points of inhibition can be thought in them, and these points consist in the gradually increasing or decreasing preponderance of one or the other force. These points of inhibition can be nicely presented in a mathematical formula which has many analogies with a numerical series.[110]

Broadly put, both Schelling and Eschenmayer agree that within nature two factors – for the Schelling of 1799, productivity and the limitation of productivity; for Eschenmayer, repulsive and attractive force – generate an infinite series of simple, immaterial and irreducible 'points' that account for the apparent qualitative diversity in nature. For Schelling, this series is the series of actants; for Eschenmayer, it is a series of ratios of forces.

Eschenmayer's argument that actants *are* in fact constructible within a Schellingian metaphysics is therefore one of the stronger arguments that he makes in *Spontaneity = World Soul*, since these actants are – *by Schelling's own lights* – various points of inhibition generated by the tension between nature's most basic activities. Nevertheless, there remains a difference between them on this issue which Eschenmayer fails to fully consider. For the former, productivity and its limitation must issue from a single principle that self-bifurcates. Although it is not until the *Presentation* of 1801 that Schelling fully commits to the view that duplicity proceeds from sheer identity, his difference from Eschenmayer's dualism is already apparent in the *First Outline*'s claim that 'antithesis must be assumed to have sprung from a universal identity' and that 'we find ourselves driven to a cause which no longer *presupposes* heterogeneity, but itself *produces* it'.[111] Thus, for all of Eschenmayer's efforts to bridge the gap between actants and the ratios of forces, the *origin* of the differentiated series of points remains a bone of contention between these nature-philosophical systems. Does nature bottom out at an irreducible duplicity of forces? Or is duplicity itself generated by nature?

In Chapter 3, we consider the relationship between duplicity and identity in more detail. Up to this point, we have considered Eschenmayer's defence of his own dynamical philosophy and his attempt to convince Schelling that he ought to return to the fold of dynamic construction in the philosophy of nature. But *Spontaneity = World Soul* goes further than this. In an attempt to justify the view that 'specific density and the determination of quality are one in the ontological essence of matter',[112] Eschenmayer finds it necessary to explain the *appearance* of material qualities which do not seem to have anything to do with specific density. The correspondence (or lack thereof) between qualitative change and change in density had briefly worried Eschenmayer in 1797 (as mentioned above), but had since been raised forcefully by Schelling in the *First Outline*. Indeed, the Schellingian critique is straightforward: it is *in fact* just not the case that differences in quality correspond in any way to differences in density. But, rather than softening his position and making room for qualitative determinacy that cannot be reduced to the two forces of nature, Eschenmayer tries to solve the problem by adding a supplementary level of complexity to his mathematical philosophy of nature, locating the apparent discrepancy between quantity and quality on the side of the *embodied subject*. That is, in order to show why *in experience* differences in density and differences in quality do not correspond, Eschenmayer turns to epistemology and puts forward a new theory of sensation.

Eschenmayer's theory of sensation

Hence, once more in 1801, Eschenmayer raises the question of the discrepancy between his a priori model and actual experience – just as he had in 1797. He writes, his initial model 'does not enlighten us at all as to the question of why the claim "that the empirical qualities of matter with their specific densities are variable" is contradicted so frequently by experience'.[113] However, rather than skate over this discrepancy, dogmatically prioritising the mathematical over empirical investigation as in 1797, Eschenmayer now gives it his full attention; indeed, he attempts to show that such a discrepancy 'which hinders all our progress here' is in fact 'a mere semblance and ultimately reducible to a ratio of degree'.[114] That is, the problem will be dissipated once experience itself is shown to result from something like the potentiated series of quantitative ratios first proposed in the *Principles*.

Thus, Eschenmayer again attempts to collapse the dualism Kant maintained between a priori reasoning about matter and empirical investigation, but he now does so by attending to the origins of the empirical. As in 1799, it is the status of chemistry that is ultimately at stake. Eschenmayer articulates the challenge for making chemistry into an a priori science as follows:

> Experience (I mean here, specifically, in chemistry), when it speaks concisely, says the following: sulphur and alkalis, for example, are substances with specific compositions; the qualities which I perceive in one are highly differentiated from the qualities of the other.[115]

In other words, the challenge for Eschenmayer is to explain why differences in quality appear phenomenally to the chemist as irreducible, as distinct 'specific compositions'. This is Eschenmayer's rewriting of the provocation he extracts from Schelling's *First Outline*: to explain that which is irreducibly qualitatively distinct as, in fact, reducible to differences in quantity.

Eschenmayer's reduction of qualitative determinacy here turns on an account of how various 'specific compositions' are experienced.[116] That is, Eschenmayer specifies the above problem as a problem pertaining to sensation: we *perceive* differences as irreducibly qualitative, so any ultimate answer will need to show how such sensations of 'specific compositions' are reconcilable with the potentiated series of ratios of natural forces. This is how he sets up the problem:

> Qualities are relations to an individual being with senses (sensation). As many types of sensation as there are, there are that many different relations. These relations, however, are so heterogeneous that they do not allow for any parallelism at all, indeed not even oppositions. For – what does a colour have in common with a sound, or a sound with a taste or a scent, etc.? However, not only are the types of sense different, but each sense has specifically different sensations: the multiplicity of colours, sounds, sensations of smell, taste and touch are proof enough. Now are these differences merely differences of degree?[117]

There are three problems posed here that Eschenmayer attempts to solve. First, there is a problem of the sheer heterogeneity of sensations: it is not only that sensations do not seem to be arrangeable into a quantitative series, but that they seem to have no relation to each other whatsoever – 'not even [as] oppositions'. The first task is thus to show that it is even possible to compare sensations of different types. Secondly, if this were possible, it would still be difficult to see how different types of sensations could be related quantitatively; it seems, at first blush, absurd to speak of the relations between sound and vision, or smell and touch, as matters of one being greater or lesser than the other. Finally, even if it were possible to reduce these relations quantitatively, there still remains the diversity of sensations within each sense, for example the question regarding the relation between red and blue.

The first problem – that of the sheer heterogeneity of sensation – is quickly solved through an idealist argument that fits with the general Fichtean reasoning of *Spontaneity = World Soul* as a whole: all sensations are sensations for one consciousness; this consciousness is self-identical and thus all its acts, including its various forms of sensation, must be 'homogenous' and 'converge in it'.[118] Thus, the multiplicity of sensations is bound into unity in consciousness, and this means that there must be some relation that holds between them. Eschenmayer quickly moves on to the second and third problems, which he finds more challenging: whether sensations can be serialised.

There is some preliminary evidence, Eschenmayer notes, that sensations within any given sense are indeed quantifiable. He writes, 'All other colours are mere compositions of the seven fundamental colours and so also stand to each other in a proportion of degree.'[119] There appears, then, some reason to think that the series of colours, for example, can be arranged quantitatively. And yet, Eschenmayer is well aware that this is to conclude prematurely, for – notwithstanding such a reduction to degree – 'a *specific difference* still inheres within them, e.g. the colour blue with which sulphur burns is specifically different from every other colour blue'.[120] Eschenmayer is acute enough to note that this fact 'is not superficial; it has full and true significance.'[121] The experience of qualitative determinacy possesses something seemingly irreducible to quantity.[122]

Nevertheless, Eschenmayer thinks he has discovered a way to reduce quality to quantity by distinguishing between an arithmetical and geometric series. Both are series which posit quantitative relations between their terms, but, while in the former the quantity separating successive terms remains constant (1, 2, 3, 4, etc.), in the latter it is only the proportion of the quantity between the terms that is constant (1, 2, 4, 8, etc.). This distinction allows Eschenmayer to describe two kinds of difference in sensation:

> There are two kinds of degree – one which progresses arithmetically and another which progresses geometrically. The multiplicity of sounds from the same sound-producing body maintain among themselves merely an arithmetical proportion, the multiplicity of sound-producing bodies, on the contrary, maintain among themselves a geometric proportion. I take this latter proportion for the energy or geometric intensity of the sound. Each sound-producing body therefore has its own energy or intensity, whereas the arithmetical series of its tones can agree precisely with the series of tones of another sound-producing body. Energy or geometric intensity is therefore the specific difference between sound-producing bodies.[123]

For example, a flute can produce different notes (C, F-sharp, etc.), but there is also a difference between an F-sharp played on the flute and the same note played on the piano. Or, to return to the example of colour, sulphur can appear as different colours, but there is also a difference between the blue produced by burning sulphur and the blue produced by burning ethanol. The former kind of difference is best described in terms of an arithmetical progression, according to Eschenmayer's conjecture; the latter – a difference in 'energy' – is a matter of geometric intensity.

Of course, Eschenmayer does not think he has provided an adequate argument for this model; it is presented merely as a 'hypothesis'.[124] Nevertheless, it is possible to see 'that the problem is capable of mathematical solution – a conclusion which is usually an extremely desirable one for philosophy of nature'.[125] According to Eschenmayer, it is at least conceivable to reduce differences in sensation to these two distinct kinds of quantitative difference (arithmetical and geometric). As he points out, 'My aim here is merely to show how the concept of a *specific composition* is to be entirely discarded from dynamics, and replaced by some kind of magnitude.'[126] He continues,

> By means of the above hypothesis we have now at least demonstrated that the obscure concept, *specific composition*, can be transformed into the constructible concept, *energy*, as is appropriate for a dynamics that hopes for universal comprehension.[127]

From this perspective, Schelling's philosophy of nature is misguided in holding fast to the view that there is an irreducible difference between qualitative and quantitative determinacy. Chemistry can once again be salvaged as a 'proper science', despite the appearance of 'specific compositions' to the chemist's eyes.[128]

Schelling in January 1801

On the True Concept, Schelling's 'appendix' to *Spontaneity = World Soul*, marks a partial retreat from some of the more trenchant positions of the *First Outline*. Indeed, by January 1801, Schelling is rolling back on his blanket rejection of the quantitative explanation of quality and particularly on his replacement of it with a dynamic atomism. Instead, he now reinterprets the dynamic atomism of the *First Outline* as a 'natural' way for a philosopher to describe nature, but one which he is entirely willing to surrender. After all, the mechanical atomism from which Schelling had drawn inspiration in the *First Outline* is incapable of 'play[ing] a role in *any* true philosophy of nature',[129] and there is no need to transform such an anti-philosophical atomism into something properly philosophical. Thus, in the *Universal Deduction*, Schelling criticises any postulation of 'ideal atoms' in the philosophy of nature;[130] and in *On the True Concept*, he explicitly reconciles with Eschenmayer when it comes to the latter's critique of actants. Atomism is now abandoned and retrospectively identified as a propaedeutic device. This means, moreover – and again Schelling is startlingly explicit on this point – Eschenmayer's criticisms of the theory of actants and specific composition 'annul themselves'.[131] In Schelling's words, the difference between his philosophy of nature and that of Eschenmayer 'does not lie [here]'.[132]

Nevertheless, Schelling still intends to substantially distance his newly revised philosophy of nature from Eschenmayer's dynamics. And so, *On the True Concept* continues:

> The difference between my viewpoint and Eschenmayer's ... [lies] in the fact that, in the proportion of original forces to each other, he has claimed that solely a quantitative difference ... is possible ... Moreover, by these different quantitative proportions, as well as the formulae through which they are expressed, he believes that he has derived *all* specific differences of matter, although they will never give him anything except differences in specific degrees of density, and so a host of other determinations [of matter] remain entirely indeterminate.[133]

He goes on: '*I* try to construct the qualitative determinations of matter from another relation of two forces to each other than [this quantitative ratio] which determines specific weights.'[134] Despite Schelling's acknowledgement of the success of some of the criticisms from *Spontaneity = World Soul*, he still rejects Eschenmayer's own construction of qualities. The defining issue is again the density–quality correspondence. Once more, Schelling rejects the idea that material qualities are reducible to 'quantitative proportions' when such proportions are to be understood in terms of the excess or deficit of one of the two fundamental forces. Yet, while Schelling here rejects quantitative explanation based on Eschenmayerian dynamics, this is not a rejection of quantitative explanation *tout court*: it leaves open the possibility that other quantitative means of explaining the natural world might be adequate – a position that will inform, partly at least, Schelling's *Presentation* of May 1801. In short, in so far as Schelling becomes open to conceiving quality in terms of a *certain* type of quantity, he can be seen to have been greatly influenced by Eschenmayer's attempt to ground qualitative determinacy in quantitative difference. This makes sense of the fact that, at this stage in his intellectual development, Schelling begins to appropriate key mathematical concepts from Eschenmayer. Foremost is the idea of the potentiated series, which begins to take centre stage in Schelling's metaphysics and allows Schelling to understand both qualitative determinacy and organic processes in terms of quantity (see Chapter 2).[135]

However, one key difference that remains throughout 1801 needs to be emphasised. While Eschenmayer's series is constituted out of two factors (the attractive and repulsive forces of dynamics), the Schellingian series is generated out of one factor alone – the productivity of the subject-object or absolute. This shift from dualism to monism is a long-standing tendency in Schelling's philosophy of nature: the *First Outline* postulates an identity of productivity with itself underlying all of the various dualities in nature; the *Universal Deduction* claims that all antithetical activities are unified in a more fundamental identity;[136] and, in *On the True Concept*, Schelling argues that the series of stages in nature which proceeds from the inorganic to the organic is propelled by the productivity of the subject-object alone, and not the interplay of two fundamental forces. Indeed, although the subject-object of *On the True Concept* may appear as though it is composed out of the synthesis of two components – namely, the subjective and the objective – Schelling is explicit that the 'subjective' and 'objective' are derivative of their primordial identity, a thesis that becomes essential to the metaphysics of the *Presentation*.

And yet, even this difference between Schelling and Eschenmayer – a difference we explore in detail in Chapter 3 – involves a significant amount of overlap. In arguing that the diversity of nature is generated by a single principle and not, as Eschenmayer has it, two fundamental forces, Schelling finds himself turning to something like the Eschenmayerian model. From the *Universal Deduction* onwards, the magnet's neutral point starts to grow in theoretical significance within Schelling's system, since this point, which is 'neither + nor –' but 'complete indifference', is the basis of all magnetic polarity.[137] In *On the True Concept*, Schelling even appropriates Eschenmayer's concept of the zero potency: 'The pure-subject-object from which [the philosophy of nature proceeds] is precisely that which is simultaneously the ideal and the real in the potency 0.'[138] The 'potency 0' will turn out to be the indifference point of the absolute itself, a point at which – as in Eschenmayer's 1797 work – no qualities are manifest, and from which the construction of qualities must begin.

In the final few pages of *On the True Concept*, Schelling reflects on Eschenmayer's new epistemological model for sensation, and here again a qualified agreement is palpable.[139] Schelling slyly notes that when it comes to 'the question of the basis for the specific properties of matter', Eschenmayer 'has tried to move the investigation forward in the preceding treatise . . . [and] now takes into account relations which he elsewhere has not'.[140] Although he is not entirely convinced, Schelling goes on to praise these developments in Eschenmayer's account,[141] and he expresses interest in some of the specific concepts Eschenmayer employs in his sensualist supplement to *Spontaneity = World Soul*. Indeed, Schelling seems to particularly value Eschenmayer's doubling of the quantitative series (i.e. the arithmetic and the geometric): 'It appears to us that we are no longer so far from Eschenmayer, now that he allows for the validity of another proportion than the merely arithmetic.'[142] And he goes on to suggest that Eschenmayer's new-found openness to *different* series can be seen to resemble his own conception of the dynamic process as consisting in multiple stages or discontinuous potencies, such that quantitative differences between material objects might be conceived as belonging to *one* series of proportions while *qualitative* differences between material objects might be conceived as belonging to a *second* series. In other words, Schelling is suggesting that, by 'admitting' to the possibility of different 'levels of reflection' in the construction of matter,[143] Eschenmayer may be close to converging with his own position – at least regarding the construction of quality in the philosophy of nature. This is the reason why, at this point in *On the True Concept*, Schelling launches into a summary of his own conception of the dynamic process: not to directly rebuke Eschenmayer, but to encourage him to take the final step towards a Schellingianism that is already half-anticipated in the final sections of *Spontaneity = World Soul*.

After January 1801

When Schelling came to revise the *Ideas* into a second edition in 1803, his attitude towards the nature-philosophical construction of material qualities had stabilised, after the mercurial shifts of the earlier periods charted in this chapter. He proclaims,

> With [the true philosophy of nature] there is an end to all those qualitative differences of matter which a false physics fixes and makes permanent in the so-called basic substance: All matter is intrinsically one, by nature pure identity; all difference comes solely from the form and is therefore merely ideal and quantitative.[144]

In 1803 – at the height of the identity philosophy – Schelling wholeheartedly affirms the reduction of apparent qualitative differences in the natural world to quantitative differences. He attacks any view that 'proclaims absolute qualitative differences' by returning to a quasi-Eschenmayerian position which interprets material qualities as epiphenomena of underlying quantitative features of reality.

However, this does not mean that Schelling has forgotten all of his problems with Eschenmayer's dynamics. Indeed, with explicit reference to

Kant, he criticises dynamics in much the same way as he had done since 1799: the 'defectiveness of the Kantian' position rests on (1) its failure to recognise 'the *third* principle of the construction' or gravity, (2) its fixation on attractive and repulsive forces as the only manifestation of duality in nature and (3) its purely analytic method of explanation.[145] Moreover, as in 1799, Schelling praises Kant – and implicitly criticises the early Eschenmayer – for recognising the impossibility of constructing specific material qualities on the basis of dynamics alone. Additionally, just as in *On the True Concept*, Schelling alludes to the need for something more than an 'arithmetical ratio' to explain specific material qualities.[146] Quality may be reducible to a series of quantitative relations, but not those identified by Eschenmayer's early dynamics; a different notion of quantitative relation is required to make sense of qualitative diversity in the natural world.

At this point in the 1803 *Ideas*, Schelling refers the reader back to his *Presentation of my System of Philosophy*, published in May 1801 just after *On the True Concept*. And, on a superficial level, the 1801 *Presentation* – the opening salvo to the identity philosophy – does foreground many features of Eschenmayerian philosophy of nature: it explains difference quantitatively; it places the point of indifference between two magnetic poles at the heart of its metaphysics; it uses the language of equilibrium and preponderance, of relative and absolute indifference and of potency. Moreover, Schelling himself acknowledges his debt to Eschenmayer in the Preface to the text. It is therefore little wonder then that many scholars have insisted on a substantial Eschenmayerian influence on the *Presentation*; indeed, the editors of the ongoing *Historisch-Kritische Ausgabe* of Schelling's works have spoken of the *Presentation* as a 'return' to Eschenmayer, since both 'work with a concept of degree or quantitative difference',[147] and Rang has gone so far as to claim that any proper appreciation of the *Presentation* depends on a precise reconstruction of Eschenmayer's philosophy of nature.[148] In many ways, what this chapter has tried to show is that this 'return' to Eschenmayer is not particularly surprising: it had been prepared by their ongoing conversations from 1799 onwards.

Eschenmayer's application of his mathematical model to magnetism in the 1798 *Investigations* is particularly influential on Schelling in May 1801. Although other influences, such as Brugmans, should not be overlooked,[149] it is Eschenmayer's suggestion of a neutral point which might possibly act as an originary generator of difference that comes to shape Schellingian metaphysics of the period. His influence is tangible in Schelling's 'fundamental schema of our whole system', the magnetic line of § 46 of the *Presentation*:

Absolute identity's form of being can thus be universally conceived through the image of a *line*

$$\frac{^+A = B \qquad A = B^+}{A = A^0}$$

wherein the very same identity is posited in each direction, with predominant A or B in the opposite directions, while A = A itself falls at the point of equilibrium.[150]

According to the *Presentation*, difference can be understood as a quantitative imbalance within an original identity – the neutral or indifference point. Reading § 46 of the *Presentation* in light of the earlier dispute over material qualities, Eschenmayer's influence becomes apparent. The mathematical notation, the distribution of being across a linear series, the privileging of the neutral point of the magnet as an originary moment of indifference – all of this seems to be appropriated from Eschenmayer's early writings.[151]

Nonetheless, what had been one of the most important criticisms of the Eschenmayerian model in *On the True Concept* remains in full force in the 1801 *Presentation* and becomes essential to Schelling's metaphysics of the period. The Schellingian series is not produced out of a synthesis of two factors (A and B), but is the product of one alone: identity (A = A). Whereas, in Eschenmayer's dynamics, the zero potency merely appears along the potentiated series of proportions of repulsive and attractive force, indifference is original for Schelling, and all other potencies are determinate formations of this primordial indifference. More details will be provided in Chapter 3, but it is worth noting that it is precisely this point – the transformation of dualism into monism – that is stressed in *On the True Concept* when Schelling announces the advent of the identity philosophy and the forthcoming publication of the *Presentation*:

> In the following issue, I hope to begin the new presentation of my system . . . and to show how in the end one is forced to solely affirm that view which I have characterised above, namely that in which all dualism is forever annihilated and everything becomes absolutely one.[152]

The Eschenmayerian series may appear in Schelling's identity philosophy, but the dualistic philosophy of nature that underlies it does not.

Chapter 2

Potency

Schelling's *On the True Concept* rejects in no uncertain terms Eschenmayer's reduction of material qualities to various proportions of repulsive and attractive force. And yet, as suggested above, in this same text Schelling also comes to see the value of constructing qualities in a quasi-Eschenmayerian – that is, quantitative – fashion. Indeed, *On the True Concept* proposes that Eschenmayer's series of proportions might be supplemented with further series, thereby adding depth to Eschenmayer's single-dimensional, nature-philosophical construction: for Schelling, differences regarding the proportions of force constitute only the most basic stage or level of a more general, *vertical* series that extends from the dynamic to the qualitative and culminates in the organic. And if natural qualities, such as chemical properties, belong to a more complicated series of stages – 'higher' or 'greater' than the more basic, dynamic stage – then it is possible to conceive such qualities in terms of quantity. Schelling identifies the general stages or levels of reality as 'potencies' or 'powers', and in this chapter we consider Schelling's adoption and transformation of this concept, a concept that begins to take centre stage in his metaphysics, at least in part, thanks to the controversy with Eschenmayer.

The concept of potency at the end of the eighteenth century

In his 1796 *Der polynomische Lehrsatz*, Carl Friedrich Hindenburg, the leading figure of the Leipzig combinatorial school – the 'most influential' mathematical movement in Germany during the 1790s[1] – remarks on the introduction of the term 'potentiation' into his text as follows:

> This is, as far as I am aware, a word that has, until now, been quite uncommon ... but nonetheless seems exactly fitting. If only all neologisms in mathematical language were always so blameless and never harmed its precision and simplicity! – a wish that could be extended to many phenomena in the unsettled domains of letters.[2]

It has been frequently remarked that Novalis (and consequently many of those he influenced in Jena during the late 1790s) owes the term 'potentiation' to Hindenburg.[3] It is also likely that Eschenmayer was heavily influenced – directly or otherwise – by the combinatorial school when it comes to his own appropriation of the terminology of potency and potentiation.

For Hindenburg and his school, potentiation designates 'the operation of raising an infinite series to an exponential power and the attempt to find formulas for the coefficients of the new series through a combinatorial calculus' – a mode of mathematical serialisation 'which was all the rage in Germany in the 1790s'.[4] This use of an algebraic series has evident Leibnizian roots (indeed, the very name of the *combinatorial* school evokes Leibniz) and found success in the works of Lagrange and Euler. Of course, the significance of the potency or exponent in mathematical calculation long preceded late eighteenth-century algebra and was central to the Cartesian revolution in mathematics (a point to which we return below). Moreover, concepts cognate to potentiation were readily available in the natural and metaphysical sciences of the time, such as Goethe's concept of intensification and Oetinger's dynamics of spiritualisation. Nevertheless, Hindenburg's popularisation of the language of potentiation in the field of mathematics explains, at least partially, the eruption of this language within philosophical discourse in the 1790s.

At any rate, the concept of potentiation was in the air for anyone interested in mathematics in the 1790s. It is thus unsurprising that this concept was employed by Eschenmayer as the very cornerstone of his philosophy of nature, even in his earliest writings. As outlined in Chapter 1, Eschenmayer accounts for the qualitative determinacy in nature by constructing an infinite series of proportions between repulsive and attractive force, a series in which each apparent quality is interpreted as a higher or lower potency. And Eschenmayer does not stop here; indeed, when he turns his attention to *any* phenomenon, he seeks to reduce it to the result of the interplay of two fundamental principles, whose various relations can be enumerated in a potentiated series of the form: $A^{-n}.B \ldots A^{0}.B \ldots A^{+n}.B$. The two principles (A and B) give rise to an infinite number of terms on the basis of the ratios by which they relate – and each of these terms is characterised by a specific potency. Eschenmayer repeats this basic schema in his construction of matter, in his construction of mechanical motion, in his construction of electricity and magnetism and in his constructions of the fundamental activities of the human mind. Indeed – as Chapter 4 will explore – the potentiated series generated out of the interplay of the mental activities of production and reflection acts as the transcendental ground of the potentiated series discerned in nature. In every domain, Eschenmayer utilises the conception of potentiation and conceives this potentiation as 'the increase of one force and corresponding decrease of the other'.[5]

The similarities with Hindenburg's formulation of potentiation are striking. Both employ the concept as part of an overall mechanism of serialising what had, until then, not been properly serialised: Hindenburg serialises specific problems in the calculus of his day; Eschenmayer transforms the whole of the natural and mental world into series of potencies. Both, moreover, serialise these phenomena using the same model: a polynomial set of terms arranged according to a gradual and continuous process of exponentiation. And, finally, both understand this potentiated series to be the key to resolving disputes in their respective disciplines and setting calculus, on the one hand, and philosophy of nature, on the other, on a firm foundation. Eschenmayer, then, is a child of the 1790s in his use of the concept of potency.

The same can also be said for Schelling, although here the situation is – as always with Schelling – far more complicated. By 1801, Schelling has famously adopted the language of potency and potentiation, and these terms will go on to serve as master-concepts in his metaphysics until the end of his life. Despite the many significant shifts that Schelling's thought undergoes during the first half of the nineteenth century, 'potency' remains one of his fundamental terms – even when it takes on new meaning. As we saw in Chapter 1, however, Schelling's attitude towards Eschenmayer's mathematicisation of the philosophy of nature was ambivalent, to say the least, and this is by extension true of his attitude towards Eschenmayer's concept of potency. Indeed, critics insist that Schelling is the philosopher 'to rid potency of its mathematical baggage'.[6] This makes it far more difficult to assess the extent to which Schelling may have been influenced by the Hindenburgean–Eschenmayerian conception of potentiation. And if we consider the fact that Schelling was much closer than Eschenmayer to the creative and often metaphorical uses of the concept by the Jena Romantics – as well as to cognate concepts such as Goethean intensification – the picture becomes all the more complicated. The reasons behind Schelling's appropriation of the concept of potency are not, therefore, straightforward.

Nevertheless, it seems clear that Eschenmayer plays some role in Schelling's adoption of the term. This can be gleaned not only from the testimony of Schelling's contemporaries (e.g. Hegel) and Schelling's own comments (see below), but also from a brief history of Schelling's early use of the concept. Although he uses the term in *On the World Soul* to refer to the 'exciting powers' [*erregenden Potenzen*] of John Brown's physiology,[7] it is not until the *First Outline* and its *Introduction* that Schelling begins to develop his technical conception of the potencies as the essential structures of reality. Thus, when Schelling states that 'sensibility is only the higher power of magnetism; irritability only the higher power of electricity; formative drive only the higher power of the chemical process', he is laying the groundwork for a distinctive nature-philosophical perspective in which the concept of potency plays a central role.[8] In the *Universal Deduction*, Schelling significantly elaborates upon the ideas sketched in the *First Outline*, and *On the True Concept* provides a sustained account of the role of potentiation and depotentiation in nature-philosophical methodology. Most significantly, however, in the *Presentation*, he does not only refer to the *concept* of potency, but – as he himself puts it in the Preface to that work – he '[makes] quite frequent use . . . of a general symbolic notation that was previously employed by Herr Eschenmayer in his essays on natural philosophy'.[9] It is here that the basic levels of reality are expressed symbolically (i.e., as $A = B$, A^2, A^3).

Schelling is explicit, then: it is owing to Eschenmayer that the concept of potency comes to the fore. While he may have experimented with the concept in earlier texts, it is only in 1801, motivated by the controversy with Eschenmayer, that his employment of potency becomes formalised through the 'general symbolic notation' of algebra. In Tilliette's words, only in 1801 does potency 'form the internal armature of Schelling's philosophy'.[10] It is therefore reasonable to suggest that Eschenmayer's provocation causes Schelling to settle on an explicit understanding of potency that holds good for his identity philosophy and, in many important ways, for his later writings as well.

Potentiation in the 1801 *Presentation*

As we explored in Chapter 1, Eschenmayer employs the potencies to signify various proportions between the fundamental forces (A and B signifying attraction and repulsion and the exponents signifying various levels of their imbalance). In 1801, Schelling adopts this notation in order develop a more complete philosophical system of nature, one which includes not only an account of the relationship of the forces (still represented as A and B or $A = B$), but also distinctive branches of qualitative physics (A^2) and speculative biology (A^3). Generally put, the use of these potencies signifies an Eschenmayerian commitment on Schelling's part, namely, a commitment to the general notion that quality – and everything else in nature – can be constructed on the basis of some form of quantitative difference. But crucially, Schelling rejects the idea that it is through the conflict between attraction and repulsion that diversity in nature arises; instead, this conflict is only the lowest level of a more general movement in which *absolute identity* (A = A) expresses itself at various levels of intensity. Each of these levels is a different potency or power of identity.

One of the difficulties presented by Schelling's use of the potencies is that he conceives them as recursive. At the most general level, the spiritual realm is a higher potency of nature, and the absolute indifference or unity of nature and spirit is a still higher potency. But, at a more specific level, the potencies are expressed *within* the domains of nature and spirit as ascending levels of natural and spiritual determinacy. In nature, the potencies are expressed as gravity (and quantitative difference more generally), light (and qualitative difference more generally) and organic life; in spirit they appear as cognition, action and art.[11] And, although Schelling does not conceive the further specification of each of the potencies in nature and spirit as potencies proper, the tripartite structure of the potencies is repeated again at these even more specific levels. Thus, nature in the first potency is constituted by three distinct moments or stages, as is nature in the second potency, and so forth. This whole recursive structure is important, for Schelling, because it exhibits the manner in which the potencies recapitulate themselves throughout the whole of natural reality and spiritual life. Since we are here concerned with Schelling's speculative physics, we can set aside the recursion of the potencies within the domain of spirit and focus exclusively upon their recursion within nature.

The first potency: A = B and its potentiation

Schelling describes A = B as 'the general expression of potency as such'.[12] This is because potency is some instantiation of identity (A = A) in which difference is exhibited. In so far as A = A can be said to involve difference, then, it can be expressed as A = B, the most basic potency of identity. To the extent that identity involves difference, this is a quantitative difference – that is, an imbalance between its subjective and objective aspects – such that either A in the subject position (i.e. 'A') or A in the predicate position (i.e., 'B') predominates. A and B are nevertheless essentially identical (A = B), because this difference is strictly quantitative; they are the *same being*. It follows from this that identity does not *negate* itself in its potentiation as A = B. For A = B *is* A = A in which the subjective and objective aspects of this identity have become imbalanced.

The first potency, therefore, is an instantiation of identity in which there is a quantitative difference within that identity. In its most basic material exhibition, this potency is gravity. And, just as the potency has three aspects (i.e. A, B and their identity, '='), gravitational motion has three aspects: attraction, repulsion and gravity proper. Schelling associates attraction with A, because it is the dynamic tendency in which the subjective (i.e. the *inner*) aspect of identity predominates. Likewise, since repulsion is an outward-directed tendency, it constitutes the objective aspect of identity – that is, B. Gravity, then, is the *unity* of A and B – that is, the indifference of attraction and repulsion.[13] For in gravitational motion, a material body – which both repels other objects from its place (B) and yet does not scatter infinitely outwards but remains *the material it is* (A) – seeks to unite with other material bodies and thereby achieve maximal identity within the strictly quantitative dimension of nature: in their immanent gravitational motion, material bodies seek to become absolutely *one*.

Since this potency – taken as a whole – seeks indifference *in matter*, it can be expressed as $A = B^+$ – that is, first potency with a preponderance of objective being (as opposed to cognition, the first potency of spirit, which can be expressed $^+A = B$ given its preponderance of subjectivity).[14] Different elements of nature, however, exhibit more subjectivity than the minimal subjectivity of gravitational motion. And the potentiation of $A = B$ to A^2 constitutes an increase in nature's subjective element. The second potency in nature is light, which is an immaterial principle of expansion. Unlike gravity – the striving of all material bodies to become *one* material body – light expands outwards in order to achieve indifference through an immaterial process of bringing matter *to light*: everything is one in the light of day in so far as everything is made apparent. From this perspective, it *seems* as though light (A^2) is 'in conflict with the being of $A = B$' – that is, matter or gravity.[15] However, Schelling insists that 'the opposition between A^2 and $A = B$ is not an intrinsic opposition'.[16] For both potencies are potencies of *the same identity* – that is, $A = A$. Moreover, A^2 is nothing other than $A = B$ *duplicated* with itself. The second potency of nature *just is* the first potency in an intensified form. As Schelling writes, '$A = B$ is posited anew through A^2.'[17] And what is brought out in this new form of $A = B$ is the subjective (or non-objective) element.[18] It is within this second potency that Schelling locates the 'universal categories of physics', namely, magnetism, electricity and the chemical process.

The second potency: A^2

Schelling's association of magnetic, electrical and chemical phenomena with light (A^2) is complicated, but, in the most general sense, it rests on the fact that they all require nature-philosophical construction that goes beyond the play of repulsive and attractive force.

This first thing to note about the second potency is that it involves the intensification of the *subjective* element of subject-object identity in a *strictly physical* manner. This means that the most basic element in A^2 is a 'relative identity' of the subjective or ideal (A) and objective or physical (B) poles of identity. Consequently, Schelling argues, A and B are 'posited under the form of the line',[19] the two ends of which signify the two poles of relative identity. The natural phenomenon that exhibits this kind of identity is magnetism, since a magnet is constituted by two poles which cannot be separated from one another. Whereas magnetism exhibits the relative identity of the two poles of A = B, electricity intensifies the *difference* between the poles, hence Schelling's identification of electricity with 'relative duplicity'.[20] Material bodies do not exhibit *both* positive and negative electrical charge as magnets exhibit both positive and negative poles; a material body is either positively or negatively charged, and it relates to *other* bodies through this specific difference. The third moment of the second potency concerns chemical transformation, and it intensifies the relationship between material bodies which is already exhibited in the phenomenon of electricity. In chemical interaction, bodies are not only affected by one another on their *surface* (as in electrical discharge), but their entire structure is altered through their relationship. Through such an intensification of A^2, natural objects do not only exhibit intrinsic polarity (magnetism) and a superficial relationship to other objects (electricity), but a thoroughgoing relationship to bodies that appear qualitatively distinct from them. Importantly, however, the chemical process is identical to magnetism and electricity to the extent that each of these phenomena displays qualitative determinacy in nature by exhibiting *indifference*, albeit in different ways. Whereas magnetism exhibits indifference by merging the two poles (A and B or + and –) into one and electricity exhibits indifference by separating the positive and negative as equally powerful and intrinsically related in their opposition, chemical processes – specifically processes of chemical combination – exhibit indifference by eradicating the qualitative specificity of two bodies, and therefore polarity, altogether.[21]

Schelling describes the three moments of the second potency as the universal categories of physics, because magnetism, electricity and chemical process are 'functions of *all* matter'.[22] In 1801, Schelling continues to hold the view – first expressed in the earlier texts on the philosophy of nature – that the universality of the physical categories signifies the fact that all material bodies have the *potential* to be magnetised and electrified.[23] By 1803, Schelling has taken this universalism even further by arguing that all material bodies *in fact* exhibit such qualities. That is to say, every single material body exhibits the qualities of magnetic polarity, electrical charge and chemical constitution, even if the degree to which these qualities are expressed is barely perceptible in certain instances.[24] The idea that all material bodies are magnetic, electrical and chemical is closely related to Schelling's claim that there is no special kind of 'force' or 'matter' in nature, but that *all* of nature expresses the same functions to varying degrees. Magnetic phenomena, for instance, do not depend upon the existence of a 'special magnetic force – or even one, or two, magnetic matters'.[25] In other words, the natural world is not constituted by qualitatively distinct substances; rather, the natural world is made up of one and the same material which expresses the same three qualities at different levels of intensity, thereby producing what appear to be qualitatively distinct phenomena.

Schelling's universalism regarding the categories of physics does not end here. Not only is all matter potentiated as qualitatively determinate in the threefold manner described above, but the moments of quality *themselves* constitute a series of various intensities of *one and the same physical process* in which inorganic nature exhibits subject-object identity. This is why 'there is no intrinsic opposition between relative identity [i.e. magnetism] and relative duplicity [i.e. electricity]; with equal correctness, we can consider the magnet to be composed of two bodies and the two bodies of the electrical process to be one (= magnet).'[26] When put this way, it becomes clear once again that the potencies are meant to express a form of differentiation in nature that proceeds via an intensification of one and the same being. Just as nothing is cancelled out in the movement from first to second potency – only an intensification of A – so too the development *within* the second potency is a development without negation.

The Third Potency: The Potentiation of A^2 and the Determinacy of A^3

The subjective dimension of subject-object identity is further intensified in the third potency (A^3), which Schelling identifies with the organism. The transition from second to third potency, therefore, constitutes nothing less than Schelling's account of the relationship between inorganic matter and organic life. One of the most important lessons of the *Introduction to the Outline* is that all attempts to discover a third principle and common source of the inorganic and the organic fail, because such attempts – despite the effort to unify these two aspects of nature – presuppose a qualitative ontological distinction between the two.[27] Against such dualism, Schelling argues, life must be understood to be inorganic nature raised to a higher power. Thus, the key moments in life will be *intensified* forms of magnetism, electricity and the chemical process, the three categories of physics.

Magnetism is raised to the organic potency in the form of sensibility.[28] Just as the two poles of a magnet are inseparable, the subjective and objective features of sentient life constitute a 'relative identity': for an organism can only *sense* external (and internal) stimuli if it actively relates to itself as a passive object capable of being affected by the world. Without the subjective dimension of sensibility, an organism would not experience anything at all; and yet, without the objective dimension of sensibility – that is, the capacity to be affected – an organism also would not experience the world. Thus, in so far as a natural object is sentient, it must be subject and object at one and the same time, the difference between the active and passive elements of sensibility being equally necessary.[29]

The second moment of the third potency is irritability – that is, an organism's ability to move of its own accord. And just as the qualities of the magnet are intensified in the phenomenon of electricity, so too does sensibility lead to irritability. In particular, an organism's receptiveness to stimuli makes possible an even more active – that is, subjective – engagement with the world: the organism can *act*. And because an organism can direct its action either *outwards* or *inwards* – for example, the metamorphosis of an insect issues from an alternation of expansive and contractive motion[30] – irritability recapitulates the 'relative duplicity' of electricity. If we attend to the purpose of such action, however, we see that an organism always acts in the service of forming, maintaining and reproducing itself. The third and final moment of the organic process, therefore, is the formative drive (*Bildungstrieb*), the organism's inner striving to maintain itself as a subject over and against the objective world.

From a certain perspective, then, the formative drive is the highest moment of the highest potency in nature: in the drive of the organism, the subjective element of subject-object identity is intensified to such a great degree that it achieves absolute *indifference* with the objective element.[31] In this way, the organism exhibits *more* subject-object identity than do chemical processes. Whereas the latter achieve indifference through the nullification of duplicity in what is a relatively *objective* nature, the organism maintains itself as a living *subject* that is *also* a natural object. The subjective and objective aspects of identity (A = A) are thus equally expressed in an organism's drive to maintain itself as the life it is. That being said, although organisms exhibit identity to a greater degree than inorganic processes, living things are not special kinds of objects, set apart from the non-living on account of some *élan vital* or substantial, material difference between inorganic and organic bodies. Life is nothing more than intensified inorganic matter.

Reflections on the above schema

We are now in a position to consider some of the key metaphysical principles of Schelling's early doctrine of the potencies. First, it is important to note that the lower potencies ground the higher potencies. This means that, *without* the appearance of qualitative features in the material world, organic life *would not exist*; likewise, and at a more basic level, the qualities in material nature would not exist were it not for nature's activity in the first potency – that is, attraction, repulsion and their unity in gravitational motion: 'A^2 subsists only insofar as A = B does.'[32] This does not mean that, as Eschenmayer argues in the *Principles*, qualities can be constructed with exclusive reference to the play between the fundamental forces; but it *is* the case that the forces in some sense ground the being of magnetism, electricity and chemical processes for Schelling.[33] Indeed, if there were no material bodies repelling other material from their place, then those bodies *could not express* the universal categories of qualitative physics. The development from one potency to another, then, suggests that there is a grounding relationship between the more basic structures of nature and its more complex structures.[34]

However, if we focus exclusively upon the fact that the lower potencies ground the higher potencies, we can easily lose sight of the fact that the higher and lower potencies are all potencies *of the same being*, namely, identity (A = A). And this is a central feature of Schelling's early doctrine of the potencies which cannot be overstated. By conceiving the most general structures of nature as potencies of identity, Schelling insists on an extreme form of monism, in which even the most general categories of nature, such as the inorganic and the organic, are understood to be identical. Nature is essentially *one*.

Schellingian identity (A = A) potentiates itself as *Stufenfolge*.[35] It is therefore necessary to recognise the processual character of Schellingian identity and the way that the concept of potentiation does not only allow Schelling to understand the general forms of nature as united; it also allows him to understand identity itself as a process of differentiation. In other words, the idea that the general structures of reality emerge from one another does not only commit one to monism in the philosophy of nature; this idea also implies that the philosophy of nature must attend to the immanent genesis of these structures. To be sure, in 1801, Schelling does not conceive this genetic process as a *historical* development.[36] Nevertheless, the genetic character of the *Stufenfolge* is clear. Potentiation names an atemporal process of self-duplication, through which identity intensifies itself and thereby expresses itself in gradually more complex forms – and, significantly, identity only *is* in so far as it *does* this.

Schelling's employment of the concept of potency to develop an account of the self-differentiation of nature distinguishes him in a fundamental way from the Hindenburgean–Eschenmayerian tradition. As Moiso emphasises, potentiation in Schelling's system expresses the relations between *discontinuous* stages or levels of reality, and this is radically different from the continuous polynomial series in which Hindenburg and Eschenmayer embed the process of potentiation.[37] In other words, while Eschenmayerian potentiation describes the different possible permutations within any given domain of reality, Schellingian potentiation makes radical jumps across domains, such that the material, qualitative and organic structures of reality can be presented as more and less complex stages of one and the same nature. Oddly, then, Schelling's rejection of Eschenmayer's reduction of quality to the forces of attraction and repulsion goes hand in hand with his discovery that Eschenmayer's potentiated series can be extended to encompass different domains of reality *at once* and thereby *unite* these domains as stages of a single series ($A = B, A^2, A^3$). Instead of reducing the more complex features of nature to the more basic features, Schelling conceives the former as quantitative intensifications of the latter – thus affirming, in a novel manner, the broadly Eschenmayerian commitment to interpreting natural phenomena on the basis of quantitative determinacy.

Throughout the remainder of this chapter, we focus on what might conditionally be called Schelling's Eschenmayerianism – that is, his sympathy for algebraic notation as a means of nature-philosophical expression. In doing so, we hope to further shed light upon Schelling's doctrine of the potencies. First, we attempt to distinguish Schelling's algebraic conception of potency from the Aristotelian conception of the same. We then go on to defend Schelling against the Hegelian charge that mathematical formalism, such as we find in Schelling's use of the potencies, has no place in philosophical reasoning. Throughout the following, however, it should be kept in mind that, despite his use of a *generally* Eschenmayerian concept, Schelling's doctrine of the potencies is unique in all of the ways outlined above.

A different kind of power

One of the more significant recent trends in scholarship on Schelling's philosophy of nature has been to place it into conversation with contemporary powers-ontology. And given the centrality of the potencies in Schelling's thought, his philosophy of nature can rightly be described as an ontology of powers.[38] However, while there is much to be valued in this trend, it is still important to recognise that the meaning of power, for Schelling, is – in a number of fundamental ways – different from the way power is understood in contemporary anglophone metaphysics.

Largely inspired by Aristotle, a handful of contemporary metaphysicians have sought to reaffirm the notion that powers are an irreducible feature of the natural world. Against the Humean orthodoxy in anglophone philosophy, which refuses the reality of causal powers, these metaphysicians argue that 'inanimate matter is not passive, but essentially active'.[39] There are more and less traditional versions of this view, and some which appear to entirely overturn Aristotelian substance ontology; for example, George Molnar argues that, at the basis of all phenomena – that is, at the subatomic level – there are 'ungrounded' powers – that is, powers which do not inhere in any substance at all.[40] The idea uniting all powers-realists, however, is that powers are irreducible elements of reality, and that a philosophical understanding of nature must attend to the ontological character of such powers.

As Alderwick has noted, Molnar's discussion of ungrounded powers raises the question as to whether the whole of nature is not, at bottom, constituted by powers. Alderwick goes on to argue that contemporary metaphysicians would benefit significantly from drawing upon Schelling, who *does* conceive nature as being 'composed of powers in process, all the way down'.[41] Of course, Schelling is not the first philosopher to suggest that powers can be found in the depth of nature; his own influences in this regard include Bruno, Leibniz, Herder, Goethe, Kielmeyer and Oetinger. Thus, when Schelling rejects mechanical conceptions of nature for failing to grasp the dynamism at work within the natural world, and when he argues that matter is *active* in gravitational motion, magnetic polarity, electricity and chemical processes, he is drawing upon a long tradition of thought. From this perspective, Schelling's philosophy of nature – and the larger movement of modern German philosophy within which it plays an integral role – may be a significant resource for further discussions in contemporary metaphysics regarding the ineliminable powers at work in the natural world, particularly since these discussions tend to draw exclusively upon ancient sources for inspiration.[42]

Nevertheless, it is noticeable that Alderwick's argument for Schelling's relevance to contemporary powers ontology largely draws on the *First Outline*. This text, and especially the qualitative atomism presented therein, may well be a significant resource for thinking about the irreducible nature of causal powers. However, one of the contentions implicit in the foregoing commentary is that the *First Outline* is a transitional and experimental work, in which many doctrines key to Schelling's mature philosophy of nature remain nascently formulated and others are not present at all. It is only in the wake of the controversy with Eschenmayer in January 1801 that Schelling fully develops his conception of potency, and a switch in focus to the texts of 1801 shows that the structure of nature, for Schelling, is unintelligible with reference to forces and actants alone. By focusing on the technical use of the term 'potency' in 1801, therefore, we are seeking to draw out a significant difference between Schelling's metaphysics and contemporary powers ontology, a difference that concerns not only the extension of the concept of potency to the very depths of nature, but the meaning and function of the concept as well. Simply put, we suggest that it is philosophically significant that Schelling adopts an algebraic, as opposed to Aristotelian, use of the term *dunamis*, and that this is a testament to the importance of the Eschenmayer controversy for Schelling's metaphysics of the period.

Like all philosophical concepts which have their roots in ordinary language, *dunamis* is said in many ways.[43] Generally speaking, however, philosophers following Aristotle have used the term (and its equivalents in other languages) to signify a thing's intrinsic power or capacity to undergo a change, whether that change is initiated by the thing itself or by some other thing.[44] It is this conception of *dunamis* as an immanent principle of change that is of interest to contemporary philosophers seeking to overturn Humean philosophy of nature. There is certainly a sense in which this conception of power makes its way into Schelling's thought. For example, it is presumably what Schelling has in mind in § 52 of the *Presentation*, which states that 'the essence of absolute identity, insofar as it is immediately the ground of reality, is power [*Kraft*]'.[45] However, when Schelling refers to the *Potenzen*, he has something else in mind. It is necessary, then, to consider the way that *dunamis* has, historically, signified something other than the potential, capacity or power for something to perform an action.

In a number of dialogues, Plato uses the term *dunamis* within the context of geometry. In the *Theaetetus*, for example, *dunamis* designates squares[46] as well as lines which are incommensurable in length and yet commensurable 'in respect of the plane figures which they have the power [*dunantai*] to form'.[47] Euclid uses the term in a related although somewhat different manner in Book X of the *Elements*: 'Straight lines are commensurable *in square* [*dunamei*] when the squares on them are measured by the same area.'[48] That is, incommensurable lines are commensurable *in power* if the areas of the squares constructed by those lines can be measured by the same unit without remainder. *Dunamis* can therefore refer to a line, in so far as it can be swept out to construct a square, or it can refer to a square itself.

In *Metaphysics Θ*, Aristotle suggests that the geometrical term *dunamis* should be ruled out of metaphysics proper, since the geometrical and metaphysical terms are related in name alone.[49] In *Metaphysics Δ*, he suggests a closer connection, yet one which still separates the metaphysical from the geometrical: 'potentiality [*dunamis*] in geometry is spoken of metaphorically'.[50] Whether or not Aristotle is right to make this claim, it does raise the question: what is it about the everyday conception of a 'capacity' that allows it to be translated into a geometrical concept meaning either a square or one of the sides of a square (i.e. a root)? Put simply, a line can be understood in terms of power if one attends to the line's *capacity to be squared*. There is, then, a connection between the geometrical conception of power and the everyday use of the term. However, it is important to emphasise the novelty of the geometrical usage. First, it transforms the concept into a quantitative feature of an abstract entity, as opposed to a qualitative feature of a concrete substance.[51] Secondly – and related to this first point – the 'change' that is suggested by the power of a line (or the line 'in power') has nothing to do with a natural object's capacity to undergo a change of state, but is rather far more abstract: it is simply the change that results from the squaring of the line. Such a change is quantitative, but it should be noted that this quantitative change brings about a significant shift. In the 'movement' from the line to the square, a real differentiation occurs, since a line – when duplicated with itself – generates a plane. The same can be said of the movement from the line to the cube, in which the line that is triplicated with itself generates a solid.[52] Although we have not yet arrived at the modern mathematical conception of potency, it can already be noted that the abstractness of the geometrical conception of power and the fact that it is connected to a conception of development which arises through self-relation will prove to be of particular interest to Schelling.

In the third century AD, Diophantus began to give symbolic expression to this mathematical concept, using Δ^Y to signify the square of an unknown number (i.e., Δ for *dunamis*).[53] But it was not until Descartes's *Geometry* of 1637 that a fully symbolic algebraic system became popularised, a system containing the exponential notation used to this day – and, of course, the same notation appropriated by Eschenmayer in his Kantian philosophy of nature.[54] Importantly, for Descartes, a^2 and b^3 signify 'only simple lines, although, in order to make use of the names used in algebra', he refers to a^2 and b^3 as 'squares, cubes, etc.'[55] Descartes thus forgoes the Euclidean procedure of diagram construction in favour of a strictly symbolic formalism, stating that 'often one has no need so to trace . . . lines on paper, and it suffices to designate them by certain letters.'[56] In doing so, he develops a novel way to think about mathematics itself. Macbeth is helpful in describing this transition from pre-Cartesian to Cartesian thought:

> Whereas traditional mathematics . . . concerns objects, that is, geometrical figures, kinds of numbers (conceived as collections of units), and so on, Descartes's new mathematics is to be a science of order and measure. What Descartes means . . . is that mathematics is now to be conceived as a science not of things, objects, but of the relations and patterns that objects can exhibit.[57]

And since mathematics no longer concerns objects – however abstract – but, rather, relations and patterns which *may be exhibited* by objects, it follows that the symbolic forms of mathematical language are meaningful without referring to any objects whatsoever. The Aristotelian conception of power implicit in the early geometers' employment of the term is thereby diminished, if not fully extinguished, in Cartesian mathematics. Powers – from a Cartesian perspective – signify neither the capacities of natural objects nor even the capacities of abstract lines, but refer *only to themselves* – that is, to the sheer relations that such powers *are*.

It is this Cartesian conception of power that Hindenburg and Eschenmayer are exploiting for their own ends in calculus and philosophy of nature respectively; and it is this conception that Schelling takes over from Eschenmayer and substantially revises in 1801. In order to fully grasp the specificity of Schelling's powers metaphysics, then – and to fully distinguish it from neo-Aristotelian philosophies of nature – it is helpful to enumerate the ideas that he seeks to express with the concept of potency:

1. *Abstractness.* The potencies are not the contingent capacities of various particular objects, but the *fundamental structures or patterns in nature*. Because the 'powers of nature' can be fully understood in abstraction from individual things, the philosopher can exhibit the structure of reality through a profoundly abstract form of philosophy. That is, the potency is 'a functional [form which is] not affected by content',[58] and this means that Schelling can present the structures of reality in abstraction from the particular.
2. *Radical Universalism.* The algebraic notation employed by Schelling also signals the fact that the stages or structures of nature are universal in their extension: *all matter is magnetic, electrical, and chemical; all living things sense the world outside them, respond to that world, and are driven to reproduce themselves.* Expressing these essential structures of reality in formal language therefore helps to demonstrate that these potencies apply to the whole of nature. Moreover, the potencies recur at all stages of reality, which means that it is not only nature that is structured by the potencies but spirit as well.[59]
3. *Monism.* The potencies are intrinsically connected to one another and cannot be separated as fully independent structures of reality. But

rather than conceiving the connections between the stages of nature in terms of a harmonious interaction between ontologically distinct kinds, Schelling understands these connections to be far more thoroughgoing: each and every general feature of nature is an expression of *the same being*. The language of the potencies thus allows Schelling to convey the idea that the irritability of an organism *is* electricity and that the reproductive process *is* a chemical process. A, A^2 and A^3 are all instances of *A*.

4. *Duplication*. Monism does not rule out difference, and the language of the potencies also allows Schelling to symbolise the differences between the various features of reality. Although A, A^2 and A^3 are all instances of A, they are A *raised to various levels of intensity*. Zeltner expresses this nicely in stating that 'potency is defined as designating determinate forms or modes of being of absolute identity, corresponding to their respective quantitative difference of subjective or objective [being]'.[60] In order for such difference to fit within a monistic system, Schelling argues that it arises immanently through nature's relationship *to itself*. This is precisely what is represented in the movement from one potency to another: A duplicated with itself – and without any mediation through some *other* reality – generates A^2.

Thus, (1–2) the potencies describe the general stages of reality as a whole – rather than the particular capacities of individual things – and (3–4) these general stages are themselves lower and higher intensities of *the same being*.

This is a very different way to think about the 'powers of nature'. Schelling does not utilise this concept in order to focus on the capacities *of things* to act in one way or another, but rather to understand the connections between the most general elements that structure the whole of reality – that is, the *Stufenfolge* or series of stages *that nature is*. With such an approach to speculative physics, the philosopher need not concern herself with how a plethora of dispositions do and do not manifest themselves in causal interaction, but rather, how the most general kinds of processes in nature are different intensities of the same reality. Algebraic notation is therefore extraordinarily useful in making explicit the identity and quantitative differences between these fundamental elements of reality.

Formalism in the philosophy of nature

In 1986, Walther Zimmerli resuscitated an old opposition in German Idealism studies with an essay entitled 'Potenzlehre versus Logik der Naturphilosophie'. As such a title suggests, Zimmerli presupposes

– initially at least – a stark opposition between the Hegelian logic of nature and Schelling's metaphysics of potency, in order to illustrate two very different ways of pursuing a philosophy of nature. In other words, Zimmerli sets up his essay according to the very terms of the Hegelian polemic against Schelling, in which the former's proper logical approach to natural categories is to be opposed to the latter's use of a mathematical concept in the domain of metaphysics.[61] For, although the young Hegel may have occasionally followed Schelling in employing this concept to describe the structure of reality,[62] the mature Hegel was persistently critical of philosophical uses of potency. In his 1825/6 *Lectures on the History of Philosophy*, for example, he argues that 'the philosophy of nature has fallen into particular disrepute', in part 'because it takes a ready-made schema for its basis and imposes it on natural phenomena'. He goes on to specify that 'for Schelling these forms [or ready-made schemas] were the potencies'.[63] And, according to Hegel, drawing upon non-philosophical categories in this way does serious harm to the philosophy of nature; in particular, it makes philosophy formal, such that the philosopher is unable to exhibit the determinate content that abounds in nature.[64]

The first thing that is important to keep in mind when considering these criticisms is that there are a number of different ways in which the concept of potency entered philosophical discourse in the 1790s (by means of Eschenmayer, Novalis and others), and Schelling's use of the concept is marked by his wariness of its mathematical baggage. As Chapter 1 made clear, Schelling, in fact, wages war against Eschenmayer's mathematicisation of philosophy of nature, criticising the attempt to reduce natural categories to purely quantitative relations between the forces of nature. This is what Novalis dubs Schelling's 'feud with the mathematicians', a feud that reaches its zenith in the *First Outline*'s criticisms of Eschenmayer. Even in 1802, when Schelling comes to see philosophy as intimately connected to arithmetic and geometry, he rejects the reduction of philosophical procedures to sheer mathematical operations. In no way is Schelling exemplary of a mathematicised philosophy of nature.

Hegel himself recognises that Schelling did not intend to reduce philosophy to mathematics, but rather, to simply '[make] *use* of the form of potencies' in order to comprehend the rational structure of nature.[65] Hegel's critique of Schelling's alleged formalism cannot, therefore, be dismissed by simply distinguishing Schelling from the more mathematically-minded philosophers of the period. The crux of the critique comes down to two interconnected issues. The first concerns the idea that, if we understand the natural world in terms of ready-made forms, we will fail to grasp the rich ontological content which is immanent to natural phenomena. This is why, according to Hegel, there is a certain tendency in Schellingian philosophy to reduce determinate difference to self-same identity. To conceive the absolute as A = A – and to conceive the different stages of reality as different powers of this same A = A – is to evacuate reality of its determinacy and thereby fall into a 'monochromatic formalism'.[66] Thus, on Hegel's view, whenever a philosopher understands the natural world in terms of algebraic symbols, she will inevitably fail to grasp the differentiated character of nature.[67]

The formalist, of course, does not seek to obscure all difference, but to make such difference intelligible. And it is this which brings us to the second problem, according to Hegel, with the formalist approach: the natural diversity that *is* acknowledged by the formalist is simply presupposed – a presupposition that allows the philosopher to then impose algebraic forms onto nature from without. Against this view, Hegel proposes that a philosophy of nature ought to immanently derive the wealth of, and connections between, natural forms by attending to the inner *logic* of nature. Hegel's own system seeks to accomplish precisely this. Because the logical structure of any given form of nature is immanent to that form, Hegel argues that a logical explication of natural forms secures the philosopher's understanding of nature's determinacy. By contrast, a formalist, algebraic exhibition of nature's diversity simply presupposes the connections between various forms. As Hegel puts it, 'the *progression* of the forms appears more as an *outwardly imposed schema*. The logical aspect of the progression is not justified on its own account.'[68]

The second apparent problem with Schelling's use of the potencies, then, is that they fail at their appointed task: the formalist philosophy of nature only '*seems* . . . to have matured into an expanded science' which exhibits the vast range of nature's fundamental structures.[69] However:

> A closer inspection shows that this expansion has not come about through one and the same principle having spontaneously assumed different shapes, but rather through the shapeless repetition of one and the same formula, only externally applied to diverse materials, thereby obtaining merely a boring show of diversity.[70]

In other words, the reason Schellingian philosophy of nature yields either a monochromatic formalism or a merely superficial display of natural diversity is that it fails to proceed via a logical and therefore genuinely immanent method. Hegel goes on to argue that a truly speculative science will exhibit the spontaneous development of one shape of reality to another via the movement of *negativity*, a process in which an oppositional difference internal to being itself is sublated precisely through that opposition.[71] And, for Hegel, it is only by attending to this dialectical process that the philosopher of nature can grasp nature's differentiated structure.

Form and content

We can begin by considering a potential Schellingian response to Hegel's first and seemingly most straightforward criticism, namely, that formalism in the philosophy of nature tends to obscure rather than illuminate the determinacy of the natural world. As we will see, this criticism, and the way it differentiates Schelling from Hegel, is not in fact as straightforward as it appears at first blush.

The first thing that must be noted is that Schelling is equally concerned about this tendency of formalist thought to blind the philosopher to nature's determinacy. As he puts it in *On the World Soul*, 'I hate nothing more than the mindless striving to eliminate the multiplicity of natural causes through fictitious identities.'[72] Indeed, his critique of Eschenmayerian dynamism is partly motivated by its inability to provide a genuine ground of determinate difference, as opposed to reducing natural phenomena to merely formal differences in density.[73] Although Schelling and Hegel both accept that *some* amount of determinacy must be passed over by a philosophy of nature – since neither philosopher ever tasks philosophical thought with the existential derivation of individual, determinate things – they agree that the general *kinds* of beings and processes that constitute the whole of reality ought to be grasped in philosophical thought, and this means that philosophy fails when it ignores the determinate differences between those general kinds. As we will see below (and in even more detail in Chapter 3), Schelling rejects the idea that these various kinds are differentiated according to a logic of negation. Nevertheless, he thinks that organic processes are different, in some respect, from the inorganic processes of which they are the higher potencies. Likewise, the human mind is different from the organic life of which it is an intensified expression. Moreover, the two philosophers agree that it is a problem when ideas are, as Schelling puts it, 'clumsily imported into philosophy from mathematics'.[74] The point of conflict between Schelling and Hegel on the question of form and content does not, therefore, concern either the problems with *excessive* formalism or the *failed* attempts to import mathematical concepts into philosophy. The disagreement is ultimately over formal symbolism – that is, whether philosophical ideas can *ever* exhibit the determinacy of nature's stages in any form that was originally mathematical.

The Schelling of 1801, in contrast to Hegel, thinks that formal symbolisation *is* capable of illuminating the determinate features of reality. Part of Schelling's reasoning here is that some amount of formalisation is always necessary in order to philosophically illuminate the determinacy of reality – that is, to allow the different stages of natural and spiritual life to immanently reveal themselves in philosophical science. In principle, the Hegelian ought to affirm this Schellingian point: Hegel also thinks that the universal structures of reality are generative, in some sense, of determinacy – even if, on first glance, philosophical thought appears 'abstract', 'colourless' and empty, a 'realm of shadows' contrasted with the determinacy of reality.[75] And yet, even if Hegel may be sympathetic to Schelling's general line of thought, he still thinks that mathematical forms are not very good at exhibiting determinacy in nature. It is harmless, Hegel thinks, to 'take numbers and geometrical figures . . . simply as symbols', yet one should not be confused about the fact that 'it is foolish to fancy that in this way more is expressed than can be grasped and expressed by thought'.[76] For it is thought alone – that is, logic – which can explain what these forms *mean*.

There are two main reasons why Hegel thinks that logical forms are superior to mathematical forms when it comes to expressing philosophical truths. First, the logical forms are present within our everyday language, and this means that they are – in principle – intelligible without having to be translated into a different conceptual register. As difficult as it is to understand the logical claim that 'essence is reflection, the movement of becoming and transition that remains internal to it, in which the differentiated moment is determined simply as that which in itself is only negative, as illusory being [*Schein*]',[77] Hegel believes that it is, in principle, entirely intelligible without any further elucidation – so long as one has understood the dialectical progression up to the appearance of this claim in the *Science of Logic*. With mathematical notation, on the other hand, things are different: the philosopher must explain – *in ordinary language* – what *ideas* are being expressed by mathematical symbols. In other words, mathematical symbols are less transparent than logical concepts. According to Hegel, therefore, 'Philosophy . . . stands in no need of a special terminology', such as the mathematical potencies, since 'the forms of thought are, in the first instance, displayed and stored in human language'.[78]

Hegel is certainly correct that, absent any elucidation in ordinary language, the use of mathematical symbols in philosophical writing would be perplexing. Simply staring at Schelling's magnetic line, without any interpretive aid, would most likely lead to an impoverished understanding of Schelling's ontology – even though the image of the line is *supposed* to disclose 'the form of being of absolute identity'.[79] But, importantly, Schelling does not write exclusively in algebraic notation. On the contrary, he always seeks to elucidate the meaning of these symbols. For example, after exhibiting the image reproduced above in § 46 of the *Presentation*, Schelling goes on to offer multiple notes of explanation and additions to the text in order to make fully apparent the significance of the image of the line. Significantly, Hegel *also* finds it helpful to add supplementary remarks to the logical development of his system. While the logical progression is, in principle, self-sufficient, he nevertheless draws upon historical events, the ideas of other philosophers, and even logical forms yet to be properly derived in the system, all in the service of further elucidating the immanent movement of the dialectic. For both Schelling and Hegel, then, supplementary explanation – that is, explanation external to the essential ontological series (algebraic or logical) – can assist one in comprehending what is, in principle, fully intelligible in its own right.

The second reason for Hegel's critique of mathematical symbols is that they are excessively *sensuous*, and this sensuous element of the mathematical forms, Hegel thinks, distances them from the purely intelligible, conceptual meaning that they seek to elucidate.[80] Whereas logical forms simply *say what they mean*, mathematical forms – weighed down by their sensible expression – mean something that only logical forms can properly say. Surprisingly, then, central to Hegel's critique of formalism in the philosophy of nature is the idea that formalist thinking – such as algebraic notation – is an overly sensuous way of presenting the essential structures of reality.[81]

Schelling, by contrast, does not think that the sensuousness of symbolic language distances it from that which it seeks to express. On the contrary, given the fact that the philosopher of nature is aiming to understand processes that are physical and *not* conscious, it seems appropriate that the philosopher's language will be immersed in the sensible. From a Schellingian perspective, limiting oneself to strictly logical concepts is to miss out on a whole range of forms of expression that are equally 'natural' – that is, linguistic forms which immanently express the structure of reality itself, even if these forms do not appear in ordinary, everyday language. Indeed, according to Schelling, there are languages *of nature* that the philosopher must first *discover* in order to think:

> Nature is like some very ancient author whose message is written in hieroglyphics on colossal pages ... Even those who investigate nature only empirically need to know her language in order to understand utterances which have become unintelligible to us.[82]

Pace Hegel's critique, then, Schelling's argument is not that the philosopher comes to an indeterminate nature and applies forms that make it intelligible; rather, the philosopher allows nature's determinacy to arise before her eyes by making explicit the rational, formal connections and differences between natural phenomena. And to whatever extent symbolic forms are steeped in materiality – that is, to whatever extent they are not one-sidedly ideal – so much the better. Thus, whereas Hegel's logical formalism seeks to shed light upon the determinacy of nature in ordinary language that has sublated the sensuous element of symbolic thinking, Schelling's algebraic formalism aims to illuminate nature's determinacy by abstracting from the language of ordinary, conscious life and utilising symbols immersed in the sensible.

Schelling's distinctive brand of formalism can perhaps be better understood from the perspective of 1802, when he stipulates that arithmetic, geometry and philosophy share the same object of inquiry, namely, reason itself (understood as the structure of reality rather than a capacity of the mind). Because the object of arithmetic, geometry and philosophy is reason, these sciences must themselves be rational, a priori sciences. In geometry, one rationally constructs in the mode of finitude; in arithmetic, one constructs in the mode of infinity; and in philosophy, one constructs in the mode of eternity.[83] Thus, unlike the empirical sciences, which set out from the way finite human beings experience the world, a priori science (whether mathematical or philosophical) abstracts from consciousness and seeks to account for the universal truths of reality, those rational truths which are more fundamental than consciousness itself. Read from the perspective of 1802, then, Schelling's adoption of mathematical symbols is not in any way arbitrary: arithmetic, geometry and philosophy each concern themselves with the same rational content, and such rational content demands the implementation of rational symbols, symbols which drive home the fact that the philosopher is *not* discussing our ordinary experience of the world but the essential, rational structure of reality that undergirds all experience.

Negation and duplication

Hegel's insistence on the specificity and superiority of logic is not unrelated to his second criticism of Schellingian formalism: the supposed lack of any explanation regarding the development from one stage of nature to another. According to Hegel, a formalist system that uses ready-made symbols to explain the relationships *between* natural phenomena will necessarily fail in this explanation, because those connections will not arise immanently. That is to say, a formalist system such as Schelling's will not be capable of accounting for the progression from A to A^2 and A^2 to A^3. And this is because mathematical symbolism cannot express the logical development that necessitates the movement from one stage of reality to another — that is, the development in which one stage of reality proves to *not* be what it *is* and thereby generates a *new* logical structure.

Like Hegel, Schelling conceives the process of nature's self-differentiation as an atemporal, ontological development,[84] but he does not conceive the development from one stage of reality to the next in terms of *logical* explication. Nor does Schelling understand this development to be motivated by an immanent process of self-negating negativity, where one logical form immanently *negates* itself and thereby generates a new form, one which is qualitatively distinct form the first. As we saw above, Schelling conceives the development from A to A^2 to proceed by way of the *duplication* of A with itself. The novel form that is generated in this atemporal process, then, is not something which is a '*not*-A' but an *intensified* 'A'. And the *reason* 'A' expresses itself in more intense forms – such as A^2 – is not because the more intense forms are *logically implicit* in the less intense forms, but because the absolute itself– that is, A = A – *just is productivity*. In the *Freedom* essay of 1809, Schelling makes this point entirely clear when he refers to the 'creativity' of the law of identity. But already in the works of 1801, it is clear that Schelling understands nature to be stratified or differentiated because identity *only is* in so far as it *expresses* itself, and a *maximal expression* of identity will involve the expression of identity at as many degrees of intensity possible. At the very least, then, what Schelling suggests is that there is more than one way to conceive nature's immanent development. In order to fully unpack Schelling's argument regarding the way A = A determines itself, however, we will have to consider his unique conception of identity, and it is to this task we turn in the next chapter.

From the perspective of the twenty-first century, as well as from the perspective of the Aristotelian, Kantian and Hegelian traditions, it is certainly strange to read philosophers who employ mathematical methods and terminology in their metaphysics. And perhaps Hegel is right to be suspicious of this general tendency in the history of philosophy. But, as we conclude our discussion of the concept of potency, it should be kept in mind that Schelling is in good philosophical company when he draws upon mathematics for philosophical inspiration.[85] For Plato, Descartes, Spinoza, Leibniz, Fichte and Novalis – to name only a handful from this counter-tradition – mathematics provides the philosopher with key insights about the practice of philosophy itself. And if the language of potentiation can indeed express the view that nature differentiates itself as dynamic (A = B), qualitatively determinate (A^2) and organic (A^3), then Schelling's adoption of Eschenmayerian terminology should be seen as a significant event in the history of speculative thought.

Chapter 3

Identity

In this chapter, we retain the focus of Chapter 2 on the significance of the 1801 controversy with Eschenmayer for Schelling's subsequent metaphysical constructions, focusing on another central concept of his emergent identity philosophy – identity itself. Attending to the concept of identity allows us to examine the essential viewpoint of the *Presentation* and various reactions to it: Eschenmayer's Fichtean response in a letter penned to Schelling in July 1801 (translated in Appendix 1 of the present volume); Fichte's own response to the *Presentation* in correspondence and unpublished notes; and finally, Hegel's *Differenzschrift*, written in late spring 1801 with a copy of *On the True Concept* and perhaps the *Presentation* in front of him. What will prove most significant about this triangulation of the 1801 Schelling–Eschenmayer controversy with Schelling's identity philosophy and subsequent reactions to it by Eschenmayer, Fichte and Hegel is the way it recasts Schelling's thinking of identity: it foregrounds the radical manner in which Schellingian philosophy of the period severs any analytic connection between difference and *non*-identity. Differences, Schelling maintains in 1801, can be constructed without appeal to the non-identical or antithetical.

Identity and difference from *On the True Concept* to the *Presentation*

As we have seen, in the wake of Kant, Eschenmayer seeks to reduce the multiplicity of material qualities to various quantitative ratios between two opposed forces. Eschenmayer's models always presuppose this foundational dualism – that is, the fundamental opposition between repulsion and attraction – and, as he will readily admit in a letter penned to Schelling in July 1801, the models thereby presuppose that non-identity (between the two forces) is to be postulated as a primary ontological principle.[1] This is significant, because – from the *First Outline* to the *Presentation* – Schelling expresses dissatisfaction with such a dialectical ontology: he wishes to retain Eschenmayer's idea of a series of potencies *without their dialectical ground*. Part of Schelling's initial polemic against Eschenmayer in the *First Outline* and its *Introduction* is directed precisely against the latter's use of repulsive and attractive forces to construct qualitative determinacy, and his short-lived appeal to actants is meant as an alternative to Eschenmayerian dynamics – a way to construct natural diversity without perpetual recourse to a dialectical interplay of antithetical forces. In other words, there is already in 1799 a tendency in Schelling's philosophy of nature towards explaining diversity in the natural world without recourse to a fundamental dualism. The same tendency can be seen in his quest for the source of duplicity in nature: 'If nature is originally identity – and its striving to become identical again proves it, then it is without doubt the highest problem of natural science to explain the cause that brought infinite opposition into the universal identity of nature.'[2] As Schelling begins to argue in his *Universal Deduction*, 'When speculations are raised concerning [the] absolute unification of antithetical activities that we think in the concept of nature, we no longer have any object other than the absolutely identical.'[3] It is this project of developing a model for understanding difference (or, more specifically, the diversity of natural qualities) without appeal to the principle of non-identity that is undertaken most concertedly in *On the True Concept*.

In *On the True Concept*, Schelling's refusal to postulate a dialectical interplay of forces to explain the basis of reality comes to the fore: 'All dualism is forever annihilated and everything becomes absolutely one.'[4] In its place, Schelling insists throughout the text that *one always already finds oneself in identity*: there is no escaping it, no creating or destroying it.[5] Everything is always already identity and only identity; this includes both nature potentiated into consciousness (the 'nature' of Fichtean transcendental idealism), as well as nature at lower, non-conscious levels of potency (the nature with which the speculative philosopher of nature begins). Hence, in *On the True Concept*, the task of the philosopher of nature is not to explain the genesis of duplicity out of a pre-existing identity as it had been in 1799,[6] nor to construct material products out of two irreducible and fundamental forces as for Eschenmayer; rather, it is to chart the potencies of identity – that is, to map the process of potentiation by which the higher potencies of identity arise out of the lower potencies, or, in Schelling's own words, 'to let the subject-object of consciousness emerge from the pure subject-object'.[7]

In sum, Schelling seeks to construct a potentiated series constituted out of one factor, rather than two— that is, a series of powers of *identity*, rather than of ratios of opposed forces. The intensity of identity alone is increased or decreased across the series to account for the multiplicity of ontological forms.[8] Schelling thus writes:

> With nature-philosophy I never emerge from that identity of the ideal-real; I continually preserve both in this original connection, and the pure subject-object from which I proceed is precisely that which is simultaneously the ideal and the real in the potency 0.[9]

Every point in the series is always an affirmation of the self-same identity of 'the ideal-real'. As Schelling was later to put it, 'Identity recurs at all possible stages, changing in form only.'[10] The only difference between various forms – that is, the only difference between various points in the series – is the specific potency at which such identity posits itself.

In May 1801, four months after the appearance of *On the True Concept*, Schelling published the *Presentation of my System of Philosophy*. In this text, the very same model of identity without non-identity receives its canonical formulation in § 46, as we have seen.[11] In § 46, Schelling definitively articulates the model first sketched in *On the True Concept* – the model that had emerged out of his ongoing exchanges with Eschenmayer; indeed, the presentation of the magnetic line in May 1801 is one of the most significant consequences of the Schelling-Eschenmayer controversy. As Rang puts it, 'It is the series constructed by Eschenmayer that forms the basis of Schelling's own linear construction in the *Presentation* . . . Schelling comes to integrate identity-metaphysics into the Kantian–Eschenmayerian theory of matter, and from there he grounds it anew.'[12] According to Schelling's magnetic line, the very same identity is repeated at higher and lower potencies across a series or line; what changes is not the identity itself but the potency at which it is expressed.

The model for the relation of identity and difference propounded in *On the True Concept* and the *Presentation* turns on the assertion that the law of identity is 'the ultimate law' of all being. In other words, 'We never emerge from A = A.'[13] Every point in the series *is* identity, an expression of A = A – without exception. On such a model, reality is described solely by this thetic law (A = A), leaving no room for an antithetical law that would describe the difference between A and that to which it is *not* identical (-A ≠ A): since nothing *is* but one and the same being, identity 'cannot be negated anywhere and in no manner'.[14] In so far as forms of reality do appear to be ontologically distinct, they are nothing other than A = A with a preponderance of either A in the subject position or A in the predicate position, a *quantitative* difference that Schelling represents as A = B: 'Each

A = B considered in itself or as referred to itself is an A = A, therefore something absolutely self-identical.'[15] Without recourse to the category of negation, there is no means to distinguish various forms of being in a *fundamentally* qualitative manner; quality can, in the end, be reduced to quantity. Such is the very scandal of identity philosophy: negation, qualitative difference and opposition have no purchase in a metaphysical account of what *is*, for all there is is *identity*.

Varieties of identity in German Idealism

It is important to emphasise just how radical Schelling's model is in comparison to contemporaneous experiments in thinking about the relationship between identity and difference. This is, of course, not the place for a potted history of early German Idealism's construction of the absolute out of the remnants of Kant's critical philosophy; but it is necessary to note that, by late 1800, it had become clear to a number of philosophers in Jena and beyond that, in order to make sense of the possibility of knowledge and thus the practice of philosophy itself, an original identity of subject and object had to be either postulated or proven. Any adequate description of reality must have recourse to such identity, and understand the world – both mind and nature – on the basis of it. As Schwab puts it, '*one* logical ground stands at the heart of early post-Kantian philosophy – namely, the grounding of philosophy as a system from a first principle of "absolute identity", oriented around the proposition A = A', and to elucidate the presuppositions, structure and implications of this A = A was, he continues, the 'common objective of early idealism'.[16] Of course, there were huge discrepancies over whether such an identity was to be figured as the transcendent ground of reality or reality itself, whether it held good only within the I or in relation to being as a whole, whether it had regulative or constitutive significance, whether it had causal power, and so on. However, in the first months of 1801, Bardili, Reinhold, Schlegel, Hegel (newly arrived in Jena at Schelling's invitation), even Fichte in Berlin – in addition to Schelling himself – all saw an adequate account of identity as one of the most pressing tasks for contemporary philosophy.

Accordingly, it is a shame that many accounts of German Idealism tend to reconstruct this diversity as a teleological movement towards one standard, successful template: the dialectical model. That is, the Hegelian model is often taken as a norm against which all other conceptions of identity are judged.[17] On the dialectical model, in order for identity to count as *absolute*, it must overcome the self-same and finite identity which is simply *opposed* to the non-identical and, instead, become truly identical by becoming *other* than itself. Absolute identity can therefore only be properly understood as the identity of identity and non-identity. As Hegel puts it in *The Difference between Fichte's and Schelling's System of Philosophy*, 'The claims of separation must be admitted just as much as those of identity... Philosophy must give the separation into subject and object its due ... Hence, the Absolute itself is the identity of identity and non-identity; being opposed and being one are both together in it.'[18] Identity includes itself and its other; otherness and difference are therefore part of what it means to be identical.

For the early Hegel, the exemplary case of the identification of opposites in the absolute is that of subject and object – or the I and nature – which he describes as follows:

> These two opposites, whether they are called I and nature, or pure and empirical self-consciousness, or cognition and being... are together posited in the Absolute. Ordinary reflection can see nothing in this antinomy but contradiction; Reason alone sees the truth in this absolute contradiction through which both are posited and both nullified, and through which neither exists and at the same time both exist.[19]

The opposition of subject and object – the stark qualitative difference between them – is both preserved and annulled in absolute identity. It is only from a lower cognitive viewpoint, – that is, 'reflection' – that the identity of the two cannot be understood as united in their opposition. Such a failure of thinking results in a merely pejorative use of the language of 'contradiction' and 'antimony'. However, Hegel argues, from a genuinely speculative standpoint, identity and non-identity are held together as identical; the difference between subject and object thus makes possible their unity. From this standpoint of speculative thought, contradiction becomes 'the purely formal appearance of the absolute' itself and antinomy 'the highest formal expression of knowledge and truth'.[20] For the Hegel of 1801, to philosophise properly is to recognise the constitutive role of difference (conceived as non-identity) at the very heart of absolute identity.

The *Differenzschrift* was Hegel's friendly response to Schelling's philosophy of early 1801. It was intended – explicitly at least – as a defence of the position Schelling had developed in the first months of that year against Fichte's supposed subjectivisation of absolute identity. In consequence, Hegel presents the above as a summary of the Schellingian position, an explication of the concept of identity presupposed in Schelling's own texts. However, this is evidently to downplay the fact that in the *Differenzschrift* Hegel amends, rewrites and attempts to improve upon the Schellingian position – and this corrective process is nowhere more discernible than in the account of identity.[21] Hegelian dialectical identity is not a faithful transcription of Schelling's metaphysics of the *Presentation of my System of Philosophy*, or even of *On the True Concept*. There are radical differences between the two positions that cannot be effaced. To put it bluntly: Schelling's engagement with Eschenmayer gave rise to a distinctly non-dialectical conception of identity.

Indeed, preliminary indications of such a radical difference between Hegel and Schelling on identity can be discerned in the above description of Schelling's expulsion of the non-identical from identity: when he speaks of the 'identity of identity' in the *Presentation*,[22] he is intending thereby to exclude what is non-identical from metaphysics. Indeed, § 2 of the *Presentation* ('Outside reason is nothing, and in it is everything'[23]) is entirely clear that what is not identity can only be understood from a non-philosophical perspective, since the philosopher is only concerned with what *is*, and not with what is *not*. Elsewhere, Schelling is even more insistent: 'The absolute is absolute only through the absolute exclusion of difference from its essence.'[24] As we will see below, this does not mean that *all* forms of difference are excluded from the absolute, but antithetical, oppositional difference – that is, difference that proceeds from negation – simply *is not*, for Schelling. In this respect, the *Presentation* is an adventure in Eleatic philosophy.[25]

Responses to the *Presentation* I: Hegel

The story of Hegel's and Schelling's competing understandings of identity in 1801 does not end there. Rather, despite the stark differences separating them during the first months of 1801, *by the end of the year* Schelling had come round – however temporarily – to espousing a version of the dialectical model himself. Schelling's shift towards this dialectical model is first manifest in the lectures he gave at Jena in the summer semester of 1801 to accompany the publication of the *Presentation of my System of Philosophy*,[26] but it becomes far more evident in the next major work on which he embarked: *Bruno, or On the Natural and Divine Principle of Things*. In this text, Schelling writes,

> To make identity the supreme principle, we must think of it as comprehending even this highest pair of opposites and the identity that is its opposite as well, and we must define this supreme identity as the identity of identity and opposition, or the identity of the self-identical and the non-identical.[27]

Just as in the *Differenzschrift*, absolute identity is constituted dialectically as 'the identity of identity and opposition' or 'the identity of the self-identical and the non-identical'. Just as for Hegel, opposition and contradiction play a constitutive role in a composite notion of identity. In *Bruno*, then, Schelling is in broad agreement with Hegel's reasoning that, for identity to be absolute, it has to make everything – including opposites, such as the opposition between identity and opposition itself – identical.

The overwhelming likelihood is that it was Hegel himself (whether via the *Differenzschrift* or conversations in Jena) who brought Schelling round to such a dialectical model of identity in late 1801. And this is obviously a significant piece of evidence for those who wish to construe the Hegelian identity of identity and non-identity as the norm by which German Idealist constructions of the absolute are to be judged. There seems to be an implicit acknowledgement on Schelling's part that the Hegelian model is correct and conceptually superior to his own earlier attempts to make sense of absolute identity. A classic retelling of this story is given by Klaus Düsing, for whom Schelling's development during 1801 is to be understood as a shift from an 'indifference model' of identity to a 'Hegelian' model, motivated by the inadequacies of the former. Düsing writes,

> The definitions of this absolute identity vary in Schelling; he retains two different fundamental models which he attempts to unite with each other . . . Alongside Schelling's original model a second – Hegelian – model increasingly gains significance during the early phase of the identity philosophy.[28]

In *Bruno*, 'Schelling clearly grounds this model of unity very close to Hegel', for in this text, unlike in the *Presentation*, 'indifference and difference are simultaneously posited in the absolute'.[29] Hence, Düsing can conclude that 'the model for unity which stems originally from Hegel is increasingly observed by Schelling from the first articulations of the system of identity onwards'.[30] Accordingly, Düsing stands in a tradition of scholarship for which, according to Engels, 'it was Hegel who made Schelling realise how far he had already gone beyond Fichte without knowing it'[31] or for which, according to Lukács, Hegel 'rendered Schelling's own discoveries . . . philosophically conscious to him'.[32]

A more nuanced version of this basic position can also be discerned in Manfred Frank's interpretation of the identity philosophy. While Frank certainly does not consider Schelling's mature account of identity to be the same as Hegel's,[33] he nevertheless contends that Hegel's introduction of the dialectical model in the *Differenzschrift* is closer to what Schelling's actual position should have been than anything Schelling himself had written in early 1801. In Frank's own words, 'In his *Differenzschrift*, Hegel tried to sum up the central thought of Schelling's philosophy by characterising it as "the identity of identity and non-identity", and Schelling himself not only accepted this characterisation of his Absolute System of Identity without demurral, but enthusiastically endorsed it.'[34] According to Frank, Hegel's dialectical model in the *Differenzschrift* may seem at first blush to distort Schelling's earlier thinking about identity, but in fact it should be understood 'simply as the expression of the basic idea his friend had in mind when he spoke, as he repeatedly did, of "the identity of identity" or of "identity duplicated within itself"'.[35] On this interpretation, Hegel provides a helpful clarification that Schelling appreciated.[36] The implication of Frank's position is that Schelling's writings from early 1801 should be taken with more than a pinch of salt; the *Presentation of my System of Philosophy* is, in fact, 'hastily written' and thus does not sufficiently express 'the thought of an identity that is sensitive to difference'.[37] On Frank's account, both Hegel and Schelling in 1801 are involved in a common project of making sense of an absolute identity that includes opposition within itself; they may differ significantly in the details, but both are committed to a broadly dialectical model.[38]

Later in the chapter, we wish to show, first, that, *pace* Frank, Schelling does hold a distinct understanding of absolute identity in early 1801 that cannot be reduced to or clarified by the Hegelian dialectical model.[39] Indeed, central to Schelling's non-dialectical conception of identity is the idea that non-oppositional, determinate differences can be produced through identity alone. Secondly, *pace* Frank, Düsing and many others, we will suggest that this distinctive non-dialectical model for identity is not obviously inferior to any of its competitors. That is, whatever did motivate Schelling's experimentation with a dialectical model in late 1801, it was not blatant inadequacies and inconsistencies in the metaphysics of the *Presentation*. In fact, Schelling will return wholeheartedly to the non-dialectical 'indifference-model' in the most complete presentation of the identity philosophy, the *System* of 1804.

Responses to the *Presentation* II: Fichte

A second front in Schelling's 1801 attempt to formulate a distinctive model for identity is his combat with Fichte and Eschenmayer and their insistence that antithesis is as formally fundamental as identity in metaphysical constructions. That is, whereas the Schelling of early 1801 stands opposed to Hegel's incorporation of non-identity into the *interior* of identity (as a constitutive principle of it), he also stands opposed to Fichte and Eschenmayer's insistence that the principle of non-identity is distinct from yet equally as fundamental as the principle of identity. For both Fichte and Eschenmayer, one reason that Schelling's *Presentation* fails is because it excludes opposition from philosophy, and thus, for both of them, an alternative model is required that recognises opposition as a basic principle. Indeed, this idea that Schelling's exclusion of antithesis from his 1801 ontology leads evidently and necessarily to its abject failure recurs throughout the scholarship: it is implicit in Düsing's account of Schelling's migration from the indifference-model to dialectics and it is explicit in Nassar's recent Fichtean critique of the *Presentation*. For all these readers, Schelling fails because of his refusal to countenance antithesis as a primary explanatory tool.

The fundamental difference between the Fichtean and Schellingian conceptions of identity is apparent in Fichte's unpublished notes written upon first reading the *Presentation* in early summer 1801.[40] Fichte observes, 'It is not clear how the one and absolute reason ... cannot be the *indifference* of the subjective and objective, without at the same time and in the same indivisible entity also being the *difference* of the two.'[41] He continues: 'Why can't one and the same exist in genuine opposition? Nothing is said about this incredibly important relation!'[42] This is Fichte's response to § 1 of the *Presentation* in which Schelling argues that, through abstraction, reason comes to occupy a position of indifference between the subjective and the objective. This is an essential moment in Schelling's early logic of identity, for it is from this standpoint of indifference alone that he seeks to construct a philosophical account of reality. Fichte certainly recognises that the purpose of the early propositions of the *Presentation* is to seek to establish a description of the world that proceeds solely from the law of identity, without any appeal to a law that establishes antithetical difference: 'Absolute reason dissolves into the law of absolute identity; another law, another determination, is not absolutely appropriate for it, because it [would] already fall within the difference. This much is clear.'[43] Nevertheless, it is precisely Schelling's insistence, at the commencement of the identity philosophy, to philosophise from identity *without opposition* that Fichte questions. For Fichte, this seems to be an arbitrary limitation that restricts philosophy's explanatory power by failing to make use of a second, equally fundamental principle of antithesis.

According to Fichte, a corollary of this criticism is that Schelling's appeal to quantitative difference in his *Presentation* as a substitute for oppositional differences is utterly insufficient. In Chapter 1, we considered how Schelling ultimately follows Eschenmayer – at least in part – in privileging a certain form of quantitative difference in nature-philosophical explanation. We also explored how, in the *Presentation*, this explanation of quality in terms of quantity is extended beyond the apparent qualities of material bodies to include all aspects of being – inorganic, organic and spiritual. Against the *Presentation*'s approach, Fichte contends that 'quantitative difference also cannot help, for difference, indeed opposition, always posits this'.[44] In other words, either quantitative differentiation is a consequence of (or posited by) antithesis or it is no difference at all. For

Fichte, Schelling's appeal to quantity is an attempt to smuggle substantial differences into a system that pretends to exclude any principle of difference. In August 1801, he expands on this criticism in a letter to Schelling:

> I can tell you our point of difference in a few words. – You say 'the absolute' (concerning *which* and whose *determination* I completely agree with you, and whose intuition I have possessed for a long time) 'as I claimed in my *Presentation*, exists under the form of quantitative difference.' This is indeed what you assert; and it is *precisely because of this* that I found your system to be in error and rejected the *Presentation* of your system – because no inference or discussion can be correct which is based on a principle that does not hold.

Fichte continues, if the absolute is conceived as indifference, then there 'cannot be any quantity and relation in the absolute'.[45]

Nassar's *The Romantic Absolute* takes Fichte's criticisms as a springboard for reflecting on the identity philosophy. Just like Düsing and Frank, she understands the indifference-model articulated by Schelling in *On the True Concept* and *Presentation* as an inadequate first draft partially abandoned and partially improved upon in Schelling's subsequent trajectory. However, unlike Düsing and Frank, rather than seeing Hegel's intervention in the *Differenzschrift* as the crucial catalyst for improvement, Nassar turns to the Fichte-correspondence: Schelling's transition to new models of identity in *Bruno* and beyond are responses to Fichte's criticisms. She reconstructs these criticisms as follows:

> Fichte accuses Schelling of a contradictory conception of the absolute on several levels. As indifference, it is entirely negative. In addition, although it does not contain difference within itself, it is situated within a larger framework that assumes difference – difference from the rational thought structure in which it is presented. In turn, as an indifferent absolute, it does not *explain* the origin of difference, of the transition from the one to the many, but wishes away the problem by positing the notion of the 'form of quantity'. This form of quantity, however, does not only *not* resolve the problem of transition, but also accentuates the contradictory nature of the absolute. Insofar as the absolute is 'under' the form of quantity (or any form), it is not absolute, rather, by placing the absolute under a form, Schelling inadvertently objectifies it.[46]

Nassar thus extracts three substantive and related criticisms from Fichte's correspondence: (1) that, if the absolute is different from, for example, 'the rational thought structure in which it is presented', oppositional differences are already presupposed and therefore such difference is an equiprimordial principle standing alongside identity, *pace* Schelling's explicit commitments; (2) that the indifference of the absolute fails to make sense of differences in the world, and that the recourse to quantitative difference certainly does not make up for this failure; and (3) that quantitative difference forms the absolute, for Schelling, but what is absolute must exist without form.

Below, we consider some defences of Schelling's model against such criticisms; nevertheless, it is perhaps worth preliminarily noting that each criticism begs the question somewhat: why should the philosopher presuppose that the absolute is different from the philosophy which presents it? Why should the philosopher assume that difference is inexplicable if all that is is identity? And why should the philosopher suppose that formation necessarily results in a loss of absoluteness (rather than formation being an intensification of the absolute)? We do not claim to provide a sustained engagement with these questions here. What is more pertinent to our present concern is that Nassar sees Fichte's criticisms not only as compelling, but as providing the stimulus for Schelling's abandonment of the indifference-model in late 1801. She writes:

> With those critiques in mind, Schelling begins to rethink the nature of the absolute... In the two works that follow the *Darstellung*, the dialogue *Bruno* and the *Fernere Darstellungen*, his aim is to respond to Fichte's critiques... [In *Bruno*] Schelling details the difficulties that arise from different conceptions of the absolute and explicitly concedes the problems with the notion of a self-identical indifferent absolute as elaborated in the *Darstellung*.[47]

Nassar concludes: 'Schelling implicitly recants and disagrees with some of the basic premises of the *Darstellung* [in response] to Fichte's critiques.'[48]

What changes after early 1801, according to Nassar, is that more substantial categories of difference come to form part of metaphysical construction, such that later writings make reference to a new type of philosophically pertinent difference – a 'difference that is inherent to the existence, the reality, of the absolute'[49] – that is, these texts make reference to a type of difference completely absent from the *Presentation*. Just as for Düsing and Frank, Schelling's seemingly reckless constitution of identity without antithetical difference in early 1801 is judged inadequate, a stumbling-block that he spent the rest of the identity philosophy endeavouring to overcome. Schelling's trajectory during 1801 is thus recast as a narrative of successive improvements in the wake of the failure of the *Presentation*, a growing realisation on Schelling's part – brought about by the challenges issued from his new philosophical rival (Fichte) and his friend and collaborator (Hegel) – that a metaphysics of identity without antithesis is unsustainable.

Responses to the *Presentation* III: Eschenmayer

At this point, Eschenmayer's name should be added, alongside Fichte's and Hegel's, to those who directly confronted Schelling with the (supposed) inadequacies of his indifference-model. A few weeks before Fichte sent Schelling his criticisms of the *Presentation* and before the publication of Hegel's *Differenzschrift* in autumn 1801 (although, most likely, contemporaneously with Schelling first reading the manuscript), Eschenmayer had already written to Schelling with a fully developed critique of the *Presentation* that revolved around its exclusion of antithetical difference. Eschenmayer's criticisms are thus an important addition to those found in Hegel's and Fichte's responses, and one of the final documents of the 1801 Schelling–Eschenmayer controversy.

Eschenmayer's letter sent on 21 July 1801 (and translated in full in Appendix 1 to this volume) affirms a broadly Fichtean model for understanding the relation of identity and difference, and it proposes this model as the solution to those problems taken to be inherent in Schelling's indifference-model. Eschenmayer is, indeed, the first of Schelling's critics to take on his elimination of antithesis (which is hardly surprising, of course, considering that such an elimination was undertaken, in part, as a response to Eschenmayer's own dualistic philosophy of nature). Eschenmayer opens by stating very clearly the precise stakes of Schelling's 1801 metaphysics:

> Since you take absolute identity for the exclusive basis of your system, then your $A = A$ is indeed in agreement with *Fichte's* first principle which in form and content is unconditioned, but *Fichte's* second principle, $-A$ does not $= A$, is no longer to be found in your system. That is, Fichte assumes an original opposition, and his $-A$ does not $= A$ is thus a principle which according to content is conditioned by the first [principle], and yet according to form is just as unconditioned as the first. In your work, the original opposition falls away completely; for you, there is nothing originally positive or negative, but only a difference in the magnitude of being (quantitative difference) or a preponderance of identity with itself, in which preponderance consists your $A = B$ or subjective and objectivity.[50]

Referring to Fichte's presentation of the fundamental principles of the *Wissenschaftslehre* in Part One of the 1794 *Grundlage*, Eschenmayer identifies Fichte's second principle ($-A \neq A$) as that which is conspicuously missing from Schelling's account. 'Opposition falls away completely.'[51] And all that is left for Schelling is something like Fichte's third principle which has been transformed into a non-oppositional, quantitative means to account for differentiation through preponderances of identity (or, to use the terminology of *On the True Concept*, the various potencies at which identity posits itself).[52] Eschenmayer then goes on to side firmly with Fichte: 'I confess to assuming with *Fichte* the A = B in an original opposition, and – according to form – just as unconditionally as the A = A.'[53] Moreover, he draws a substantial link between this metaphysical position and the nature-philosophical debates around quality and dynamist dualism: within the domain of metaphysics, the Fichtean is 'a bit like the dynamist who cannot resolve the infinite multiplicity of directions in space into one direction but only into two opposed [directions]'.[54]

From this position, Eschenmayer makes two criticisms of Schelling. First, according to Eschenmayer, differences in nature can only be understood from the standpoint of a Fichtean subjective idealism. As early as his March 1801 review of the *First Outline* in the *Erlanger Litteratur-Zeitung*[55] – before he had yet read Schelling's *Presentation* – Eschenmayer foregrounds his Fichte-inspired insistence that the only way to account for material differentiation is through a formally original opposition *within the self*. In the *First Outline*, Schelling had, according to Eschenmayer, already smuggled in forms of difference and negation without being able to account for them (such as the inhibition of productivity and 'the negation of all movement'[56]); and this is, Eschenmayer claims, because such processes cannot in fact be explained from nature at all: they are 'completely foreign to nature' and require recourse to something prior, namely, the activity of the self, in order to make sense of their possibility.[57] In Chapter 4, we explore the details of this argument regarding the original source of activity, and therefore difference, in nature. At this stage, the key point is that, according to Eschenmayer, only Fichtean principles can make sense of negation and difference; Schelling's cannot.[58] This line of argument is developed further in Eschenmayer's initial reaction to the *Presentation* in the summer of 1801. Here he argues once more that, in order to make sense of difference, a Fichtean brand of transcendental idealism is needed – one in which limitation and so differentiation are consequences of the positing of the self: 'Is self-cognition anything other than a self-limitation, or rather, since we are speaking of identity, a *self-differentiation*?'[59] The incorporation of a formally unconditioned 'principle of opposition' (as Fichte himself calls it[60]) is for Eschenmayer the only way to answer the pressing question: 'Whence comes this difference?'[61] For Fichte, such opposition is formally as *fundamental* as thetic identity and also indirectly *necessitated* by it. Only on the basis of this Fichtean model of the relation between identity and difference can metaphysical coherence be rescued, according to Eschenmayer. He thus concludes by reaffirming his Fichtean starting-point: 'The proofs that I have set out along the way are all of a kind to justify more securely my conviction that an absolute difference or an original opposition can be excluded from the basis of a philosophical system just as little as absolute identity can.'[62]

In addition to arguing in favour of the Fichtean model, Eschenmayer also attacks the coherence of Schelling's model for identity and difference on its own terms. Eschenmayer's second criticism proceeds in two stages: first, he assumes that Schelling's metaphysics does recognise the kinds of difference required to make sense of reality, in order to then ask whether the kind of identity Schelling also desires is thereby possible; secondly and conversely, he assumes Schelling's account of identity, in order to interrogate the possibility of difference on this basis. Overall, Eschenmayer focuses on the concept of a limit between two entities – that is, an ontological break that keeps them separate and distinct; for if entities 'are to be differentiated from one another, then this can only happen if something *heterogeneous* steps between them'.[63] He attempts to show that Schelling's various ways of articulating his identity-monism in the *Presentation* (particularly the magnetic line of § 46) all fail to account for such a limit, which means that it will be impossible for Schelling to provide a place for both identity *and* difference within his system.

These more immanent criticisms of Schelling's *Presentation*, focused on the concept of limit, are also inspired by Fichte. According to the latter, the self and not-self must mutually limit one another, and, significantly, 'to *limit* something is to abolish its reality, not *wholly* but *in part* only, by negation'. Fichte continues: 'Thus, apart from reality and negation, the notion of a limit also contains that of *divisibility* (the *capacity for quantity* in general. . .).'[64] It is only in this context that Eschenmayer's critique of Schelling's *Presentation* as not taking the concept of limit seriously is fully intelligible. Eschenmayer sees in Schelling's doctrine of quantitative difference (as represented by the magnetic line) an illegitimate appropriation of Fichte's third principle without the very concept of a heterogeneous limit that is so central to its operation. According to Eschenmayer, Schelling can construct, at best, a quantitative conception of limit. However, if one were to attempt to distinguish identity from difference in terms of a *quantitative* limit – that is, if one were to take Schelling's doctrine of quantitative differentiation seriously as the only explanation of difference in reality – then this would be insufficient to make sense of the robust heterogeneity required for a *limit* in the first place: 'To separate identities necessarily requires a difference, and a preponderance in identity cannot be thought at all without difference; this difference is, however, not quantitative.'[65]

There are, of course, ways of defending Schelling against many of Eschenmayer's more substantial criticisms; indeed, Eschenmayer's obsession with the notion of a limit separating two terms begs the question as to the very necessity of the category of 'the heterogeneous' in accounting for the genesis of difference. One response to this is to claim that, by refusing Fichte's second principle (that of antithesis), Schelling does not so much appropriate the third principle as transform it into a doctrine that functions *without limit*.[66] That is, Schelling's is a doctrine of determination that does not depend upon any limit between A and −A, since all there *is* is identity (A = A). Eschenmayer, however, remains tied to the postulation of an original duplicity – whether this is the duality of forces in physics or the antithetical principles of identity and difference.[67] He consequently misunderstands that Schelling uses the formula 'A = B' not to express the becoming-identical of two originally opposed terms, but rather as a form of A = A.[68] For all of these reasons, Eschenmayer too contributes to a narrative that reads Schelling's *Presentation* as an aberration from a norm that alone can make sense of the identity-difference relation. It is this narrative that we want to contest.

Reading the *Presentation* by way of *On the True Concept*

What the above reactions to Schelling's *Presentation* of 1801 have in common is that they write off – in one way or another – the *Presentation*'s subscription to an unadulterated version of the 'indifference-model' for identity. Schelling is better than that, goes the critical consensus, and he soon realised that he was better than that. The exclusion of the nonidentical in the *Presentation* is, so the above narratives tell us, merely a blip, a short-lived mistake that Schelling goes on to quickly rectify in his subsequent works. And, furthermore, Schelling is said to have saved his philosophy by turning to a dialectical model.

What we want to suggest is that it is possible to take the metaphysics of the *Presentation* seriously without reading it as part of a narrative of failure. Another interpretation of Schelling's development in 1801 is possible – and it is one that is grounded in an appreciation for the way in which the *Presentation* emerges out of Schelling's debate with Eschenmayer. On this reading, far from being a blip, the *Presentation* is the culmination of a longer trajectory in Schelling's writings on philosophy of nature: to philosophically construct reality from the category of identity alone. In short, where Fichte and Eschenmayer see the great weakness of Schellingian metaphysics of this period, Schelling locates the defining feature of an immanentist philosophy of nature. And, notwithstanding Eschenmayer's critical comments in the summer of 1801, this novel metaphysics of identity was forged through Schelling's readings of and responses to Eschenmayer's earlier texts in the philosophy of nature.[69] Hence, in answer to Eschenmayer's question, 'whence comes difference?',[70] one need look no further than Schelling's earlier retort to Eschenmayer in *On the True Concept*: it is here that he first explains differences in material quality from the category of identity. Indeed, the arguments in *On the True Concept* alone are enough to provisionally indicate that the *Presentation* does not naively extemporise; Schelling had already shown a profound interest in demonstrating the manner in which nature's *Stufenfolge* is immanently constructed through the principle of identity. As Vater and Wood have put it, the *Presentation* 'closely corresponds to what Schelling told Eschenmayer he was going to do – display the unity and vitality of nature without recourse to any fundamental dualism'.[71]

It is worth emphasising, however, that this is not to deny that there are other models for the constitution of identity present in Schelling's work, particularly after summer 1801. There is the indifference-model, and there is also the dialectical model in *Bruno*, the *Further Presentations*' conception of a plurality of identities constructed '*across* or *thanks to* difference'[72] and the dialectical in-forming (*einbilden*) of the finite into the infinite and the infinite into the finite in the second edition of the *Ideas*. The identity philosophy consists of a series of experiments in modelling the concept of identity. Beyond the identity philosophy too, there is, to name but a few, the synecdochical conception proposed in the *First Outline* where nature as universal productivity is identical to individual natural products but also perpetually exceeds and destroys them;[73] there is the formulation of 'an intrinsically creative kind' of identity – and the rejection of the 'general misunderstanding of the law of identity' as self-sameness – in the celebrated pages on the copula in the *Freiheitsschrift*;[74] and there is the modal figuring of identity as the subject's 'potency-to-be-other' in the later lectures.[75] If anything puts into doubt the recent vogue for the 'continuity thesis' in Schelling scholarship, it is his differing models for identity.[76]

We certainly do not wish to underappreciate this point; rather, our claim is simply that there is no obvious teleology here, no surpassing of each earlier model on the way to the genuinely 'Schellingian' position. The indifference-model of *On the True Concept* and the *Presentation* is no less valuable, coherent or 'Schellingian' than the others. In fact, despite the important differences between Schelling's various experiments in conceiving identity, the model presented in 1801 actually remains in the background of some of the most distinctive of Schelling's subsequent metaphysical formulations: the argument in the 1807 lecture *On the Relation of the Plastic Arts to Nature* that 'definiteness of form in nature is never a negation but always an affirmation';[77] the remark in the 1810 *Stuttgart Lectures* that the 'transition from identity to difference' is not a 'cancellation of identity' but a 'doubling of the essence, and thus an intensification of the unity';[78] the related account of divine creation in the first draft of the *Ages of the World*, which conceives God's self-generation as occurring without division but by self-doubling;[79] and the description of the form of judgement (A = B), in the same 1811 text, as a doubling of unity[80] – all of these central Schellingian insights can be traced back to the conception of identity first worked out in *On the True Concept* and the *Presentation* of 1801.[81]

The Opening to the *Presentation of my System of Philosophy*

The *Presentation* of May 1801 begins with a task demanded of the reader – to abstract from everything subjective and (consequently) objective, so as to constitute what is indifferent to the subjective and the objective.

> *Definition*: I call *reason* absolute reason or reason as it is conceived as *the total indifference* of the subjective and the objective ... Reason's thought is foreign to everyone: to conceive it as absolute, and thus to come to the standpoint I require, one must abstract from what does the thinking. For the one who performs this abstraction reason immediately ceases to be something subjective ... [Reason] can of course no longer be conceived as something objective either, since an objective something ... only becomes possible in contrast to a thinking something, from which there is complete abstraction here.[82]

Chapter 5 will consider this act of abstraction in far more detail; for now, what is important is that in the philosophical act of exhibiting indifference, one abstracts from all positing. All that remains is unposited identity, the 'bond' between subject and object, as Schelling will put it in 1806, or, to use a term from Schelling's very earliest writings, the 'inner form' of identity.[83]

This abstraction to the point of absolute indifference serves as a starting-point from which the text argues for identity-monism, in much the same way as the opening propositions of Spinoza's *Ethics* argue for substance-monism: a self-evident definition is followed by its logical entailments. In the *Presentation*, the argument leads to an ontological proof of the necessary existence of identity in § 8.[84] Further propositions go on to demonstrate that identity does not just necessarily exist, but that it is the only thing to exist. Schelling is at his most Spinozist in this text: both the opening twelve propositions of Schelling's *Presentation* and the first fifteen propositions of Spinoza's *Ethics* attempt to prove that there is only one thing that, properly understood, has being: in Spinoza's case it is substance, in Schelling's case it is identity. Moreover, both Schelling and Spinoza make this argument in similar stages: (1) definitions are postulated, followed by (2) a series of propositions that set out the properties entailed by such definitions – one such property being necessary existence; then (3) an ontological argument is framed on the basis of this property of necessary existence; and (4) the conclusion is reached that what necessarily exists is the only thing that exists.

To turn to the detail of Schelling's argument, §§ 1–3 of the *Presentation* consist of pre-thetic definitions of key metaphysical elements (derived from the initial act of abstraction) that generate a series of equivalences: reason = indifference of subjective and objective = in-itself = philosophy = absolute = one = identical = '=' itself. And opposed to this series is the 'non-philosophical' series of reflection, subject–object difference, appearance, succession, temporality. These are, Schelling thinks, analytically entailed from the initial performance of abstraction: all of these entailments can be asserted as *pre-thetically* valid.[85] The task of the next stage of the argument is to demonstrate their reality – that is, their corresponding validity *in* being or when *posited*.[86] In other words, there is now the question of the transition from ideality to reality, or from what is the case abstractly or pre-thetically to what is the case in being.[87] The second corollary to § 4 provides the crucial moment of transition: after having established the pre-thetic validity of A = A (since abstract reason is characterised by self-identity), Schelling now states, 'The proposition A = A is the sole truth posited *in itself*.'[88] It is thus the introduction of the concept of positing that signifies the *Presentation*'s entry into the realm of being: just as for Kant and Fichte, positing constitutes the thetic realm for Schelling.[89] The second corollary to § 4 asserts that what is posited is the law of identity (A = A) – and, what is more, that this is the only thing that truly *is* ('the *sole* truth posited in itself'). Being is governed by the law of identity: it is 'the ultimate law . . . for all being.'[90]

It is on this basis that § 6 of the *Presentation* develops a model for the mechanics of such positing. In essence, this section states that the proposition A = A is the form of being, and whatever exists comes into being by being posited through this form. Moreover, the emphasis here is placed on the concept of 'positing through' [*Durchsetzen*] in a way that is markedly different from Fichte's or Kant's understanding of the thetic. At the centre of Schelling's metaphysical construction of reality out of identity alone is this unique activity of 'positing through':

> The proposition A = A, conceived universally, says neither that A on its own is, nor that it is as subject or predicate. Instead, the unique being posited through this proposition is that of identity itself.[91]

The three elements of the process of positing in Schelling's indifference-model are thus (1) that which will be posited (essential or pre-thetic identity) – that is, the indifference of reason exhibited in § 1; (2) that through which identity is posited, the 'form' or 'law' of being (A = A); and (3) that which is *as* posited – that is, determinate being.[92]

Thus, to understand Schelling's account of difference in 1801, § 6 of the *Presentation* is crucial: it establishes a model of the genesis of reality without appealing to the category of antithesis. Instead, § 6 proposes that being is constituted through the category of identity alone – as three forms of identity: essential identity, formal identity and determinate identity. In Hennigfeld's words, Schelling's later appeal to the 'identity of identity' in § 16 'is no empty tautology if one understands the claim as: identity posits itself as identity'.[93] More precisely: identity is posited, through identity, as identity. Nothing else is required to understand the production of being. Wherever being is posited – that is, wherever something *is* – identity is posited through identity as identity. Hence, while Vater might be correct that it is in these propositions, above all, that Schelling sows 'the seed of difference', 'smuggl[ing] difference into the absolute' with the distinction between identity as essence and identity as form,[94] it is important to emphasise that such difference arises simply out of a rational consideration of identity itself. Indeed, one of Schelling's most fundamental, albeit implicit, claims in these opening propositions of the *Presentation* is that difference does not necessarily mean non-identity. That is, the two concepts are not, as usually thought, analytically related; there are forms of difference that can be explained without any recourse to non-identity.[95]

We return to this below, but to briefly summarise what follows in the subsequent propositions of the *Presentation*: the burden of the next set of propositions is to demonstrate the validity of this model for being, and this takes the form of 'something like an ontological proof'.[96] Thus, the argument of § 8 runs: absolute identity is necessarily posited whenever A = A (the form or law of identity) is posited; A = A is, according to § 4, a necessary truth and so must be posited; therefore, absolute identity must necessarily be posited as well. In other words, the very essence of identity is to come into being: 'It belongs to the essence of absolute identity to be.'[97] In a corollary Schelling expresses it thus: there is a mutual entailment between essential identity and the form of identity, such that to posit essential identity is necessarily to posit it under the form of A = A, while to posit A = A is necessarily to posit essential identity through it.[98] The two – form and essence – are inseparably connected, and one cannot subsist without the other. A few propositions later in the *Presentation*, Schelling is even clearer. 'Absolute identity *is* only under the form of the proposition A = A, or this form is immediately posited through its being . . . This form is immediately posited along with the being of absolute identity.'[99] Moreover, what is thereby proven in § 8 is the very task of the first part of Schelling's argument: to show that identity alone *does* explain that there is being. After such a conclusion, all that remains to be demonstrated is identity-monism.[100]

In this second part of the argument, Schelling follows Spinoza very closely: identity possesses the property of absoluteness, for it cannot be limited in its own kind – that is, in being. It is unconditionally true and therefore infinite (§ 10). § 11 goes on to show that absolute identity is always and necessarily absolute identity, that it cannot be abolished as absolute identity: it is eternal and unchanging. Hence, if absolute identity is all that there is at one moment in time, it is always all that there is. § 12 provides the triumphant conclusion – there is nothing but absolute identity: 'Since identity is infinite and can never be abolished as absolute identity, everything that *is* must be absolute identity itself.'[101] Reality in all of its aspects – inorganic, organic and spiritual – is identity and only identity.

Difference in the *Presentation*

Crucially, Schelling has established a model for the formation or determination of being that makes no reference to antithesis. It is in fact ironic that Schelling's Spinozism in 1801 leads him to reject the Spinozist principle – so central to German Idealism from Jacobi onward – that 'all determination is negation'. For Fichte as well as for Hegel, 'To determine . . . is to negate, i.e. to establish the identity of a thing over and against other things that it is *not*.'[102] The 1801 *Presentation* contests this tradition and, indeed, in 1804 Schelling will continue to argue against this Jacobian orthodoxy. For example, Schelling's whole polemic in the metaphysical sections of *Philosophy and Religion* is directed against those like the Eschenmayer of 1803 (to whom he is directly responding) and the Neoplatonists who consider the formation or determination of being to necessarily involve appeal to antithesis or substantial difference. The idea, Schelling writes, that the self-determination of the absolute is 'a splitting of itself' is 'a misinterpretation that must be corrected'.[103] Moreover, as in the 1801 *Presentation*, Schelling's model for ontological determination in *Philosophy and Religion* involves a triad of identical components: (1) essential identity or 'pure absoluteness without any further determination'; (2) 'eternal form'; and (3) identity as posited or 'the real'.[104] And, again, none of these categories presuppose antithetical difference: on the one hand, 'form is as eternal as essence and as inseparable from it as absoluteness is from the idea of God' and, on the other hand, the real is in fact absolute identity 'represented in the real, although in it both are *one*, without difference'.[105] Schelling alludes at this juncture to the phenomenon of mirroring: 'Is it not, in fact, impossible to think of a more perfect identity than the one between a thing and its reflected image?'[106] Thus, in 1804, Schelling continues to understand being as positing itself without antithesis, which provisionally suggests that, whatever else is the case, the indifference-model was not wholly abandoned or radically 'improved upon' after summer 1801: Schelling reaffirms many of its key principles towards the end of the identity philosophy in 1804.

It is important to note, moreover, that while the indifference-model worked out in early 1801 excludes antithetical difference, it nonetheless allows for a minimal form of difference – a non-antithetical difference that can be explained from the category of identity alone. More specifically, the indifference-model admits of the quantitative differentiation of identity that is introduced in § 23 of the *Presentation*: 'None other than quantitative difference is at all possible between subject and predicate.'[107] And this is because – and here Schelling is broadly following Fichte's construction of his third principle in the 1794 presentation of the *Wissenschaftslehre* – when identity is posited, it is formed according to the law of identity (A = A): being is, as it were, distributed across this form, across all of its elements. Posited through A = A, identity tends in three directions: towards the 'A' of the subject position, the 'A' of the predicate position and the '=' of indifference. This becomes clear in the proof to § 23. First, 'Any qualitative difference ... is unthinkable', because 'it is the same equal absolute identity that is posited as subject and object'.[108] As Schelling puts it in the Explanation, 'We admit no opposition between subject and object.'[109] And he is no less insistent on this point at the end of the period of the identity philosophy: '*We can nowhere in the universe conceive of an essential or qualitative difference ... The subjective and objective are only the same.*'[110] In consequence, the second part of the proof to § 23 states:

> Since there is no possible difference between the two in terms of being itself, there remains only a quantitative difference, i.e. one that obtains with respect to the *amount* of being, such that the same identity is posited, but with a predominance of subjectivity or objectivity.[111]

Quantities of identity – or potencies – are the units by which philosophers make distinctions. Schelling thus reverts to the category of quantity to avoid that of antithesis. And this takes us straight back to his depiction of the magnetic line:

$$\frac{{}^+\!A = B \qquad\qquad\qquad\qquad A = B^+}{A = A}$$

As Chapter 1 suggested, Schelling's doctrine of quantitative difference as formulated in the magnetic line retains forms of difference – a difference in direction or polarity between the various points on the line, that is, a difference which is often taken as an opposition (between +A and -A). However, by transforming Eschenmayer's potentiated series, Schelling comes to interpret the apparent opposition between A and -A as an imbalance within A = A: a quantitative difference that even Eschenmayer – the mathematical reductionist *par excellence* – could not appreciate. Indeed, Eschenmayer's commitment to the *original* duplicity of A and -A led him to construct a series of quantitative differences (i.e. proportions of the fundamental forces) *grounded upon qualitative negation*; despite his efforts to reduce sensible qualities to quantitative difference, he ultimately falls back upon an antithetical relationship to explain determinacy in nature. But the difference between A and B need not be understood as essentially antithetical, according to Schelling. Indeed, the difference between 1 and -1 does not involve a binary opposition, but can be reduced to a sheer quantity – that is, 2. For Schelling, all apparent differences in reality – even those which appear as oppositional – can be understood in terms of quantity, so long as one focuses upon the zero potency or point of indifference (A = A) and subsequently interprets apparent oppositions (A and B) in terms of the more and the less (+A and -A). From this perspective, identity can be seen to express itself at various degrees of intensity, thereby generating the different potencies or structures of nature.

The *Presentation* therefore accounts for determinate difference in reality without the need for the category of non-identity; the self-differentiation of identity is sufficient for the philosopher. This is why it makes sense for Schelling, at this juncture, to refuse the dialectical and Fichtean accounts of the relation of identity and difference. Reality can, Schelling insists in the *Presentation*, be fully described as 'the identity of identity'.[112] The indifference-model developed during the early months of 1801 accounts for the relation of identity and difference in a way that refuses to make the principle of opposition (-A ≠ A) an equiprimordial principle in the constitution of reality – in a way, then, that is resolutely irreducible to Hegel's, Fichte's or Eschenmayer's contemporaneous experiments in the formation of identity.[113]

Chapter 4

Drive

In the first three chapters of commentary, we focused on various ways philosophers of nature have accounted for the qualitative differences that abound in the natural world. We sought to demonstrate that Schelling's engagement with Eschenmayer on this topic led him to adopt the mathematical concept of 'potency' and articulate the metaphysical position of the 1801 *Presentation*, in which all determinacy in nature is explained in terms of quantitative difference or varying degrees of 'identity'.

We now turn to what Schelling and Eschenmayer understood to be the crux of their debate: the possibility, significance, and methodology of an idealist philosophy of nature. In *Spontaneity = World Soul* and his later review of Schelling's *First Outline*, Eschenmayer argues that idealist philosophy of nature ought to be pursued from a transcendental perspective. In *On the True Concept*, Schelling rejects this transcendental approach to the philosophy of nature in no uncertain terms and proposes a radical method of abstraction in which the philosopher no longer identifies with the reflective activity of the I but with the activity of nature itself. The full significance of Schelling's proposal will only become apparent in Chapter 5, in which we consider Schelling's theoretical account of abstraction in *On the True Concept* and the way abstraction is put into practice in the *Presentation*. At this point, it is necessary to explore the different ways that Eschenmayer and Schelling view the aims of the philosophy of nature and the manner in which these aims are shaped by a fundamental metaphysical disagreement between them. While Eschenmayer locates the original source of nature's activity in the spontaneity of the I, Schelling argues that there is a more fundamental activity in the inorganic world, an activity which only achieves consciousness – that is, only *becomes* an I – as a result of an atemporal, ontological development of non-conscious being. The former view leads Eschenmayer to understand the philosopher's task as the derivation of the diverse range of natural processes from the original activity of consciousness; the latter view leads Schelling to argue that the philosopher of nature must bracket the structure of consciousness altogether in order to exhibit, in philosophical reason, the activity of nature *qua* nature. Thus, against Eschenmayer's transcendental approach to the philosophy of nature, Schelling argues that a philosophy of nature worthy of the name must attend to the activity that is immanent to nature and logically precedes both organic life and human consciousness.

Schelling's conception of speculative physics therefore depends upon two key ideas: first, that nature is intrinsically active, and second, that philosophical thought can in fact shed light upon this activity. In his critical reviews of the *First Outline*, Eschenmayer argues that Schelling simply *presupposes* the first of these ideas, making the latter idea and the very project of a speculative philosophy of nature illegitimate from the beginning. Central to Eschenmayer's critique of Schelling, then, is his attempt to demonstrate that conceiving nature as intrinsically active – and therefore legitimising the very project of philosophy of nature – is only possible if one transposes the spontaneity of one's own activity, as a conscious being, into nature. From this perspective, a philosophy of nature must be grounded in transcendental idealism, since the latter provides the philosopher with the only possible starting point from which to conceive nature's activity.

We begin, then, with Eschenmayer's own account of the original source of activity in nature. According to Eschenmayer, the transposition of spontaneity from the I into nature is possible, because the spontaneity of the I always expresses itself *within* nature as the *drive* of an organism. As the midway point between the original activity of the I and the derivative activity of nature, the biological drive proves to be absolutely essential to a transcendental philosophy of nature.

Eschenmayer's theory of the drive

Schelling's *First Outline* and its *Introduction* describe nature as fundamentally active in two closely connected ways. On the one hand, nature is understood as absolute productivity (*natura naturans*) which, through an immanent principle of inhibition, generates natural products (*natura naturata*). On the other hand, nature's graduated sequence of stages, or *Stufenfolge*, is conceived as an atemporal development that issues from the activity of nature. These two forms of activity are related in so far as they both lead to the *differentiation* of the natural world. But, Schelling asks, *why* does nature differentiate itself in these ways?

> What is the universal source of activity in nature? What cause brought forth the first dynamic juxtaposition in nature . . .? Or what cause first cast the seed of motion into the universal rest of nature, duplicity into universal identity, the first spark of heterogeneity into the universal homogeneity of nature?

Thus, Schelling continues, 'the highest problem of natural science [is] to explain the cause that brought infinite opposition into the universal identity of nature'.[1]

In the *First Outline* and its *Introduction*, Schelling fails to answer this question in an unambiguous fashion, and the ambiguity of Schelling's position in 1799 can be seen in two distinct ways. First, as is evident from the passage above, Schelling has yet to fully commit to the radical identity-monism that he champions in 1801 and which we discussed in Chapter 3 above, and yet the impulse to ground difference in identity is already present. As explored in Chapter 1, Schelling criticises Eschenmayer's dynamic construction of quality, in part, because this dynamism cannot account for the origin of the dual forces of nature. And Schelling insists throughout the *First Outline* that nature's differentiated character must be comprehensible on the basis of nature's oneness or simplicity: the differences found in nature must ultimately emerge from a single, *natural* principle. At least, this is *one* direction that Schelling's thinking in the *First Outline* is headed. It is also noteworthy that, in 1799, Schelling does not believe he has in fact discovered any single principle in nature that would account for the differentiated character of reality. And this leads him to a second ambiguity: despite his repeated insistence that nature is explicable with reference to itself alone – that is, without recourse to foreign principles – the *First Outline* nevertheless does occasionally flirt with a transcendental explanation of nature's duplicity, specifically regarding the fundamental forces. That is, in 1799, Schelling seems to leave open the feasibility of his 1797 solution, presented in the *Ideas*, to the problem of the construction of fundamental forces, suggesting that the activities of consciousness ground this duplicity in nature. It is in this vein, for example, that the closing words of the *First Outline* read:

> It was assumed that nature is a development from one original involution. This involution cannot be anything real . . . thus it can only be thought *as act*, as *absolute synthesis*, which is only ideal, and signifies the turning point, as it were, of transcendental philosophy and philosophy of nature.[2]

Despite the stated aims of the *First Outline* to explain nature's differentiation on the basis of nature alone, Schelling seems to open up a space to call into question the very idea that nature's determinate character results from an immanent principle of activity.

It should therefore come as little surprise that Eschenmayer, a transcendental philosopher, takes these passages from the *First Outline* very seriously. He plausibly follows the hint Schelling gives at the end of the *First Outline* (one pursued by Schelling himself, in fact, in the 1800 *System of Transcendental Idealism*) that what is necessary is to continue constructing a philosophy of nature out of the premises of transcendental idealism. Thus, instead of affirming Schelling's stated view that nature becomes differentiated through a process of self-determination, Eschenmayer argues that the source of activity in nature cannot possibly be natural, precisely because all activity has its source in *freedom*. Indeed, according to Eschenmayer, when Schelling acknowledges that nature must contain a 'hidden trace of freedom', he implicitly suggests that natural activity – and therefore difference – has its origin in the mind, which alone can 'begin a series of productions absolutely'.[3] In other words, according to Eschenmayer, the need to ground philosophy of nature on transcendental premises, which seems to be occasionally hinted at within the *First Outline* itself, is incompatible with the *First Outline*'s explicit commitment to the intrinsic activity of nature; one of the two principles needs to be done away with to make the project of philosophy of nature consistent – and, for Eschenmayer, it is evidently the latter that must be abandoned. Philosophy of nature requires transcendental premises to dynamically construct material diversity, and this means that it can no longer claim that the source of nature's activity and determinacy are to be found within nature itself.[4]

Nevertheless, that nature is not intrinsically active does not mean that it plays no role in the construction of natural diversity. According to Eschenmayer, the diversity of the natural world arises on the basis of an interaction between the spontaneous activity of consciousness, on the one hand, and the sheer being of nature, on the other. Eschenmayer therefore argues that it is necessary to search for a point of interaction between spiritual freedom and material nature, and he identifies this middle point as 'the original drive' (*Urtrieb*), a drive which consists of both spontaneous and natural features. As will become apparent, however, the drive which unifies nature and consciousness is systematically derived from a phenomenological consideration of consciousness itself. Thus, in his critical reviews of Schelling's *First Outline*, Eschenmayer sketches his own outline of a philosophy of nature which would disclose the inner unity of spiritual freedom and material nature in a way that is consistent with the standpoint of transcendental idealism.

The concept of drive

Eschenmayer takes up the concept of the drive from Fichte. Generally speaking, Eschenmayer's Fichteanism during this period cannot be doubted:[5] in 1803, looking back at his earlier work, he expresses regret for not having sooner transcended the standpoint of Fichte.[6] And, as mentioned in the Introduction to this volume, Fichte himself praised Eschenmayer's transcendental approach to the philosophy of nature in a letter written to Schelling in May 1801.[7] Eschenmayer's conception of the drive in 1801 is no exception. Indeed, the nature-philosophical drive theory which emerges in Eschenmayer's controversy with Schelling appears to be both based upon Fichtean principles and subsequently affirmed by Fichte himself.

What, then, is a drive, according to Fichtean philosophy? As Günter Zöller explains, 'in its widest meaning in Fichte, the term stands for the tendency of a being to determine itself',[8] and this applies to 'the natural drive', which includes the drives to self-nourishment and reproduction, as well as the 'higher', 'pure drive', which, when properly cultivated, is manifested as an ethical drive and a drive for knowledge.[9] That the natural drive is self-determining is especially important for Eschenmayer, because it rules out the idea that an organism is responsive to the external world in a merely mechanical fashion; the drive of the organism is far from passive. In fact, the drive of the organism logically precedes the existence of its environment, if an environment is a meaningful context in which the organism acts. Fichte clarifies the transcendental character of the natural drive in the 1798 *System of Ethics*: The natural drive 'originates entirely from my own nature ... I do not feel hunger *because there is food for me*; instead, something becomes food for me *because I am hungry*.'[10] To say that an organism's natural drive is self-determining thus means that it is *original*, and that the material reality upon which the drive acts is derivative. That is, material reality is derivative to the extent that it is a *meaningful* reality, a reality that lights up as an environment containing various opportunities for a living thing to express its biological urges or drives. Fichte goes on to extend this account of a living thing's self-determination beyond the drives of the human animal:

> The situation is no different in the case of any of the organised products of nature. It is not the presence of materials that pertain to the plant's substance that stimulates the plant to absorb these materials; instead, precisely these materials are demanded by the plant's inner structure, independently of their actual presence; and if such materials were not present in nature at all, then the plant could not exist in nature either.[11]

On a Fichtean account, a drive logically precedes that at which it aims.

The second important feature of the Fichtean concept of the drive is that, despite the fact that it is original and self-determining, the drive is not absolutely independent. On the contrary, the drive only manifests itself *within* an environment and, more specifically, as a response to certain phenomena. Fichte explains this by comparing the self-determination of the drive to the 'striving' of a compressed steel spring to 'push back against what presses upon it'.[12] According to Fichte, the spring does not seek decompression simply because something external to it is pressing upon it. Rather, the spring is structured in such a way as to seek decompression whenever it is compressed. The inner 'striving' to decompress, then, is 'the ground of [the spring's] elasticity', analogous to the organism's drive to maintain itself.[13] But the steel spring will not *manifest* this outward directed activity if no external pressure is in fact applied. While immanent to the spring itself, the striving to decompress only ever expresses itself in particular situations. And the same goes for the natural drives of an organism: 'Just as in the case of the steel spring, the drive will result in a self-activity as soon as the external conditions are present.'[14]

The image of the steel spring is therefore helpful in demonstrating that a drive is, at one and the same time, *self-determining* and *responsive to the external world*. And this brings us to the idea, central to Eschenmayer's philosophy of nature, that the original drive that animates all organic processes is the midway point between the spontaneity of the I and the passivity of nature. For the drive 'bears the character of both spontaneity and nature in itself'.[15]

The unity of nature and consciousness

In *Spontaneity = World Soul*, Eschenmayer begins by noting that spiritual freedom, on the one hand, and material nature, on the other, appear to be entirely different from one another. If the I is characterised by absolute spontaneity, nature is characterised by purely passive being.[16] And yet, the I does not in fact find itself to be an exclusively spontaneous, non-natural being; it is also part of *nature*. Indeed, a human being is not a purely free activity but also a *thing*, namely, a material body that is responsive to its environment. In this way, consciousness is characterised by a certain degree of passivity, which allows it to intuit the external world.[17] This is what Eschenmayer means when he claims that 'nature forces the products of its lawfulness on to me'.[18] Furthermore, because nature acts upon an intuiting consciousness, it is not a merely passive being after all, but equally a kind of activity. Consequently, the relationship between consciousness and nature proves to be far more dynamic than appeared at first glance: when I act upon nature, the latter reveals a surplus of passive being; when nature acts upon me, I reveal my own passivity. According to Eschenmayer, this reciprocal interaction is made possible because the spontaneity of the I expresses itself as a *drive*, a kind of natural spontaneity or, as Fichte puts it, objective activity.[19]

It is important to recognise that, precisely because the drive is natural or objective, its self-determination does not achieve the absolute character of spiritual freedom. According to Eschenmayer – and, again, this follows Fichte's thought to the letter – the naturalness of the drive means that it is extraordinarily limited in its power. We can see this in three fundamental ways. First, an organism does not have a choice regarding the particular drives that motivate its actions. The drives of a self-determining, living thing are, in this sense, lacking the robust freedom of the will.[20] Second, the drive is ultimately ineffective. For as long as a living being remains *alive*, its fundamental drive continues ad infinitum.[21] This is why Eschenmayer claims that the drive, 'in striving out for the external world – never exhausts itself and, like an infinite factor, reproduces itself always anew'.[22] Eschenmayer's point is not that a particular drive, such an organism's drive to nourish itself, necessarily fails in any given instance, as if living things were always failing to achieve their goals. The point is, rather, that the *fundamental* drive to self-maintenance is never exhausted in any particular act. On the contrary, so long as an organism is *living*, it continues to be driven. Life is therefore, at bottom, the infinite striving of a natural being to remain the being it is.[23] And this is an impoverished form of freedom, precisely because it is inexhaustible; the striving of life never comes to completion, but is only extinguished in death.

The third way that the spontaneity of the drive is tempered by its natural character concerns the fact that the organism aims at self-maintenance *within a material world*. As opposed to pure spontaneity, which initiates a chain of events *ex nihilo*, the original drive of an organism only ever acts upon already existing material. A plant seeks air, light and water for the purposes of growth and self-maintenance; an animal seeks to nourish itself by ingesting plants and other animals. In both cases, the living thing acts upon some given material in order to reform its own material body. The drive to reproduce is, likewise, limited by this materiality: an animal seeks out *other* members of its species for the purpose of reproduction, and the product of the sexual act is a mere repetition of the organisms that already exist. The organic drive is not, then, truly creative, but *formative*. It is, at bottom, a *Bildungstrieb*, the striving of an individual to maintain and perpetuate itself.

It is not by accident that Eschenmayer conceives the drive as fundamentally formative. Fichte's drive theory, upon which Eschenmayer's philosophy of nature is based, is heavily influenced by Blumenbach's idea of a formative drive (*nisus formativus*).[24] For Blumenbach and his followers, living things seek to maintain and perpetuate themselves through a fundamental drive, a drive responsible for the generation, nourishment and reproduction of life.[25] Since the formative drive actively organises previously existing material, it does not, strictly speaking, create. Moreover, this drive to form and reform matter is never complete, but rather continues ad infinitum. Eschenmayer therefore sees the Blumenbachean conception of organic life as providing a way to think about the unity of consciousness and nature.[26] We become alive to the natural world thanks to our spontaneous activity *in* nature, and yet our spontaneity is diminished in its efficacy thanks precisely to the nature in which we find ourselves driven.[27] The drive is the principle that simultaneously raises the sheer being of nature to activity and extinguishes the pure spontaneity of the I.

The theory of the drive thus proves that spontaneous freedom and deterministic nature are not simply opposed to one another as two antithetical elements of reality, but that they lie on a continuum. Absolute spontaneity and absolutely passive being are two poles of an infinite series, the middle point of which is drive.[28] The closer one gets to the 'spontaneous' pole of the series, the more subjectivity expresses itself; the closer one gets to the 'natural' pole of the series, the more objectivity is expressed. The image here is extraordinarily similar to Schelling's model of identity in § 46 of the *Presentation* – and yet, one crucial difference remains: for Eschenmayer, the unity of subjective spontaneity and objective nature – that is, the unity expressed in the drive – has its source in the spontaneity of consciousness. In order to see this, we need to consider Eschenmayer's rational deduction of the original drive and its subsequent representation as the soul of the world.

The derivation of the drive

In the *Deduction of the Living Organism*, Eschenmayer eloquently outlines the task of the philosophy of organic life: 'It is not enough for us that we possess [the organism] necessarily in experience, we want to know how it necessarily arises thus.'[29] In other words, the philosopher of nature cannot be content with the empirical knowledge that intrinsically driven natural objects *exist*; she must go on to ask why this must be the case. Of course, life is not the only phenomenon that requires rational explanation (as we saw in Chapter 1, Eschenmayer is equally committed to understanding the ground of inorganic qualities in nature); yet the rational derivation of the drive is absolutely central to Eschenmayer's project, not only because he seeks to provide a transcendental grounding for medical science, but because, as we saw above, he understands the drive as the essential point of unity between spiritual freedom and nature. How, then, does philosophical science go about deriving the existence of this drive which unifies consciousness and the natural world?

In both the *Deduction* and *Spontaneity = World Soul*, Eschenmayer argues that the existence of the drive can be derived from the sheer fact of consciousness.[30] Attending to the structure of ordinary consciousness, the philosopher notices two distinct faculties of the mind: a faculty of *production* and a faculty of *reflection*. And, although both of these faculties are free powers of the mind, they are opposed in orientation. Whereas production is directed *outward* as a positive activity of creation or synthesis, reflection is directed back upon the mind as a negative activity of analysis. Eschenmayer's description of the relationship between the faculties of production and reflection calls to mind his earlier dynamic philosophy of nature, in which repulsion and attraction are described as two principles of infinite activity opposed in their spatial orientation – although, importantly, the 1799 deduction of the drive is in no way dependent on such nature-philosophical principles: the dynamic conflict between the faculties of production and reflection is derived from their appearance in consciousness alone.

Given the antithetical character of production and reflection, and given the fact that each of these faculties is equally powerful, it follows that these faculties would, left unchecked, cancel one another out.[31] Indeed, if the faculties of production and reflection were to act simultaneously, then neither would act at all – that is, the result would be an *absolute equilibrium* in which neither production nor reflection occurs; there would be no freedom at all, but merely passive being or nature.[32] In other words, the equilibrium of the mind's tendencies would annul spiritual freedom and yield a nature entirely devoid of spontaneity.

Recall that our starting point is ordinary consciousness, and that Eschenmayer claims that it is obvious from the perspective of consciousness that production and reflection *do* exist. It follows that 'nature' – the passive being in which production and reflection cancel one another out – does *not* in fact describe the activity of consciousness. What, then, accounts for the fact that this dual cancellation fails to occur, despite the fact that production and reflection are infinitely opposed in orientation? In order to answer this question, Eschenmayer reproduces the logic of dynamic conflict at a higher level: the 'natural' tendency, in which the faculties of production and reflection simply cancel one another out, must *itself* be opposed by a second tendency, a tendency that seeks to keep the faculties separate from one another. This second tendency issues from *spontaneity*, precisely because the faculties, when kept apart, remain the infinitely free faculties that they *are*. In the *Deduction*, Eschenmayer describes this principle of spontaneity as seeking to employ the faculties in 'succession' rather than in 'simultaneity'.[33] The idea is that, so long as the I freely produces, this production must be unencumbered by reflection, and so long as the I freely reflects, this reflection must be unencumbered by production. Importantly, however, the faculties prove extreme in isolation: left unchecked by production, reflection 'proceeds to *annihilation*', and left unchecked by reflection, production 'proceeds to *creation*'.[34] That is, the reflective faculty, since it tends inwards and away from the objective world, would – left to its infinite power alone – 'annihilate' the stuff of the external world. By the same token, employing the productive faculty without reflection would yield the same lack of determinacy: without a counterforce to limit its power, the productive faculty would extend infinitely outwards as a 'creativity' that fails to engender any determinate, finite products.

It can be helpful to once again recall that Eschenmayer's derivation of the drive begins with the facts of ordinary consciousness. According to Eschenmayer, in addition to explaining the fact of *self*-consciousness, we must explain the fact that consciousness is a 'consciousness of things outside of us and of representations in us'.[35] That is to say, in our everyday experience we are aware of objects in the world as well as our representations of those objects. It follows from this fact that we do not employ production or reflection in the truly infinite manner described above. To be sure, consciousness freely reflects and produces, but it does so in a limited fashion. For, as we have seen, if either faculty were to be employed with limitless power, no determinacy would result. In actual reflection, reality is not *annihilated*; rather, a concept is extracted from but nonetheless connected to the material world. Likewise, in actual production, one does not creative *infinitely* – which would result in indeterminacy – but synthesises and modifies already-existing material in order to form a determinate product. In ordinary experience, each of the faculties proves to be 'limited by *matter*'.[36]

It is the existence of material nature, then, which prevents spontaneity from being absolute – that is, from enabling the faculties of reflection and production to operate in isolation from one another. And importantly, at this stage, Eschenmayer has argued that nature is nothing other than the absolute *equilibrium* of production and reflection – that is, their negation. The spontaneity which seeks to keep the faculties of production and reflection distinct is itself tempered by *nature*, which seeks to cancel out the independence of the faculties and therefore freedom as such. Eschenmayer thus argues that ordinary consciousness acts in a manner that is neither strictly natural nor strictly free. That is, the faculties are employed neither in absolute simultaneity (which would cancel them out) nor in succession, but in an intermediate manner. Consciousness always acts with *both* faculties, and in this way is pulled in the direction of nature. And yet, through the spontaneity of consciousness, one of the two faculties always *predominates*. Every action, then, is some combination of productive and reflective activity, with a surplus of one of the two faculties. In the *Deduction*, Eschenmayer calls this middle point the 'striving' of the I:[37] consciousness *strives* to achieve absolute freedom, but such absolute freedom is always out of reach. In the final pages of the *Deduction*, Eschenmayer argues that the striving of the I appears *within* nature as an organism's formative drive, and that it is such striving which accounts for the very *life* of the organism. In *Spontaneity = World Soul*, he is even more direct, simply identifying the original middle point between spontaneity and nature as the drive.[38] According to Eschenmayer, it must be the case that consciousness is 'driven' – that is, that consciousness is neither purely spontaneous nor purely passive but a natural or objective spontaneity, a form of freedom that is fundamentally limited in its material existence. The condition for the possibility of consciousness, then, is the drive of the organism.

At this point, we simply want to point out the fact that Eschenmayer's derivation of the drive is based upon a proto-phenomenological description of consciousness. Since 'self-consciousness is an undeniable fact',[39] the philosopher *begins* by reflecting upon how she 'finds man typically engaged'.[40] Eschenmayer, therefore, neither begins with nature as it exists in itself, nor with the drives of living things, but with ordinary consciousness and its faculties of production and reflection. Indeed, it is only through a transcendental investigation into the conditions of phenomenal consciousness that Eschenmayer arrives at his discussion of the drive.

The drive and the quantitative series

Importantly, the above derivation of the drive is not the end of the story for Eschenmayer. And this is because, rather than simply settling on a given proportion between the faculties of production and reflection, the drive produces *various* proportions of the faculties. Eschenmayer describes this in the following way: through our *receptivity*, we become aware of an imperative to maintain an absolute equilibrium between the faculties of production and reflection. Indeed, as receptive beings, we are aware of ourselves as natural beings who neither reflect nor produce but simply sense and intuit and thus implicitly seek to maintain an absolute equilibrium between our reflective and productive capacities. And yet, we do not *want* to maintain such an equilibrium, precisely because this would amount to the cancellation of our spontaneity.[41] It is this tension that generates a *series* of relationships between production and reflection, a series that extends infinitely between two ideal poles, that is, two poles which are never actualised: (1) the absolute equilibrium and therefore cancellation of the faculties and (2) the absolute separation and therefore independence of the faculties. Marking a middle point of this infinite series, we see that there are two basic types of proportions: proportions that tend towards absolute equilibrium and proportions that tend towards absolute separation. The half of the series in which production and reflection achieve greater independence is constituted by our 'concepts and their corresponding products'.[42] And because the other half of the series contains proportions of the faculties that tend towards their equilibrium, the points along this half of the series can be understood as 'objective' as opposed to 'subjective'.[43] It is therefore within this latter domain that the I senses and intuits the objective world. Significantly, Eschenmayer claims that the drive does not only generate the infinite series, but it also separates sensation and intuition from one another, thereby initiating a further dynamic conflict. Sensation and intuition thus emerge as distinct and yet reciprocally related. It is in this way, Eschenmayer argues, that 'consciousness of an external world becomes possible', for it is the relationship between sensation and intuition that 'produces in us a multiplicity of material'.[44] Indeed, it is through this relationship that all reality as well as all magnitude emerges.[45]

In Chapter 1, we discussed the series of magnitudes as it relates to Eschenmayer's metaphysical account of qualitative difference in nature. We now learn that, for Eschenmayer, sensible qualities are not only reducible to proportions of force, but that proportions of force have their origin in the activity of the drive. Indeed, the drive – as 'the limit between two series'[46] – generates the entire quantitative series which is ultimately perceived as a qualitatively differentiated nature. Consequently, the objective reality one perceives in everyday life owes its vast range of qualities to the tension, within the organism, between its natural and spontaneous tendencies.

World soul: the transcendental perspective

The systematic priority of consciousness in Eschenmayer's philosophy of nature should now be apparent. As a transcendental philosopher, Eschenmayer begins with ordinary consciousness and seeks to derive the conditions that make consciousness possible. In so far as the transcendental philosopher ventures into the domain of nature, then, it is always on the basis of a prior and presupposed familiarity with consciousness. Moreover, the vast diversity of qualities perceived in the natural world is understood, on this account, to be dependent upon the activity of the I. Indeed, without assuming the existence of a conscious subject from which the organic drive is deduced, the transcendental philosopher cannot explain the reality of either the organism or its qualitatively differentiated environment.

Of course, it is not as if a person is ordinarily aware of their active role in diversifying the natural world in which they exist. The process through which nature takes on its determinate features proceeds at an unconscious level. And, according to Eschenmayer, this has significant consequences for how one actually experiences the world. Indeed, because I do not typically reflect upon the fundamental activity of my drive, I am unaware of the fact that the natural determinacy I encounter in the world proceeds from *my* drive. Consequently, I assume that the source of activity which engenders a differentiated world is located *in nature*. As Marchetto puts it, 'through the unconscious activity of the intelligence a drive enters into nature and then becomes known from the point of view of a consciousness as objective, and independent of the I, as a World Soul'.[47] In Eschenmayer's words, the drive 'is represented *immanently* do nature as the *world soul*', thereby accomplishing the complete unification of consciousness and nature.[48] Marchetto continues, 'this does not mean that this drive properly *belongs* to nature',[49] but that nature merely *appears* as spontaneous to an embodied consciousness. What appears to consciousness as an activity intrinsic to nature has its ultimate origin in the depths of consciousness.

It is worth noting that Eschenmayer has not gone beyond Fichte here. In the *System of Ethics* and the 'Propositions towards the Elucidation of the Nature of Animals', Fichte also argues that we are compelled to conceive nature *as though* it were intrinsically active, and that this follows from the basic character of the drive. According to Fichte, self-determining drives *only exist* within environments that *support* them, and this leads him to his fundamental nature-philosophical thesis: if we understand ourselves and other living things as immanently driven, and if drives only ever exist in so far as they are supported by the nature which is external to them, then it follows that we must conceive nature as a realm of 'harmony, reciprocal interaction, and not, as it were, mere mechanism'.[50] Indeed, that we perceive self-determining individuals existing in environments which allow those individuals to flourish requires that we conceive nature *as a whole* to be organised and self-determining – that is, as a whole in which self-determining parts relate in harmonious interaction. From this perspective, 'nature as such is ... an organic whole and is posited as such'.[51] It is the self-organising activity in nature – or, rather, the representation of such an activity – that Eschenmayer identifies as the 'world soul'. And if we conceive nature as such a self-organising whole, we can understand our own organic drives as products of *nature's* productivity.[52]

On this account, nature appears to us as a holistic system organised by an immanent, productive activity. But it is necessary to recognise that this world soul thesis is a *transcendental* thesis. It claims nothing whatsoever about nature as it exists in itself, but exclusively concerns how we are compelled to *conceive* nature.[53] Thus, Fichte writes, 'a rational being is *forced* to think of nature in this manner'.[54] We must think of ourselves as products of nature, and, significantly, the compulsion to conceive nature as productive issues from the activity of the I. Indeed, the I unconsciously transfers *to nature* its self-conception as immanently driven.[55] The world soul thesis of the transcendental idealist is therefore clear: we must conceive nature as intrinsically active and, indeed, even productive of our own organic existence. We cannot, however, make any claims about nature as it is in itself. Thus, although Fichte entertains the idea that 'intelligence is a higher power [*Potenz*] of nature',[56] he insists that, 'when that proposition is made to signify that in a system of nature the intelligence is itself a higher power or manifestation of nature, then it is evidently incorrect, and is refuted thoroughly in transcendental philosophy'.[57] Eschenmayer makes precisely the same argument in *Spontaneity = World Soul* in order to contend, *pace* Schelling, that the organic drive that issues from the spontaneity of the I is the original source of activity and determinacy in the natural world (as it is given to us in experience). As for nature *in itself*, the philosopher has nothing to tell us.

On the feasibility of transcendental philosophy of nature

The above interpretation of Fichte and Eschenmayer does not rule out the possibility that these philosophers are, at the end of the day, naturalists of some stripe or, at the very least, that their thought is consistent with a version of philosophical naturalism. Moreover, to ground philosophy of nature in transcendental philosophy is not necessarily to invalidate the philosophy of nature that is so grounded. Fichtean–Eschenmayerian philosophy of nature is still a variant of philosophy of nature. Instead, what follows from the above account is merely that, from the perspective of the transcendental philosophy of nature: (1) consciousness must be granted systematic priority; (2) the variety of natural qualities is understood as being dependent upon the existence of a practically-engaged form of life;

and (3) the idea of a world soul is legitimised via the transposition of the organism's self-determining activity into nature writ large. It does not follow from this transcendental perspective, however, that nature lacks reality or that consciousness is essentially a disembodied, purely spiritual entity. On the contrary, the view promoted by Eschenmayer seeks to demonstrate the *reality* of nature and its *inseparability* from spiritual freedom in a living and breathing I. In other words, for Fichte and Eschenmayer, all that is being asserted is that a proper philosophy of nature must attend to nature via a phenomenological description of conscious life and a transcendental investigation into its necessary conditions.

In further support of the feasibility of a transcendental philosophy of nature, one could refer to Fichte's discussion of the difference between the natural drive and the purely spiritual drive. According to Fichte, it is only through an act of thought that the natural and spiritual drives can be seen as separate from one another. They are, at bottom, united in what Fichte calls the 'original drive':

> From the transcendental point of view, the two are one and the same original drive, which constitutes my being, simply viewed from two different sides. That is to say, I am a subject-object, and my true being consists in the identity and indivisibility of the two.[58]

It is therefore somewhat misleading to even describe the purely spiritual drive as 'higher' than the natural drive. As Soller remarks, 'A hierarchy of the pure and natural drives is thus ruled out in advance by the fact that the two are essentially identical!'[59] If the original drive is, as Fichte claims, simultaneously spiritual and natural, then this has significant consequences for how he conceives ethical and intellectual life. For the purely spiritual drive *would not be possible* without the natural activity to which it is identical. Thus, Fichte argues – and this is also what Eschenmayer attempts to demonstrate in the *Deduction* – the natural drive of the living organism is a condition for the possibility of moral and intellectual life.

Kosch helps to clarify the manner in which practical reasoning in particular is dependent upon the natural drive. She notes that the pure drive, to the extent that we posit it as separate from the natural drive, is unique in that it 'lacks a determinate content of its own'.[60] Indeed, considered in its purity, this spiritual aspect of the original drive is not even properly *ethical*, since it lacks determinacy altogether; it simply aims at formal independence – that is, self-activity for its own sake. Consequently, the pure drive 'must operate on the content provided by *nature*'.[61] In doing so, the pure drive can be seen to 'mix' with the natural drive, the combination of which yields a genuinely *ethical* drive 'directed toward determinate actions'.[62] Fichte thus insists that 'all our acting occurs *within* nature;

[only] in nature is our acting possible, and only in nature can it become actual for us.'[63] Additionally, our theoretical activity – our *drive* to *know*[64] – necessarily takes place within nature for Fichte. In order to seek the truth, one must be a self-determining being that finds itself in the natural world.[65] Both the moral and intellectual life of the I are thus inseparable from its organic, animal existence.

Emphasising this aspect of Fichte's idealism therefore casts the transcendental project in a more naturalist light. The nature-philosophical account of the unity of the natural drive and more complex forms of mental activity suggests that our moral, political and scientific activities are utterly dependent upon our embodied, animal existence. Fichte can thus be seen as having developed a philosophy of life that elucidates the inseparability of theoretical reason, practical reason and biological impulses.

Contrary to his reputation as an anti-realist, then, Fichte may have a great deal to teach us about the animal nature that undergirds our moral and theoretical activity. As Scribner has suggested, Fichte's idealism can be read as a precursor to subsequent philosophies of nature, such as Uexküll's biosemiotics and Merleau-Ponty's phenomenology of the body.[66] Nevertheless, it is still important to stress the limitations of such a Fichtean–Eschenmayerian variation on the nature-philosophical project. As Grant has taken great pains to demonstrate, a philosophy of nature that places the living organism at the centre of its analysis ultimately reproduces the metaphysics of Cartesian dualism *within* nature.[67] This should come as no surprise given Fichte and Eschenmayer's recourse to Blumenbach's concept of the formative drive. For Blumenbach himself claimed ignorance regarding the original source of the formative drive and thereby set into motion a dualist philosophy of nature in which there is no apparent connection between life and unorganised matter.[68] It is true that, unlike Blumenbach, Fichte and Eschenmayer claim that the mind posits the drive in the *whole of nature*, and in this way the gap between the inorganic and organic is apparently closed; however, it is also true that, from a transcendental perspective, we are only justified in claiming that consciousness must *represent* nature as being determined by a world soul. The metaphysics of Fichtean philosophy therefore remains implicitly dualist, even if it is naturalist: the organism which thinks and acts is immanently driven, and the nature in which that organism finds itself is only ever posited *as* active. Moreover, the difference between life, which is intrinsically active, and inorganic matter, which is only *conceived* as intrinsically active, is a *fundamental* difference. As Müller-Sievers remarks, the 'material flip side of the transcendental activity of the I' is a 'generative, yet *ungenerated* activity of striving'[69] – that is, a striving which is not actually shown to emerge from nature even if we *posit* nature *as* productive of the organism. Consequently, even if a transcendental philosophy of nature is feasible in some respects, by means of it we still never achieve metaphysical knowledge regarding the inorganic ground of life.

In order to return to Schelling's very different approach to the philosophy of nature, we can simply ask the following: what can philosophy teach us about the natural world? Can philosophy merely demonstrate that *we posit* nature as the ground of organic life and consciousness? Or can philosophy demonstrate that nature *is* in fact such a ground? If we simply reject this last question as naive or dogmatically metaphysical, then our philosophy of nature will only ever shed light upon the *concepts* we utilise in understanding the natural world and the organic drives which make our worldly actions possible. For Schelling, this severely limits the scope and significance of the philosophy of nature.[70]

The autonomy and autarchy of nature

From Schelling's perspective, the problem with the Fichtean–Eschenmayerian approach to nature is clear: on such a model, the philosophical significance of nature is entirely dependent upon its relationship to consciousness and its biological, intellectual and ethical interests. Such a system is therefore only concerned with nature in so far as it is given to a living subject. According to Schelling, this effectively subordinates the task of theoretical reason – that is, to grasp, in thought, what *is* – to practical reason, since it reduces the *being* of nature to its relationship to a living subject. And, from a Schellingian perspective, limiting the philosophical significance of nature in this manner is disastrous for philosophical science: not only does it mean that thought lacks access to the being of nature as it is *in itself*, but the transcendental philosopher's knowledge of the I proves to be utterly impoverished, since she has no way of explaining the emergence of living consciousness from inorganic nature. So long as consciousness is merely taken *as given*, neither nature nor consciousness is fully understood.

Schelling's proposal to overcome the shortcomings of transcendental philosophy of nature is relatively straightforward: one can only develop a realist philosophy of consciousness *and* nature by deriving the ontological specificity of conscious life from nature's activity. Thus, Schelling argues, what is required of philosophy is to provide a 'physical explanation of idealism'– that is, a *purely* theoretical philosophy that is in no way influenced by the practical interests of the thinking subject.[71] By describing the ontological structure of nature as it is in itself, such a speculative physics would shed light upon that which makes life and consciousness possible.

A philosophy of nature of this sort, however, cannot *begin* with the potencies of life and consciousness. Instead, it must begin with the more basic potencies in nature, for this is the only way to exhibit in philosophical thought: (1) the atemporal emergence of the higher potencies from the lower; and (2) the interconnectedness (or absolute identity) of all of the potencies. It follows from this that the philosophy of nature must detail how non-organic, non-spiritual nature is active in such a manner as to immanently raise itself to higher degrees of reality in biological and anthropological life. Schelling utilises a range of terms to signify this non-organic, non-spiritual activity. In the *First Outline*, he conceives this activity as nature's 'subjectivity' and as the generation or 'becoming' of beings; in the *Introduction to the Outline*, he understands nature's activity not only in terms of subjectivity and becoming,[72] but also as an *unconscious productivity*;[73] and, as we argued in Chapter 3, *On the True Concept* and the *Presentation* describe this activity as the atemporal productivity of sheer subject-object 'identity'. But, despite these changes in Schelling's terminology, the fundamental thesis remains consistent: nature owes its structure to nothing other than its own self-formation. Whether he is discussing the metaphysics of individuation and flirting with a philosophical description of natural-historical development, for example in the *First Outline* and the *Freedom* essay, or he is focusing exclusively on the eternal forms of being, for example in the *Presentation* and the late negative philosophy, Schelling continues to insist that theoretical philosophy must attend to the self-formation of nature.[74]

It is therefore possible to take certain claims on this topic in the *First Outline* as representative of Schelling's mature philosophical view. In the First Division of the text, referring to the 'autonomy of nature', he states:

> Since nature gives itself its sphere of activity, no foreign power can interfere with it; all of its laws are immanent, or *nature is its own legislator*.[75]

Nature determines itself to be the nature it is; it is 'self-legislating' in the sense that all of the laws of nature – mechanical, physical and organic – have their source in nature's activity. Consequently, Schelling argues, anything that occurs *within* nature is explicable with reference to nature alone. This latter feature is what Schelling calls the 'autarchy of nature':

> Whatever happens in nature must also be explained from the active and motive principles which lie in it, or *nature suffices for itself*.[76]

We can identify these propositions as the principles of nature's *independence* and *immanence*, which, Schelling claims, can be expressed together in a third proposition:

Nature has unconditioned reality, a proposition which is precisely the principle of a philosophy of nature.'[77]

In *Spontaneity = World Soul*, Eschenmayer explicitly rejects these Schellingian propositions. Before going on to reflect upon this, however, it is worth addressing whether or not Schelling's description of nature as autonomous, autarchic and, indeed, subjective, commits him to the view that nature is also *alive*. Because one might think that, given Schelling's claim that everything that occurs within nature is caused by nature itself, he is conceiving the natural world as some kind of living thing. Indeed, Schelling himself proposes in 1798 that nature be understood as a 'universal organism' intrinsically animated by a world soul, and he continues to describe nature as an organism throughout the *First Outline*. On our reading, however, the system sketched in this text does not allow for an organicist interpretation of nature's fundamental activity. Exploring why this is the case will help us to bring to light one of the key contributions of Schellingian thought to the philosophical study of nature.

According to Schelling, organic nature – nature raised to the third power – is defined by three distinct yet interrelated activities: sensibility, irritability and the formative drive. Each of these activities is a different way that an organism engages with its environment. In order to sense the external world, in order to respond to external stimuli and in order to reproduce, an organism must be in a relationship to something which is different from it. Moreover, the organism *depends* upon this exteriority for its very existence.[78] It is significant that these higher-order activities are only expressed within individuals that are ontologically dependent upon some external environment. Because if Schelling were to understand nature *as a whole* on the model of the living organism, then nature would necessarily be dependent upon an *outside* to which it would be responsive in the mode of sensibility, irritability and reproduction. But, as the above makes explicit, for Schelling, nature is entirely self-sufficient. Unlike the animal, nature does not exist within an environment from which it differs; nature does not depend upon some *other* nature – whether inorganic or organic – that exists outside of it. On the contrary, the organisation of nature is absolutely autonomous and thus structurally distinct from the organisation of living things. It would therefore be mistaken to regard Schellingian nature as an individuated being, such as the earth, the activities of which could be said to be analogous to those of an animal.

Our discussion above regarding Fichte and Eschenmayer on the significance of the drive now acquires a new layer of significance. For Schelling, the connecting tissue between the various levels of reality – natural and spiritual – cannot be understood on the basis of a *drive* within nature, for drive is a concept that only describes the *higher* levels of reality. We can see more clearly now that, when Eschenmayer identifies the drive as the key concept for understanding spontaneity in the natural world, he refuses to countenance the possibility that there is a more basic process at work in nature that is ultimately responsible for the *emergence* of organic drives. *Pace* Blumenbach, Fichte and Eschenmayer, Schelling seeks to explain the existence of the *Bildungstrieb* on the basis of a more fundamental activity, an activity that expresses itself as a drive only in the most complex natural products. Speculative philosophy of nature thus flies in the face of transcendental orthodoxy by aiming to understand nature as it exists *separately* from the practical and intellectual activity of any living subject. To think philosophically about nature – and not just about the nature of the *organism* – requires that one attend to a form of self-determining activity that is more basic than the activity of a living thing. From this perspective, we can see that – despite his occasional employment of organicist language – Schelling's speculative physics fundamentally opposes biocentrism and organicism in the philosophy of nature.

'The tomb of empiricism is the resurrection of rationalism'

Of course, not every philosopher will be convinced of nature's autonomy and autarchy – that is, that nature is self-determining and that all aspects of the natural world are explicable on the basis of nature's activity alone. In order to criticise this Schellingian view, Eschenmayer focuses on a number of comments in the *First Outline* that appear to identify the method of speculative physics as an 'unconditional empiricism'.[79] According to Eschenmayer, Schelling's failure to grasp the original source of activity in nature as the spontaneity of the I results from his apparent commitment to an empiricist epistemology. He thus claims that the 'tomb of empiricism' – that is, Schelling's failed speculative philosophy of nature – immanently leads one back to the rationalism of transcendental philosophy.[80] The specific failure of speculative physics proceeds from its claim to 'unconditioned' or 'absolute' status, when in fact the entire speculative system can be developed 'only under the condition of excluding that *principle of becoming*' which transcendental philosophy alone can illuminate.[81] From Eschenmayer's perspective, Schelling adopts the idealist's conception of rational self-determination and transposes it into nature, all the while ignoring the fact that this 'first principle' has its source in the transcendental philosopher's account of consciousness.

It is entirely understandable that Eschenmayer suspects the Schelling of the *First Outline* of smuggling a principle of transcendental philosophy into the philosophy of nature. We considered evidence of this kind above. Schelling claims, for example, that 'the active in nature' is the 'first *supposition*' of the philosophy of nature,[82] and, given his idealist background, it is fair to assume that this supposition is at the very least partially inspired by transcendental philosophy. That being said, even if the transcendental philosophy of consciousness happened to provide Schelling with the occasion to conceive nature in terms of an immanent 'principle of becoming' – and even if Schelling recognises that the philosophy of nature simply *begins* with this principle – it does not follow that nature can only be represented as self-determining on the basis of the self-determining activity of the mind. In other words, the presupposition of nature's activity does not require the additional transcendental commitment to the systematic priority of consciousness. In fact, the idea that nature is immanently active can be seen as a necessary principle for any philosophical explanation of the existence of things that does *not* appeal to the productivity of the mind (or a transcendent creator). Indeed, the principle of nature's self-determination – even if the terminology used to describe this self-determination is adopted from transcendental philosophy – is a prerequisite for any realist and 'immanentist' metaphysics.

Moreover, the 'first supposition' of the *First Outline* is not the end of the story. Indeed, in the texts which follow the *First Outline* and its *Introduction*, Schelling seeks to *justify* the idea that nature is intrinsically self-determining. As we will see in Chapter 5, Schelling employs a unique philosophical methodology precisely in order to exhibit the activity of nature at the most basic stages of reality. Following the *First Outline*, then, Schelling does not presuppose that nature is immanently active; he seeks to show that this is necessarily the case, and he does so by exhibiting the atemporal development that proceeds from one stage of reality to another as a rational development, because identity *is* identity by differentiating itself in a quantitative manner, thereby generating the potentiated series (A, A^1, A^2). Schelling thus understands nature to be structured via a thoroughly rational process of potentiation.[83] And this means that the task of the *philosophy* of nature is to explicate the rational forms which are immanently generated through this rational process. In this way, Schelling's system of nature is as rationalist as the Neoplatonist *scala naturae*, with the significant caveat that, for Schelling, the rationale at work in nature moves from the lower to the higher forms of reality.

The transcendental idealist cannot accept this idea, because she assumes that rational self-determination – like all spontaneity – has its origin in the *mind*. From this perspective, the notion that the rational laws of nature could be determined by nature itself is fantastical, since all rational principles are derived from consciousness. This is why Eschenmayer thinks that, if the philosopher of nature *begins* with nature, then her method will necessarily be *empirical*.[84] There is perhaps no better example of this dispute between Schelling and Eschenmayer than their differing views on the philosophical ground of mathematical truths.[85] Whereas Schelling argues that the principles of mathematics – despite being discovered in abstraction from physics – must ultimately be grounded in a philosophy of *nature*,[86] Eschenmayer insists that these principles 'owe their origin to our mind's necessary manner of acting'.[87] Thus, for Eschenmayer, since the principles of reason – mathematical and otherwise – have their source in the mind, then a truly *rational* philosophy will be a science of consciousness.

We should note the irony, then, in Schelling's suggestion that it is in fact Eschenmayer who has implicitly given too much over to empiricism. In response to Eschenmayer's suggestion that 'it seems still too early to speak of a system of philosophy of nature, before a propaedeutic for it is available',[88] Schelling counters:

> I would be anxious to know how long we will have to wait and how we shall know in the future that the time for this science has come? – Perhaps when experience has progressed further? – But *how far* are we really with experience? – This can only be judged from philosophy of nature. Experience is blind and must first learn to see its own richness or lack through science. Moreover, a completely a priori science cannot be dependent on contingent conditions like that of the progress of experience; rather, on the contrary, the latter must be accelerated onwards by the former, which presents ideas that lead to invention. One can never say of a self-sufficient science: it is not yet time to invent it, for it is always time for it to be invented.[89]

Schelling is clearly not arguing against empirical investigation into nature, but against the idea that the philosophy of nature should be constructed *on the basis* of empirical science. We find a similar argument in the *Introduction to the Outline*, where Schelling argues that experimentation seeks to test out speculative (that is, rational) hypotheses about nature.[90] On the surface, the questions Schelling poses to Eschenmayer are odd, since Eschenmayer never argues that empirical research should lead our investigations into nature. On the contrary, Eschenmayer seeks to ground the philosophy of nature in transcendental idealism. But, having considered the philosophers' dispute regarding the locus of rationality, we can make sense of Schelling's point. His claim is that, if one conceives the fundamental principles of reason as residing solely in the mind, then any philosophical knowledge of *nature* will have to be extra-rational and therefore based, in part, upon experience. For the transcendental philosopher, a strictly rationalist philosophy of nature is not possible, even if the propaedeutic to philosophy of nature is thoroughly rational in its derivation of the structure of consciousness. For Schelling, however, things are otherwise: speculative physics, when it is truly speculative, accesses nature itself and thereby generates hypotheses that, while falsifiable in principle, will always prove to be true given their source in the rational structure of the natural world.[91]

Eschenmayer was correct, therefore, in stating that the tomb of empiricism is the resurrection of rationalism; it is, however, Eschenmayer's transcendental perspective which dies on the cross of empiricism by simply assuming the fact of consciousness. As we saw above, despite Eschenmayer's claim that 'no aspect of experience creeps into the investigation here',[92] the entire a priori deduction of life is pursued on the basis of an experiential fact: that consciousness *is*. Schelling's speculative physics, by contrast, makes no assumptions whatsoever regarding the existence or structure of consciousness; it thereby seeks to overcome the remnant empiricism of transcendental idealism by sinking into the self-determining structure of non-conscious nature.

But if Schelling is indeed correct that nature is self-determining and intrinsically rational, what kind of philosophical reasoning will allow one *access* to nature as it is in itself? What will a philosophy of nature look like if it does not proceed from a self-conscious being driven by practical concerns? How does one philosophise if not as an organic and, indeed, spiritual being? According to Schelling, the philosopher must *abstract* from consciousness in order to construct, via the reason of nature, the series of powers that leads from the unconscious activity of inorganic processes to conscious life. In the following chapter, we explore this method of abstraction.

Chapter 5

Abstraction

In the Preface to the *Phenomenology of Spirit*, Hegel contrasts the proper 'coming-to-be' of science – which, 'in order to become genuine knowledge . . . must travel a long way and work its passage' – with 'the rapturous enthusiasm which, like a shot from a pistol, begins straight away with absolute knowledge, and makes short work of other standpoints by declaring that it takes no notice of them'.[1] While Hegel's targets remain unnamed throughout this preface, there is little doubt that something like the Schellingian position of 1801 is here intended.[2] It is, indeed, one of the most persistent prejudices against the variant of Schelling's philosophy under discussion in this volume that it lacks method, that it installs itself in the absolute straightaway ('like a shot from a pistol') without any concern for how to get there, that it enthusiastically and naively affirms immediate certainty of the absolute.

A classic anglophone repetition of this Hegelian attack is to be found in Michael Forster's *Hegel and Skepticism*. In order to rescue Hegel from the criticism that he 'acknowledged no epistemological responsibilities toward his philosophical system', Forster converts Schelling into the true culprit instead:

> Schelling, whose philosophy of identity had a decisive and lasting influence on Hegel, really was guilty of being cavalier in matters epistemological in much the way that Hegel is often wrongly supposed to have been. Thus, Schelling accepted his philosophy of identity in a crudely dogmatic manner as the gift of an alleged faculty of 'intellectual intuition,' understood as an unteachable, absolute precondition of philosophical insight the possession of which justified the philosopher in a complete disregard of all other viewpoints.[3]

Forster goes on to accuse Schelling of 'dogmatic appeal to intellectual intuition' and 'epistemological shortcuts'.[4] More recently, in 'Schelling and Skepticism', Forster has revisited this critique: the Schelling of 1801 (the Schelling of *On the True Concept* and *Presentation of my System of Philosophy*) is presented once again as an epistemologically naive dogmatist. That is, Forster insists that Hegel's criticism of Schelling as rehearsed above is applicable at least to 'certain phases of Schelling's career, especially to the period when Hegel first came to Jena to collaborate with Schelling, i.e., roughly 1801–2'. Forster continues: 'Thus, Schelling's *Presentation of My System of Philosophy* shows no real interest in skepticism, and instead presents its highest principle of absolute identity in a dogmatic way as a principle that stands in no need of demonstration.'[5]

To put it bluntly, according to this tradition of which Forster is representative, the Schelling of 1801 fails to grasp the significance of the problem of *beginning* in philosophy, of how to get going with due methodical and epistemic care so as to safeguard knowledge of the metaphysical structure of reality against sceptical attack. And the purpose of the present chapter is to contest this accusation – in part, at least – by demonstrating how, in *On the True Concept* and other writings that emerge out of the 1801 Schelling–Eschenmayer controversy, Schelling is not only aware of the problem of the beginning and the need to justify his methodology, but he does so at length in robust conversation with other idealists. The aim of this final chapter is, then, to show the methodological complexity in Schelling's philosophy of early 1801 and the central role *On the True Concept* must play in any defence of it. For this essay is one of his most extensive treatments of methodological questions in the 1800s, and yet its contribution to this issue is virtually ignored, especially in comparison to the attention given Schelling's contemporaneous doctrine of construction.[6] Schelling's practice of philosophical construction is certainly important for understanding his unique methodology, but there remains the question of how, according to Schelling, the philosopher is supposed to initially reach that position from which she can then construct reality in its absoluteness. That is, the significant studies of Schelling on construction by commentators such as Breazeale, Krings, Verra and Ziche (among others) do not fully address the above critique of Schelling as epistemologically 'cavalier' when it comes to the *beginning* of philosophy – that is, when it comes to finding a place from which the metaphysical structure of reality can be constructed. The following is meant to address this precise epistemological issue.

More concretely, our task is to demonstrate the centrality of the concept of abstraction to Schelling's methodological considerations of the period, for, as we shall see, it is with an act of abstraction that philosophy is to begin. And, indeed, this very appeal to abstraction already exhibits Schelling's radical difference from Hegel when it comes to the question of beginning. While this chapter, then, will argue that the Schelling of 1801 is not as epistemologically 'cavalier' or 'crudely dogmatic' as usually supposed, it will not do so in a way intended to please those sympathetic to Hegel. Schelling has an alternative vision of philosophical methodology, one that self-consciously and deliberately refuses the 'long passage' of Hegelian mediation.[7] In what follows we will suggest that Schelling has, in fact, a quite compelling methodology underlying his works of 1801, one that should be taken seriously as a genuine alternative to Hegelian beginnings.

'The reproach of abstraction'

'Think abstractly? *Sauve qui peut!*'[8] If there is one thing to be learned from German Idealism – particularly its Hegelian 'culmination' – it is the poverty of the abstract. The 'reproach of abstraction'[9] has become theoretical second nature, for 'the abstract universal . . . is an isolated, imperfect moment of the Notion and has no truth'.[10] However, as always, orthodoxy here obscures diversity: while 'abstract' does indeed sometimes function pejoratively in the writings of the German Idealists, this is not the whole story. A case in point is Hegel's own *Differenzschrift*, which is ambivalent on the nature of abstraction. On the one hand, there are anticipations of the mature Hegel in the critique of Spinozist identity as 'originating in abstraction' and of 'abstract reasoning [in which] the intellect drifts without an anchor'.[11] On the other hand, Hegel suggests that there is a positive form of abstraction, a kind of abstraction which provides the key to accessing the 'true identity of subject and object' as the casting off of what is 'peculiar' and 'one-sided' in scientific forms.[12] What is more, Hegel is explicit that not only is such a positive conception of abstractive methodology taken directly from Schelling; it comes, in fact, straight out of Schelling's dispute with Eschenmayer in *On the True Concept*:

> Abstraction from what is subjective in the transcendental intuition is the basic characteristic formula of Schelling's philosophy. This is inherent, not only in the passages quoted,[[13]] but in the very principle of his whole system. It is expressed even more definitely in the *Journal for Speculative Physics*, vol. II, no. 1, in the discussion of Eschenmayer's *Objections to the Philosophy of Nature*, objections which are *derived from the grounds of transcendental idealism* where the totality is posited only as an Idea, a thought, or in other words as something subjective.[14]

Taking Hegel's positive appraisal of Schellingian abstraction as our clue, we want to suggest in what follows that, in opposition to many orthodoxies concerning German Idealist suspicions of the abstract as stultifying, there is a *productive* conception of abstraction to be found in Schelling's philosophy of early 1801, and that this productive conception provides the basis for his distinctive account of how philosophy should begin. It is here one will find – beyond mere quasi-Hegelian 'reproaches of abstraction' – a properly Schellingian reflection on the starting point of philosophy.

One way to understand Schelling's method of abstraction is to turn again to Hegel, specifically the mature Hegel's 'limit argument' which he repeatedly deploys against the abstract thinking of transcendental philosophy. Although Hegel is profoundly critical of this form of abstraction – and although Schelling, too, will criticise significant aspects of this method – it nevertheless helpfully illuminates the existence of a distinctive methodology of abstraction at work in early German Idealism. For it is this methodology, ultimately rejected by Hegel, that Schelling will transform and promote as the starting point for a speculative philosophy of nature.

The version of the limit argument found in Hegel's *Encyclopaedia* runs as follows:

> It is the supreme inconsistency to admit, on the one hand, that the understanding is cognizant only of appearances and to assert, on the other . . . cognition *cannot* go any further, this is the *natural*, absolute *restriction* of human knowing . . . Something is only known, or even felt, to be a restriction, or a defect, if one is at the same time *beyond* it . . . There can be no knowledge of limit unless the Unlimited is *on this side* within consciousness.[15]

Or, as Hegel summarises it in the *Lectures on the History of Philosophy*, 'Kant says that we must remain at what is one-sided, at the very moment when he is passing out beyond it.'[16] Hegel accuses Kant of transcending the limits of human cognition at the same time as deeming such transcendence impossible; in order to discover the limits of knowledge, Kant must himself have already gone beyond such limits to recognise them *as* limits. Kant's entire critical project, therefore, seems to depend upon an impossible transcendence.

If the impossibility of such an identification of limits were not enough, Hegel's 'limit argument' suggests two further problems with transcendental thought. First, in so far as the transcendental philosopher *immediately posits* herself beyond the limits of cognition in order to determine those limits, the very method of critical philosophy lacks justification. Thus, echoing the *Phenomenology*'s line about 'a shot from a pistol', Hegel remarks that, on the Kantian standpoint, 'there soon creeps in the mistaken project of wanting to have cognition before we have any cognition, or of wanting to go into the water before we have learned to swim'.[17] The moment of discovering the limits of thought always occurs too soon: not only is it impossible, then, but it is also premature.

Finally, Hegel goes on to identify this impossible task of premature knowing with the *production of the abstract*: transcendental philosophy gives rise to 'the empty abstractions of an understanding which keeps itself in the abstract universal'.[18] That this is 'a radically abstract thinking'[19] is a direct consequence of the above. The philosopher who immediately transcends the limits of knowledge in order to determine them prematurely from outside can know them merely externally. She imposes properties on to phenomena from above, rather than making them explicit from within. Cognition is forever *abgesehen von*, set apart from, what is known. It is against such a paradigm of abstract and impossible transcendence that Hegel puts forward the model of immanent dialectic, which 'is not brought to bear on the thought-determinations from outside' but 'must be considered as dwelling within them'.[20] Dialectic is immersive.[21]

Generative abstraction in Fichte

Although Kant sets the critical project in motion, it is Fichte who first explicitly articulates the kind of transcendental methodology that is under attack in Hegel's arguments above, specifically in so far as Fichte thematises the philosopher's act of abstraction. In what follows, we consider this tradition of abstractive method in its own right – following the path set out by Hegel's critical indications above – as an enduring *alternative* to dialectical strains of German Idealism. Ultimately, it will be this method of abstraction that Schelling will transform into a radically anti-subjectivist practice that grounds a non-dialectical form of speculative philosophy of nature.

Abstraction lurks only in the background of Kant's epistemology. According to the *Jäsche Logic*, it is – along with comparison and reflection – an 'essential and universal condition for the generation of every concept whatsoever'.[22] It is on this basis that Osborne has argued that Kant gives an 'unequivocally positive epistemological value to abstraction as constitutive of the object of knowledge':[23] it is through abstraction that experience achieves objectivity.[24] Nevertheless, throughout both the pre-critical and critical periods, the essentially *sterile* role of abstraction is constantly stressed by Kant: while a necessary condition of the generation of the concept, abstraction is never sufficient – hence, the *Blomberg Logic*'s assertion that 'through abstraction not the least cognition arises'[25] and the *Jäsche Logic*'s claim that 'no concept *comes to be* through abstraction'.[26]

As so often with the Kantian legacy, it fell to Fichte to challenge the letter of the critical philosophy in order to do justice to its spirit. In this case, Fichte affirms the importance of discovering a form of abstraction sufficient for the generation of philosophical insight. Beginning in his very earliest sketches of the *Wissenschaftslehre* and culminating in the *First Introduction*, Fichte resorts repeatedly to abstraction to explain how philosophising is epistemically possible. For our purposes, it is worth considering four key components of the Fichtean methodology of abstraction.

Experiments in transcendence

Just as the young Hegel occasionally comments upon the productive capacity of abstraction, so, too, does Fichte recognise a form of abstraction that is generative in so far as it makes apparent aspects of reality that are not ordinarily evident. This is precisely the kind of act of impossible transcendence, implicit in Kant's methodology, that the mature Hegel will criticise. In the *First Introduction*, Fichte writes:

> A finite rational being possesses nothing whatsoever beyond experience. The entire contents of his thinking are comprised within experience. These same conditions necessarily apply to the philosopher, and thus it appears incomprehensible how he could ever succeed in elevating himself above experience. *The philosopher, however, is able to engage in abstraction.* That is to say, by means of a free act of thinking he is able to separate things that are connected with each other within experience . . . and when he does so he has abstracted from experience and has thereby succeeded in elevating himself above experience.[27]

For Fichte, abstraction designates precisely that free act by which the philosopher *incomprehensibly* rises above experience.[28] The human is defined as what is limited to experience and this limitation 'necessarily applies to the philosopher' – and yet, almost miraculously, the philosopher abstracts from her experience and thereby generates an impossible space beyond experience, a space from which genuine philosophy can be conducted. The philosopher thus manages to achieve what no human – as merely human – can achieve.

Hence, the impossible but successful experiment of abstraction founds philosophy, according to Fichte, and to this extent he adheres to the Hegelian caricature of transcendental methodology rehearsed above. However, Fichte counters the Hegelian position *avant la lettre* by contending that the type of knowledge that arises from this initial act of abstraction is not one-sided, empty or poor, but more contentful than it otherwise would have been. As Breazeale makes clear, central elements of our very being – for example the unity of our subjective activity and objective nature – 'become objects of thetic consciousness *only* within philosophical reflection, where they are *abstracted from* the full, rich context of lived experience'.[29] This rich context of lived experience is not *obscured* in abstraction; rather, by neutralising 'lived experience', its inner content becomes properly *philosophical* content – that is, content that can come to consciousness.

This initial act of abstraction is always 'an experimental enterprise',[30] a performance that one must freely undertake for oneself. Such an emphasis on the performativity of philosophising is, of course, a theme running through the whole of Fichte's works: one cannot be given the results of abstraction by another; philosophical thinking must continually begin anew with personal acts of abstraction until this becomes 'a new habit'.[31] What is more, for Fichte, it is the thoroughness of such experiments in abstraction that provides one of the crucial criteria for philosophical success. To quote Breazeale once more, Fichte 'believed that the purity of the philosopher's inner intuitions and hence the universality of his descriptions is, so to speak, *guaranteed* by the *completeness* of the initial act of free abstraction which precedes his series of self-observations'.[32] Thoroughgoing abstraction provides the warrant for proper philosophy.

Beginnings

For Fichte, therefore, abstraction initiates the practice of philosophising. Part One of the *Grundlage*, for example, opens with the statement that, 'Our task is to discover the primordial, absolutely unconditioned first principle of all human knowledge' and that 'this makes it necessary to ... *abstract* from everything that does not really belong to it'.[33] Fichte continues: 'Let any fact of empirical consciousness be proposed; and let one empirical feature after another be detached from it, until all that remains is what cannot any longer be dismissed, and from which nothing further can be detached.'[34] Or, as he programmatically puts it elsewhere:

> There is certainly no one among you who does not know that under the name *Wissenschaftslehre* I have labored upon a rigorously scientific transcendental philosophy, and that this philosophy is erected upon *what remains after one has abstracted from everything possible* – that is, upon the I. A science of this type can furnish no rule except the following: One should continue to abstract from everything possible, until something remains from which it is totally impossible to abstract.[35]

As we will see below, the Schelling of 1801 agrees with Fichte that a proper philosophical method begins in abstraction and then proceeds to self-construction.[36] On Fichte's version of the process, the philosopher must abstract from ordinary consciousness in order to attain the pure self-positing I, before going on to watch the I reconstruct reality before the philosopher's eyes. Philosophy thus 'retraces the path of abstraction, or rather, it permits the I to retrace this path, while it observes this process'.[37] To proceed with philosophical construction, one must first abstract.

An indifferent epochē

Abstraction is not negation. One does not actively cancel that from which one abstracts, but becomes indifferent to it. In Fichte's words, abstracting from being does not mean that one conceives of *non*-being, 'for by doing so one would succeed only in negating the concept of being, not in abstracting from it. Instead, the concept of being is here not thought of at all – either positively or negatively.'[38] The abstracted element is not posited in any form; there is a suspension of judgement (an *epochē*), rather than an antithetic judgement.

Fichte's insistence on the fundamental difference between abstraction and negation should be contrasted with Hegel's collapsing of abstraction into an impoverished mode of negation. Here, for example, is Hegel's definition of abstraction in 'Who Thinks Abstractly?': 'This is abstract thinking: to see nothing in the murderer except the abstract fact that he is a murderer, and to *annul* all other human essence in him with this simple quality.'[39] For this reason, Hegel argues that a properly speculative standpoint is not achieved through abstraction, but requires the philosopher to enter into the concrete experience of consciousness and follow the way that the logic of this experience negates *itself* and immanently generates the standpoint of absolute reason (a phenomenological process that involves self-negating negativity as opposed to sheer negation). For Hegel, it is by attending to the concreteness of consciousness – and unpacking what logically follows from the details of conscious experience – that one arrives at a speculative position in which consciousness is put out of play. This ultimate 'putting out of play' of consciousness is part of Hegel's Schellingian heritage – that is, his commitment to absolute as opposed to subjective idealism. But what is Hegelian through and through – and what has, in the years after Hegel, become orthodoxy among philosophers inspired by German Idealism – is the idea that to simply abstract from consciousness is to negate consciousness, and that proper thinking requires that one attend to the concreteness of experience.

There is, however, a line of thought in early German Idealism that insists forcefully on the *fundamental distinction between abstraction and negation*. According to Fichte, abstraction neither affirms nor negates what *is*, but rather, rises *above* it in indifference. In 1801, Schelling follows Fichte in conceiving abstraction as an act of indifference, but one which sinks beneath – rather than rises above – the concrete. The early philosophies of Fichte and Schelling, therefore, premised as they are on this initial act of abstraction, offer something different to the hegemony of dialectic, concreteness and immanent critique bequeathed by Hegelian thought.

The immune transcendental

Finally – and it is here that the stakes of Schelling's divergence from Fichte are provisionally to be located – Fichte proposes that one begin philosophising by abstracting from the *object* of intuition to isolate the intuiting activity itself. This gives rise to a problem in Fichte's account that we dub 'the immune transcendental'. The philosopher must 'tear himself away *from what it given*',[40] and what is left once the given has been suspended is the abstracting I, which functions as a limit, the unabstractable remains of what Fichte takes to be the most thoroughgoing procedure of abstraction possible. Fichte is clear on this: 'One should continue to abstract from everything possible, until something remains from which it is totally impossible to abstract. What remains is the pure I.'[41] Fichte seems to be arguing that this I is unabstractable precisely because it is what makes the activity of abstraction possible in the first place. In Kantian terms, transcendental apperception is a necessary condition for the possibility of any thought, including an abstractive one. In Fichte's words, 'You cannot think at all without subjoining in thought your self, as conscious of itself; from your self-consciousness you can never abstract.'[42] The transcendental condition of abstraction cannot itself be abstracted; it is itself immune from the process. The self therefore remains untouched by its own operation of abstraction. And this is how such methodological beginnings succeed at situating the philosopher immediately in front of the activity of her own self.

Immersive abstraction in Schelling

Schelling's *On the True Concept* marks a new stage in the thinking through of this practice of generative abstraction in German Idealism. However, what is strange is that Schelling makes use of this concept of abstraction as the primary means of *breaking with* Fichte. That is, he opposes Fichte through recourse to a concept that in large part was inherited from him. In particular, Schelling develops an understanding of abstraction as a method of *immersion* as opposed to transcendence – a version of abstraction that appears contradictory from the perspective of the mature Hegel's distinction between abstract thinking, on the one hand, and immersive, dialectical thinking, on the other.

As we have sought to demonstrate in this volume, from the very beginning of *On the True Concept*, Schelling is clear that a Fichtean interpretation of philosophy of nature of the kind propounded by Eschenmayer is false: 'Many people misled by the term 'philosophy of nature' expect transcendental deductions of natural phenomena . . . For me, however, philosophy of nature is a self-sufficient whole and is a science fully differentiated from transcendental philosophy.'[43] The radicality of Schelling's contention here should not go unremarked. It is sometimes thought that what unifies the German Idealist tradition, if nothing else, is fidelity to transcendental argumentation. However, Schelling is here denying that his practice of philosophy of nature can be situated in that tradition; it marks out an alternative, one based on rejection of this Kantian heritage. As Grant has put it, 'Schelling's post-Kantian confrontation with nature itself begins with the overthrow of the Copernican revolution . . . [Schelling precipitated] the fast overthrow of the entire transcendental structure Kant bequeathed his philosophical successors.'[44] Philosophy of nature is not only liberated from the dead hand of the *Wissenschaftslehre*, but from the argumentative framework of the *Critique of Pure Reason* itself – in the name of something different.

If philosophy of nature no longer involves a form of transcendental argumentation, what exactly is the alternative? Schelling goes on to aver that his alternative is so different from orthodox methods within German Idealism that it becomes almost incomprehensible to those accustomed to them: 'The reason that those who have grasped idealism well have not understood philosophy of nature is because it is difficult or impossible for them to detach themselves from [the methodology of transcendental idealism].'[45] The question is therefore to determine the nature of this break between the two methods.

To begin to determine it more precisely, Schelling first details what exactly is wrong with transcendental idealist explanation: transcendental argumentation remains bound by the concerns and structures of the self; it can never transcend these to intuit the workings of the natural world as it does *not* appear to the self. Schelling writes: 'If I [try] to find out what philosophising itself is, then I see myself merely as something known in myself – and during this entire investigation I never get out of myself.'[46] The transcendental idealist – that is, Eschenmayer as well as Fichte – remains trapped in 'the circle of consciousness' which is 'inescapable'.[47]

Such a philosopher is both the subject and object of her philosophical interest: she is the one philosophising and she is also the one being philosophised about, even when she is philosophising about nature, since nature is understood as that which is given to consciousness. As we saw in Chapter 4, this leads the transcendental philosopher to locate the source of the identity of subjective mind and objective nature *in the mind*. This identity of subject and object *in the subject* is the very core of the Fichtean system to which Eschenmayer subscribes. And, for Schelling, this marks that system's inherent limitation: it cannot account for a subject-object identity outside of or prior to the subject.

As became evident in Chapter 3, Schelling is not denying that nature is also a subject-object identity; he is merely asserting that the manifestation of the subject-object called 'nature' is partially obscure to the subject-object *of the finite I*. In Schelling's own words:

> The following objection [has been] frequently made to me: I *presuppose nature* without asking the critical question of how we thus come to suppose a nature ... I presuppose nothing for the construction but what the transcendental philosopher likewise presupposes. For what I call *nature* [is] the pure subject-object, what the transcendental philosopher posits as = I.[48]

He continues:

> I have therefore not presupposed what *you* think of as nature, but rather derived it ... In general, I have presupposed nothing but what can immediately be taken from the conditions of knowing itself as a first principle, something originally and simultaneously subjective and objective.[49]

Schelling's philosophy of nature will thus seek to derive nature *as given to consciousness* ('what *you* think of as nature') from nature *as such* ('the pure subject-object'). In Chapter 4, we considered in more detail this argument that a philosophy of nature worthy of the name must attend to the activity at work in nature itself, an activity more fundamental than the activity of the mind. At this point, we want to focus on the epistemological framework which allows for this turn to nature – and Schelling's methodological innovation becomes apparent when one notes that grasping the 'pure subject-object' can be understood as a version of intellectual intuition. What is known must be identical with what knows (the identity of subject and object); this premise, shared by Schellingian and Fichtean idealists alike, grounds the idea of intellectual intuition. However, at first blush, nature (in so far as it remains unperceived or is hidden from consciousness) is *non-identical* with the conscious I. How, then, is intellectual intuition of nature and so philosophising about nature possible?

In *On the True Concept*, Schelling explores two solutions, the Fichtean and his own. According to Schelling, the Fichtean solution implicit in Eschenmayer's version of philosophy of nature consists in altering (or potentiating) the object (i.e. nature) until it becomes identical to the subject: to raise nature into the mind and make it into a sensation or perception that can be fully explained in terms of the mind's operations. Yet, this is in fact no solution at all, since that which is not raised to the potency of consciousness still remains hidden from the philosopher. '[For the Fichtean] I can behold nothing objective other than in the moment of its entry into consciousness . . . and no longer in its *original* coming-into-being at the moment of its *first* emergence (in *non-conscious* activity).'[50] Schelling's own view is that reality exists at non-conscious as well as conscious potencies, and the latter are derivative. To limit philosophical method merely to the raising of reality into consciousness is therefore to foreclose the study and description of the lower, non-conscious potencies *as non-conscious*. Schelling thus writes that, by means of the transcendental method, 'I assume *myself* already in the highest potency, and therefore the question is also only answered for this potency.'[51]

The Schellingian solution to this epistemological problem is to proceed in the opposite direction: to alter consciousness so that it becomes identical to (and can therefore intuit) non-conscious reality. That is, instead of bringing nature into identity with consciousness (a process of potentiating nature), what requires changing is consciousness in order to make it identical with nature (a process of 'depotentiating' consciousness). The philosopher must reduce her intuiting down to the lower potencies, so as to become one with the unperceived, hidden natural world. That is to say, she must become like nature, must immerse herself in nature, to philosophise from the point of view of nature (the objective genitive implied in 'philosophy *of* nature'). Thus, for Schelling, the question of the possibility of philosophy of nature in fact runs: what need the philosopher do to herself in order to become nature? And the answer is found in *abstraction*. In On the True Concept, abstracting from consciousness is the practice that makes philosophy of nature possible by immersing the philosopher in the natural world:

> To see the objective in its first coming-into-being is only possible by *depotentiating* the *object* of all philosophising, which in the highest potency is = I, and then constructing, from the beginning, with this object reduced to the first potency. This is only possible through abstraction.[52]

Nature at *all* of its levels of productivity, not merely the conscious, can only be philosophically grasped through a process of abstractive depotentiation; philosophy shifts away from the high potencies in which Fichte's *Wissenschaftslehre* had been undertaken and scours the low potencies for clues as to how the higher potencies come to be. This form of abstraction fundamentally differentiates Schellingian philosophy of nature from Fichtean *Wissenschaftslehre* (and, by extension, Eschenmayerian philosophy of nature): 'With this abstraction one moves from the realm of the *Wissenschaftslehre* into *pure-theoretical* philosophy.'[53]

According to Schelling, this means that, in opposition to Fichte, philosophy of nature begins with abstraction from the subjective, *as well as* the objective – that is, from the consciousness of the philosophising subject as well as what is given to that subject – so as to access nature as it does not appear to consciousness. According to the true concept of philosophy of nature, philosophy must be taken to the potency 0, to its very depths, before gradually reconstructing reality through all its potencies, mimicking the productive force of nature. For Schelling as for Fichte, the philosopher must abstract and then construct; however, abstraction can take the philosopher in very different directions.

This difference is made particularly clear in passages from Schelling's contemporaneous correspondence with Fichte that closely parallel the presentation of the doctrine of abstraction in *On the True Concept*. Here, Schelling speaks of his project as 'the *material* proof of idealism' – as opposed to Fichte's formal proof – and he claims that this proof is achieved by means of an abstraction. Here is the full passage:

> The task is to deduce nature with all its determinations, indeed in its objectivity, its independence not from the I, which is itself objective, but from the I that is subjective and does the philosophising. This occurs in the theoretical part of philosophy. It arises through an abstraction from the general *Wissenschaftslehre*. Specifically, it is abstracted from the subjective (*intuiting*) activity that posits the subject-object as identical with *itself* in consciousness, and through that identical positing, it first becomes = I. (The *Wissenschaftslehre* fails to suspend this subjective identity and is for that very reason ideal-realistic.) What remains after this abstraction is the concept of the *pure* (solely objective) subject-object . . . The *I* that is the subject-object of consciousness or, as I also put it, the potentiated subject-object, is only the higher power of the former.[54]

This passage (sent to Fichte in November 1800) anticipates the argument set out in *On the True Concept*, particularly in its presentation of abstraction as both a suspension of subjective activity and a neutralisation of the *Wissenschaftslehre* itself.[55] It also emphasises the idea that such abstraction depotentiates: it brings the philosopher into contact with the same subject-object that is potentiated into the conscious I, but instead at a much lower potency – that is, the potency of nature. 'This ideal-real I, which is *merely* objective but for this very reason simultaneously productive, is in its productivity nothing other than *Nature*, of which the I of . . . self-consciousness is only the higher potency.'[56]

Perhaps most significant in the correspondence, though, is Schelling's further insistence that Fichte's own doctrine of abstraction 'is entirely and absolutely my view'. However, he goes on to argue that what Fichte does not realise is that,

> after this abstraction there remains an *ideal-real* item, but *as* such something purely objective, not grasped in its own proper intuition. In a word, what is left is the same that appears *in a higher power* as I; except you can easily see that it is not a matter of indifference for the result whether the philosopher takes up his object in the higher power (as I) or in the root.[57]

The idea of abstracting might be the same, but Schelling considers himself to have undertaken it in a more thoroughgoing manner (and one should remember that such thoroughgoingness was for Fichte himself the warrant of proper philosophising) as a means to take the philosopher to 'the root' – that is, subject-object identity prior to its potentiation. Thus, Schelling's more thoroughgoing abstraction, in which the philosopher does not merely abstract from experience, but also from the transcendental I immune to abstraction in Fichtean idealism, results in a fundamental change in the orientation of philosophical practice. For Schelling, abstraction is not a means of transcending to something higher, but to immerse the philosopher more deeply in the natural world.

Nassar has recently emphasised this immersive aspect of Schellingian methodology during this period. While, as she points out, for both Fichte and Schelling the possibility of philosophy 'depends on an original *postulation* or summons to abstraction',[58] what is distinctive about such abstraction for Schelling is that it is a call to '*participate* in the work of nature'.[59] This is precisely what Schelling is getting at with the immersive direction in which his doctrine of abstraction takes him – an immersion that justifies philosophy of nature as a distinct science, independent from those disciplines beholden to transcendental argumentation that remain trapped in 'the circle of consciousness'. The very possibility of Schelling's autonomous philosophy of nature depends upon his concept of immersive abstraction.

Förster's critique I: subject-object identity

Schelling's appeal to immersive abstraction – as a means of distinguishing his method from Fichte's – has recently come under criticism. In *The Twenty-Five Years of Philosophy*, Eckhart Förster argues from Schelling's appropriation of the Fichtean methodology of 'abstract first, then construct' to the ultimate incoherence of philosophy of nature as an autonomous philosophical project. Indeed, Förster goes so far as to base his entire critique of Schelling's philosophy on the doctrine of abstraction proposed in *On the True Concept*.

Förster's basic thesis throughout *The Twenty-Five Years* is that there are two forms of immediate cognition at play in German Idealism that scholarship has forever failed to distinguish, both originating in the *Critique of the Power of Judgement*: Fichtean intellectual intuition and Goethean (or, more properly perhaps, Spinozist) intuitive understanding.[60] And, Förster continues, Schelling's philosophy fails because it employs Fichtean intellectual intuition (based on a prior process of abstraction) in philosophy of nature when only Goethean intuitive understanding would be successful in making contact with nature. Förster thereby establishes his critique of Schelling in terms of the Fichtean argument already encountered above and eloquently expressed in Eschenmayer's *Spontaneity = World Soul*: (1) Schelling's philosophy is premised on the identity of subject and object; (2) but, in knowing nature as something unavailable to consciousness, the two are not identical; (3) therefore, there can be no speculative philosophy of nature. Here is how Förster puts it:

> As Schelling himself writes in the *System of Transcendental Idealism* – 'one always remains both the intuited and the one who is intuiting'. This is *obviously* not so in the case of nature: here that which is intuited and the one doing the intuiting are not identical. The intellectual intuition adapted from the *Wissenschaftslehre* is of no use in *Naturphilosophie*.[61]

Förster goes on to insist, moreover, that it is with *On the True Concept*'s doctrine of abstraction that this methodological problem becomes most acute:

> If intellectual intuition is to be retained as the method of our intuition of nature, that is only possible on the basis of a depotentiation (a suppression or neutralization) of the intuiting subject. The question however remains whether an intellectual intuition in which one abstracts from the intuiting subject can really amount to more than word-play . . . What exactly would such an intuition be, assuming it possible? [Schelling's] methodology, however, is wholly insufficient. And he is fundamentally mistaken when he infers that the method of cognition must be the same for both nature and the I, namely intellectual intuition, for he has clearly failed to learn the lesson of what I referred to above as Fichte's central insight: that 'I am' and 'it is' express two wholly distinct modes of being.[62]

Thus, according to Förster, Schelling's method of abstraction goes awry: it is an attempt to redeploy Fichtean intellectual intuition within an illegitimate domain.

Förster's resolutely Fichtean critique of Schelling is, therefore, ultimately threefold.[63] First, when it comes to philosophy of nature, intellectual intuition is impossible, since in this domain subject and object are non-identical. Secondly, Fichtean intellectual intuition is made possible by abstraction from what is objective; therefore, Schelling's claim that philosophy should abstract from 'the intuiting subject' is 'mere wordplay'. Thirdly and relatedly, abstraction is 'insufficient' in the domain of nature, for this method is only valid – as Fichte demonstrated – in relation to the I.[64] In what follows, we make use of each of Förster's criticisms as jumping-off points to understand Schelling's conception of immersive abstraction more fully.

As described above, programmatically at least, Schelling is committed to the identity of subject and object in philosophy of nature, and he is thus committed to the idea that abstraction does not violate this key epistemic presupposition for two reasons. First, because the 'pure' subject-object that Fichte labels 'I' is *also* nature, and thus philosophy of nature (as nature's self-construction before the eyes of the philosopher) remains subject-object throughout. 'With nature-philosophy I never emerge from that identity of the ideal-real', Schelling insists.[65] Secondly, as rehearsed above, the Schellingian solution to the possibility of an intellectual intuition of nature involves the knowing subject altering herself so as to become identical with the object of knowledge (i.e. the objective subject-object). Therefore, *pace* Förster, the central tenet of the *System of Transcendental Idealism* that 'one always remains both the intuited and the one who is intuiting' remains equally in force in *On the True Concept*.

However, the question of *how* subject-object identity remains in force has yet to be determined: we have still to adduce any evidence that it is possible, for example, for the philosopher to alter herself in such a way that she becomes – in some sense – one with nature. And, at an even more basic, logical level, it does not seem that abstracting from subjectivity would give one access to subject-object identity. That is, if what occurs in philosophy of nature is abstraction from the subject, then the subjective element of the subject-object (and so the identity of subject and object) seems to have been removed from the remit of philosophy of nature. For example, Schelling writes, 'If I now abstract . . . there remains something *purely objective*'[66] and 'I demand . . . an abstraction which leaves behind for me the purely objective [element] of this [intuiting] act.'[67] Such passages seem, at first blush, to put in jeopardy the identity of subject and object. We consider this issue in depth before going on to address to question of the possibility of abstraction.

One needs to be very careful in reading Schelling's claims about attending to the 'purely objective'. This is the second quotation excerpted more fully: 'I demand... an abstraction which leaves behind for me the purely objective [element] of this [intuiting] act, which in itself is merely subject-object, but in no way = I.'[68] That is, there are two notions of subjectivity (and so objectivity too) at stake here: one subjectivity which is removed in the act of abstraction and another which forever remains constitutive of the subject-object that is left behind after abstraction has taken place. Subjectivity as it exists *for* a finite, conscious self is suspended, *not* subjectivity *tout court*. To put it another way, according to Schelling, the Fichtean principle underlying intellectual intuition consists of the identity of subject and object *in the subject*, and so what immersive abstraction suspends is merely the 'in the subject' component of this principle – that is, merely the human subjectivity *for which* intellectual intuition occurs. The identity of subject and object *in itself* is left intact. In other words, Schelling wants to claim that the requirement for an identity of subject and object in philosophy of nature is not affected by the fact that philosophy begins with an abstraction from the subjective.

It is no surprise, then, that Schelling explicitly draws attention to the double meaning of the 'objective':

> Many philosophical writers... appear to have taken this *objective* [element], from which philosophy of nature should proceed, I don't quite know for what, but certainly for something objective in itself. So, it is no wonder if the confusion in their representations proliferates substantially on the back of this... For me... the objective is itself *simultaneously the real and the ideal*; the two are never separate, but exist together originally (even in nature).[69]

Just as there are two senses of the term 'subjective', there are two senses to the term 'objective' in *On the True Concept*. Schelling insists that these two senses must be kept separate. The argument can be reconstructed as follows. The very process by which the subject-object attains a higher potency is the process of nature *becoming an object* for a subjective *consciousness*. Hence, to abstract – or to depotentiate – is to undo this process whereby the subject-object as nature is cast as an objective correlate to subjective consciousness. Abstraction seeks to return the philosopher to the source of both objective nature and subjective mind, that potency of the subject-object at which no subject stands opposed to an object. One then reaches a point 'where the opposition between I and nature, which is made in ordinary consciousness, completely disappears, so that nature = I and I = nature.'[70] This is achieved when the philosopher manages to depotentiate to potency 0, or that being which is not potentiated at all. At this level, subject and object no longer stand opposed, for there is no consciousness to take a stand as subject over against an object. It is this merely oppositional deployment of subjectivity from which Schelling's philosophy of nature abstracts, not the subjective *in itself*.

Thus, when Schelling writes, '[Through] abstraction, I reach the concept of the pure subject-object (= nature) from which I then rise to the subject-object of consciousness (= I)',[71] one can clearly see that the task is not to abstract from something subjective to reach what is purely objective. Both consciousness and nature are *subject*-objects at different potencies. Abstraction reduces the potencies, immersing the philosopher in the subject-object identity of nature; it does not divest reality of subjectivity as such. The point being, to return to Förster's first criticism, that there remains an identity of subject and object even in the intuition of non-conscious nature (and so Schelling's tenet from the Preface to the *System of Transcendental Idealism* holds good in this domain).

Similarly, the above also puts into question Förster's third criticism, which runs: abstraction is insufficient to function in the domain of nature, since nature is a realm of the 'it is', whereas Fichte had already shown that abstraction, and indeed the whole process of philosophical construction which follows, applies merely to the realm of the 'I am'. As has become evident in the above, the very idea that the 'nature' of philosophy of nature is something lacking subjectivity altogether is false. It is only *human* subjectivity – in its biological and spiritual specificity – which the philosopher of nature brackets or puts out of action.

Förster's critique II: the impossibility of abstraction

The ultimate consequence of Schelling's commitment to immersive abstraction seems to be as follows: just as the transcendental idealist raises herself above the adulterated 'I' of ordinary experience through an act of abstraction, so, too, in a mirror image or subversion of the idealist, the philosopher of nature transcends 'beneath' the limits of consciousness into the depths of nature. Schellingian abstraction performs a kind of transformational enactment of the origins of natural becoming, in which, as Nassar described above, the philosopher participates in the very productivity of nature. The methodological opposition that emerges here correlates roughly to what is described by Deleuze in the Eighteenth Series of *The Logic of Sense* as two images of philosophers: the Platonic philosopher, who is 'a being of ascents', acts as 'the one who leaves the cave and rises up',[72] or, as Fichte himself puts it, 'Just as we were ushered by birth into this material world, so philosophy seeks – by means of a total rebirth – to usher us into a new and higher world.'[73] The Nietzschean philosopher, by contrast, 'place[s] thought inside the caverns and life in the deep ... [and so recognises] the absolute depth dug out in bodies and in thought'.[74] There should be no question, at this point, that Schelling follows this latter path, a path that leads into the material world and its creative activity.

And yet, this is perhaps too sympathetic a description of Fichtean abstraction, at least from Schelling's perspective. Schelling does not quite present abstraction in *On the True Concept* as twofold, consisting in either a practical abstraction that ascends or a theoretical abstraction that descends. In fact, he argues that the theoretical abstraction of the philosopher of nature is *the only* possible form of abstraction. The reason for this has become clear in the preceding: to abstract is to suspend forms of consciousness; abstraction is therefore subtractive or, in Schellingian terminology, it depotentiates. Thus, to rise to the highest potency of pure self-consciousness through abstraction, as Fichte wishes to, is to misunderstand the nature of the abstracting process as such, which takes one down the ladder of the potencies away from consciousness.[75] From this perspective, Fichtean abstraction is not only lacking in the thoroughness it seeks; it is not a genuine form of abstraction at all. This is the Schellingian rebuttal to Förster's second criticism – that is, that immersive abstraction is impossible.[76] Perhaps it is impossible to abstract from consciousness – and we will explore this below – but in so far as abstraction is, by definition, an abstraction *from conscious experience* – as the Fichtean herself recognises – then Fichtean abstraction is *necessarily* impossible, since it abstracts from consciousness in order to find itself, once again, within consciousness. As we argued in Chapter 4, Schelling's speculative physics aims to overcome – or, perhaps, abstract from – the remnant empiricism of transcendental idealism.

Of course, this does not blunt the full force of Förster's second criticism entirely; there are still ways to present Schellingian abstraction that quickly draw attention to its seeming impossibility. After all, it seems that Schelling is arguing that one gains knowledge of the natural world through a loss of consciousness! To philosophise, Schelling writes, he had 'to posit [the I] as *non-conscious* ... not = I'.[77] As one depotentiates or decreases the intensity of one's conscious attention, one intensifies one's intuition of nature. More is intuited through less – less action, less personality, less thinking; and the full reality of nature is grasped only when all of these elements of spiritual life are fully put out of play. Describing the Schellingian programme in this way makes Förster's second criticism particularly acute, for how can one know nature without consciousness? How can one philosophise thoughtlessly? That is, how is Schellingian abstraction possible?[78]

There are a number of ways to frame this objection to Schelling's doctrine more determinately, and we will consider one that particularly worried Schelling below; to begin, however, it is worth putting it in Fichtean form. For Fichte, one can abstract from everything in experience except for the act of abstracting itself. This is what we have dubbed Fichte's problem of 'the immune transcendental' above. To repeat the key quotation, 'All that remains after the abstraction has been completed (i.e. after we have abstracted from everything we can) is the *abstracting subject* itself'.[79] The activity of the abstracting self posits a limit to abstraction, a limit that Schelling's doctrine blatantly transgresses. Fichte's argument here is essentially Cartesian. Just as, in the activity of doubting, one cannot doubt the existence of the being that doubts, so too in abstraction one can never abstract from the being that abstracts.

The Schellingian response is simple: Schelling is in no sense *denying* the activity of abstraction, for *it is not a modality of negation*. Above, we pointed to this crucial characteristic of abstraction as elucidated *in Fichte's own writings*. Abstraction suspends; it does not negate. To abstract from the positing of the I is not to deny that it occurs, but to merely become theoretically indifferent to it. Therefore, it is perfectly possible to abstract from what is self-evidently necessary, like the activity of abstracting itself. There is no latent performative or pragmatic contradiction here, and therefore no limit to the act of abstraction: *pace* Fichte (and critics of Schelling such as Förster), it may in fact be possible for a conscious being to abstract from her own consciousness.

Even granting the above, however, there still remain problems for the possibility of Schellingian abstraction, chief among them: how can one be said to know or to be doing philosophy while abstracting from consciousness? To think while one has abstracted from thought sounds a fairly tricky, if not downright ridiculous, endeavour. This was a problem to which Schelling returned again and again: the possibility of non-conscious philosophy.[80] And his solution was always to search for models or exemplars for this kind of activity. One line of thought leads from *On the True Concept* to the mystical themes of his middle period. His interest in Swedenborg, for instance, has to do with the fact that this 'spirit-seer' gains knowledge even while extinguishing the self.[81] Likewise, Schelling's fascination with animal magnetism and other occult practices can be read along this trajectory. In *Clara*, particularly, Schelling explores the idea of a moment of 'waking sleep'[82] brought about by hypnosis through which genuine philosophical insight is possible: 'Only he who could do while awake what he has to do while asleep would be the perfect philosopher.'[83] All such experiments are to be understood as means to self-abstract, to depotentiate, and so to philosophise as a not-I. They are specific practices intended to induce something like the theoretical abstraction described in *On the True Concept*; through them philosophy of nature becomes possible. Moreover, these unorthodox methods are not the only practices

Schelling finds inspiring: more traditional (yet no less radical) inspirations for Schellingian abstraction include Platonic *anamnesis* and Spinoza's third kind of knowledge, both of which abstract from ordinary, empirical consciousness in order to access the essential truth of being. Here too, the self is temporarily suspended in the name of intuiting; philosophy is pursued by means of a loss of consciousness. Perhaps Förster is correct to claim that we cannot perform such a suspension of consciousness. But, if this is the case, then purely theoretical philosophy, philosophy 'without any subjective admixture',[84] is itself impossible. Throughout the whole of his life, Schelling fought against such a view. His doctrine of abstraction is nothing less than a defence of the possibility of philosophy.

In addition to addressing all three of Förster's criticisms, we are now in a position to acknowledge the sophistication of Schelling's methodological approach to the problem of the beginning of philosophy. It is true that some of the foregoing may never satisfy those sympathetic to Hegel, such as Michael Forster, for whom Schelling's Spinozist desire to reach the absolute 'as quickly as possible'[85] will always be suspect. Nevertheless, Schelling does not proceed naively: to the problem of how to begin in philosophy he responds with a doctrine of abstraction that is subtly wrought out of his debates with Fichte and Eschenmayer. Schelling may still get to the subject-object 'like a shot from a pistol', but the pistol he uses is nonetheless an impressive feat of engineering.

Abstraction and indifference

One of the key claims to emerge from the above analysis is that, in so far as one abstracts from what is subjective for consciousness, one abstracts from what is objective for consciousness, too. This is for the simple reason that one is abstracting from consciousness as such, and so from the structural opposition of subjectivity and objectivity that consciousness establishes. It is not the case that Fichtean abstraction merely suspends what is objective, while Schellingian abstraction merely suspends the subjective; rather, Schelling shows that the true process of abstraction – and the only one that is ultimately coherent – is one which suspends both the subjective and the objective *in so far as they stand opposed*.

While this feature of immersive abstraction remains merely implicit in *On the True Concept* itself, four months later, in the next issue of the *Journal for Speculative Physics*, Schelling returns to the idea of abstraction, founding his mature identity philosophy on an initial methodological moment of abstraction from *both* what is subjective *and* what is objective. The opening proposition of the *Presentation* reads:

> I call *reason* absolute reason or reason as it is conceived as the total indifference of the subjective and the objective . . . Reason's thought is foreign to everyone: to conceive it as absolute, and thus to come to the standpoint I require, one must abstract from what does the thinking. For the one who performs this abstraction reason immediately ceases to be something subjective . . . [Reason] can of course no longer be conceived as something objective either, since an objective something . . . only becomes possible in contrast to a thinking something, from which there is complete abstraction here.[86]

Abstraction is an act of depotentiation where both the subject and the object (in so far as they are opposed) are suspended, so as to isolate what Schelling here calls 'the total indifference of the subjective and the objective'. As outlined in Chapter 3, this opening to the *Presentation* is intended to turn philosophical attention to an a-thetic domain in which the logic of identity can be described prior to its positing in being. And the point here is that it is through an operation of abstraction that this domain is attained. By means of abstracting, Schelling discovers a philosophical space *indifferent to all positing*.[87] Indeed, according to § 1 of the *Presentation*, reason names that which remains after an act of total abstraction. This is the totalising form of absolute abstraction with which Schelling begins the identity philosophy. In opposition to Fichte's limit of the 'immune transcendental', Schelling conceives abstraction *without limit*, a totalising process that not only neutralises all that is given to the subject, but the subject – in so far as it is opposed to the objective – as well. Whereas abstraction reaches a limit in transcendental idealism, Schelling transgresses this boundary in the name of pure indifference.[88] Once again, therefore, philosophy is premised for the Schelling of 1801 on the disappearance of the philosopher; as he will go on to put it in 1804, 'In *reason* all subjectivity ceases . . . In reason, eternal identity is at once the knower and the known – it is not *me* who recognises this identity, but it recognises itself, and I am merely its organ. Reason is *reason* precisely because its knowledge is not subjective; instead, an identity in it comes to recognise itself as the self-same.'[89]

Here the identity philosophy begins – in abstraction. And it is a doctrine of abstraction, moreover, which Schelling most fully and explicitly works out in *On the True Concept*, in response to Eschenmayer's Fichtean provocations. Once again, it is to this short text from January 1801 that we should look to make sense of much of what Schelling is doing in subsequent years.

Appendices

Appendix 1

A. C. A. Eschenmayer and F. W. J. Schelling, Correspondence, 1799–1801[1]

[III/1 207] F. W. J. Schelling to A. C. A. Eschenmayer

Jena, 28 March [17]99

Next summer I will begin to issue a journal for speculative physics.[2] I wish very much to obtain some essays by your hand for it. I ask you to send me your answer on this soon. [208] As a fee, I can only initially promise 8 Saxon rt[hl]r.,[3] although I know that this consideration will not determine the matter for you.

I will happily undertake something in return for you, if it is within my power, and am respectfully,

Your most loyal,
Schelling

[III/2.1 184] F. W. J. Schelling to A. C. A. Eschenmayer

Jena, 10 Feb. 1800

For a long time now, I have been keen to remind you of the gracious promise you made to me some time ago to send me contributions for the journal for speculative physics.[4] A mass of other works, as well as other difficulties, have recently delayed the appearance of this journal – and thus an answer to your letter as well. Now, however, the printing has begun and further issues should appear at Easter. Might I now remind you of your pledge? – If you should have some treatise lying ready, then I ask you to send it to me as soon as possible, in which case it can still be inserted into the second issue.

I would love to write to you much about your excellent *Presentation of Transcendental Philosophy* in *Röschlaub's Magazine*.[5] It is the most perspicuous and penetrating [presentation] yet to exist. How very much I would enjoy receiving something similar from you soon.

Forgive me that this letter contains so little that is interesting for you. With the delivery of the first issue of the journal, I hope to write more to you.

With the warmest respect,
Yours,

Schelling

[237] F. W. J. Schelling to A. C. A. Eschenmayer

Bamberg,[6] 22nd September 1800

Is it permitted to stay silent almost half a year after a letter and such an agreeable present as your treatise[7] which I have received from Röschlaub through your efforts? At the time I received both [your letter and your treatise], I was on the point of leaving Jena to spend the summer here, and so was prevented [from replying]; scarcely after arriving here, circumstances impelled me to journey home, where I definitely hoped to speak to you in person, but the turmoil of war forced me, sooner than I thought, to depart.[8] And since this time, I have lived in much turmoil, and am now convalescing from an illness which made me quite inactive for many weeks.

[238] You will receive [with this letter] both first issues of my Journal for Speculative Physics, and I ask you to accept them from me with the friendship I have otherwise demonstrated and as proof of my truest respect. I very much wish to hear your judgement on many of the ideas expressed in the treatise on *dynam.[ic] process*, particularly your opinion on the whole idea of equating the 3 stages of the dyn.[amic] proc.[ess] with the 3 dimensions of matter.[9] – You have perhaps read my system of transc. [endental] ideal.[ism],[10] and I would enclose [a copy] if I had any to hand. Perhaps it has convinced you that, between then and now, I have not been idle in expanding the transcendental viewpoint across all the main objects of knowledge.

The reason why your treatise has yet to be printed is because there was no space for it in either issue. I did not want to break off for a second time the treatises interrupted in the first issue, and this, then, took up so much of the second issue that there was simply not enough space for your treatise, still less for an addition [to it][11] that I wish to make, so as to come to a complete understanding with you. However, it is now in press, and the first in the third issue.[12] Please accept my warmest thanks, in the meantime, for your frank and perceptive assessment that has done justice to a part of my *Outline*, as well as for the many superb ideas with which you have enriched me.[13] – Permit me still the wish to see you agreeing to definite participation in the *Journal*; [such a wish] is made out of the purest interests of science, to which I promise the truest benefits. Gradually, I hope that everyone concerned with nature-phil.[osophical] ideas will be able to unite in collaborative activity, and thus reach a middle point for the new physics from where it can spread and gain in scope. Ultimately, even the empiricists will be forced to think ideas that they now call incomprehensible, when they see that infinitely hard-headed and stubborn nature will be impelled to unlock itself for them.

Let me know soon whether I can assure myself of your continued participation in the Journal. Please send your letter here only with the address *bei Herrn Prof. Röschlaub*, as if it were to no longer find me here, it would in this case be immediately forwarded to me.

I commend myself to you warmly, and be convinced of my warmest respect and friendship, with which I am devotedly yours,

Schelling

[256] A. C. A. Eschenmayer to F. W. J. Schelling

Sulz a/Neckar, 20 Oct. 1800

Accept my thanks for the two first issues of your Journal which I received. They met me just as I had begun to rest after studying your transcend.[ental] idealism. What should I say of the splendid method of the latter? Your move into art and history,[14] which is as true as it is unique, provides merely a new proof of how harmoniously the principles of all science come together towards a single point. More and more the idea that philosophy works for its own annihilation becomes reality – that is, insofar as it squeezes its own life out into its various organs; in the end, it will no longer have anything for itself except the deduction of different constructing principles, each of which apportions its own sphere from human cognition [as a whole]. If philosophy's achievements in philosophy of nature, morality, art and history were to be replicated in mathematics, then nothing more that I know about would be missing. However, the latter still lays claim [257] to its inner autonomy against all philosoph.[ical] attacks, and protects its evidence (as it is usually called) against all probabilities. I am convinced that the success and favourable acceptance which philos.[ophy] strives to attain – in part for itself and in part for speculative physics – still depends, for the most part, on showing the mathematician that his principles owe their origin to our mind's necessary manner of acting, just as much as in any other science.

By means of the many bold and new things with which you have enriched physics in your Journal, you have led us, it seems, into an immeasurable field of investigation. Even without meticulous examination, your main idea that the three moments of the dynamic process are designated by the three dimensions is accompanied by a certain harmonious feeling that, in the universal system, things could only be arranged thus and in no other way. With this thought, you have without doubt completed the physical construction of the dimensions of matter, but the pure mathematical construction of the dimensions is still lacking.

With that, I will give my opinion that in the necessary and original actions out of which general arithmetic, pure geometry and the geometry of bodies all result the three dimensions of space are also present, and thus it must be shown that your first moment – magnetism – can be expressed through the principle of universal arithmetic, your second – electricity – through the principle of pure geometry, and your third – the dynamic process – through the binding of the previous two or the geometry of bodies. Before long I am going to undertake an attempt of this kind.

For some time, I was uncertain about your location and it pleases me very much to know that you are with our friend *Röschlaub*, to whom I ask to be commended.

Be well

Entirely yours,
Eschenmayer

[270] F. W. J. Schelling to A. C. A. Eschenmayer

Jena 3rd Nov 1800

Your letter, my dearest friend, indeed found me no longer in Bamberg, but was immediately sent on to me here. For me, your assent to the idea of the three dimensions of the filling of space is a strong external proof of its correctness. Because of mathematics, I left a great lacuna in the *Idealism*, which I feel acutely; it would please me so much more, then, to see it filled. It seems to me that the mathematician, just as much as the logician, has until now asserted his exceptionality by establishing his propositions – *the principles of which really emerge in another science* – in complete abstraction from [this other science]. This other science is undoubtedly natural science. It must be deduced how arithmetic, geometry, etc., come into *nature*. Your idea strikes [me] at first glance as an exceptionally happy one. I am already thinking of the magnet as the original 1, 2, 3 and as the image of the arithmetic line ascending and descending in one dimension.[15] With your perspicuity, you have to succeed at extending this idea far wider than I have so far been able to conceive, and I ask you to [271] get on with this work very soon. I would also ask you in advance to keep hold of your ideas on this for a scientific-critical institute that I will be editing in collaboration with Fichte from next year,[16] and which will critically consider all sciences in their relation to philos.[ophy] only in the highest potency – completely purged of all empiricism. For this, we are very much counting on you, since we know so few who value science so highly; and the discipline of *philosophy of mathematics* is particularly blank, so it should therefore fall completely to you, if you wanted to take it on.

In the near future, I hope to be able to send over to you the advance sheets of your treatise.[17]

Keep me in friendship, and live well,

Completely yours,
Schelling

[342] F. W. J. Schelling to A. C. A. Eschenmayer

Jena 8th May [18]01

I know my fault towards you, most revered friend. – The issue of my Journal, in which your essay is printed alongside my response, already appeared at the beginning of this year. Uncertain how soon I could write to you, – for I wanted to write at length, and in addition to lots of work, struck down with an illness which left me good for only the most necessary tasks – I gave the publisher the instruction to enclose an exemplar for you with the usual dispatch. I only realised that – owing to his carelessness – this was not done when the most recent issue appeared, which I now have the pleasure of sending to you together with that first one.[18] This perhaps relieves me of [the need] to set out at length the fundamental reasons for our differences, and [why] I am unreceptive to your repeated reproofs from the standpoint of idealism. Even in the most recent review of my Outline in the Erl.[anger] Lit.[teratur] Z.[eitung],[19] for which I give you my sincerest and warmest thanks, you still keep assuming that I *admit* idealism in the same sense you do, and because of this you always send me back to this system.[20] The Presentation of my System, published in the most recent issue, will show you that what is at stake lies still further back, and that we must return [343] to investigations of the first ground of philosophy as such in order to persuade each other. If I were so fortunate as to dislodge you to some degree or move you away from the point that you have now taken as definitively fixed, then our exchange could certainly pursue a much freer and more liberal path than possible until now.

I have thought of you a lot over the past winter. You know of Hufeland's departure.[21] He has yet to be replaced. It was obvious to think of our friend Röschlaub; however, everyone here is opposed to him. Other circumstances have meanwhile brought so much to pass that the position has not at all been filled for the time being, which is to be considered a genuine bit of luck, since otherwise we would have been stuck with some new mediocrity. – In the meantime, the good cause can gain strength, and I do not deny that I have often wished that *you* were inclined to enter on such a career. It would be far easier for you to be called[22] than Röschlaub[23] – and, for this reason, I wish at the very least to know your views on this, on giving up your connections with home – and entering into the new situation which, I can assure you, would soon be pleasant and desirable to you. What *you* – could be *here* for *science*, what you would be, I will not elaborate on. I am in the position to be able to take steps to this end, as soon as I am certain of your consent. You will find many friends here. – Your review of Hufeland[24] has aroused universal admiration. It was found to be fine, clear, deep and devastating in the politest way.

Goethe knows you and respects you. With one word, it is not impossible that you will be called; and it is quite certain that if particular circumstances do not prevail, you would find yourself here in a very desirable situation – one that would be utterly suited to your mind and character. – Answer me soon. – Your verdict on the 'Presentation' is very important to me, and I ask you to soon favour me with something. Be assured of my warmest respect.

Schelling

P.S. I count on you not forgetting the *Journal*, but rather adorning it further with essays by your hand. Do it from love of science. – You will receive the honorarium of 60 fl. soon either through Cotta's bookstore or by other means.

[357] A. C. A. Eschenmayer to F. W. J. Schelling

Kirchheim, 21 July 1801

The last issue of your *Journal*[25] has pleasantly interrupted the mental poverty in which I have been living for some time. Permit me to write below some reflections I have made.

Since you take absolute identity for the exclusive basis of your system, then your A = A is indeed in agreement with *Fichte's* first principle which in form and content is unconditioned,[26] but *Fichte's* second principle, –A does not = A, is no longer to be found in your system. That is, Fichte assumes an original opposition, and his –A does not = A is thus a principle which according to content is conditioned by the first [principle], and yet according to form is just as unconditioned as the first.[27] In your work, the original opposition falls away completely; for you, there is nothing originally positive or negative, but only [358] a difference in the magnitude of being (quantitative difference) or a preponderance of identity with itself, in which preponderance consists your A = B or subjective and objectivity.[28]

I confess to assuming with *Fichte* the A = B in an original opposition, and – according to form – just as unconditionally as the A = A, a bit like the dynamist who cannot resolve the infinite multiplicity of directions in space into one direction but only into two opposed [directions].[29]

The difference between the two premises is already expressed in the first construction and, in this respect, I am struck by your fundamental formula:

$$\frac{A^+ = B \qquad A = B^+}{A = A}[30]$$

The demand underlying your claims seems to run as follows. A and B should be one and equally identical, but, in the quantity of their being, the two should be so differentiated that, on one side, A and, on the other, B possess the same preponderance. This demand is satisfied by means of the construction of a line, in the middle of which falls an indifference-point, and on the left side of which the same A is posited in a specific potency over B, and on the right side of which B is posited in a proportionate potency over A. According to your construction, this line is:

$$\frac{A^+ = B \qquad A = B^+}{A = A}$$

Since, however, A and B are identical and their difference consists merely in preponderance, that preponderance must have a point of rest or limit, and so, on both sides of the line, a limit is to be inserted between A and B – a limit which, in terms of distance, is proportionate to the potency of A and B. Your line can thus also be expressed literally as follows: first, there comes a greater portion of identity (A^+), then a limit, after this follows a lesser portion of identity (B) and again a limit, and after this the point of indifference, A = A. Then comes a lesser portion of identity (A) and again a limit, and finally a greater one (B^+). The limit must always determine the preponderance and, according to your claims, separate subjectivity from objectivity.

[359] In order to now make clear what the mathematician will object to [in the above], it must be laid down that, according to your system, A^0 or $1 = B$, thus $A = B^2$, $A^2 = B^3$, $A^3 = B^4$, etc.

Objections to the constructed line:

1. How can $A^+ = B$ be posited, since $A^0 = B$. That is, there emerges a misuse of the (=) sign of equality. As much as I grasp that the left-hand side of the indifference point is meant to mark a preponderance of A and the right-hand side a preponderance of B – since both factors on both sides are connected by means of the (Ɛ) sign of equality – how can a preponderance emerge? If it were meant to be constructed according to the (=) sign of equality and with the lowest exponential A^2, instead of A^+, then the line would look like this:

$$\frac{A^2 = B^3 \qquad\qquad A = B^2}{A = A}$$

But then there would be no preponderance in the factors and much less in the way of equilibrium between the poles.

2. If one has no regard for the (=) sign of equality, but on the contrary [attends to] the demand that there is meant to be equilibrium between the two poles, then this too cannot be realised by means of the constructed line presented above.

Let one posit the lowest exponent A^2, instead of A^+, then the first part of the line is labelled $A^2 = B$, since in $A^0 = B$, then $A^2 = B$, [i.e.] B is three potencies lower than A^2. The second part of the line must then be re-oriented according to this proportion, and so will have the following shape.

$$\frac{A^2 = B \qquad\qquad A = B^4}{A = A}$$

Thus, just as in the first part [of the line] B is three potencies lower than A, so in the second part B is three potencies higher than A, and therefore there is no equilibrium between the poles, because B^4 is 1 potency higher than A^2 and A is one potency higher than B. In order to produce this equilibrium perfectly, the series must evidently look like this

$$\frac{A^2 = B \qquad\qquad A^0 = B^3}{A = A}$$

which deviates considerably from your line.

3. If you do not want to express mathematical equality by means of the sign (=) between A and B, but rather the metaphysical identity of A and B – and to do so irrespective of the fact that the preponderance of two factors requires a mathematical expression which one does not find precisely defined in this series – then you will [360] concede that the values of A and B in your system could be substituted for one another. For your $A^0 = B$ signifies no metaphysical but mathematical equality. If one now undertakes this substitution for that line where alone there is equilibrium between the poles, then instead of the line

$$\frac{A^2 = B \qquad A^0 = B^3}{A = A}$$

there arises the following two lines:

$$\frac{A^2 = A^0 \qquad A^0 = A^2}{A = A} \qquad \frac{B^3 = B \qquad B = B^3}{B^2 = B^2}$$

Since as a result of this substitution of the values of A and B – which the mathematician has an undeniable right [to undertake] – there is still absolutely no ratio that might be comprehensible [to the mathematician] evident in either identical line, then [one must conclude that] the philosopher alone must be able to justify this line – and so I now come to the philosophical part of it.

The philosopher will say: there is an absolute act in reason through which identity excludes one part of itself from itself, and thus a preponderance over itself is brought about – and through this, subjectivity is separated from objectivity. Therefore, on both sides of the above series, a limit or point of rest between A and B must be inserted – a limit which, according to the extent of the excess of the potencies, separates the greater identity from the lesser one, and in this way the above series can be justified.

Thus, the philosopher. He is to be replied to in the following way.

A and B are one and the same identity, only, here, A and, there, B marks a preponderance over the other (quantitative difference), but a preponderance absolutely requires, in the metaphysical as well as in the mathematical sense, a limit or a point of rest. If two identical [terms] are to be differentiated from one another, then this can only happen if something *heterogeneous* steps between them; for a limit is nothing in and for itself, it is only a negation for space. To separate identities necessarily requires a difference, and a preponderance in identity cannot be thought at all without difference; this difference is, however, not quantitative.

The question, whence comes this difference?, will now bring us closer to the truth.

Into absolute identity you insert *cognition* as an act, which – because nothing is outside of identity – is born from it. This cognition [361] is without doubt a self-cognition, which is infinite or rather can be repeated infinitely. Now, is this self-cognition anything other than a self-limitation, or rather, since we are speaking of identity, a *self-differentiation*? Since you insert this act of self-cognition *absolutely* into identity, is not difference just as absolute as identity itself?

In this way, I have now returned to the point from which I started, and the proofs that I have set out along the way are all of a kind to justify more securely my conviction that an absolute difference or an original opposition can be excluded from the basis of a philosophical system just as little as absolute identity can.

I don't intend to raise here what the logician has objected against it: that the concept of absolute identity has content only in opposition to absolute difference, that neither concept precedes or derives from the other. Just as little do I intend to start on the counter-proof which the psychologist has objected – namely, that the great diversity between subjectivity and objectivity, between thought and extension, is nothing but the preponderance of the identity of each – which is just as unlikely as if one were to say that time is merely the preponderance of space over itself.

With the remaining formulae that you have applied in your system, it stands the same as with the fundamental formula. For since A and B can be substituted for each other, then either subjectivity or objectivity can be completely discarded from your equations, and thus the formulae lose their true significance. This criticism does not affect my series and I believe it could be justified against the mathematician – something which I have already attempted in private. Since, in the construction of my series, I proceed from an absolute opposition, then A can absolutely not be expressed through B, except by means of complete opposition or, what is the same, by means of a complete cancellation of all identity between the two. For me, there is an unalterable limit between subjectivity and objectivity, and the point of indifference always falls in the middle – such that within the middle, what falls on the negative (ideal) series pertains to subjectivity, and outside of the middle, what falls on the positive (real) series pertains to objectivity.

I am limiting myself to the mathematical part and the basis of your system. Everything else is extremely interesting to me. As soon as you [362] have arrived at the separation of subject and object and assume opposing poles, I follow you with indescribable pleasure.

My work on philosophy of nature, which I intend to take up in the future, will proceed such that, as soon as aspects of the construction go beyond philosophy, they thereby enter into mathematics, and although I have for now only a narrow perspective on such a field, this narrow [perspective] is still so inviting to me that I have decided to subordinate all my other occupations to it. Within this narrow perspective, there is already contained the [hope] that I will be able to make use of many of your recent claims correctly. If, through my method, I have previously gone about it all in an empty fashion, then I believe myself compensated by the fact that my idea was a means to, at the very least, make myself more familiar with all parts of mathematics – and this has granted me abundant pleasures in and for itself.

The second half of your letter contains one of the most precious proofs of your amicable sentiments towards me,[31] and although in the present case I can make no use of your gracious offer, it places me in a debt to you that I will never be able to forget. In your amicable sentiments I immediately see that my judgement about your work should in future be submitted to you privately – something I prefer much more, since when it comes to literary differences, I would like to get beyond appealing to the public; for what does it concern the world if we want to better understand each other?[32] I will always make use of your responses to my doubts – which, owing to the economy of your time, may turn out as short as they like – to rectify my standard. This way of understanding each other seems to me far more affectionate and frank than any other, and the road to communication far shorter than if it were to occur by means of so many Midas-ears through which every judgement loses its achromatic effect.

Seeing myself in Hufeland's place would not seem to me too audacious an undertaking – especially as the literary focus in Jena may be extremely pleasant for me – if it were not at times so hot as to burn one's wings on it, and, really, I can't guarantee that my feathers, just like Icarus', might not here and there be stuck on with wax. Yet, I do realise that through the quicker and more liberal turnover of ideas my annual revenue of them would be greatly increased.

However, the worst is that I have no system for my science. My path to medicine passes through philosophy and I am still not far from the beginning. So far, I pursue my science *con amore* [363] and forget the systematic. Though I am familiar with all these systems, I think it worse to cobble something new out of them all, a bit like Hufeland,[33] than to have none at all. In brief, at present I am not suitable for a Chair of this kind; – I would have to wield a continual scepticism, yet for everything I attacked could suggest nothing better: this is to empty a Chair, rather than fill it. What is more, there are other objections, particularly my pleasant situation, which, besides my intimate family relations and a sufficiently busy practice, which is attractively confined within my excellent region, is eminently precious to me in [affording me] complete leisure and doing away with the need to act *ex officio*, learned and proper all of the time. Also, my last change, which was my third in three years, is still too new to wish for another one already. At any rate, accept my warmest thanks for your kindness and be sure that I hold very highly the loss I suffer by not relocating to Jena into close contact with you and other excellent men. Perhaps in 5–6 years I would have seized such an opportunity eagerly. Nevertheless, I admit that to gain a vocation importunely is for me an indelicate thing, as it means permitting oneself a judgement on one's own capabilities – something for which one can never be a competent judge.

Be assured of my respect and friendship.

From your,
Eschenmayer

Appendix 2

Principles of Nature-Metaphysics Applied to Chemical and Medical Subjects

A. C. A. Eschenmayer

[Extracts][1]

On Chemistry

[1] After getting rid of the particular empirical determinations of external objects, there remains for us still the concept of matter in general. It is now to be asked how, by means of the analysis of this concept, there could be established a priori principles suitable for providing unity to the systematic treatment of natural science, such that all its parts converged in one idea, as it were.

Among the natural sciences it is pre-eminently chemistry that makes a claim to the principles that set out the metaphysics of nature for the doctrine of nature. [Chemistry] is the doctrine of the qualitative relations [*Verhältnisse*][2] of matter and of the processes nature undergoes that alter [such relations]. [2] From this it is apparent that it will be the principles of dynamics above all to which chemistry devotes itself.[3] Dynamics teaches us that the existence of matter can be thought only under the assumption of the concurrence of two original forces – these forces are the force of attraction and the force of repulsion. This is not the place to prove this premise; instead, what follows is merely a brief glance at its salient features:

All matter is an empirical filling of space within determinate limits.[4] In this claim, there are two aspects at play: first, the cause of empirical filling; secondly, the cause of the determination of the limits of empirical filling. The first can only be grasped if we assume that matter fills its space by means of repulsive forces in all its parts, i.e. by means of its own force of extension. The second aspect, on the contrary, indicates [3] to us the assumption of an original force of attraction that attempts to limit the force of repulsion.

It needs to be remarked at this point that it is only from the metaphysician of nature's standpoint — which is to say, [from the standpoint] of proving the necessary assumption of these forces — that the duplicity of matter and forces, introduced so frequently into explanations of phenomena in natural science, can here be justified. Theoretical dualism in the natural sciences is actually postulated by dynamics, even though these origins are usually ignored. It is in this way that acids and alkalis, two electric materials, [or] two magnetic materials have come to be opposed to each other. Thus, Gren[5] assumes a gravitational force and an expansive force, de Luc[6] a gravitating fluid and a receptive fluid, Voigt[7] a male and female fuel, Prevost[8] a magnetic fluid formed out of two disparate elements. When properly understood [4] – whatever the concepts – the names are all that differ. The assumption of such a dualism is necessary as soon as one analyses the concept of matter in respect to the category of quality. However, this happens only inasmuch as we reflect on the principles under which we could classify the causal convergence of natural phenomena. Ultimately, such a dualism is to be deduced from the original positing and counter-positing that form the conditions of possibility of our very consciousness. It is because, in the past, scientists frequently did not perceive the origins of this dualism that different empirical determinations were regularly arranged into opposed concepts, which either could not be made to agree with [the determinations themselves] or, at the very least, were unproven. Thus, the correct principles were hypothetical. In fact, the pure expression for all these concepts, when applied to natural science, is [5] attractive and repulsive force, and it follows for the metaphysics of nature that [at least] one of these [forces] must act as a norm for the scientist from which he cannot depart, on pain of contradiction, when laying out his explanations.

Dynamic Principles

Matter is only to be comprehended by means of the assumption of two fundamental forces, and matter fills space not through its mere existence, but through [these] forces. Since the empirical filling of space is given in infinitely different ways to our intuition and [since] the multiplicity of a force consists merely in a matter of degree, these differences are also to be seen as [different] degrees. *Qualities* are thus degrees, and a degree of matter is some specific ratio [*Verhältnis*] of the forces of attraction and repulsion.

It is on this point that the dynamic [6] philosophy of nature is to be distinguished from the mechanical.[9]

In the explanation of specific differences in matter, the latter seeks refuge in what is absolutely full [i.e. atoms] and what is absolutely empty [i.e. the void], in the insuperability of figure in basic bodies. The former assumes a merely relative impenetrability, a mere ratio of degree between two original forces, and there is for it, in consequence, no empty space, even when [there is] uneven dynamic dispersal. In so far as the existence of matter is comprehensible only under the presupposition of two forces, the figure of the bodies cannot be given prior to the activity of these forces. Thus, the mechanical way of thinking must return to the dynamic. According to the dynamic, differences in matter can be just as great as the host of ratios that hold between the forces of attraction and repulsion.

In accordance with the various specific densities [7] of matter, differences in other sensible proportions [*Verhältnisse*] occur.

Since every possible proportion of repulsive force to attraction can just produce an inverse proportion between the space which matter occupies and mass, the differences in degree of those forces must express themselves in specifically different densities. If now the qualities are given with the degrees, then they must also change with the different densities.

This proposition might not appear to be fully in agreement with experience, but it follows immediately from the above. For that matter, if one runs through the tables of specific densities of bodies, one will find that not one specific density is ever completely parallel to another, although, on the other hand, it cannot be denied that the magnitude of this difference does not fully appear to stand in relation to [8] the magnitude of the difference in sensible qualities.

Chemical processes are changes in the ratios of degree in matter.

Chemical movement depends on the freedom of both the attractive and the repulsive force – chemical rest [depends] on their being in a state of constraint.

There is only relative freedom or constraint in matter, when one degree is compared with another. In the first case, the repulsive force has preponderance; in the other case, it is the attractive force.

There is no absolute freedom or constraint of these forces in matter. – For the concept of matter would thereby be annulled. In absolute freedom, the forces would be independent of each other, and an infinitely great or small degree of matter would exist, i.e. absolutely no degree. In absolute constraint, likewise the series of degrees would be annulled and the sensation = 0.

[9] Freedom of the repulsive force in some degree of matter is bound to deficiency of the attractive force, and, vice versa, [freedom] of the repulsive force is bound to excess of the attractive force.

We estimate the level of a degree of matter from the magnitude of the empirical filling of space. The repulsive force is proportional to the space;

the attractive force, on the contrary, inversely [proportional] to it. Thus, in any [body of] matter, the more the attractive force is deficient, the freer the repulsive force appears.

There is a maximum and a minimum in degrees of matter. All the degrees in between are middle-degrees.

It is in the metaphysics of nature that one proves that the force of attraction must be ascribed to a tendency to bring matter back to a point and the repulsive force to a tendency to expand matter into the immeasurable[10] – or that one without the other gives rise to the notion either of the infinitely big or of the infinitely small [10] in itself. If we designate the force of attraction with the letter A and the force of repulsion with B, then $A = 1/\infty$, $B = \infty$. Since matter is only comprehensible through the concurrence of both forces, then $A.B = M$,[11] if M refers to matter. M thus designates a unity – that is, $1/\infty \cdot \infty = 1$ generally signifies a finite number. As a unity, matter is capable of a maximum and a minimum in its degrees – if this were not the case, then it would be infinite and the concept of matter would be annulled. The degrees that lie in between are middle-degrees.

The force of repulsion is, with respect to our faculty of intuition, a positing, the attractive force a negation, because the former fills space, whereas the latter determines the limits of this filling.

Where the positive degree passes over into the negative, a zero must be posited in the ratio of degrees in matter.

[11] Finitude is no degree, but an indeterminable host of degrees can be thought within the finite; similarly, unity is no degree, but the increase or decrease of unity has a degree. $A.B = M$ thus expresses no degree, but in general only a substrate which is capable of a series of degrees. Since empirical intuition of matter occurs only in so far as there are ratios of degree in which the possibility of sensible attributes lie, M is to be considered as a zero, since it presents no determinate qualities itself. Since the positive series of degrees increases as the negative decreases, and vice versa, there must be a point at which the two are equal. Since the series of degrees is to be considered annulled in it, this point must present no qualities to our intuition; rather, M is, in respect to a series of degrees, raised at this point to the potency = 0.

From these properties, a general [12] series of degrees can be formed in analogy with a general series of numbers:

$$A.B^{+n}, \ldots A.B^{+3}, A.B^{+2}, A.B^{+1}, M^0, A.B^{-1}, A.B^{-2}, A.B^{-3}, \ldots A.B^{-n}$$

In this series, a common magnitude X is thought of as raised to a potency, and its value is the same whether I posit A or B as an unaltered magnitude.

For $A.B^{+n} = B.A^{-n}$. If I thus posit B as unaltered instead of A and reverse the series, then the two series are equal to one another. A and B are posited in this series merely as opposed magnitudes and nothing more, since the common X – through which the terms are raised to potencies – is undetermined. The task was merely to show, in virtue of a geometric progression, how a positive series of degrees passes over into a negative one.

If one further asks at this point how this series of degrees can be applied to nature, then for now it can merely be added:

[13] If M is raised to the potency = 0, then it imparts no sensible quality in intuition. But if it is thought in continuous degrees and series, then the empirical determinations of matter are given to us. If there are now types of sensations received through intuition, then they could correspond to the progressive terms [of the series], and the various types would be found each time through the interpolation of the two next terms.

Deficiency of the attractive force in one order is tied to the strength of the same force in another order and freedom of the repulsive force from one order is tied to the constraint of this force from another order.

If we posit that the substrate of degrees = M and also if the ratio of the fundamental forces is altered in M, it always [follows that] $A.^{-1/8}$ [14] is given with $A.B^{+1}$. When analysed, each middle degree decomposes into a higher and a lower degree. Hence, the higher orders in the upper series are given simultaneously with the lower orders.

What follows are now only a few proportions – fragments, as it were – extracted from dynamics, but which should act as the conditions under which chemical laws are to be further investigated.

It is self-evident that, among the remarkable properties that the metaphysics of nature derives from each force, we will possess fruitful material for the laws of natural science.

For example:

That the force of repulsion is a force of surfaces, while the attractive [force] is a penetrating force.[12]

That the former operates across three dimensions, whereas the latter only in one [15] dimension; that the former fills space, whereas the latter occupies a space without filling it.

That the former is a positing and the latter a negation, insofar, that is, as it expresses a limit, a negation of the real.

That the former incorporates the notion of the infinitely big and the latter the notion of the infinitely small, whereas both together incorporate the notion of the finite in itself.

All these properties can be valuable in their application to natural science and supply new results; at the very least, the philosopher of nature will necessarily make recourse to their empirical laws and their conditions, if he wants to give them the stamp of necessity. And it is impossible to find the unity of the manifold in knowledge of nature anywhere but in such principles.

[. . .]

Appendix 3

Deduction of the Living Organism

A. C. A. Eschenmayer

[Extracts]¹

Preface

[329] [To describe] which systematic approach to take in medicine, from the standpoint at which the progress of the last decades has placed us, is a task that places us in no small discomfort.

We have seen a manifold struggle before us, systems followed by systems, theories, hypotheses – here set against one another, there united together into a third – principles inferred back from experience, which, when established as principles, soon lost their universality after further observation. Always driven on by the need for a unity of principles, we seized onto this or that opinion, held to it for a while, before returning unsatisfied to ourselves. Always we strove to circumscribe the outer limits of our scientific domain, insert the middle terms, so that [the limits] could finally touch in the middle. But this task soon broke down with the insight [330] that our domain was still too restricted, that our outer limits were themselves still middle terms. From the comparison of a host of experiences emerged a rule, from the comparison of a host of rules emerged a principle. We saw that such a principle expressed the unity of all our experiences even less than our source of experience was able to be thereby exhausted; and yet we seduced ourselves with the hope that what we have yet to experience would conform to this principle, even if later observations taught otherwise. Tired of these unavailing attempts we even intervened in a foreign domain (chemistry),² which presented itself as just as empirical as our own, but in this case because of the novelty of its conquests; we searched for principles there, this lasted a while and we returned discontented.

With all these efforts, we were unable to acquire anything of nature, to walk alongside the tranquil movement of the living organism, always identical with itself yet always changing in itself according to unchangeable laws, and it returned as a problem, always renewing itself from one decade to the next.

[331] Where now to begin? Where to end? The sum of knowledge has grown into a mass; to sort it out is [a task which] we must completely abandon out of hand. Before we may even contemplate such a burden, we need to know our own capacity for all of this – and, thus, there is left to us only one remaining refuge – *philosophy*: it is not merely intimately acquainted with our art [of medicine], it is its mother, regardless of what people may have said about its limited influence.

Opinion is divided over whether one should raise our art to the worth of a science, whether our reasoning could extend beyond an experience that had been heightened by induction and analogy – this is as fiercely disputed as it is defended. Meanwhile, it must be worth the attempt nonetheless.

Without now investigating in any detail the main points of contention for the two parties, I just want to bring to light in a few words the whole remarkable task.

Self-consciousness is an undeniable fact in us; it is just as certain as the expression: that we are we. The object of the medical arts is the living organism.

[332] If now it can be proven that the living organism must be included precisely among the necessary conditions of self-consciousness – that, without [the living organism], no explanation at all of this fact [of self-consciousness] would be possible – then we would have secured for medicine its object in a completely a priori manner.

No aspect of experience creeps into the investigation here: the organisation [i.e. organism] lies in experience, of course, but in order for it to be found to be a necessary condition of self-consciousness, we must reason to its existence completely a priori. I understand this procedure as the *deduction of the living organism*.

Now it must be remembered. – This investigation precedes all medical arts: the physician finds his object solely at the end, as the result of it. It is here not at all an issue of a law, of a principle for the medical arts, but merely of its object and, before this is given, there is also no speculative activity on the part of the physician: he can find no law, no principle, if the object of this activity has not already been made available to him.

It might of course appear odd that I want to discover in a merely a priori way the physician's object, which has been manifest [333] for thousands of years in experience: my intention is merely to make medicine philosophical and, to this end, this *deduction* is the *absolutely first step*. It is not enough for us that we possess such an object necessarily in experience, we want to know *how* it necessarily arises thus. Whoever there are among physicians who may not wish to merely and exclusively philosophise for philosophy's sake should not be too troubled by this essay: for as a physician, he will learn nothing here at all except what he has already experienced from time immemorial – *his object*.

What is more, in this essay, I have touched on the main features of the whole of philosophy, and, with regard to this magazine's remit, this requires some apology.

If the claims of our principal philosophers besides *Kant*, e.g. *Fichte*, *Schelling* and many others (who have already provided so many excellent useful hints for medicine), were to be widespread among physicians, then I would be able to take them for granted and so the deduction would be much shorter.

My excuse thus runs as follows – I am claiming to secure the physician's object a priori; this is done by showing him that [334] just this object is found under the necessary conditions of self-consciousness. Now there is, on the other hand, no self-consciousness without spontaneity and no consciousness of the represented thing without self-consciousness, and thus everything is intertwined as mutual conditions. Therefore, I hope that it will not cause the thinking physician, to whom this magazine is devoted, any displeasure to join me in describing the brief outline of the main features of philosophy, so as to gain a more complete insight into the deduction which secures his object for him, nor [any displeasure] to tarry with me among the truths of more profound speculation, which are so perfectly tangled up in the connections between all the sciences.

Main Features of Philosophy

[335] The path which philosophy is given to describe is a circle. The *I*, intuiting itself in its *original productions* and *limitations*, must itself return once more to the point from which the philosopher begins, before reason yet exists for itself. The philosopher thus begins with *all of the I's original acts*, which he can only watch from his higher point of reflection, and reaches an end in *self-consciousness* in which precisely *those acts* exist for the *I* itself. If he remains merely at the initial point, then his system is incomplete. The I is evidently made present in the knowledge of the philosopher, and this might be transmitted from philosopher to philosopher, but it has not yet been shown how reason itself arrives at the expression of the *I* (where the predicate is left empty to infinity): it is not yet conscious. Only with the deduction of this [element] is the system complete in itself, and for this insight [336] we have the more recent philosophy to thank.

The philosopher explains *facts*. In his theoretical capacity, two such facts exist (all others are contained in one or other of them). One of these facts is *consciousness of things outside of us and of representations in us*, the other is *self-consciousness*. To explain these facts is to specify the unique possible conditions under which they arise.

The most obvious objection against this, but also the only objection, runs as follows: who is claiming to explain it? Presumably consciousness itself. – Consciousness is claiming to enter into consciousness and explain itself from itself; it is claiming to become its own object – how is this possible? If this objection cannot be resolved, then the condition of all philosophising falls away, for – if consciousness is posited, then its original acts have already been undertaken; if the fact is posited, then its emergence from its conditions has already occurred – but these are precisely what the philosopher wants to explain. It will be shown that this objection is well founded to some extent. Consciousness is *finite*, and it needs to be explained; when we say: *explain*, [337] we are already in the domain of the finite. From our customary point of reflection, everything in consciousness is already occurring as a determinate finite thing, which is to be explained from another determinate finite thing. [However,] the *finite in general* cannot be further explained from the finite, but only from the infinite; [yet] the infinite cannot be encompassed in consciousness, otherwise it becomes finite. Hence, it is clear that consciousness cannot grasp its condition of possibility, and for this reason cannot be explained on the basis of such a condition. Now, it is equally certain, on the other hand, that such *explaining* is, at the very least, given as a demand of our synthetically progressing reason. The idea of the infinite is no product of the theoretical faculty, but of the practical faculty, and is just posited at the foundation of the theoretical faculty: [this demand] is thus not one of explaining, but of receiving, just as the idea of *pure duty* is also not explainable, but is only perceptible within our breast. Insight into this demand is now the very higher point of reflection for the philosopher: he stands at the transition from the transcendent to the transcendental, just as [338] the customary points of reflection stand at the transition from the transcendental to experience.

Now a glance at how this dense exposition progresses.

The first fact – *the I posits things outside of itself* – is without doubt completely opposed to the second – *the I posits itself*. Thus, the principle which grounds the first fact is also to be opposed to the principle that grounds the second. However, the whole is a circle: the second principle is thus to be placed at the point at which the deduction returns [to the beginning] after finishing with the first [principle]. There are thus two essential viewpoints: the first from which the philosopher merely watches reason acting; the second from which he shows how the *I* itself commits to its acts. In his doctrine of science [*Wissenschaftslehre*], *Fichte*, who first clearly established the original acts of the *I*, always placed the deductions from the two principles next to each other: he always first reflected as a philosopher on the acting *I*, and then made a reflection on that reflection, by which reason could raise itself to expression: I feel, [339] I intuit, I represent, etc. In this presentation, the two viewpoints have been separated, so [will] perhaps thereby gain some clarity.

It is now sufficiently well known within philosophy that without our practical faculty the theoretical [faculty] would not be present, that even the deduction of *representation* cannot be completed without the concept of striving (which concerns only what is practical); and so, that the I really rests on the reciprocity [*Wechselwirkung*] of *intelligence* and *freedom*, i.e. on its reciprocal relation with itself. I have initially just recorded these ideas in this presentation, [but] it will be shown how everything that pertains solely to the theoretical faculty arises from them in complete harmony.

Without doubt, he who freely decides to philosophise is conscious of the sphere of his free reflection and free production. The philosopher attends to them and, as a result, ascribes these two opposed faculties to reason as such.

However, the I is only *free* to the extent that there is also *something necessary* which does not depend on it but, on the contrary, [340] on which it depends: free activity is opposed to necessary [activity]. To the extent that the I acts necessarily, it is *intelligence*: it must include the given in its representation; – to the extent that it acts freely, it is *spontaneity*: it produces something in itself (the intended-concept) and something outside of itself (the product of art). However, in general, the I must act and the philosopher expresses it conveniently with the imperative: *you shall act*.

[. . .]³

Deduction of Consciousness

[343] To begin, some fundamental principles. –

The faculty of achieving the infinite [i.e. production] is, according to its product, equal to the infinitely large $= \infty$. The faculty of returning into oneself from the infinite [i.e. reflection] is in respect to the product equal to [344] the infinitely small $= 1/\infty$. In their unity, they give something finite in general, $\infty \cdot 1/\infty = 1$.

Just as these principles are valid, so too must the following be.

If the I were to act with both faculties *at the same time* [i.e. the imperative of necessary activity], the expressions of the two faculties would cancel each other out: finitude in general would be the result of this mutual cancelling-out. However, nothing would come into being for the I, because these faculties would stand in absolute equilibrium. For absolute finitude is an idea, and the I can only grasp a determinate finite thing.

If the I were to express itself with its faculties successively or individually [i.e. the task of free activity], once again nothing would come into being: its [faculty of] infinite production would dissipate into the infinite and so would differentiate nothing there; its [faculty of] infinite reflection would return to one point and likewise nothing would be present.

We go further: the imperative [of necessary activity] states: you should act [with all your faculties] *at the same time*. The task [of free activity] states: I want to act [with my faculties] *one after the other*. Each, however, stands in reciprocal influence to the other; as a result, the two faculties cannot express themselves either *at the same time* or *one after the other*: between simultaneity and succession, [345] a middle term must be inserted, and thus a third emerges which consists neither completely in simultaneity nor completely in succession. The imperative demands acting simultaneously; the I tries, it becomes inhibited by that part of spontaneity that [participates] in the reciprocal influence, and which the I cannot be conscious of in this position [of absolute freedom] – hence the feeling of necessity in these concerns. [The I] cannot therefore express itself simultaneously with two opposed faculties; in fact, it is precisely the fact that it *should* and *cannot* that brings about a conflict in it – a conflict which is now distinguished as a *striving* that demands to be causal yet cannot achieve it. And it is precisely this striving that is now the middle term that steps between simultaneity and succession. What is more, it is a conflict which sometimes gives *preponderance* to one faculty of the *I* and sometimes to the other, even if according to a strict rule – and precisely this preponderance resolves the most difficult task of our whole theoretical faculty.

We will keep to formulae, and it will all become clearer.

Let one take A for infinite production, [346] B for infinite reflection, and construct the following series.

$$A^{-\infty}.B \ldots A^{-n}.B \ldots A^{-2}.B \quad A^{-1}.B \quad A^{0}.B \quad A^{+1}.B \quad A^{+2}.B \ldots A^{+n}.B \ldots A^{+\infty}.B$$

The nature of this series is as follows: B is constant throughout; A on the contrary is raised in both the negative and positive potencies to a specific magnitude = x. It describes a dynamically increasing series in reason, and it would be real if the interpolation between every two terms were continued into the infinite. The side of the negative terms designates the negative direction of the series, the side of the positive terms the positive direction. The application of the series is as follows: in $A^0.B$, the two infinite faculties of the I, posited as opposed to each other, are bound to each other; in potency = 0, they are equal to one another and so become absolute finitude or unity, $\infty.\frac{1}{\infty} = 1$. If you alter the absolute equality pertaining to $A^0.B$, as occurs in virtue of the *striving* in reason, there arises the positive and negative terms in both directions, in which one of the faculties is preponderant.

I will be clearer still. – Say reason expresses itself with faculty A and simultaneously – [347] as a result of the imperative [of necessary activity] – with faculty B. What then comes about? The former strives into the infinite, the latter strives to a point; both would therefore meet in the middle and maintain absolute equilibrium – this would be $A^0.B = 1$, absolute finitude thought as unity. I call this state, in respect to the above imperative, the *tendency* to *absolute equilibrium*.

Now, according to the above, this [absolute equilibrium] cannot be the case; each [faculty] cannot annul the other in its expression. It is prevented by the task [of free activity] which stands in a reciprocal relation to [the idea] that they should merely be mutually exhausted in each other. With production (A), the *I* thus proceeds necessarily beyond the limit of $A^0.B$; now reflection (B) converges with production (A) and there now arises $A^{+1}.B$ – a state in which the faculty of production has preponderance.*[4]

However, both faculties should be equal to one another in their expressions and the demand for equality [348] endures, for they are both infinite, and [it is] only in virtue of having to [act] and being unable to [act] that one faculty remains preponderant. They must balance each other. Once again, the I acts with faculty A, but this time faculty B has preponderance; production can no longer reach the middle, but must remain within the limit of $A^0.B$, just as previously it proceeded beyond it – and so there now arises $A^{-1}.B$ – a state in which the faculty of reflection has preponderance.

Thus, from having to [act] and being unable to [act] there necessarily follows a preponderance of one faculty over the other, just as necessarily as, from the very same reason, there follows the *momentary balance* of both faculties, and thus their reciprocal exhausting in each other without ever losing equilibrium. For $A^{-1}.B$ stands in equilibrium with $A^{+1}.B$, and this I call *relative equilibrium*.

[349] Now we have three terms in this series, which can be extended indeterminately on both sides:

$$A^{-1}.B \quad A^0.B \quad A^{+1}.B$$

These three terms arise initially from the original, necessary acts of reason; they themselves contain the *schema of consciousness*. The terms are the

---

* One could ask why faculty A should express itself first, and there is no other reason [for this] except that the positive precedes the negative, positing [348] precedes opposing. In his *Doctrine of Science [Wissenschaftslehre]*, this is what *Fichte* means to express with the first, absolute principle.

ladder along which occur appearing and disappearing accidents, and, to this extent, consciousness is nothing but constant mutation. The limit is the middle point at which [consciousness] is identical with itself; at [this middle point] there is a mere reciprocal relation between two opposed terms, and the productive imagination is the wonderful faculty that holds the mutating terms together. What lies beyond the limit $A^0.B$ is revealed as the thing; what lies within the limit as the representation; each stands in a necessarily reciprocal relation to the other. In the thing, production has preponderance; in representation, reflection; but both together give a unity: $A^{-1}.B \times A^{+1}.B = A^0.B = 1$ – and this is the *unity of consciousness*.

[...]

Short Overview

[376] In our nature, just as we are this particular human being and can recognise the humanity of one another, there are two indubitable facts that pertain to our faculty of cognition: *consciousness of represented things* and *self-consciousness*. Whoever means to philosophise (and this is a decision made without any compulsion) must explain them. How does the philosopher explain? The philosopher is a human; he has already long been acting; in him occurs the *serialisation of conditions* from which the above [two] facts result and which has already long been there. He proceeds from this point, from the *customary point of reflection on the facts*; however, the conditions lie beyond the facts. The theoretical philosopher must therefore raise himself above [this viewpoint], and this is the *higher point of reflection*. This elevation is obviously no theoretical act, but a practical one; it is merely present in us as *a demand*. Hence, the *conditions of the facts* are not capable of being *explained*, but *only of being received*, such as a *commandment of pure duty*. [The conditions] lie [377] in the infinite, but the *serialisation of those conditions* is a theoretical act, which means: *theoretical philosophy*. The philosopher pursues his deductions until all the explanatory grounds of those facts are exhausted; and at the moment they are exhausted, he arrives once more at that point from which he began – and so it is in this way that the *limit and content of all theoretical philosophy* are determined.

From the common standpoint, the philosopher is conscious of a necessary and a free manner of acting: in free acts, he is conscious of his free reflection (forming concepts) and his free production (realising concepts); he notes this and ascribes himself these two opposed faculties. In the necessary manner of acting, he must think away this freedom, abstract from it and this is done by presupposing an imperative: you shall. However, what does the freedom that should be annulled consist in? Exclusively in the choice to reflect or to produce: in the free use of the former or latter faculty for itself. Freedom can thus be expressed as the task: *I want to use these faculties* [378] *individually*, or *I want to act with all my faculties one after another*. The choice is annulled by the opposite [claim]: you shall not use a faculty for itself, or I want to act with all of my faculties – *you shall act with all your faculties – simultaneously*. Thus, we have an imperative for the necessary manner of acting, and a task for the free [manner of acting], and each stands in reciprocal influence to the other.

Concerning the imperative –

The philosopher does not explain these faculties, but only their necessary manner of acting: in order to discover this, he must construct, but he must also possess the moments of the construction – and here something very beautiful is shown, that is, the descent through three fundamental principles from the practical to the theoretical terrain, from the transcendent to the transcendental.

The first fundamental proposition is: *both of the opposed faculties are infinite – (practical demand, – transcendent).*

Second fundamental proposition: *because they are both infinite, they are equal to each other – (transition to the transcendental).*

[379] Third fundamental proposition: *because they are equal, they cancel each other out in their expressions (theoretical cognition, transcendental).*

No investigation of these principles is possible any longer; they are valid because there is a fact and the fact is there because they are valid. We must remove all predicates – something achieved by means of the expression 'infinite' – in order to come to a fact (consciousness) which contains all predicates. We must go beyond everything finite, in order to come to a fact which contains everything finite. These principles are the conditions of all philosophising: whoever does not know them can be anything except a philosopher.

They are the conditions of all analysis and all synthesis; two opposites are equal to each other – this is the condition of all synthesis – the equal consists of two opposites, this is the condition of all analysis. In them lies the identity of the I and its opposition with itself.

From the customary point of reflection, one says merely: two infinite forces are equal to each other – but these forces are products of masses at speed. [380] From the higher point of reflection, there are no finite products – our first product is finitude itself, and then forces first occur. The imperative [of necessary activity] and the task [of free activity] stand in a reciprocal relation; they thus limit each other: the imperative demands absolute finitude, the task strives to the infinite; therefore, a middle term must be inserted to bind the two. However, within this middle term, where is the limit separating necessary acts from free acts? We already know from the [above] inferences that when simultaneous acting has the upper hand, the series emerges on the side of the necessary [manner of acting]. Because spontaneity inhibits the imperative [pertaining to the necessary manner of acting], a striving is produced, and from this follows that which is derived from the necessary manner of acting – that is, consciousness, sensation and intuition, space and time. The categories or reason paved the way for the transition from absolute necessity to spontaneity. Reason is the middle faculty which lies between the imperative [of necessity] and the task [of freedom]. Because of the imperative which constrains spontaneity, there emerges – instead of annihilation – mere separation, abstraction from representation; instead of creation, the mere binding and formation [381] of material – and from this follows what is derived from the free manner of acting, that is, the entire series of the ideal whole, intentional concepts and their corresponding products.

This, then, is how the deduction of the philosopher goes, in so far as he watches the I in its necessary and free acts. However, the I exists for itself; it forms at any given moment the expression: *I* – and the philosopher exhibits this fact in his deduction of self-consciousness.

Thus, at both ends of the line the two facts are grasped: the I proceeds to one of them from itself and at the other returns to itself.

[. . .]

Appendix 4

Review of F. W. J. Schelling's *First Outline of a System of Philosophy of Nature* and *Introduction to his Outline*

A. C. A. Eschenmayer[1]

[529] *Introduction to his Outline of a System of Philosophy of Nature*, by F. W. J. Schelling. 83 pp. Jena and Leipzig, C. E. Gabler 1799.
First Outline of a System of Philosophy of Nature. For the purpose of his lectures by *F. W. J. Schelling*. 10 lectures and sketch. 321 pp. Jena and Leipzig, C. E. Gabler 1799.

Among the philosophers of our age there are two, above all, whose results remain equally (although in different ways) at the highest [point] that the human mind is capable of scaling. – I mean Fichte, the earlier founder of the doctrine of science [*Wissenschaftslehre*], and Schelling, the author of the [System of] Transcendental Idealism. Chance can have very little to do with this concurrence, for – what power does [chance] have when it is a matter of finding, under so many disparities, the true proportion; nor can it have much to do with dead and lifeless imitation, light borrowed from empty letters. This is the very point at which things cannot be learned, but [only] actively produced. What you are at this level, you can be only by active self-production. – What you create here passes through an organ which, like that of the aesthetic artist, is sustained on Prometheus' frugal flame; when it comes to intellectual intuition, there are no instructions. The relation these two men have to *Kant* remains always, in respect to originality of thinking, one of inferiority, for to claim that even without *Kant's* laborious study such heights could yet have been scaled is to repudiate the history of the human mind; in respect to principles, however, the relation is one of superiority. What *Fichte* achieved from a higher standpoint in the fields of natural right, morality and some related doctrines, *Schelling* has done entirely for philosophy of nature (principally for chemistry and physiology), art and history.

It is here our aim to keep to the consideration of philosophy of nature. *Schelling* has already dealt with this important subject in a series of writings. Furnished with fundamental philosophical principles, the highest tasks of this science were always going to stimulate him [530], but since he takes analysis into the detail of natural phenomena, a deeper knowledge of physics was also essential for him. Consider also the [current intellectual] situation – unsuitable for the discipline of philosophy of nature – and you will, in fact, find his entrance into this rich abundance awe-inspiring. The kindled glimmer had, indeed, already been stoked in one of *Kant's* most beautiful products – his metaphysics of nature – but to bring life and form to this formless mass, to unite the most distant parts of nature through a continuous construction, and to bring the rubble of all doctrinal systems into a new configuration, for this was required a wide-ranging intellect. Whatever may come of the level-headed testing of all the principles with which *Schelling* presents us (the time for this is not yet at hand), we will not underestimate such an extraordinary force which has thrown its rays across this immeasurable expanse.

No. 1: It was to be expected that, in his Introduction to his Outline, the author would give some explanation of the relationship between transcendental philosophy and philosophy of nature. That is, if the former possesses the task of subordinating the *real* to the *ideal*, then the latter, on the contrary, deals with the task of explaining the *ideal* from the *real*.[2] Both are thus opposed to each other in terms of direction. The author rejects the *idealistic* type of explanation that deduces nature as a *condition of self-consciousness*, while he simultaneously remarks that such a type of explanation degenerates into the most bizarre nonsense,[3] and, instead, in his treatment of philosophy of nature observes the maxim: explain everything from natural forces.[4]

The reviewer believes he must remark here that if the directions of the two philosophies are opposed and relate [to each other] something like synthesis and analysis do, or if at the very least both opposed directions meet here as everywhere in the middle, the idealist type of explanation cannot be so very different from the realist. If the philosopher were to successfully deduce these natural forces from which *Schelling* begins his construction as *necessary conditions of our self-consciousness*, then the idealist standpoint would have to coincide with the realist one; the treatment of philosophy of nature [531] would continue on its way undisturbed by such a deduction, and if it were to be altered by [such a deduction], then this could only be for the benefit of the development of the system. Is there other evidence, another a priori than its coincidence with some immediately certain fact of our self-consciousness? Even geometry has only conditional evidence – that is, under the supposition of certain postulates and axioms. Should the philosopher stand still because of this? Must he not demonstrate that the setting of limits and the drawing of lines are nothing but necessary acts of an intelligence?

On p. 10, there is a passage which precisely coincides with the pretence of doing away with the idealist standpoint. The passage is summarised in the following claim: 'Because nature as a whole is not merely a product, but also productive, then it ultimately follows that universal duality is just as necessary a principle of natural explanation as the concept of nature itself.'[5] I now ask from where does the concept of nature come to me? If it is a priori, then it is a condition of my self-consciousness and idealist. If, however, I receive it from experience, then the principle of duality which results from it cannot be universally valid, since I cannot circumscribe the whole of nature in experience, – I have no guarantee of its applicability to hand. Now, [on the latter option] if philosophy of nature includes the task of creating nature itself, or, as *Schelling* puts it, of overhearing it in its own self-construction, I must thus derive the aspects of the construction from the sphere of experience – which is necessarily something limited and precisely as I come upon it – in order for this sphere to be able to arise successively from the aforementioned principles. I am sceptical whether this is a genuinely philosophical procedure and not in fact a circle.

In regard to the *empirical testing* on which the author relies, I admit that it all must necessarily add up, just as numerical double-checking does in calculus, but, since this can only be established once the final calculation has penetrated the natural phenomena themselves, then the construction, if it began from natural forces, would still have possessed its highest value only from experience – which is much too high a price to pay to chance. And besides, the reviewer also believes that at present the author is not yet authorised to have recourse to the empirical testing of his system.

To connect the idealist standpoint to the realist one appears to require merely a small bridge, and, in fact, possibly no one is in a better position to make this passage than the author of the transcendental-idealism. For this reason, the reviewer does not see why the philosophy of nature should take the reverse path to transcendental philosophy, since it seems suited to the nature of the thing to, rather, posit the former in continuity with the latter and to treat it [532] merely as one part of the latter – this long ago justified the revered *Kant's* use of the division: he opposed metaphysics of nature to metaphysics of ethics, but intended to derive both from a common source – transcendental philosophy, through which self-consciousness is cognised as the innermost root of both worlds, the moral and the natural, as the highest attainable unity of a system.

No. 2: With these presuppositions put forward in his Introduction, the author delves into the Outline of his philosophy of nature itself. In setting out this system, two methods could have been followed: one is the dynamic kind of representation or construction from fundamental forces, from the standpoint of intuition; the other is the atomist or construction from individual qualities (fundamental material), from the standpoint of reflection. The author prefers the latter, although he does not exclude the former.[6] The reviewer believes that secure results can be obtained from both ways, and that the difference between the atomist and dynamic methods is the same as that between algebraic and geometric construction. In reality, every construction brings both together, and just as intuition cannot do without reflection, so reflection cannot do without intuition; it is merely that the one of them has preponderance on each occasion.

The following are the author's basic principles:[7] the unconditioned constitutes the object of philosophy of nature: there is no individual thing of which one says that it is, but only being itself, and in so far as nature is [being itself], it is unconditioned. However, being itself is – absolute activity and designates an individual being only as a point of inhibition of this activity. The oscillation between infinite productivity and absolute product is the fundamental character of nature; infinite productivity is activity; it tends to absolute product; if it were to actually attain the latter, it would be fully extinguished in [such a product], and nature would come to absolute rest, which is not to be thought of as relative rest with just an infinitely small velocity, but solely as completely annihilated movement. Both [infinite productivity and absolute product] are the outer limits of a series, the continual conflict of which produces those infinitely many gradations which make up the whole we call nature.

This appears to be the basic viewpoint taken by the author in his Outline. The reviewer is for the most part in agreement with it; only he [533] believes that he can prove in the following that there are already aspects of this viewpoint which could originate solely from idealism.

The mechanism of nature rests on a mutual give and take of movement. We are not inquiring into this here; instead, the question is: what is the original dynamic source of these movements? What is it that constantly inhibits the transition of productivity into an absolute product? I am asking here for some attention to be given to the following inference: since the absolute product = absolute rest and so = the negation of all movement, then the tendency to it is also something *negative*; and so nature's productivity, in so far as it tends to an absolute product, involves the concept of a *negative* activity. From this it now follows that the *inhibiting* of this tendency is something *positive*, and this, the reviewer contends, is completely foreign to nature – that is, what constantly hinders the transition of productivity into absolute product no longer pertains to the essence of nature. In an earlier passage, the author says it would be impossible to view nature as something unconditioned if the hidden trace of freedom could not be discovered in the concept of being.[8] Whence comes this trace of freedom in nature? To begin a series of productions absolutely belongs solely to the character of a free intelligence; to try to attach this character to nature stifles all philosophy at its root. The reviewer will here attempt to respond to this difficult point from [the perspective of] idealism in what follows:

The *unconscious* activity of an intelligence turns into an outlook in which ideal activity and real activity are united and both limit one another. However, ideal activity is infinite; hence, by means of constant reproduction, it expands beyond that limit. And it is by this means that consciousness of the limit is first possible, even if not yet actual. Therefore, in *unconscious* activity two things are present: (1) an incessant inhibition of ideal activity, and (2) a continual reproduction of [the activity] itself that expresses itself in the crossing of the limit. How can we now designate both aspects in one concept? Evidently, only through the concept of *drive*, in which is to be found a constant striving beyond and also an incessant inhibition of its effectiveness. *Unconscious* activity is opposed to *conscious* [activity], which arises through the reflex of free acts of an intelligence. As soon as the I is raised to spontaneity, as occurs in the state of ordinary consciousness, then it knows itself as *subject* and opposes itself to its *unconscious* activity, which becomes *objectivity*. In *unconscious* [534] activity, however, these two aspects (that is, the limits produced by the union of the ideal and the real and the continual crossing of these limits) are both present, and this constitutes the *original drive* – such that the drive itself becomes *objective*. In short, what follows is this: by means of the unconscious activity of an intelligence, an *original drive* comes into nature, but only as opposed to spontaneity, or: from the standpoint of ordinary consciousness (subjectivity), it is cognised as *objective* and independent of us. And it is now this *drive* which is represented *immanently* in nature as the *world soul*.

Through this deduction of the original drive (the world soul), transcendental idealism passes its basis over into philosophy of nature, and on this basis [the latter] can construct further.

One can now see how, in general, the author presupposes in his basic viewpoint the original drive together with the deduction of it, and fraudulently obtains the basis from which he begins to construct by *equating being itself*, which can be thought only as *absolute rest*, with *absolute activity*, and by this means inserting the *principle of becoming* or the hidden trace of *freedom* into nature itself. Of course, when it comes to [my] deduction of the original drive, the philosopher of nature will ask what he thereby gains for his construction, and I admit – nothing at all. The gain is, first and foremost, solely negative; – for the philosopher of nature will now at the very least stop asking after some universal matter and [also stop] considering the world soul merely as the uppermost link in a chain which runs throughout nature. However, the gain will also become positive, and in the original drive itself lie the aspects of the construction. The deduced drive is in no way lawless, but contains rather all lawfulness in itself, and one only needs to analyse it to uncover the laws of its development. Indeed, one could even claim that its laws are already found, but not yet deduced and applied. The activity of an intelligence is only unconscious and blind because it operates according to a necessary law or rather according to a necessary, progressive ratio [*Verhältnis*], while conscious and free activity is raised above all laws. The *original drive* is, to express myself like Schelling, nothing but the *absolute involution of the universal organism*.[9]

After [considering] the presupposition of this deduction, we can pass over a number of the author's claims which would otherwise require extensive discussion. Among these claims I count the following: nature is its own law-giver; nature [535] is sufficient to itself; nature has unconditional reality, etc.[10] In general, the hypothesis of unconditional empiricism now appears in its true light for the first time.

On p. 15, the author, who is here pursuing the atomist mode of explanation, says: the original points of inhibition of universal natural activity are to be found in original qualities.[11] And, further, on p. 16: the original qualities are original negative exhibitions of the unconditioned; they themselves are the principles of all filling of space and are thus not themselves in space.[12] The reviewer is in agreement with these principles; however, the question arises: where are these qualities if they are not in space? That which is not in *space* and still has value can only possess it in *time*, and so too for these original qualities: they only have value for sensation, but none for intuition – and *what is positive for sensation is accordingly negative for intuition*. Heeding this opposition is important for the whole of philosophy of nature, and it can justifiably be claimed that a great part of recent errors have originated from not respecting this opposition. From the above it appears that the atomist abstracts completely from intuition in the first moment of his construction, while, on the contrary, the dynamist abstracts completely from sensation in his first moment. If now both modes of representation are bound to each other, as a rigorous philosophy of nature demands, then the atomist must show how the intuitable corresponds to the sensible – how, for example, the three dimensions of space result from the original and sensibly-cognised forces, e.g. magnetism, electricity, etc. – and the dynamist must show how the intuitable corresponds to the sensible – how basic material results from the original fundamental forces and their ratios. In this way, atomism would be the algebra of nature and dynamics the geometric construction of it.

With his atomist viewpoint, the author (p. 14 II[13]), in quick succession, conceives of the cohesion of matter, the production of original figures and shapes, and original liquidity. The formless comes into conflict with form and the individual tries to affirm itself against the universal. On this view, different forms could only be seen as different stages of development of one and the same organisation.

All differences in natural products can only rest on the various proportions [*Verhältnisse*][14] of actants (qualities) (p. 28 III[15]). From this claim [536] the author attains absolutely incomposable and absolutely indecomposable substances; but the direction of natural activity tolerates neither one extreme nor the other, and so it always tends to the middle products alone and, in addition to the appearance of a free [process of] formation, they stand in a perfect reciprocal union.[16]

Since infinite natural activity, which is kindled in all individual actants, is to be exhibited *empirically*, which can only occur through determinate formation, it is therefore necessary for the infinite product to be fixed at each stage of development. And from this emerges the following task:

[To show] how nature could inhibit its product at particular stages of development without ceasing to be active (p. 41 IV[17]). According to the author's opinion, this inhibition is to be located in the diremption of actants into opposed directions (sexual difference)[18] – that is, since nature cannot attain the collective product, it strives to form the individual perfectly.

The above is indeed perceptive, but some errors lie in the proof. That is, the reasoning which leads the author to this result can be formulated in two ways: (1) because there is sexual difference, nature's infinite activity, which strives to exhibit the whole manifoldness of the actants in a collective product, must fail to find such a proportion and so has to divide itself into opposed directions; or (2) because there is in nature permanent, individual products, infinite natural activity must be fixed in its stages of development, which, however, can only occur through the diremption of actants, or through sexual difference. In both cases, a not-quite-philosophical procedure is apparent to me. In the first case, sexual difference and, in the second case, the permanence of the individual products are presupposed *instead of being deduced*. However, in both cases, the fundamental aspect remains unknown: in the first, the reason why nature fails to exhibit its collective product; in the second, the cause which produces a diremption of actants; indeed, how, according to the latter view, does sexual difference occur when it comes to permanent inorganic products, e.g. the very precisely and individually determined crystallisations of the earth? The reviewer is merely giving one example here of how quickly, on many occasions, the author hurries over the most important subjects, leaving behind him a pile of questions.

[537] On p. 66 (V),[19] the author delves into the main problem of philosophy of nature: to derive the dynamic graduated series [*Stufenfolge*] in nature a priori. Nowhere does the author's genius show itself more fruitfully than here, developing a series of ideas which were for the most part still unknown until now.

The author begins with a universal organism that encompasses within itself the organic and inorganic worlds, which are differentiated from each other as the inner is to the outer.[20] However, the inner or organic is always a reciprocal determination of receptivity and activity. From this claim the author obtains proof of systems that until now appeared opposed to each other and in conflict: (1) the system of chemical physiology; (2) the system of physiological immaterialism, and (3) the union of both of them in a third.[21]

The outer or inorganic is thinkable in terms of what exists next to or outside one another, only as the tendency to interpenetrate. The cause of this tendency is gravity. Here the author passes over proof of the opposed systems: (1) the mechanical; (2) the metaphysical [system] of attraction, and (3) the union of both in the system of physical attraction.[22] The last [option] the author probably does not value higher than a hypothesis. For if one assumes with the author (in order to touch on only one part of the hypothesis) that the sun out of which the planets exploded is also that very mass which unites the central point of attraction in itself, then it is difficult to see how the planets pursue an elliptical path, since both repulsion and attraction work only in a straight line between two points. To explain this one must further assume some foreign impulse which lies neither in the sun nor in the planets.

I pass over once more the series of principles which the author develops. It has already been remarked that gravity is the cause of the tendency to intussusception.[23] Since, however, this does [538] not fully exhaust the conditions of intussusception, there must still be added a further, distinct actant. Intussusception exists only in the chemical process, but that which is a principle of the chemical process cannot, in turn, be a product of it. In this way, one postulates, in addition to gravity, another chemical influence of the sun; and this is what occurs by virtue of oxygen, and the phenomenon [produced by] this chemical influence is light. The earth substances – electrical proportions of bodies – are inversely proportional to this actant. On p. 156,[24] after the author has determined the organic and inorganic [worlds] individually, he moves on to their reciprocal determination, which comes to completion in the concept of irritability. By means of this concept, duplicity is brought into the organism and individual organic functions are derived from it. This derivation is one of the most beautiful parts of the Outline. Just as the dynamic graduated series in universal nature runs from light to electricity [and] from electricity to magnetism, it is repeated in organic nature: the same series in a higher potency, as it were – and it proceeds from technical drive to irritability, from irritability to sensibility, and thus at the end of the argument it emerges that it is one and the same product which passes downwards from the highest stage of sensibility until it is ultimately lost in the reproductive power of plants.

In an appendix to the Outline,[25] the author deduces a theory of illness and the universal theory of chemical process from the above principles.

The reviewer has here merely laid out some of the Outline's highlights, in order to direct attention to the significance of the many investigations in which its author is engaged. Even if one agrees with the foundations of this Outline and the basic principles from which the author begins (and this is indeed, partly, what the above proof employs), much still remains for closer scrutiny: [e.g.] whether a rigorous coherence is to be found in these investigations; whether there does not creep in a gradual change in meaning or an unnoticed contradiction in the middle term between two principles; whether the numerous novel aspects introduced into philosophy of nature [539] are actually of the kind that admits the type of construction that the author introduces; and whether this construction does not, in fact, contravene mathematics: all of this would require closer inspection. Nevertheless, this reviewer admits that it appears to him still too early to be able to reach a definite judgement on this work, and it would in fact demand a proof whose scope would far exceed the present pages. Anyhow, all the ideas that the author lays out for us still exist merely in outline. If the author will now provide us with the system itself, we will seemingly possess a full revision of his nature-philosophical concepts: many that appear obscure to us would be illuminated and the mass of constructible aspects would be arranged into something more easily surveyable. Justification for our expectation is to be found in a passage from the first issue of the second volume of his Journal,[26] where the author says: if we succeed, at the very least, in specifying an initial layout [of the system], others will soon find it comprehensible and even reasonable that the structure has been constructed from different sides and that we first attempted to pursue the individual investigations before going on to establish them in one and the same whole. One implication of this passage is that *Sch.[elling]* does not yet consider his outline to be such a whole and is aware of the higher demands of a system. The author even appears, in fact, to have changed his method of construction in a way more fruitful for a system of science, as illuminated, in particular, in his Deduction of the Dynamic Process or the Categories of Physics in his Journal.[27] It is precisely because the three originally potentiated states – magnetism, electricity and the chemical process – are posited in reciprocal dependence on the three dimensions of space[28] that the standpoint of reflection coincides with the standpoint of intuition: the atomist and the dynamist are no longer separated one-sidedly from each other; the sensible and the intuitable are originally united and precisely this original unity, taken as the foundation of a nature-philosophical system, will necessarily provide us with the most fruitful implications.

The author has perfectly achieved all that can be reasonably expected from a mere outline: the seeds of the system are scattered everywhere therein; the language of a refined philosophy is everywhere prevalent; a huge number of new aspects are introduced; each of them has been assigned a part within the whole; and the aspects that had already been familiar appear, at the very least, in more significant connections. Let us now relinquish [the work] to the directing spirit himself, for him to set us free from the tangled web into which philosophy of nature leads us and to fully illuminate that path which [540] leads straight to the majesty of sublime subjects – a path down which he has already stepped with so much originality.

Notes

Preface

1. Jean-François Marquet, *Liberté et existence: Étude sur la formation de la philosophie de Schelling* (Paris: Gallimard, 1973), p. 110.
2. Alexandra Roux, 'Introduction' to A. C. A. Eschenmayer, *La Philosophie dans son passage à la non-philosophie*, ed. and trans. Roux (Paris: Vrin, 2005), p. 14. Ziche likewise stresses the significant role Eschenmayer played in the development of Schelling's philosophy of nature. Paul Ziche, *Mathematische und naturwissenschaftliche Modelle in der Philosophie Schellings und Hegels* (Stuttgart: Frommann-Holzboog, 1996), p. 213.
3. Michael G. Vater, 'Schelling's Philosophy of Identity and Spinoza's *Ethica more geometrico*', in E. Förster and Y. Melamed (eds), *Spinoza and German Idealism* (Cambridge: Cambridge University Press, 2012), p. 171.
4. Iain Hamilton Grant, *Philosophies of Nature after Schelling* (London: Continuum, 2006), pp. 106–7.
5. John H. Zammito, *The Gestation of German Biology: Philosophy and Physiology from Stahl to Schelling* (Chicago: University of Chicago Press, 2018), p. 327.
6. Eckhart Förster, *The Twenty-Five Years of Philosophy: A Systematic Reconstruction*, trans. Brady Bowman (Cambridge, MA: Harvard University Press, 2012), pp. 248–9.
7. See Christopher Lauer and Jason Wirth's translation of Schelling's 1812 letter to Eshchenmayer, along with Lauer's accompanying essay, in Wirth, *Schelling's Practice of the Wild: Time, Art, Imagination* (Albany: SUNY Press, 2015), pp. 173–208.
8. For justifications of the splitting of the Schelling–Eschenmayer controversies into three, see Bernard Gilson, 'Présentation', in F. W. J. Schelling, *La Liberté humaine et controverses avec Eschenmayer*, ed. and trans. Gilson (Paris: Vrin, 1988), pp. 7–8.
9. Bernhard Rang, *Identität und Indifferenz: Eine Untersuchung zu Schellings Identitätsphilosophie* (Frankfurt am Main: Klostermann, 2000), p. 116.
10. Editors' comments in *HKA* III/2.2, p. 77.

Introduction: Schelling and Eschenmayer in 1801

1. It was later shortened by the editor of Schelling's *Sämmtliche Werke* to its canonical form: *On the True Concept of Philosophy of Nature and the Correct Way of Solving its Problems*.

2 H. A. M. Snelders, 'Romanticism and *Naturphilosophie* and the Inorganic Natural Sciences, 1797–1840: An Introductory Survey', in *Studies in Romanticism* 9.3 (1970), p. 196.
3 Zammito, *Gestation of German Biology*, p. 301.
4 Schelling, *On the True Concept*, p. 47 below.
5 Quoted in Monica Marchetto, 'Drive, Formative Drive, World Soul: Fichte's Reception in the Early Works of A. C. A. Eschenmayer', in *Fichte-Studien* 43 (2016), p. 299. Goethe indeed went on to read Eschenmayer's works – see Zammito, *Gestation of German Biology*, p. 301 and Schelling's comment in Eschenmayer and Schelling, *Correspondence*, p. 192 below.
6 For Novalis's 'Eschenmayer-Studies', see *Schriften*, ed. Richard Samuel (Stuttgart: Kohlhammer, 1975), vol. 2; for Ritter, see Walter Wuttke, 'Materialien zu Leben und Werk Adolph Karl August von Eschenmayers', in *Sudhoffs Archiv* 56.3 (1972), p. 267.
7 Fichte's May 1801 letter to Schelling, received in August of that year, in *Rupture*, p. 58. See Marchetto, 'Drive, Formative Drive, World Soul', pp. 313–14.
8 For fuller biographies of Eschenmayer, see Jörg Jantzen, 'Adolph Karl August von Eschenmayer', in Thomas Bach and Olaf Breidbach (eds), *Naturphilosophie nach Schelling* (Stuttgart: Frommann-Holzboog, 2005), p. 153; Wuttke, 'Materialien zu Leben und Werk Adolph Karl August von Eschenmayers', pp. 258–60; Cristiana Senigaglia, 'Einleitung' to A. C. A. Eschenmayer, *Einleitung in Natur und Geschichte*, ed. Senigaglia (Stuttgart: Frommann-Holzboog, 2016), pp. ix–xiv.
9 Quoted in Zammito, *Gestation of German Biology*, pp. 265–6. See also Kielmeyer's fairly favourable response to Eschenmayer's *Principles*: C. F. Kielmeyer, *Gesammelte Schriften*, ed. F. H. Holler (Berlin: Keiper, 1938), p. 42. Eschenmayer's closeness to Kielmeyer also put him in a strategic position among philosophers of nature in later years because of the inaccessibility of Kielmeyer's mostly unpublished corpus; he became a key mediating figure in disseminating Kielmeyer's thought to Schelling and others. See Thomas Bach, *Biologie und Philosophie bei C. F. Kielmeyer und F. W. J. Schelling* (Stuttgart: Frommann-Holzboog, 2001), p. 63.
10 Eschenmayer, *Deduction*, p. 206 below.
11 Marchetto, 'Drive, Formative Drive, World Soul', p. 299.
12 Jantzen, 'Eschenmayer', p. 153.
13 Ziche, *Mathematische und naturwissenschaftliche Modelle*, p. 213.
14 Jantzen, 'Eschenmayer', p. 161.
15 Marchetto, 'Drive, Formative Drive, World Soul', p. 303. Emphasis modified.
16 Urban Wiesing, *Kunst oder Wissenschaft? Konzeptionen der Medizin in der deutschen Romantik* (Stuttgart: Frommann-Holzboog, 1995), p. 151.
17 Jantzen, 'Eschenmayer', p. 154.
18 Quoted in Roux, 'Introduction', p. 13.
19 A. C. A. Eschenmayer, *Betrachtungen über den physischen Weltbau* (Heilbronn: Scheurlen, 1852), p. v.
20 F. W. J. Schelling, *Ideas for a Philosophy of Nature*, HKA I/5, p. 285; Harris and Heath, p. 249.
21 F. W. J. Schelling, *On the World Soul*, HKA I/6, p. 127.
22 F. W. J. Schelling, *Presentation of my System of Philosophy*, HKA I/10, p. 116; *Rupture*, p. 145.
23 F. W. J. Schelling, *On the Absolute System of Identity*, HKA I/11.1, p. 142.
24 F. W. J. Schelling, *First Outline of a System of Philosophy of Nature*, HKA I/7, p. 86; Peterson, p. 22.
25 F. W. J. Schelling, *Briefe und Dokumente*, ed. Horst Fuhrmans (Bonn: Bouvier, 1962–75), 3:222.
26 Schelling, *On the True Concept*, p. 61 below.
27 Schelling, *Presentation*, HKA I/10, p. 113; *Rupture*, p. 141.

28 Schelling, *Presentation*, *HKA* I/10, p. 113; *Rupture*, p. 142.
29 Schelling, *Presentation*, *HKA* I/10, p. 113; *Rupture*, p. 142.
30 Michael G. Vater, 'Introduction to F. W. J. Schelling, *Presentation of my System of Philosophy*', in *Philosophical Forum* 32.4 (2001), p. 339.
31 Xavier Tilliette, *Schelling: Une philosophie en devenir* (Paris: Vrin, 1970), 1:243.
32 Anton Braekman, 'From the Work of Art to Absolute Reason: Schelling's Journey toward Absolute Idealism', in *The Review of Metaphysics* 57.3 (2004), p. 551.
33 Dalia Nassar, *The Romantic Absolute: Being and Knowing in Early German Romantic Philosophy, 1794–1804* (Chicago: University of Chicago Press, 2013), p. 213.
34 Nassar, *The Romantic Absolute*, p. 214.
35 F. W. J. Schelling, *System of Transcendental Idealism*, *HKA* I/9, p. 24; Heath, p. 2.
36 F. W. J. Schelling, *Universal Deduction of the Dynamic Process or the Categories of Physics*, *HKA* I/8, p. 364; trans. Iain Hamilton Grant.
37 Schelling, *Universal Deduction*, I/8, p. 365; trans. Iain Hamilton Grant.
38 Grant, *Philosophies of Nature after Schelling*, pp. 3, 5.
39 Frederick C. Beiser, *German Idealism: The Struggles against Subjectivism, 1791–1801* (Cambridge, MA: Harvard University Press, 2002), p. 551.
40 Beiser, *German Idealism*, pp. 506–7. This nature-philosophical interpretation has also recently won adherents in Vater ('Reconfiguring Identity in Schelling's *Würzburg System*', in *Schelling Studien* 2, p. 9) and Breazeale ('"Exhibiting the particular in the universal": Philosophical Construction and Intuition in Schelling's Philosophy of Identity [1801–1804]', in Lara Ostaric [ed.], *Interpreting Schelling: Critical Essays* [Cambridge: Cambridge University Press, 2014], p. 92).
41 Schelling, *On the True Concept*, p. 54 below.
42 Schelling, *On the True Concept*, p. 52 below.
43 It is worth noting that, in *On the True Concept*, Schelling claims that there is a third, still-higher, manifestation of reality. The linear sequence that runs from nature through freedom and consciousness culminates in the work of art. We do not explore this comment of Schelling's in any detail, but it suggests that the aesthetics of the *System of Transcendental Idealism* is to be slightly revised to take into account the fact that the 'unconscious productivity' of nature and the 'conscious productivity' of the intelligence are not parallel activities which become unified in art, but that nature's productivity is recapitulated as consciousness and – through consciousness – recapitulated once again as art.
44 Schelling, *First Outline*, *HKA* I/7, p. 81; Peterson, p. 17.
45 Schelling, *On the True Concept*, p. 51 below.
46 Marchetto, 'Drive, Formative Drive, World Soul', p. 311.
47 As Roux summarises, 'Nature itself must be rethought as a projection of the I' ('Introduction', p. 46).
48 Eschenmayer, *Spontaneity = World Soul*, p. 25 below. As Jantzen point out, Eschenmayer is clearer on this point in his later review of the *First Outline* ('Eschenmayer', p. 80). Here, Eschenmayer further suggests that Schelling's illegitimate postulation of *becoming* in nature depends on the smuggling of the category of *negation* into nature – which takes us right to the heart of issues discussed in Chapter 3 of our commentary.
49 Eschenmayer, *Spontaneity = World Soul*, p. 25 below.
50 Eschenmayer, *Spontaneity = World Soul*, pp. 25–7 below.
51 We do not focus in this volume upon the fourth idea mentioned here, namely, the fact that Schelling's debate with Eschenmayer coincides with his turn away from thinking about the possibility of developing a speculative natural history in which nature's productivity is understood to be *essentially* historical. It is not until a few years later that Schelling once again expresses a profound interest in nature's history, and it is our view that the ahistorical metaphysics of 1801 can be understood, in

part, to be a result of Eschenmayer's influence. See Grant, *Philosophies of Nature after Schelling*, p. 203.
52. Our proposal that the texts of the Schelling–Eschenmayer controversy are particularly illuminating for the genesis of Schelling's position in 1801 is not the traditional view. Customarily, it is Schelling's correspondence with Fichte in 1800 and 1801 that has been taken to shed definitive light on his development at this period. Anyone who reads his November 1800 letter to Fichte alongside *On the True Concept* can see the same ideas – often word for word – repeated in both texts; however, considering the fact that Schelling read *Spontaneity = World Soul* long before Fichte's letters that are most critical of his philosophy of nature, it is very likely that Schelling was describing, in his reply to Fichte, a position he had already been formulating in response to Eschenmayer's essay. On this point, see Michael G. Vater and David W. Wood in *Rupture*, p. 136.

Translators' Notes to Eschenmayer, *Spontaneity = World Soul*

1. Schelling, *First Outline*, HKA I/7, pp. 198–9; Peterson, p. 132. Eschenmayer notably omits the beginning and end of the paragraph from the *First Outline* that describe these reflections as 'a powerful dream' and conclude, 'But what good is this dream of physics?'
2. Schelling, *First Outline*, HKA I/7, p. 230; Peterson, p. 158.
3. Schelling, *First Outline*: 'Empiricism to include unconditionedness is precisely philosophy of nature.' HKA I/7, p. 87; Peterson, p. 22.
4. See, for example, Schelling, *First Outline*, HKA I/7, p. 81; Peterson, p. 16.
5. A reference to Franz von Baader's recently published *On the Pythagorean Square* (1798) which was cited in Schelling's *First Outline* and forms a constant reference point in what follows, especially in discussions of gravity. On Baader, see Stefan Ackermann, 'Franz von Baader', in Thomas Bach and Olaf Breidbach (eds), *Naturphilosophie nach Schelling* (Stuttgart: Frommann-Holzboog, 2005), pp. 41–60.
6. Extracts from this text are translated in Appendix 3 of the present volume. See the notes to Appendix 3 for further details.
7. The topic of the Third Division of Schelling's *First Outline*.
8. That is, the 'central point' or, more strongly, 'source'. The term has its origins in seventeenth-century biology, where it signified the first pulsating traces of the heart in the embryo.
9. The distinction between *Gegenverhältnis and Wechselverhältnis*, where the former acts as the primary condition of self-consciousness, had been emphasised in Eschenmayer's 1799 *Deduction of the Living Organism*. See further Marchetto, 'Drive, Formative Drive, World Soul', pp. 308–9.
10. This is a recurrent claim in Schelling's early philosophy of nature; in the *First Outline*, it is postulated as the basic premise in Schelling's 'Deduction of the Dynamic Series of Stages' (HKA I/7, pp. 117–18; Peterson, pp. 53–4), and, along with terms like 'involution', recurs throughout the latter stages of the work.
11. Schelling, *First Outline*, HKA I/7, p. 81; Peterson, p. 17.
12. Schelling never makes this point with these precise words, but similar claims can be found throughout the earlier sections of the *First Outline*.
13. In what follows, Eschenmayer is simultaneously responding to two passages from Schelling's *First Outline* (in line with the non-linear structure of the work in which each division turns back to the material of the previous one from a higher potency). The two passages are Section II of the First Division, 'The Original Qualities and Actants in Nature', and the 'Second System' of the Second Division. In both of them, Schelling takes explicit aim at the kind of dynamical reasoning prominent in Eschenmayer's early philosophy of nature.
14. The relevant section from the *First Outline* begins, 'A product is only an *apparent*

product if infinity lies in it once more, i.e., if it bears the capacity of infinite development. This capacity cannot occur in it, however, without there being an infinite multiplicity of unified tendencies to it.' *HKA* I/7, p. 84; Peterson, p. 19.
15. On the translation of *Aktion* as 'actant', see the Translators' Note above.
16. See the extracts from Eschenmayer's earlier work in Appendices 2 and 3 of this volume.
17. That is, because Schelling denies the reduction of quality to quantity in the *First Outline*, he must find some other explanation for the production of complexity. See our discussion in Chapter 1 of the commentary.
18. Eschenmayer is here referring to Schelling, *First Outline*, *HKA* I/7, pp. 268–70; Peterson, pp. 189–91. The additional passage cited by Schelling in the accompanying footnote is from *First Outline*, *HKA* I/7, pp. 143–4; Peterson, pp. 77–8.
19. On the translation of *Verhältnis* as 'relation', 'proportion' or 'ratio', see the Translators' Note above.
20. A close paraphrase of Schelling, *First Outline*, *HKA* I/7, p. 84; Peterson, p. 19.
21. Schelling, *First Outline*, *HKA* I/7, p. 86; Peterson, p. 21.
22. Schelling, *First Outline*, *HKA* I/7, p. 87; Peterson, p. 23.
23. Schelling, *First Outline*, *HKA* I/7, pp. 87–8; Peterson, p. 24.
24. Eschenmayer is referring to his comments in *Principles of Nature-Metaphysics*, translated in Appendix 2 to the present volume.
25. Schelling uses this expression a couple of times in the *First Outline* when describing his 'third possible system' (*HKA* I/7, pp. 144ff.; Peterson, pp. 78ff.). See the Translators' Note above for more details.
26. Schelling, *First Outline*, *HKA* I/7, p. 141; Peterson, p. 76.
27. Despite the quotation marks, this is not a direct quotation from the *First Outline*.
28. A mixture predominantly containing the compound potassium sulphide.
29. Extracts from this essay are translated in Appendix 3 below.
30. That is, *Celeritas est Spatium per Temporum*, or speed equals distance over time.
31. See note 5 above.
32. Schelling, *First Outline*, *HKA* I/7, pp. 265–71; Peterson, pp. 187–92.
33. See Schelling, *First Outline*, *HKA* I/7, p. 117; Peterson, p. 53.
34. Eschenmayer's Latin dissertation submitted to the University of Tübingen in 1796 was entitled *Principia quaedam disciplinae naturali, in primis Chemiae ex Metaphysica naturae substernenda*. It was later adapted into German in *Principles of Nature-Metaphysics*, translated in Appendix 2 of the present volume. The following quotation from § 33 of the dissertation is in Latin in the text, except for the material in brackets which Eschenmayer interpolates in German.
35. A footnote in the *First Outline* similarly calls for the advent of 'comparative physiology' and invokes Kielmeyer's name in the process (*HKA* 1/7, p. 210; Peterson, p. 141; see also *HKA* 1/7, p. 113; Peterson, p. 50). Carl Friedrich Kielmeyer (1765–1844) was Eschenmayer's teacher at the Karlsschule in Stuttgart (see the Introduction above).
36. This is a paraphrase of the sections critical of Eschenmayer in the *First Outline*, discussed in Chapter 1 of our commentary. See, in particular, Schelling, *First Outline*, *HKA* 1/7, p. 142; Peterson, p. 76, which speaks of 'these principles' as 'a dead weight for natural science'.

Translators' Notes to Schelling, On the *True Concept of Philosophy of Nature*

1. This essay was originally titled 'Appendix to Eschenmayer's Essay concerning the True Concept of Philosophy of Nature and the Correct Way of Solving its Problems' and attributed merely to 'the Editor'. The shorter, better-known title was given to it by K. F. A. Schelling in the *Sämtliche Werke*.

2. A reference to Schelling's *Universal Deduction of the Dynamic Process or the Categories of Physics* published therein.
3. F. W. J. Schelling, *Introduction to the Outline of a System of the Philosophy of Nature*, in *HKA* I/8, p. 37; Peterson, p. 199.
4. These two points paraphrase Schelling, *Introduction to the Outline*, *HKA* I/8, pp. 37–8; Peterson, pp. 199–200.
5. See, for example, Schelling, *First Outline*, *HKA* 1/7, pp. 103–11; Peterson, pp. 36–46.
6. A reference to Eschenmayer, *Spontaneity = World Soul*, pp. 19–20 above..
7. This term is actually more common in the *First Outline* itself. See, for example, *HKA* 1/7, p. 87; Peterson, p. 22.
8. An anti-Fichtean polemic published in 1800 by Jean Paul (Richter). The initial example of the new-born child comes from Eschenmayer's *Spontaneity = World Soul*, p. 22 above.
9. For example, in Schelling's *Ideas for a Philosophy of Nature* (1797) and the *System of Transcendental Idealism* (1800).
10. Schelling's *Presentation of my System of Philosophy*, which has precisely this aim, occupied the whole of the next issue of the *Journal for Speculative Physics* (May 1801).
11. As discussed in note 52 to the Introduction above, much of the wording in the paragraphs that follow is extremely close to the letters Schelling was writing to Fichte in autumn 1800.
12. F. W. J. Schelling, *System of Transcendental Idealism*, *HKA* I/9, pp. 29–30; Heath, pp. 5–7.
13. Schelling, *System of Transcendental Idealism*, *HKA* I/9, pp. 264, 271; Heath, pp. 182, 186–7.
14. On Fichte's concept of abstraction to which Schelling is here responding, see the discussion in Chapter 5 of our commentary.
15. Eschenmayer will make this criticism even more clearly in his review of the *First Outline* translated in Appendix 4 below.
16. See Spinoza, *Ethics*, IP29S.
17. Schelling, *System of Transcendental Idealism*, I/9, pp. 25–6; Heath, pp. 2–3.
18. These two terms are defined respectively in Section 3 and Section 4 of the *System of Transcendental Idealism*.
19. This is a claim Schelling had summarised in more detail in § 63 of the *Universal Deduction* of 1800, indicating at the same time its significance for the very idea of philosophy of nature: 'In my System of Transcendental Idealism, I have shown that the three moments in the construction of matter, just as they may even be derived by mere physics, correspond to three moments in the history of self-consciousness. I have shown that what is still electricity in nature, for example, has already been swept up into intelligence as far as sensation, and that what arises in nature as matter, is intuition in intelligence. But this is a simple consequence of nature's continual potentiating, since we already see the beginnings of this in so-called inert nature, while light is already really an ideal activity which de- and reconstructs objects, just as idealism always does. And thus philosophy of nature gives both a physical explanation of idealism, and proves that the latter must erupt at the limits of nature, exactly as we see erupt out in the person of man. Man is not only idealist in philosophers' eyes, but also in the eyes of nature itself – and nature has for a long time made preparations for the heights it achieves through reason.' *HKA* I/8, p. 364; trans. Iain Hamilton Grant.
20. Eschenmayer, *Spontaneity = World Soul*, p. 41 above.
21. Schelling, *First Outline*, *HKA* I/7, p. 65; Peterson, p. 3.
22. The *First Outline* was expressly published as a course-book to accompany Schelling's lectures on philosophy of nature delivered at Jena in Winter Semester 1798/99.
23. See Schelling, *First Outline*, *HKA* 1/7, p. 265; Peterson, pp. 186–7; and *Introduction to the Outline*, *HKA* I/8, p. 67; Peterson, p. 224.

24. See Schelling, *First Outline*, HKA I/7, pp. 85–6; Peterson, pp. 20–2.
25. On the translation of *Aktion* as 'actant', see the Translators' Note above.
26. See Eschenmayer, *Spontaneity = World Soul*, p. 29 above.
27. On the translation of *Verhältnis* as 'relation', 'proportion' and 'ratio', see the Translators' Note above.
28. 'Singular' (as in: without relation) is also a possible translation.
29. Eschenmayer, *Spontaneity = World Soul*, pp. 29–30 above. See also Eschenmayer's discussion of this point in *Principles of Nature-Metaphysics*, translated in Appendix 2.
30. See Schelling, *First Outline*, HKA I/7, p. 81; Peterson trans., p. 16.
31. Eschenmayer, *Spontaneity = World Soul*, p. 25 above.
32. Eschenmayer, *Spontaneity = World Soul*, p. 40 above.
33. This claim and the following reconstruction of Eschenmayer's position is taken from *Spontaneity = World Soul*, pp. 32ff above.
34. Eschenmayer, *Spontaneity = World Soul*, pp. 36–7 above.
35. These are claims Schelling argues for in more detail in his *Universal Deduction* that had appeared in the previous issue of the journal.
36. Eschenmayer, *Spontaneity = World Soul*, p. 19 above.
37. Eschenmayer, *Spontaneity = World Soul*, p. 18 above.
38. In Latin in the original. Schelling is here quoting Eschenmayer's own quotation of his earlier dissertation in *Spontaneity = World Soul*, pp. 43-4 above (see note 31 to Eschenmayer's text above).
39. This final paragraph again rehearses material explored in more detail in the *Universal Deduction*.

Chapter 1: Quality

1. And readers have often been misled. Roux bemoans the 'habit' of interpreting *On the True Concept* 'outside of its polemical context' ('Introduction', p. 48).
2. Jörg Jantzen, 'Eschenmayer und Schelling. Die Philosophie in ihrem Übergang zur Nichtphilosophie', in Walter Jaeschke (ed.), *Religionsphilosophie und spekulative Theologie: Die Streit um die Göttliche Dinge (1799–1812)* (Hamburg: Felix Meiner, 1994), p. 74.
3. Patrick Leistner, 'Anmerkungen zur Debatte zwischen Schelling und Eschenmayer in der Jahren 1803–1804', in *Contrastes: Revista Internacional de Filosofía* 19 (2014), p. 100.
4. Beiser, *German Idealism*, pp. 506–7.
5. Ralph Marks, *Differenz der Konzeption einer dynamischen Naturphilosophie bei Schelling und Eschenmayer* (Munich: PhD Thesis Ludwig-Maximillians-Universität, 1983), p. 44.
6. See Kant's discussion of the relationship between the *Critique* and the *Metaphysical Foundations*: *MF*, *KGS* IV, p. 477; Ellington translation, p. 15.
7. For remarks on Kant's positioning of himself in this longstanding tradition of dynamical explanation, see Manfred Durner in HKA, *Ergänzungsband zu den Werken Band I/5–9*, pp. 35–45.
8. Kant, *MF*, *KGS* IV, p. 477; Ellington translation, p. 14.
9. Kant, *MF*, *KGS* IV, p. 497; Ellington translation, p. 41.
10. Kant, *MF*, *KGS* IV, p. 503; Ellington translation, p. 49.
11. As Friedman notes, this is another way in which Kant departs from Newton: although he follows Newton in championing an empirical, as opposed to principle-based approach to scientific investigation, he adopts a Eulerian conception of matter as continuum in contrast to Newton's atomistic conception of matter. Michael Friedman, *Kant's Construction of Nature: A Reading of the* Metaphysical Foundations of Natural Science (Cambridge: Cambridge University Press, 2013), p. 258.
12. Kant, *MF*, *KGS* IV, p. 508; Ellington translation, p. 57.

13. Kant, *MF*, *KGS* IV, p. 508; Ellington translation, p. 56.
14. Kant, *MF*, *KGS* IV, p. 509; Ellington translation, p. 57.
15. Kant, *MF*, *KGS* IV, p. 510; Ellington translation, p. 59.
16. Kant, *MF*, *KGS* IV, p. 510; Ellington translation, p. 59.
17. Kant, *MF*, *KGS* IV, p. 511; Ellington translation, p. 60.
18. Kant, *MF*, *KGS* IV, p. 513; Ellington translation, p. 62. Emphasis modified.
19. Kant, *MF*, *KGS* IV, p. 518; Ellington translation, p. 70.
20. Kant, *MF*, *KGS* IV, p. 523; Ellington translation, p. 76. '*Limitation* is simply reality combined with negation.' *Critique of Pure Reason*, *KGS* III, p. 96; trans. Norman Kemp-Smith (Basingstoke: Palgrave, 1929), p. 116 (B111).
21. Kant, *MF*, *KGS* IV, p. 468; Ellington translation, p. 4.
22. Kant, *MF*, *KGS* IV, pp. 468, 471; Ellington translation, pp. 4, 7.
23. Kant, *MF*, *KGS* IV, p. 471; Ellington translation, p. 8.
24. Kant, *MF*, *KGS* IV, p. 530; Ellington translation, p. 87.
25. Kant, *MF*, *KGS* IV, p. 532; Ellington translation, p. 90. Emphasis modified.
26. Friedman, *Kant's Construction of Nature*, p. 272.
27. Friedman, *Kant's Construction of Nature*, p. 273.
28. Wiesing, *Kunst oder Wissenschaft?*, p. 153.
29. Eschenmayer, *Principles of Nature-Metaphysics*, p. 199 below.
30. Eschenmayer, *Deduction*, p. 205 below.
31. In his *Eschenmayer-Studies* (*Schriften*, 2:381), Novalis remarks that nature-metaphysics refers to an 'intermediary moment' between the individual natural sciences and purely abstract metaphysics (one of a number of 'particular *transcendental philosophies*').
32. Marks, *Differenz*, p. 6. After 1801, such an aim is abandoned: Eschenmayer insists to Oken in 1803 that 'philosophy of nature is to return to the eternal, but to this standpoint can mathematics no longer accompany it . . . There is for us a limitation of the application of mathematics to philosophy of nature.' A. C. A. Eschenmayer, 'Letter to Oken, 8/3/1803', in Eschenmayer, *Einleitung in Natur und Geschichte*, p. 108.
33. Eschenmayer, *Principles of Nature-Metaphysics*, p. 199 below.
34. Eschenmayer, *Principles of Nature-Metaphysics*, p. 199 below.
35. Eschenmayer, *Principles of Nature-Metaphysics*, p. 200 below.
36. Eschenmayer, *Principles of Nature-Metaphysics*, p. 199 below.
37. Eschenmayer, *Principles of Nature-Metaphysics*, p. 199 below.
38. Eschenmayer, *Principles of Nature-Metaphysics*, p. 201 below.
39. Eschenmayer, *Principles of Nature-Metaphysics*, p. 200 below.
40. Eschenmayer, *Principles of Nature-Metaphysics*, p. 200 below.
41. Eschenmayer, *Principles of Nature-Metaphysics*, p. 201 below.
42. Eschenmayer, *Principles of Nature-Metaphysics*, p. 201 below.
43. This is one of the reasons why Grant identifies Eschenmayer as a Platonist. Grant, *Philosophies of Nature after Schelling*, pp. 106–7.
44. Eschenmayer, *Principles of Nature-Metaphysics*, p. 202 below.
45. Howard M. Pollack-Milgate, 'Gott ist bald $1 \cdot \infty$ – bald $1/\infty$ – bald 0: The Mathematical Infinite and the Absolute in Novalis', in *Seminar* 51.1 (2015), p. 64.
46. Pollack-Milgate, 'Mathematical Infinite', p. 65. Pollack-Milgate goes on to emphasise Eschenmayer's influence on Novalis in this respect.
47. Eschenmayer, *Principles of Nature-Metaphysics*, p. 202 below.
48. Eschenmayer, *Principles of Nature-Metaphysics*, p. 203 below.
49. Eschenmayer, *Deduction*, p. 211 below.
50. Eschenmayer, *Deduction*, p. 211 below.
51. Gilles Châtelet, *Figuring Space: Philosophy, Mathematics and Physics*, trans. Robert Shore and Muriel Zagha (Dordrecht: Kluwer, 2000), p. 89.
52. Eschenmayer, *Principles of Nature-Metaphysics*, p. 202 below.

53. Jantzen, 'Eschenmayer und Schelling', p. 75; see further Paul Ziche, *Mathematische und naturwissenschaftliche Modelle*, p. 214.
54. A. C. A. Eschenmayer, *Psychologie in drei Theilen* (Stuttgart: Cotta, 1817), p. 11. Reading the 1797 *Principles*, Kielmeyer will take issue precisely with this interpretation of the lever as paradigmatic of the interplay of chemical forces. See Kielmeyer, *Gesammelte Schriften*, pp. 42–50.
55. Châtelet, *Figuring Space*, p. 73.
56. Châtelet, *Figuring Space*, pp. 80–1.
57. Châtelet, *Figuring Space*, p. 99.
58. Schelling, *Ideas*, HKA I/5, p. 285; Harris and Heath, p. 249.
59. The centrality of chemistry to the nature-philosophical project is perhaps the most distinctive feature of Schelling's 1797 conception of philosophy of nature: 'The new system of chemistry, the work of a whole era, spreads its influence ever more widely over the other branches of natural science, and employed over its *whole* range may very well develop into the universal system of nature' (Schelling, *Ideas*, HKA I/5, p. 112; Harris and Heath, p. 59). Indeed, Lequan argues that 'the originality of the 1797 *Ideen*' consists in its recognition of the philosophical importance of chemical processes, and that Schelling was 'one of the first philosophers in Europe to recognise the scientific plenitude of chemistry' (Mai Lequan, '1797–1799: D'une "philosophie de la chimie" au chimisme en philosophie. Les premiers écrits de Schelling sur la nature', in *Dix-huitième siècle* 42 [2010], pp. 166, 168); Eschenmayer's name should be added to this list of philosophers.
60. Marquet, *Liberté et existence*, p. 211. See also Roux, 'Introduction', pp. 22–3.
61. Schelling, *Ideas*, HKA I/5, pp. 189–90, 208; Harris and Heath, pp. 148, 171.
62. Schelling, *Ideas*, HKA I/5, p. 189; Harris and Heath, p. 148.
63. Schelling, *Ideas*, HKA I/5, p. 208; Harris and Heath, p. 171
64. Schelling, *Ideas*, HKA I/5, pp. 210, 215; Harris and Heath, pp. 173, 177.
65. Schelling, *Ideas*, HKA I/5, p. 213; Harris and Heath, p. 176.
66. Schelling, *Ideas*, HKA I/5, p. 215; Harris and Heath, p. 177. Emphasis modified.
67. Schelling, *Ideas*, HKA I/5, p. 218; Harris and Heath, p. 183. Schelling's subjectivism here should not go unremarked: his derivation of the fundamental forces in the *Ideas* leads directly to the view that 'no objective existence is possible without a mind to know it' (*Ideas*, HKA I/5, p. 215; Harris and Heath, p. 177). Thus, in 1797, Schelling argues that matter is necessarily repulsive and attractive because of the nature of the *mind*. As this commentary will go on to argue, the 1801 debate with Eschenmayer was an occasion for Schelling to disentangle himself from the subjective idealism of the 1797 *Ideas*.
68. Schelling, *Ideas*, HKA I/5, pp. 190, 253; Harris and Heath, pp. 148, 222.
69. Schelling, *Ideas*, HKA I/5, p. 253; Harris and Heath, p. 222.
70. Schelling, *Ideas*, HKA I/5, p. 253; Harris and Heath, p. 222.
71. Schelling, *Ideas*, HKA I/5, p. 238; Harris and Heath, p. 206.
72. Schelling, *Ideas*, HKA I/5, p. 239; Harris and Heath, p. 207.
73. Schelling, *Ideas*, HKA I/5, p. 247; Harris and Heath, p. 215.
74. Schelling, *Ideas*, HKA I/5, p. 248; Harris and Heath, p. 216.
75. Schelling, *Ideas*, HKA I/5, p. 286; Harris and Heath, p. 252.
76. Schelling, *Ideas*, HKA I/5, p. 287; Harris and Heath, p. 253.
77. Relatedly, Schelling follows Kant in arguing that it is through the *regulative* use of reason that chemistry can interpret sensible qualities in terms of the fundamental forces; that is, the contingent features of the natural world can be *regarded* as 'merely different modifications and relationships of the basic forces' (*Ideas*, HKA I/5, pp. 266, 270; Harris and Heath, pp. 232–3, 237).
78. Schelling, *First Outline*, HKA I/7, p. 86; Peterson, p. 22.
79. Jantzen, 'Eschenmayer', p. 161.
80. Schelling, *First Outline*, HKA I/7, p. 86; Peterson, p. 22.

81. Schelling, *First Outline*, HKA I/7, p. 87; Peterson, pp. 22–3.
82. Novalis, *Schriften*, 4:263.
83. F. W. J. Schelling, 'Letter to Fichte, 19/11/1800', HKA III/2.1, p. 281; *Rupture*, pp. 46–7.
84. Eschenmayer, *Correspondence*, p. 190 below.
85. See Eschenmayer's letter to Schelling from 20 October 1800, in which the former claims that mathematical principles 'owe their origin to our mind's necessary manner of acting'. Eschenmayer, *Correspondence*, p. 190 below.
86. Schelling, *First Outline*, HKA I/7, p. 152; Peterson, p. 87.
87. Schelling, *First Outline*, HKA I/7, p. 268; Peterson, p. 189.
88. Schelling, *First Outline*, HKA I/7, p. 269; Peterson, p. 190.
89. Schelling, *First Outline*, HKA I/7, p. 269; Peterson, p. 190.
90. Schelling, *Universal Deduction*, HKA I/8, pp. 330–3; trans. Iain Hamilton Grant. See also Schelling, *First Outline*, HKA I/7, pp. 143–4; Peterson, pp. 77–8.
91. Schelling, *First Outline*, HKA I/7, p. 88; Peterson, p. 24.
92. Schelling, *First Outline*, HKA I/7, p. 86; Peterson, p. 21.
93. Schelling, *Introduction to the Outline*, HKA I/8, p. 49; Peterson, p. 209.
94. Schelling, *First Outline*, HKA I/7, p. 86; Peterson, p. 21. Emphasis modified.
95. Schelling, *First Outline*, HKA I/7, p. 87; Peterson, p. 22.
96. Schelling, *First Outline*, HKA I/7, p. 87; Peterson, p. 22. Emphasis modified.
97. Schelling, *First Outline*, HKA I/7, p. 87; Peterson, p. 22.
98. Schelling, *First Outline*, HKA I/8, 49; Peterson, p. 209.
99. Schelling, *First Outline*, HKA I/7, 85; Peterson, p. 21.
100. Schelling, *First Outline*, HKA I/7, 93; Peterson, p. 29.
101. Schelling, *First Outline*, HKA I/7, p. 89; Peterson, p. 25.
102. Schelling, *Introduction to the Outline*, HKA I/8, pp. 55–6; Peterson, p. 214.
103. Schelling, *First Outline*, HKA I/7, p. 98; Peterson, p. 32.
104. Schelling, *First Outline*, HKA I/7, p. 102; Peterson, p. 35.
105. Schelling, *First Outline*, HKA I/7, p. 93; Peterson, p. 29.
106. On the connection between Kant's pre-critical *Physical Monadology* and Schelling's dynamic atomism, see Michela Massimi, 'Philosophy and the Chemical Revolution after Kant', in Karl Ameriks (ed.), *The Cambridge Companion to German Idealism* (Cambridge: Cambridge University Press, 2017), pp. 188–9.
107. In the *Introduction to the Outline*, Schelling goes on to suggest that 'quality is a higher power of matter', and that 'all quality is something by virtue of which the body is, so to speak, *raised above itself*' (HKA, I/8, pp. 49–50; Peterson, pp. 209–10). In such passages, Schelling's mature nature-philosophical view begins to emerge: material qualities cannot be reduced to fundamental forces, yet they are related to one another as higher and lower powers of the *same reality*. This is the view that Schelling develops over the next two years.
108. Eschenmayer, *Spontaneity = World Soul*, p. 26 above.
109. Eschenmayer, *Spontaneity = World Soul*, p. 29 above.
110. Eschenmayer, *Spontaneity = World Soul*, p. 22 above.
111. Schelling, *First Outline*, HKA I/7, p. 256; Peterson, p. 179.
112. Marks, *Differenz*, p. 98.
113. Eschenmayer, *Spontaneity = World Soul*, p. 32 above.
114. Eschenmayer, *Spontaneity = World Soul*, p. 32 above.
115. Eschenmayer, *Spontaneity = World Soul*, p. 32 above.
116. As Jantzen points out, Eschenmayer is in many ways close to the Schelling of 1797 at this point – for both turn to 'a transcendental analysis of intuition' to justify Kant's dynamical explanation of matter ('Eschenmayer und Schelling', p. 76).
117. Eschenmayer, *Spontaneity = World Soul*, pp. 32–3 above.
118. Eschenmayer, *Spontaneity = World Soul*, p. 33 above.
119. Eschenmayer, *Spontaneity = World Soul*, p. 33 above.

120. Eschenmayer, *Spontaneity = World Soul*, p. 34 above.
121. Eschenmayer, *Spontaneity = World Soul*, p. 34 above.
122. Eschenmayer, *Spontaneity = World Soul*, p. 34 above. Marks outlines the necessity behind Eschenmayer's turn to a theory of sensation as follows, 'Since for Eschenmayer it is indubitably the case that consciousness represent natural products in terms of qualitative determinations, it is now necessary to find an explanation for the *appearance* of original qualities in matter for "normal consciousness"', that is, 'to explain qualities as subjective sensations of our senses' (*Differenz*, p. 110).
123. Eschenmayer, *Spontaneity = World Soul*, pp. 34–5 above.
124. Eschenmayer, *Spontaneity = World Soul*, p. 36 above.
125. Eschenmayer, *Spontaneity = World Soul*, p. 35 above.
126. Eschenmayer, *Spontaneity = World Soul*, pp. 35–6 above.
127. Eschenmayer, *Spontaneity = World Soul*, p. 40 above.
128. For reasons of space, we pass over the remarks Eschenmayer makes at the end of *Spontaneity = World Soul* on gravity. Eschenmayer contests this by means of a reinterpretation of Baader's *On the Pythagorean Square in Nature* and thus turns his disagreement with Schelling into a matter of who better understands Baader – a topic that takes us far beyond the limits of this chapter.
129. Schelling, *On the True Concept*, p. 55 above.
130. Schelling, *Universal Deduction*, HKA I/8, p. 364; trans. Iain Hamilton Grant.
131. Schelling, *On the True Concept*, p. 55 above.
132. Schelling, *On the True Concept*, pp. 55–6 above.
133. Schelling, *On the True Concept*, pp. 55–6 above.
134. Schelling, *On the True Concept*, p. 56 above.
135. As Jantzen notes, 'Clearly recognisable [here] is the old, Eschenmayerian schema of potentiation.' Jantzen, 'Eschenmayer und Schelling', p. 78.
136. Schelling, *Universal Deduction*, HKA I/8, p. 300; trans. Iain Hamilton Grant.
137. Schelling, *Universal Deduction*, HKA I/8, pp. 303–4; trans. Iain Hamilton Grant.
138. Schelling, *On the True Concept*, p. 51 above.
139. In fact, Marks already discerns in Eschenmayer's own account in *Spontaneity = World Soul* a 'distancing' from the model of *Principles of Nature-Metaphysics* (a 'break' even) and a corresponding 'convergence' with the outlook of Schellingian philosophy of nature (*Differenz*, p. 167).
140. Schelling, *On the True Concept*, pp. 57–8 above.
141. He writes, 'I find the whole thing very astute with individual claims of compelling truth.' Schelling, *On the True Concept*, p. 58 above.
142. Schelling, *On the True Concept*, p. 59 above.
143. Schelling, *On the True Concept*, pp. 59–60 above.
144. Schelling, *Ideas*, HKA I/13, p. 209; Harris and Heath, p. 137. See also Schelling, *Ideas*, HKA I/13, p. 307; Harris and Heath, pp. 219–20.
145. Schelling, *Ideas*, HKA I/13, p. 275; Harris and Heath, p. 192.
146. Schelling, *Ideas*, HKA I/13, p. 286; Harris and Heath, p. 202.
147. Editors' comment to HKA I/10, p. 75. Similarly, Jantzen claims that in Schelling's identity philosophy, 'reality . . . can be explained as a result of the potentiation of an indifference and also therefore can be expressed in the structure of quantitative difference. Here lies the lasting significance of Eschenmayer for Schelling' ('Eschenmayer', p. 158). Marquet similarly writes, 'As early as 1797, the *Ideas* had shown, following Eschenmayer, that each natural individuality is posited by certain quantitative differences in relation to the two constitutive forces of matter; this hypothesis is taken back up here in the framework of a global metaphysical explanation of the universe' (*Liberté et existence*, p. 211).
148. Rang, *Identität und Indifferenz*, p. 150.
149. See Sarhan Dhouib, 'Die Begriffe Indifferenz, quantitative Differenz und Endlichkeit in Schellings *Darstellung meines Systems der Philosophie*', in Mildred Galland-

Szymkowiak (ed.), *Das Problem der Endlichkeit in der Philosophie Schellings* (Münster: Lit-Verlag, 2011).
150. Schelling, *Presentation*, HKA I/10, pp. 138–9; *Rupture*, p. 159.
151. Indeed, one of the first passages in which Schelling discusses the construction of a magnetic line is in correspondence with Eschenmayer: 'I am already thinking of the magnet as the original 1, 2, 3 and as the image of the arithmetic line ascending and descending in one dimension.' Eschenmayer and Schelling, *Correspondence*, pp. 190-1 below.
152. Schelling, *On the True Concept*, p. 61 above.

Chapter 2: Potency

1. See Hans Niel Jahnke, 'Mathematik und Romantik', in Voker Peckhaus and Christian Thiel (eds), *Disciplinen im Kontext* (Munich: Fink, 1999), pp. 168–70.
2. C. F. Hindenburg, *Der polynomische Lehrsatz* (Leipzig: Fleischer, 1796), p. 150.
3. Novalis studied with Hindenburg between 1791 and 1793 and owned a number of his books, including the above. On Hindenburg and Novalis, see Jahnke, 'Mathematik und Romantik', Pollack-Milgate, 'Mathematical Infinite' and John Neubauer, 'Zwischen Natur und mathematischer Abstraktion: der Potenzbegriff in der Frühromantik', in Richard Brinkmann (ed.), *Romantik in Deutschland* (Stuttgart: Metzler, 1978).
4. Pollack-Milgate, 'Mathematical Infinite', p. 55. Likewise, Timmermans describes Hindenburg's use of potentiation as follows: 'the raising of the binomial a + b to a nth power (a + b)n was interpreted as the recitation of a series of combinations of n elements.' Benoît Timmermans, 'Novalis et la réforme des mathematiques', in Augustin Dumont and Laurent van Eynde (eds), *Modernité romantique* (Paris: Kimé, 2011), p. 80.
5. Jantzen, 'Eschenmayer', p. 157.
6. Roux, 'Introduction', p. 23.
7. Schelling, *On the World Soul*, HKA I/6, p. 196.
8. Schelling, *First Outline*, HKA I/7, p. 325; Peterson, p. 231. See also *First Outline*, HKA I/7, pp. 220–2; Peterson, pp. 150–2.
9. Schelling, *Presentation*, HKA I/10, p. 116; *Rupture*, p. 145.
10. Tilliette, *Schelling*, 1:261
11. See the 1804 *System* (SSW 6:131–576), which presents a more complicated series of natural potencies but also contains the most detailed account of Schelling's early understanding of the spiritual potencies. It should be remarked that, in *On the True Concept*, Schelling understands 'art' as neither natural nor spiritual but in terms of their higher unity.
12. Schelling, *Presentation*, HKA I/10, p. 136; *Rupture*, p. 157.
13. Schelling, *Presentation*, HKA I/10, p. 146; *Rupture*, p. 164.
14. Schelling, *Presentation*, HKA I/10, p. 147; *Rupture*, p. 165.
15. Schelling, *Presentation*, HKA I/10, p. 150; *Rupture*, p. 167.
16. Schelling, *Presentation*, HKA I/10, p. 150; *Rupture*, p. 167.
17. Schelling, *Presentation*, HKA I/10, p. 150; *Rupture*, p. 167.
18. Schelling, *Presentation*, HKA I/10, p. 151; *Rupture*, p. 168.
19. Schelling, *Presentation*, HKA I/10, p. 153; *Rupture*, p. 169.
20. Schelling, *Presentation*, HKA I/10, pp. 158–9; *Rupture*, p. 172.
21. Schelling, *Presentation*, HKA I/10, pp. 180–1; *Rupture*, p. 185. To be sure, chemical combinations ultimately generate new material bodies with their own qualitative specificity, and in this way natural objects prove once again to be constituted by a (limited) form of difference. But the philosopher can isolate the first moment of chemical combination in order to reveal the fact that, in the combination of two materials, polarity (A = B) is dissolved and indifference (A = A) is maximally

exhibited in inorganic nature. It is for this reason that Schelling describes the chemical process as gravity raised to the second power: in gravitational motion, material bodies combine with one another and thereby seek to relinquish their spatiotemporal specificity; in the chemical process, the combination of substances yields not only spatiotemporal identity but the return of a qualitatively distinct object to its more fundamental state, that is, sheer identity.
22. Schelling, *Introduction to the First Outline*, HKA I/8, p. 72; Peterson, p. 229. Emphasis modified.
23. Schelling, *Presentation*, *HKA* I/10, p. 150; *Rupture*, p. 167. Schelling discusses the process through which material bodies become magnetised in *Ideas*, HKA I/5, pp. 166–70; Harris and Heath, pp. 122–5.
24. Schelling, *Ideas*, *HKA* I/13, pp. 198–9; Harris and Heath, pp. 128–9.
25. Schelling, *Ideas*, *HKA* I/5, p. 170; Harris and Heath, p. 125. Emphasis modified.
26. Schelling, *Presentation*, *HKA* I/10, p. 182; *Rupture*, p. 186.
27. Since the texts of 1801 devote comparatively little attention to the third potency, the following draws heavily upon the nascent doctrine of the potencies presented in the *First Outline* and its *Introduction*.
28. See Schelling, *First Outline*, *HKA* I/7, p. 325; Peterson, p. 231.
29. Schelling, *First Outline*, *HKA* I/7, pp. 228–9; Peterson, p. 157. It is worth pointing out that, just as Schelling thinks the universal categories of physics are exhibited in *all matter*, he argues that sensibility is a universal feature of life: all living things – plants included – exhibit at least a minimal degree of sentience. In Schelling's words, 'The spark of sensibility' necessarily exists in '*everything* organic, even if its existence cannot be demonstrated everywhere in nature', 'e.g., in the greater part of the plant world'. Schelling, *First Outline*, *HKA* I/7, pp. 181, 215; Peterson, pp. 114, 146.
30. Schelling, *First Outline*, *HKA* I/7, pp. 190–1; Peterson, p. 125.
31. To complicate matters, Schelling notes that the reproductive drive is most intense in plant life – that is, in life which exhibits the lowest degree of sensibility. Following Kielmeyer, he argues that the scale of organisms which runs from the 'first animal' to the 'last plant' exhibits proportions of increased reproductive drive and decreased sensibility. *First Outline*, *HKA* I/7, p. 219; Peterson, p. 149.
32. Schelling, *Presentation*, *HKA* I/10, p. 150; *Rupture*, p. 167.
33. As Schelling puts it in the *Universal Deduction*: 'The particular determinations of matter that we conceive of under the name of qualities, and which I . . . call attributes of the second power, have their ground in the different proportions of those three functions in bodies, and only with this proposition is the universal principle of a construction of qualitative difference discovered.' *HKA* I/8, p. 343; trans. Iain Hamilton Grant.
34. Schelling, *Presentation*, *HKA* I/10, pp. 202–4; *Rupture*, pp. 199–200.
35. In this specific regard, the potencies of Schellingian identity are fairly similar to the hypostases of the Plotinean One. See Paul Redding, *Hegel's Hermeneutics* (Ithaca: Cornell University Press, 1996), p. 60.
36. As Schelling puts it in the *Presentation*, 'All potencies are absolutely contemporaneous' (*HKA* I/10, p. 136; *Rupture*, p. 157).
37. Francesco Moiso, 'Die Hegelsche Theorie der Physik und der Chemie in ihrer Beziehung zu Schellings Naturphilosophie' in R. P. Horstmann and M. J. Petry (eds), *Hegels Philosophie der Natur: Beziehungen zwischen empirischer und spekulativer Naturerkenntnis* (Stuttgart: Klett, 1986), p. 65.
38. See, for example, Jeremy Dunham, Iain Hamilton Grant and Sean Watson, *Idealism: The History of Philosophy* (Abingdon: Routledge, 2014), p. 143 and Charlotte Alderwick, 'Nature's Capacities: Schelling and Contemporary Power-Based Ontologies', *Angelaki* 21.4 (2016), pp. 59–76.
39. Brian Ellis, *The Philosophy of Nature: A Guide to the New Essentialism* (Montreal: McGill-Queen's University Press, 2002), p. 59.

40. George Molnar, *Powers: A Study in Metaphysics*, ed. Stephen Mumford (Oxford: Oxford University Press, 2003), pp. 125–42.
41. Alderwick, 'Nature's Capacities', p. 59.
42. Ellis, for example, appears to return to Aristotle, at least in part, because he understands the modern tradition of European philosophy as being committed to the view that natural objects are fundamentally passive. For example, he remarks that 'the founding fathers of all of the major philosophical traditions of western Europe' – 'Descartes, Newton and Hume, but also . . . Locke and Kant' – conceive natural objects as lacking intrinsic capacities for action (*Philosophy of Nature*, p. 2). It is telling that Spinoza and Leibniz do not appear on Ellis's list.
43. Aristotle, *Metaphysics*, trans. Hugh Lawson-Tancred (London: Penguin, 2004), Θ: I, 1046a.
44. Aristotle, *Metaphysics* Δ: XII, 1019a. In addition to conceiving *dunamis* as (1) a being's potential to act and (2) a being's potential to be acted upon, Aristotle understands *dunamis* as a being's potential to perform an act *well*, either (3) through its own activity or (4) through the activity of some other being. Finally, (5) Aristotle remarks that *not* having a particular *dunamis* is itself a potentiality – for example, a thing's *incapacity* to change shape can cause it to break and, in this way, can also be understood as a capacity.
45. Schelling, *Presentation*, HKA I/10, p. 146; *Rupture*, p. 164.
46. Plato, *Theaetetus* 147d; trans. M. F. Burnyeat in *Explorations in Ancient and Modern Philosophy: Volume 2* (Cambridge: Cambridge University Press, 2012), p. 43.
47. Plato, *Theaetetus* 148a–b. See also Plato's geometrical use of the term at *Republic* 587d, *Timaeus* 31c–32a and *Statesman* 266a–b. On the potential Babylonian source of the mathematical conception of *dunamis*, see Jens Høyrup, 'Dynamis, the Babylonians, and Theaetetus 147c7—148d7', in *Historia Mathematica* 17.3 (1990), pp. 201–22.
48. Euclid, *The Thirteen Books of the Elements, Volume 3*, trans. Thomas Little Heath (New York: Dover, 1956), p. 10. Cf. Ian Mueller, 'Greek Arithmetic, Geometry and Harmonics: Thales to Plato' in *Routledge History of Philosophy, Volume I: From Beginning to Plato*, ed. C. C. W. Taylor (London and New York: Routledge, 1997), p. 257.
49. Aristotle, *Metaphysics* Θ: I, 1046a.
50. Aristotle, *Metaphysics* Δ: XII, 1019b.
51. In fact, there can already be found in Plato the suggestion that 'powers' can be understood in abstraction from 'things' altogether. As Beere writes, 'the meticulous reader will have noticed that Theaetetus says that the lines *are* powers', whereas Aristotle – in his own discussion of geometry – 'say[s] that they *have* powers'. Jonathan Beere, *Doing and Being: An Interpretation of Aristotle's* Metaphysics Theta (Oxford: Oxford University Press, 2009), p. 39.
52. Plato, *Theaetetus* 148b.
53. Thomas L. Heath, *Diophantus of Alexandria: A Study in the History of Greek Algebra* (Cambridge: Cambridge University Press, 1910), p. 129.
54. This is not to suggest that between Diophantus and Descartes there is no development of symbolic notation in algebra. Rafael Bombelli, for example, employs a notation that is very similar to the one with which we are familiar today. See Victor J. Katz and Karen Hunger Parshall, *Taming the Unknown: A History of Algebra from Antiquity to the Early Twentieth Century* (Princeton: Princeton University Press, 2014), p. 223.
55. René Descartes, *Discourse on Method, Optics, Geometry, and Meteorology*, trans. Paul J. Olscamp (Indianapolis: Hackett Publishing Company, 2001), p. 178.
56. Descartes, *Geometry*, p. 178.
57. Danielle Macbeth, *Realizing Reason: A Narrative of Truth and Knowing* (Oxford: Oxford University Press, 2014), p. 127.

58. W. C. Zimmerli, 'Potenzlehre versus Logik der Naturphilosophie', in R. P. Horstmann and M. J. Petry (eds), *Hegels Philosophie der Natur: Beziehungen zwischen empirischer und spekulativer Naturerkenntnis* (Stuttgart: Klett, 1986), p. 320.
59. For a related discussion about the holism of Schelling's philosophy of nature and how a holistic, Schellingian framework might help complement work in contemporary powers ontology, see Alderwick, 'Nature's Capacities', p. 63.
60. Hermann Zeltner, 'Das Identitätssystem', in Hans Michael Baumgartner (ed.), *Schelling: Einführung in seine Philosophie* (Freiburg: Alber, 1975), p. 88.
61. Zimmerli, 'Potenzlehre versus Logik', pp. 317–19.
62. W. C. Zimmerli, 'Schelling in Hegel: Zur Potenzenmethodik in Hegels "System der Sittlichkeit"', in Ludwig Hasler (ed.), *Schelling: Seine Bedeutung für eine Philosophie der Natur und der Geschichte* (Stuttgart: Frommann-Holzboog, 1981).
63. G. W. F. Hegel, *Lectures on the History of Philosophy*, *HW* XX, p. 445; *The Lectures of 1825–1826*, vol. 3, trans. R. F. Brown and J. M. Stewart (Berkeley and Los Angeles: University of California Press, 1990), p. 270.
64. The potencies are not the only feature of Schellingian metaphysics that has its origin in the discipline of mathematics. As Hegel notes, there is a connection between Schelling's utilisation of this algebraic concept and his Spinozist method of construction in the *Presentation* (*Lectures on the History of Philosophy*, *HW* XX, p. 437; Brown and Stewart translation, 3:267–8). In both cases, Hegel thinks, Schelling improperly adopts a style of thinking from beyond the purview of philosophy.
65. Hegel, *Lectures on the History of Philosophy*, *HW* XX, pp. 437–8; Brown and Stewart translation, 3:268.
66. G. W. F. Hegel, *Phenomenology of Spirit*, *HW* III, p. 21; trans. A. V. Miller (Oxford: Oxford University Press, 1977), p. 9.
67. As Beiser points out, this is why Hegel's critique of Schellingian intellectual intuition is not a critique of apophatic mysticism – which in no way describes Schelling's project – but a critique of the use of mathematical construction within philosophy. Frederick C. Beiser, 'Mathematical Method in Kant, Schelling, and Hegel', in *Discourse on a New Method: Reinvigorating the Marriage of History and Philosophy of Science*, ed. Mary Domski and Michael Dickson (La Salle: Open Court, 2010), p. 245.
68. Hegel, *Lectures on the History of Philosophy*, *HW* XX, p. 445; Brown and Stewart translation, 3:270.
69. Hegel, *Phenomenology of Spirit*, *HW* III, p. 21; p. 8. Emphasis modified.
70. Hegel, *Phenomenology of Spirit*, *HW* III, p. 21; Miller translation, p. 8.
71. Hegel, *Phenomenology of Spirit*, *HW* III, p. 23; Miller translation, p. 10.
72. Schelling, *On the World Soul*, *HKA* I/6, p. 67; trans. Iain Hamilton Grant.
73. As late as 1812, Schelling continues to be disappointed with Eschenmayer's reliance upon 'mathematical comparisons' and his 'inclination to bring everything back to ... dead formulas'. Schelling, translated by Lauer and Wirth in Wirth, *Schelling's Practice of the Wild*, p. 185.
74. Schelling, *Further Presentations*, *SSW* 4:398–9.
75. G. W. F. Hegel, *Science of Logic*, *HW* V, pp. 54–5; trans. A. V. Miller (London: Prometheus, 1969), pp. 57–8.
76. Hegel, *Science of Logic*, *HW* V, pp. 247–8; Miller translation, p. 215.
77. Hegel, *Science of Logic*, *HW* VI, p. 24; Miller translation, p. 399. Emphasis modified.
78. Hegel, *Science of Logic*, *HW* V, pp. 20–1; Miller translation, pp. 31–2.
79. Schelling, *Presentation*, *HKA* I/10, p. 139; *Rupture*, p. 159. Translation modified. See the reproduction of Schelling's magnetic line on p. 93 above.
80. Hegel, *Science of Logic*, *HW* V, p. 248; Miller translation, p. 215.
81. According to Hegel, numbers are simply 'unsuitable mediums for expressing thoughts'. G. W. F. Hegel, *Introductory Lectures on the History of Philosophy*, *HW* 18,

p. 110; trans. J. Glenn Gray in *Introductory Lectures on Art, Religion, and Philosophy* (Indianapolis: Hackett, 1970), p. 292.
82. F. W. J. Schelling, *On University Studies*, *SSW* 5:246–7; ed. Nobert Guterman and trans. E. S. Morgan (Athens: Ohio University Press, 1966), p. 40.
83. Schelling, *Further Presentations of the System of Philosophy*, *SSW* 4:398–9; *Rupture*, p. 217.
84. Although Schelling suggests in the *First Outline* that nature's history may be philosophically significant (see, for example, *Introduction to the First Outline*, *HKA* I/8: p. 71; Peterson, pp. 227–8), his considered view of the period is clear: nature's potentiation is in no way historical, since all the potencies are contemporaneous. For a discussion of Schelling's subsequent philosophical development on this matter, see Berger, 'Schelling, Hegel, and the History of Nature', forthcoming in *The Review of Metaphysics*.
85. Badiou's distinction between 'the little style' and 'the grand style' is helpful here: the former treats mathematics as an object or regional science to be understood by philosophy; the latter 'stipulates that mathematics provides a direct illumination of philosophy, rather than the opposite'. Alain Badiou, 'Mathematics and Philosophy: The Grand Style and the Little Style' in *Theoretical Writings*, ed. and trans. Ray Brassier and Alberto Toscano (London and New York: Bloomsbury, 2004), p. 7.

Chapter 3: Identity

1. He writes, 'I confess to assuming with *Fichte* the A = B in an original opposition, and –according to form – just as unconditionally as the A = A.' Eschenmayer and Schelling, *Correspondence*, p. 193 below.
2. F. W. J. Schelling, *First Outline*, *HKA* I/7, p. 183; Peterson, p. 117.
3. F. W. J. Schelling, *Universal Deduction*, *HKA* I/8, p. 300; trans. Iain Hamilton Grant.
4. Schelling, *On the True Concept*, p. 61 above.
5. As this implies, Schelling's position here changes decisively not just from the nature-philosophical writings of 1799, but also from the *System of Transcendental Idealism* of 1800. This break in Schelling's conception of identity between early 1800 and early 1801 is similarly emphasised by Reinhard Lauth, *Die Entstehung von Schellings Identitätsphilosophie in der Auseinandersetzung mit Fichtes Wissenschaftslehre (1795–1801)* (Freiburg: Karl Alber, 1975), p. 153 and Dhouib, 'Die Begriffe Indifferenz', as well as Sven Jürgensen, 'Schellings logisches Prinzip: Die Unterschied in der Identität', in Christoph Asmuth et al. (eds), *Schelling: Zwischen Fichte und Hegel* (Amsterdam: Rodopi, 2000), p. 115. Jürgensen also helpfully identifies *On the True Concept* as 'the turning point' in Schelling's thinking on identity ('Logisches Prinzip', p. 115).
6. Schelling, *First Outline*, *HKA* I/7: 230; Peterson, p. 158.
7. Schelling, *On the True Concept*, p. 50 above. It is Paul Ziche who has most clearly tracked Schelling's evolution in this regard. He notes how Schelling 'took over Eschenmayer's mathematical terminology in a very abbreviated and, at certain key junctures, completely altered manner' (*Mathematische und naturwissenschaftliche Modelle*, p. 218) – with the key alteration involving the elimination of duality from the potentiated series. According to Schelling and *pace* Eschenmayer, 'The [terms of the series] are not the product of two (qualitatively differentiated) magnitudes, but an identity of two magnitudes which are to be thought as qualitatively and quantitatively identical.' This is a 'consciously chosen alternative to Eschenmayer' that consists in the fact that 'for Schelling it is not the balancing of different magnitudes, but in fact their identity which is decisive' (*Mathematische und naturwissenschaftliche Modelle*, p. 219). Ziche goes on to indicate how this model as first articulated in *On the True Concept* becomes determinative for the metaphysics of the 1801 *Presentation* (*Mathematische und naturwissenschaftliche Modelle*, p. 225).

8. What is more, Schelling also goes further than Eschenmayer in conceiving of philosophical methodology itself according to this potentiated line of identities. That is, while Eschenmayer's subjective idealism makes the epistemic operations of the philosopher's mind prior to – and therefore distinct from – the series of ratios of opposed natural forces, *Schelling naturalises philosophical methodology*, such that the philosopher is understood to pass up and down the line of identities, just as nature does. It is this process of naturalisation that grounds his key methodological doctrine of 'immersive abstraction' elucidated in Chapter 5. In short, the philosopher *too* is identical with nature, and she philosophises about nature by performing the processes of potentiation and depotentiation that characterise natural productivity.
9. Schelling, *On the True Concept*, p. 51 above.
10. Schelling, *On University Studies*, *SSW* 5:272; Morgan translation, p. 66.
11. See pp. 92–3 above.
12. Rang, *Identität und Indifferenz*, pp. 134, 142.
13. Schelling, *Presentation*, *HKA* I/10, p. 138; *Rupture*, p. 253.
14. F. W. J. Schelling, *System of Philosophy in General and of the Philosophy of Nature in Particular*, *SSW* 6:179; *Idealism and the Endgame of Theory: Three Essays*, ed. and trans. Thomas Pfau (Albany: SUNY Press, 1994), p. 169.
15. Schelling, *Presentation*, *HKA* I/10, p. 135; *Rupture*, p. 157. As Schelling puts it in the *System* of 1804, 'We can nowhere in the universe conceive of an essential or qualitative difference.' *SSW* 6:179; Pfau translation, p. 169.
16. Philip Schwab, 'A = A. Zur identitätslogischen Systemgrundlegung bei Fichte, Schelling und Hegel', in *International Yearbook of German Idealism* 12 (2017), p. 263. Schwab goes on to distinguish two main controversies around the law of identity in early German Idealism: first, the 'material' dispute between Fichte and Schelling in 1799–1800 over whether the proposition I = I provides the transcendental guarantee for the validity of A = A (i.e. whether transcendental idealism has priority over other philosophical pursuits); secondly, the 'structural' controversy between Schelling and Hegel in 1801 over the relation between identity and difference ('A = A', pp. 264–6). As our concern in this chapter is with 1801, we assume the Schellingian position on the 'material' dispute (that A = A grounds the system) in order to focus on the 'structural' dispute, which, we suggest, also involves Fichte and, most importantly, Eschenmayer.
17. See Schwab's corrective: 'The debates in classic German philosophy around identity and difference in no way find their end in Hegel's *Differenzschrift* and still less their fulfilment' ('A = A', p. 285), and there should certainly be no imputation of 'a teleological three-step à la Kroner' ('A = A', p. 265). Rather, what exist at this time are 'different constellations of identity and difference' ('A = A', p. 265).
18. G. W. F. Hegel, *The Difference between Fichte's and Schelling's System of Philosophy*, *HW* II, p. 96; trans. H. S. Harris and Walter Cerf (Albany: SUNY, 1977), p. 156.
19. Hegel, *Difference*, *HW* II, p. 115; Harris and Cerf translation, p. 174.
20. Hegel, *Difference*, *HW* II, pp. 39, 41; Harris and Cerf translation, pp. 108–9.
21. Grant puts it more polemically: 'When Hegel attempts the presentation of Schellingian identity, he botches it royally' (Grant, *Philosophies of Nature after Schelling*, p. 189).
22. Schelling, *Presentation*, *HKA* I/10, p. 122; *Rupture*, p. 150.
23. Schelling, *Presentation*, *HKA* I/10, p. 117; *Rupture*, p. 146.
24. Schelling, *Further Presentations*, *SSW* 4:375.
25. Hence, Uslar helpfully glosses, 'This inner movement of absolute identity, which comes so close to Hegelian dialectic, is different from the latter above all through the fundamental element that it is not a negation of the negation, but the finite potentiation of an identity of identity' (Detlev von Uslar, 'Die innere Bewegung der absoluten Identität bei Schelling', *Studium Generale* 21 (1968), p. 507). See also Beiser,

German Idealism, pp. 590–2, and Ziche, *Mathematische und naturwissenschaftliche Modelle*, p. 230.
26. See I. P. V. Troxler, 'Hauptmomente aus Schellings Vortrage nach der Stunde aufgezeichnet, 1801', in Klaus Düsing, *Schellings und Hegels erste absolute Metaphysik (1801–2)* (Cologne: Dinter, 1988), pp. 27–62.
27. F.W.J. Schelling, *Bruno, or On the Natural and Divine Principle of Things*, HKA I/11, p. 359; trans. Michael G. Vater (Albany: SUNY Press, 1984), p. 136.
28. Klaus Düsing, *Schellings und Hegels erste absolute Metaphysik (1801–2)* (Cologne: Dinter, 1988), pp. 145–6.
29. Düsing, *Schellings und Hegels erste absolute Metaphysik*, p. 148.
30. Düsing, *Schellings und Hegels erste absolute Metaphysik*, pp. 149, 151.
31. Friedrich Engels, *Anti-Schelling* in the *Collected Works of Karl Marx and Friedrich Engels, Vol. 2, Engels: 1834–42* (New York: International Publishers, 1975).
32. Georg Lukács, *The Destruction of Reason*, trans. Peter Palmer (London: Merlin, 1980), pp. 134–5.
33. He writes, for instance: 'Schelling and Hegel, to be sure, hold different views about this whole. Schelling believes that the overarching identity cannot be explained in terms of the relation between identity and difference subordinated under it. Hegel, on the other hand, thinks that this is precisely how they must be explained.' And he goes on to emphasise Schelling's 'unwilling[ness] to associate himself with the interpretation of his position his friend Hegel proposed'. Manfred Frank, '"Identity of identity and non-identity": Schelling's Path to the "absolute system of identity"', in Lara Ostaric (ed.), *Interpreting Schelling: Critical Essays* (Cambridge: Cambridge University Press, 2014), pp. 120–1.
34. Frank, '"Identity of identity and non-identity"', p. 120. A similar position is proposed by Bernhard Rang, for whom Schelling's definition of identity in *Bruno*, influenced by Hegel, is Schelling's only worthwhile word on the subject (*Identität und Indifferenz*, pp. 7–11).
35. Frank, '"Identity of identity and non-identity"', p. 120.
36. Frank, '"Identity of identity and non-identity"', p. 124.
37. Frank, '"Identity of identity and non-identity"', p. 123.
38. 'There Schelling still treats Hegel as a competitor engaged in the same project, that of trying to give the best interpretation of the formula that expresses the fundamental principle of philosophy: an identity which is enriched by virtue of including within itself its other.' Frank, '"Identity of identity and non-identity"', p. 143.
39. For a robust articulation of this position, see also Beiser, *German Idealism*, p. 565.
40. For details of Fichte's response to the *Presentation*, see Lauth, *Entstehung*, pp. 154–81.
41. J. G. Fichte, *On the Presentation of Schelling's System of Identity*, Rupture, p. 122.
42. Fichte, *On the Presentation*, Rupture, p. 129.
43. Fichte, *On the Presentation*, Rupture, p. 125.
44. Fichte, *On the Presentation*, Rupture, p. 129.
45. Fichte, 'Letter to Schelling, 07/08/1801', *Rupture*, p. 72. This critique of quantitative difference has a long reception history; it is repeated most recently by Beiser, for whom 'quantitative differences are no better than qualitative ones: both fall outside the absolute standpoint [of Schelling's metaphysics], and both . . . serve as limits on the absolute.' *German Idealism*, p. 568.
46. Nassar, *The Romantic Absolute*, pp. 238–9.
47. Nassar, *The Romantic Absolute*, pp. 239–40.
48. Nassar, *The Romantic Absolute*, p. 240.
49. Nassar, *The Romantic Absolute*, p. 242.
50. Eschenmayer and Schelling, *Correspondence*, pp. 192–3 below.
51. Eschenmayer and Schelling, *Correspondence*, p. 193 below.
52. As Schwab helpfully glosses, Schelling 'takes up the absolute identity of Fichte's first principle, but omits the absolute opposition of his second principle, in order to then

appropriate the quantitative difference of Fichte's third principle' ('A = A', p. 282). Roux ('Introduction', pp. 52–5) provides the only commentary in the scholarship on this important letter (a letter which Horst Fuhrman famously truncated in his edition of Schelling's letters, because of its 'aridity'; see Xavier Tilliette, *Schelling: Biographie* [Paris: Calmann, 1999], pp. 134–5).
53. Eschenmayer and Schelling, *Correspondence*, p. 193 below.
54. Eschenmayer and Schelling, *Correspondence*, p. 193 below.
55. See Appendix 4 below.
56. Eschenmayer, *Review of Schelling*, p. 218 below.
57. Eschenmayer, *Review of Schelling*, pp. 218-19 below.
58. If nothing else, Eschenmayer's initial foray into this kind of critique in early 1801 suggests that he, at least, saw the long-standing tendency in Schelling's work from 1799 onwards to downplay the importance of the categories of negation and opposition.
59. Eschenmayer and Schelling, *Correspondence*, p. 196 below.
60. J. G. Fichte, *FSW* I, p. 105; *Foundations*, p. 105.
61. Eschenmayer and Schelling, *Correspondence*, p. 196 below.
62. Eschenmayer and Schelling, *Correspondence*, p. 196 below.
63. Eschenmayer and Schelling, *Correspondence*, p. 195 below.
64. Fichte, *FSW* I, p. 108; *Foundations*, p. 108. On Schelling's dependence on Fichte in this regard, see Schwab, 'A = A', pp. 281–2.
65. Eschenmayer and Schelling, *Correspondence*, p. 195 below.
66. In Roux's words, 'The principle missing from the Schellingian system is the principle which limits, which installs all limits' ('Introduction', p. 54).
67. For example, Eschenmayer writes, 'Since, in the construction of my series, I proceed from an absolute opposition, then A can absolutely not be expressed through B, except by means of complete opposition or, what is the same, by means of a complete cancellation of all identity between the two.' Eschenmayer and Schelling, *Correspondence*, p. 196 below.
68. In other words, Eschenmayer does not seem to recognise the extent to which Schelling had already undertaken the modification of his potentiated series in *On the True Concept*, such that it has become a series of proportions of an original *identity*, rather than a series of proportions of an original *duplicity*.
69. That is to say, fencing off the identity philosophy as beginning *ex nihilo* in May 1801 is to miss many of the continuities at issue here.
70. Eschenmayer and Schelling, *Correspondence*, p. 196 below.
71. Michael G. Vater and David W. Wood, Editors' Comments to *Rupture*, p. 137.
72. Jean-François Courtine, *Extase de la raison: Essais sur Schelling* (Paris: Galilée, 1990), p. 116.
73. Schelling, *First Outline*, HKA I/7, pp. 77–9; Peterson, pp. 13–14.
74. F. W. J. Schelling, *Philosophical Inquiries into the Nature of Human Freedom*, SSW 7:341; trans. James Gutmann (La Salle: Open Court, 1936), p. 13.
75. F. W. J. Schelling, *Philosophie der Offenbarung (Erster Teil)*, SSW 13:228–9.
76. On the above, see further Daniel Whistler, 'Identity Philosophy', in Kyla Bruff and Sean McGrath (eds), *The Palgrave Handbook to Schelling* (Basingstoke: Palgrave, forthcoming).
77. F. W. J. Schelling, *Concerning the Relation of the Plastic Arts to Nature*, SSW 7: 303; trans. Michael Bullock in Herbert Read, *The True Voice of Feeling* (London: Faber & Faber, 1953), p. 334.
78. F. W. J. Schelling, *Stuttgart Seminars*, SSW 7:424–5; trans. Thomas Pfau in *Idealism and the Endgame of Theory*, p. 200.
79. F. W. J. Schelling, *Die Weltalter Fragmente: In den Urfassungen von 1811 und 1813*, ed. Manfred Schröter (Munich: Biederstein und Leibniz, 1946), p. 56.
80. Schelling, *Die Weltalter Fragmente*, p. 28.
81. We do not mean to suggest that these ideas have no *other* sources. Chief among the

many influences on Schelling's logic of identity include Böhme's theosophy, which conceives God's immanent development precisely as a process of self-duplication, and Goethe's philosophy of nature, which places the intensification of life at the centre of analysis.

82. Schelling, *Presentation*, *HKA* I/10, p. 116; *Rupture*, p. 145. Emphasis modified. This proposition is helpfully clarified in 1804: 'The proposition A=A [does not] claim that A exists as subject or as predicate. In fact, it states the opposite: that A does not exist as predicate, and not as subject in particular, but only that their *identity* exists. Hence, this proposition allows us to abstract from everything, from the reality of the A as well as from its reality as one of a subject and predicate; the only thing from which we cannot abstract, and which remains as the only reality in this proposition, is the *self-sameness* or the *absolute identity* itself.' Schelling, *System of Philosophy in General*, *SSW* 6:146–7; Pfau translation, p. 147.

83. On the pertinence of the 1794 concept of 'inner form' to the *Presentation*, see Nassar, *The Romantic Absolute*, pp. 168–70, 228. It is owing to similarities such as this that Nassar insists that the 1801 *Presentation* 'closely resembles Schelling's earliest writings, especially *Vom Ich*' and so constitutes 'a *return* to his first philosophical goals' (Nassar, *The Romantic Absolute*, pp. 228–9).

84. In May 1801, Schelling writes to Goethe apologising for keeping hold of his edition of Spinoza while 'further working out my *Presentation*' ('Letter to Goethe, 25/5/1801', *HKA* III/2.1, p. 352). And it is for this reason, above all, that the idea of a 'return to Spinoza' in the *Presentation* (Tilliette, *Schelling*, 1:458) has become standard in Schelling scholarship – a return to the 1795 exclamation, 'Ich bin indessen Spinozist geworden!' ('Letter to Hegel, 4/2/1795', *HKA* III/1, p. 22). Recently, in contrast to traditional views that see the *Presentation* as only 'superficially' mimicking Spinoza (e.g. Lauth, *Entstehung*, p. 150), Melamed and Vater have affirmed the Spinozist character of the *Presentation*, but disagree over the precise extent of Spinoza's influence on it. For Vater, 'despite formal similarities between Spinoza's geometric method and Schelling's numbered mathematical-geometrical construction, Schelling's direct debts to Spinoza are few' ('Schelling's Philosophy of Identity and Spinoza's *Ethica more geometrico*', p. 158). Melamed, by contrast, insists that 'the beginning of the *Presentation* has much more in common with the *Ethics* than what first meets the eye' (Yitzhak Melamed, 'Deus sive Vernunft: Schelling's Transformation of Spinoza's God', in G. Anthony Bruno [ed.], *Freedom, Nature and Systematicity: Essays on F. W. J. Schelling* [Oxford: Oxford University Press, 2020]). On this latter view, 'despite appearance to the contrary, Schelling's 1801 *Presentation* essay is deeply indebted to Spinoza, not only in form and rhetoric, but also in its core metaphysics'. In what follows, we argue for a position similar to Melamed's.

85. Jürgensen's comments on the opening proposition should be borne in mind here: 'The beginning of the *Presentation* is neither a concept nor a (sensible or intellectual) intuition, but a word: "reason", which as word neither posits itself nor is posited'; the propositions that follow therefore have a 'purely logical structure' ('Logisches Prinzip', p. 116).

86. This is an idealist mutation of the transition from *in mentu* to *in re* in the traditional ontological argument of which Spinoza makes use

87. See F. W. J. Schelling, *Philosophy and Religion*, *SSW* 6:34; trans. Klaus Ottmann (Putman, Conn.: Spring, 2010), p. 22.

88. Schelling, *Presentation*, *HKA* I/10, p. 118; *Rupture*, p. 147.

89. For example, Schelling follows Fichte's assertion (minus the restriction to the self) that, '*To posit oneself* and *to be* are, as applied to the self, perfectly identical' (*FSW* I, p. 98; *Foundations*, p. 99).

90. Schelling, *Presentation*, *HKA* I/10, p. 118; *Rupture*, p. 147.

91. Schelling, *Presentation*, *HKA* I/10, p. 119; *Rupture*, p. 147. Emphasis modified.

92. See Marquet, *Liberté et existence*, p. 210: 'If A as subject and A as predicate are not

posited as such by the principle of identity, they are no less *presupposed* by it: they form an integral part of its utterance [*énoncé*] and constitute the *form* under which the existence of identity can be revealed. So, all actual identity is in fact the identity of two terms . . . [Therefore] the apparent simplicity of the principle reveals three elements: the essence of identity (the subject of the utterance), . . . the existence of identity (the object of the utterance) [and] the two terms A (the form of the utterance).'

93. Jochem Hennigfeld, *F. W. J. Schellings 'Über das Wesen der menschlichen Freiheit'* (Darmstadt: WBG, 2001), p. 19.
94. Vater, 'Schelling's Philosophy of Identity', p. 163.
95. Schelling is not far here from Deleuze's Spinozist concept of expression: 'Expression presents us with a triad . . . Substance expresses itself, attributes are expressions, and essence is expressed' (Gilles Deleuze, *Expressionism in Philosophy: Spinoza*, trans. Martin Joughin [New York: Zone, 1990], p. 27). Dodd has considered Schelling's relation to this notion of expression at length, although his conclusions about the identity philosophy depart from ours insofar as he insists on 'a minimum of discontinuity' between the three terms on Schelling's model (James Dodd, 'Expression in Schelling's Early Philosophy', *Graduate Faculty Philosophy Journal* 27.2 [2006], p. 28), whereas we will emphasise their identity *as* multiple forms of identity.
96. Vater, 'Schelling's Philosophy of Identity', p. 163. Vater and Wood similarly speak of 'something like the old metaphysical idea of the ontological proof of God's existence, but this time done from God's stance, not from the outside' (*Rupture*, p. 19).
97. Schelling, *Presentation*, *HKA* I/10, p. 119; *Rupture*, p. 148.
98. Schelling, *Presentation*, *HKA* I/10, p. 119; *Rupture*, p. 148.
99. Schelling, *Presentation*, *HKA* I/10, p. 121; *Rupture*, p. 149. Emphasis modified. This is a version of the key Spinozist tenet: 'There is no being beyond the level of the production of being.' Gregor Moder, *Hegel and Spinoza: Substance and Negativity* (Evanston: Northwestern University Press, 2017), p. 102.
100. To return to the parallel with Spinoza's *Ethics*, this point in the argument corresponds to the end of IP11 and the shift from the proof of the existence of one substance to the proof that one substance alone exists. Correspondingly, Schelling has shown that identity exists; he now needs to demonstrate that identity alone exists.
101. Schelling, *Presentation*, *HKA* I/10, p. 120; *Rupture*, p. 148. The demonstration (mainly found in § 10) goes as follows (and again the parallels to Spinoza are palpable): imagine something that is not identity; in this case, identity would be limited. But identity cannot be limited because it is infinite. Therefore, nothing but identity exists.
102. Fred Rush, 'Schelling's Critique of Hegel', in Lara Ostaric (ed.), *Interpreting Schelling: Critical Essays* (Cambridge: Cambridge University Press, 2014), p. 229. On the Jacobian tradition of *omnis determinatio est negatio*, see Robert Stern, '"Determination is negation": The Adventures of a Doctrine from Spinoza to Hegel to the British Idealists', *Hegel-Bulletin* 37.1 (2016) and Yitzhak Melamed, '"Omnis determinatio est negatio" – Determination, Negation and Self-Negation in Spinoza, Kant, and Hegel', in Eckart Förster and Melamed (eds), *Spinoza and German Idealism* (Cambridge: Cambridge University Press, 2012). On Schelling's contestation of this tradition, see further Daniel Whistler, 'Schelling on Individuation', *Comparative and Continental Philosophy* 8.3 (2016).
103. Schelling, *Philosophy and Religion*, *SSW* 6:32; Ottmann translation, p. 20.
104. Schelling, *Philosophy and Religion*, *SSW* 6:29–30; Ottmann translation, pp. 18–19.
105. Schelling, *Philosophy and Religion*, *SSW* 6:32, 30; Ottmann translation, pp. 21, 19.
106. Schelling, *Philosophy and Religion*, *SSW* 6:32; Ottmann translation, p. 22.
107. Schelling, *Presentation*, *HKA* I/10, p. 125; *Rupture*, p. 151.
108. Schelling, *Presentation*, *HKA* I/10, p. 125; *Rupture*, p. 151.
109. Schelling, *Presentation*, *HKA* I/10, p. 125; *Rupture*, p. 151.
110. Schelling, *System of Philosophy in General*, *SSW* 6:179–80; Pfau translation, p. 169.

111. Schelling, *Presentation*, *HKA* I/10, p. 125; *Rupture*, p. 151.
112. The productive logic of the 'identity of identity' recalls God's statement in Exodus 3:14, 'I am that I am', as well as Jesus' statements of identity in the Johannine Gospel, each of which recapitulates the Christ *through* identity.
113. Cf. Giovanelli's arguement that the reduction of quality to quantity can, in fact, already be seen in Fichte, and that this tendency in post-Kantian thought has its source in Kant's Principle of Anticipations of Perception. Marco Giovanelli, *Reality and Negation – Kant's Principle of Anticipations of Perception: An Investigation of its Impact on the Post-Kantian Debate* (Dordrecht: Springer, 2011), especially pp. 71–124.

Chapter 4: Drive

1. Schelling, *First Outline*, *HKA* I/7, p. 230; Peterson, p. 158.
2. Schelling, *First Outline*, *HKA* I/7, p. 271; Peterson, p. 192. Similarly, when Schelling writes in the *Introduction to the Outline*, 'This duplicity cannot be further deduced physically; for, as the condition of all nature generally, it is the principle of all physical explanation' (*HKA* I/8, p. 45; Peterson, p. 205) and 'the philosophy of nature does not have to explain the productive power of nature' (*HKA* I/8, p. 46; Peterson, p. 206), he seems to imply that a non-naturalistic – that is, transcendental – deduction might be necessary from a perspective external to philosophy of nature.
3. Eschenmayer, *Review of Schelling*, p. 219 above.
4. It is remarkable that this aspect of the Schelling–Eschenmayer debate echoes – in an idealist key – early modern debates about whether motion is intrinsic to nature. Just as counter-Enlightenment philosophers contested the radical Enlightenment assertion that motion is intrinsic to matter in order to ensure that another discourse – in this case, the theological – retained explanatory priority in the natural world, so in an analogous manner does Eschenmayer.
5. More difficult to determine is how far back in Eschenmayer's work this Fichteanism reaches. The scholarly consensus is that the 1799 *Deduction of the Living Organism* marks a turning-point from a fairly classical paradigm of Kantian dynamics to a dynamics heavily grounded in Fichtean transcendental idealism (e.g. Marchetto, 'Drive, Formative Drive, World Soul', pp. 304–5, Gilson, 'Présentation', p. 21). Marks goes further in suggesting that it is Schelling's criticisms of Eschenmayerian dynamics in the *First Outline* which converted Eschenmayer to Fichteanism in *Spontaneity = World Soul* in 1801: at this juncture, Eschenmayer 'necessarily turns to the Fichtean *Wissenschaftslehre*' to overcome Schelling's critique (*Differenz*, p. 55). Nevertheless, Senigaglia ('Einleitung', p. xv) plausibly argues that Fichtean features are evident in Eschenmayer's earlier 1797 writings. Roux problematises the standard account from another angle, noting that even when the Fichtean influence seems strongest, Eschenmayer is still creatively appropriating him: in regard to his account of production and reflection, 'Eschenmayer here believes he owes everything to Fichte, but in reality he inverts the terms in which Fichte himself thinks of these two tendencies. Infinite reflection has become, in his text, the limiting tendency' ('Introduction', p. 28).
6. A. C. A. Eschenmayer, *Die Philosophie in ihrem Übergang zur Nichtphilosophie* (Erlangen: Walther, 1803), pp. 8–11.
7. J.G. Fichte, 'Letter to Schelling, 31/5/1801', *Rupture*, p. 58.
8. Günter Zöller, *Fichte's Transcendental Philosophy: The Original Duplicity of Intelligence and Will* (Cambridge: Cambridge University Press, 1998), p. 66.
9. J. G. Fichte, *System of Ethics*, *FSW* IV, p. 152; trans. Daniel Breazeale and Günter Zöller (Cambridge: Cambridge University Press, 2005), p. 144. See also J. G. Fichte, 'On Stimulating and Increasing the Pure Interest in Truth', *FSW* VIII, pp. 349–52; trans. Daniel Breazeale in *Early Philosophical Writings* (Ithaca: Cornell University Press, 1988), pp. 228–31.

10. Fichte, *System of Ethics*, *FSW* IV, p. 124; Breazeale and Zöller translation, p. 118. Emphasis modified. In addition to demonstrating Fichte's conception of the self-determination of the drive, this statement is closely related to his commitment to the primacy of practical reason. As he writes in the *Vocation of Humanity*, 'Something *comes to be* food and drink for me not through concepts but *through hunger, thirst, and satisfaction.*' *FSW* II, p. 260; *The Vocation of Man*, trans. Peter Preuss (Indianapolis: Hackett Publishing Company, 1987), p. 77. Emphasis modified.
11. Fichte, *System of Ethics*, *FSW* IV, p. 124; Breazeale and Zöller translation, pp. 118–19.
12. Fichte, *System of Ethics*, *FSW* IV, p. 26; Breazeale and Zöller translation, p. 32.
13. Fichte, *System of Ethics*, *FSW* IV, p. 30; Breazeale and Zöller translation, p. 34.
14. Fichte, *System of Ethics*, *FSW* IV, p. 41; Breazeale and Zöller translation, p. 44.
15. Eschenmayer, *Spontaneity = World Soul*, p. 20 above.
16. Eschenmayer, *Spontaneity = World Soul*, p. 18 above.
17. Eschenmayer, *Spontaneity = World Soul*, p. 19 above.
18. Eschenmayer, *Spontaneity = World Soul*, p. 18 above.
19. Fichte, *System of Ethics*, *FSW* IV, p. 105; Breazeale and Zöller translation, p. 101.
20. Fichte, *System of Ethics*, *FSW* IV, p. 112; Breazeale and Zöller translation, p. 108.
21. See Fichte, *FSW* I, p. 296; *Foundations*, p. 260.
22. Eschenmayer, *Spontaneity = World Soul*, p. 22 above.
23. The Fichtean conception of striving is, of course, closely related to Spinoza's conception of *conatus*. See Allen Wood, *Fichte's Ethical Thought* (Oxford: Oxford University Press, 2016), pp. 63, 115, and Tom Rockmore, 'The Traction of the World, or Fichte on Practical Reason and the *Vocation of Man*', in *Fichte's Vocation of Man: New Interpretive and Critical Essays*, ed. Daniel Breazeale and Tom Rockmore (Albany: SUNY Press, 2013), p. 147.
24. See Fichte, *System of Ethics*, *FSW* IV, p. 121; Breazeale and Zöller translation, p. 116.
25. Johann Friedrich Blumenbach, Über den Bildungstrieb, 3rd edn (Göttingen: Johann Christian Dieterich, 1791), p. 32.
26. In *On the World Soul*, Schelling also remarks that the concept of the formative drive allows us to understand the inner unity of freedom and natural necessity (*HKA* I/6, p. 216).
27. Eschenmayer, *Spontaneity = World Soul*, p. 20 above.
28. Eschenmayer, *Spontaneity = World Soul*, p. 22 above.
29. Eschenmayer, *Deduction*, pp. 206–7 below.
30. Eschenmayer, *Deduction*, pp. 206–7 below.
31. Eschenmayer, *Spontaneity = World Soul*, p. 21 above and *Deduction*, p. 209 below.
32. Eschenmayer, *Spontaneity = World Soul*, p. 22 above.
33. Eschenmayer, *Deduction*, pp. 210-11 below.
34. Eschenmayer, *Spontaneity = World Soul*, p. 21 above.
35. Eschenmayer, *Deduction*, p. 208 below.
36. Eschenmayer, *Spontaneity = World Soul*, p. 21 above.
37. Eschenmayer, *Deduction*, p. 210 below.
38. Eschenmayer, *Spontaneity = World Soul*, pp. 21–2 above.
39. Eschenmayer, *Deduction*, p. 206 below.
40. Eschenmayer, *Spontaneity = World Soul*, p. 20 above.
41. Eschenmayer, *Spontaneity = World Soul*, pp. 21–2 above.
42. Eschenmayer, *Deduction*, p. 214 below.
43. Eschenmayer, *Spontaneity = World Soul*, p. 22 above.
44. Eschenmayer, *Spontaneity = World Soul*, p. 23 above.
45. Eschenmayer, *Spontaneity = World Soul*, p. 23 above.
46. Roux, 'Introduction', p. 41.
47. Marchetto, 'Drive, Formative Drive, World Soul', p. 313.
48. Eschenmayer, *Spontaneity = World Soul*, p. 25 above.

49. Marchetto, 'Drive, Formative Drive, World Soul', p. 313.
50. Fichte, *System of Ethics*, *FSW* IV, p. 124; Breazeale and Zöller translation, p. 119.
51. Fichte, *System of Ethics*, *FSW* IV, p. 115; Breazeale and Zöller translation, p. 110.
52. Fichte's argument in 'Concerning the Nature of Animals' runs as follows: we do not only attribute a drive to other *organisms*, but we attribute a drive to 'each atom in nature' – which allows us to understand chemical affinity (J. G. Fichte, 'Concerning the Nature of Animals, *FSW* XI, pp. 363–4; trans. A. E. Kroeger in *The Science of Rights* [London: Trübner & Co., 1889], pp. 497–9). When atomic drives are conceived as combining in such a manner as to 'merge together into a new *whole*' – that is, into an 'organisation' – we understand this to constitute a 'higher power [*Potenz*] within nature' (Fichte, 'Concerning the Nature of Animals', *FSW* XI, p. 364; Kroeger translation, pp. 499–500. Translation and emphasis modified). We thus attribute the existence of organised beings – that is, living things – to a more *fundamental* self-organising activity in nature. Yet, as similar to Schelling as this might superficially appear, it must be kept in mind that, for Fichte, *consciousness only attributes* the existence of living things to a more basic activity in nature.
53. 'Everything that is thought in the concept of nature is thought of *as* a drive. Everything . . . that is thought as nature is thought of *as* determining itself.' Fichte, *System of Ethics*, *FSW* IV, p. 113; Breazeale and Zöller translation, p. 109. Emphasis modified.
54. Fichte, *System of Ethics*, *FSW* IV, p. 119; Breazeale and Zöller translation, p. 114. Emphasis modified.
55. Fichte, 'Concerning the Nature of Animals', *FSW* XI, p. 362; Kroeger translation, p. 495.
56. Fichte, 'Concerning the Nature of Animals', *FSW* XI, p. 362; Kroeger translation, p. 495. Translation modified.
57. Fichte, 'Concerning the Nature of Animals', *FSW* XI, p. 362; Kroeger translation, p. 496.
58. Fichte, *System of Ethics*, *FSW* IV, p. 130; Breazeale and Zöller translation, pp. 124–5.
59. Alois K. Soller, *Trieb und Reflexion in Fichtes Jenaer Philosophie* (Würzburg: Königshausen and Neumann, 1984), pp. 108–9.
60. Michelle Kosch, *Fichte's Ethics* (Oxford: Oxford University Press, 2018), p. 27.
61. Kosch, *Fichte's Ethics*, p. 27. Emphasis modified.
62. Fichte, *System of Ethics*, *FSW* IV, p. 151; Breazeale and Zöller translation, p. 144.
63. Fichte, *System of Ethics*, *FSW* IV, p. 215; Breazeale and Zöller translation, p. 204.
64. Fichte, 'On Stimulating and Increasing the Pure Interest in Truth', *FSW* VIII, p. 342; *Early Philosophical Writings*, p. 223.
65. 'Our thinking is not founded on itself, independent of our drives and inclinations; a human being does not consist of two parts running parallel to each other, but is absolutely a unit. All our thinking is founded in our drives.' Fichte, *Vocation of Humanity*, *FSW* II, pp. 255–6; Preuss translation, p. 73.
66. F. Scott Scribner, 'A Plea for (Fichtean) Hypothetical Idealism', in *Fichte and Transcendental Philosophy*, ed. Tom Rockmore and Daniel Breazeale (Hampshire: Palgrave Macmillan, 2014), pp. 322–6.
67. Grant, *Philosophies of Nature after Schelling*, p. 10.
68. According to Blumenbach, we can discuss the formative drive in terms of its phenomenal effects, but its ultimate cause is entirely unknown; it is a *qualitas occulta* (*Bildungstrieb*, pp. 32–4). Why some material happens to be self-organising is not something that the natural philosopher can explain; it is thus no wonder that Kant was so interested in this text. See Marjorie Grene and David Depew, *The Philosophy of Biology: An Episodic History* (Cambridge: Cambridge University Press, 2004), pp. 121–2.
69. Helmut Müller-Siever, *Self-Generation: Biology, Philosophy, and Literature around 1800* (Stanford: Stanford University Press, 1997), p. 80. Emphasis modified.

70. See Grant, *Philosophies of Nature after Schelling*, especially pp. 97–102, which demonstrates the limits of Fichte's biocentric philosophy of nature.
71. Schelling, *Universal Deduction*, HKA I/8, p. 364.
72. Schelling, *First Outline*, HKA I/7, pp. 283–4; Peterson, pp. 201–2.
73. Schelling, *First Outline*, HKA I/7, p. 271; Peterson, p. 193.
74. See Whistler, 'Schelling on Individuation'.
75. Schelling, *First Outline*, HKA I/7, p. 81; Peterson, p. 17.
76. Schelling, *First Outline*, HKA I/7, p. 81; Peterson, p. 17.
77. Schelling, *First Outline*, HKA I/7, p. 81; Peterson, p. 17.
78. It is this point regarding ontological dependence which fundamentally distinguishes the organic from the inorganic potencies.
79. Schelling, *First Outline*, HKA I/7, pp. 87–8; Peterson, pp. 22, 24.
80. Eschenmayer, *Spontaneity = World Soul*, p. 18 above.
81. Eschenmayer, *Spontaneity = World Soul*, p. 18 above.
82. Schelling, *First Outline*, HKA I/7, p. 82; Peterson, p. 17.
83. Schelling, *On the True Concept*, p. 53 above.
84. Eschenmayer, *Spontaneity = World Soul*, pp. 17-18 above.
85. In addition, of course, to their differing views on the uses of mathematics in philosophy of nature, as set out in Chapter 1.
86. See Eschenmayer and Schelling, *Correspondence*, p. 190 below.
87. Eschenmayer and Schelling, *Correspondence*, pp. 189–90 below.
88. Eschenmayer, *Spontaneity = World Soul*, p. 41 above.
89. Schelling, *On the True Concept*, p. 54 above.
90. Schelling, *First Outline*, HKA I/7, pp. 276–7; Peterson, pp. 196–7.
91. See Schelling, *First Outline*, HKA I/7, p. 277; Peterson, pp. 197–8. It is important to note that, while Eschenmayer and Schelling each, in their own way, criticise the apparent empiricism of the other, neither of the philosophers is *anti*-empiricist. As Eschenmayer writes: 'It is indeed true that if we are not capable of setting down our conclusions in a way in which experience can comfortably take them up, then their mistrust is fully justified. We want to give experience itself a speaking role' (Eschenmayer, *Spontaneity = World Soul*, p. 22 above). And in the *Introduction to the Outline*, Schelling argues that we only become aware of the a priori principles of nature via some form of experience. His rationalism can thus be formulated as follows: 'It is *not, therefore,* that WE KNOW nature as a priori, but nature IS a priori; that is, everything individual in it is predetermined by the whole or by the idea of a nature generally' (*HKA* I/7, p. 279; Peterson, p. 198).
92. Eschenmayer, *Deduction*, p. 206 below.

Chapter 5: Abstraction

1. Hegel, *Phenomenology of Spirit*, HW III, p. 31; Miller translation, pp. 15–16.
2. Despite the doubts of those like H. S. Harris ('The Cows in the Dark Night', *Dialogue: Canadian Philosophical Review* 26.4 [1987], pp. 627–44), Ziche has set out the most convincing case that Schelling himself is strongly implicated in Hegel's attack (*Mathematische und naturwissenschaftliche Modelle*, p. 107).
3. Michael N. Forster, *Hegel and Skepticism* (New Haven: Harvard University Press, 1989), p. 101.
4. Forster, *Hegel and Skepticism*, p. 101.
5. Michael N. Forster, 'Schelling and Skepticism', in Lara Ostaric (ed.), *Interpreting Schelling* (Cambridge: Cambridge University Press, 2014), pp. 32–3.
6. For the most helpful discussions of Schellingian construction, see Breazeale, '"Exhibiting the particular in the universal"'; Hermann Krings, 'Die Konstruktion in der Philosophie: Ein Beitrag zu Schellings Logik der Natur', in J. Stagl (ed.), *Aspekte der Kultursoziologie* (Berlin: Reiner, 1982); Valerio Verra, 'La "construction" dans la

philosophie de Schelling', in G. Planty-Bonjour (ed.), *Actualité de Schelling* (Paris: Vrin, 1979); and Paul Ziche, 'Die "eine Wissenschaft der Philosophie" und die "verschiedene philosophischen Wissenschaften": Wissenschafts-systematik und die Darstellung des Absoluten', in K. Viewig (ed.), *Gegen das 'unphilosophische Unwesen': Der Kritische Journal von Schelling und Hegel* (Würzburg: Neumann, 2002).

7. As Fischbach insists, 'Schelling's procedure is radically different from and even diametrically opposed to [Hegel's].' Franck Fischbach, *Du commencement en philosophie: Étude sur Hegel et Schelling* (Paris: Vrin, 1999), p. 218.
8. G. W. F. Hegel, 'Who Thinks Abstractly?', *HW* II, p. 575; trans. Walter Kaufmann in *Hegel: Texts and Commentary* (New York: Anchor, 1966), p. 463.
9. Peter Osborne, 'The Reproach of Abstraction', *Radical Philosophy* 127 (2004), pp. 21–8.
10. Hegel, *Science of Logic*, *HW* VI, p. 278; Miller translation, p. 604.
11. Hegel, *Difference*, *HW* II, pp. 29, 45; Harris and Cerf translation; pp. 97, 113. Even in the mature Hegel, 'abstract' sometimes assumes a similar ambivalence; see note 21 below.
12. Hegel, *Difference*, *HW* II, p. 100; Harris and Cerf translation, p. 160.
13. In the previous paragraph, Hegel has just quoted freely from the conclusion to the 1800 *Universal Deduction*, in which Schelling speaks of philosophy of nature as 'the physical explanation of idealism', but an explanation that is obscured and misunderstood by most philosophers who only contemplate their object 'in the highest power'; there is thus an imperative, Schelling notes and Hegel quotes, 'to think purely theoretically, merely objectively, without any subjective admixture' (*HKA* I/8, pp. 364–5; trans. Iain Hamilton Grant).
14. Hegel, *Difference*, *HW* II, p. 118; Harris and Cerf translation, p. 176.
15. G. W. F. Hegel, *The Encyclopaedia Logic*, *HW* VIII, Remark to § 60, pp. 143–4; trans. T. F. Geraets et al. (Indianapolis: Hackett, 1992), pp. 105–6.
16. Hegel, *Lectures on the History of Philosophy*, *HW* XX, p. 381; trans. E. S. Haldane and Francis H. Simson in *Hegel's Lectures on the History of Philosophy* (London: Routledge, 1955), 3:472. An early version of this argument is also to be found in G. W. F. Hegel, *Faith and Knowledge*, *HW* II, pp. 325–6; trans. Walter Cerf and H. S. Harris (Albany: SUNY Press, 1977), p. 89. For a recent reconstruction of the limit argument that places it at the centre of Hegel's philosophy, see A. W. Moore, *The Evolution of Modern Metaphysics: Making Sense of Things* (Cambridge: Cambridge University Press, 2011), pp. 164–6.
17. Hegel, *Encyclopaedia Logic*, Addition to § 41, *HW* VIII, p. 114; Geraets translation, p. 82.
18. Hegel, *Lectures on the History of Philosophy*, *HW* XX, p. 379; Haldane and Simson translation, 3:472.
19. Hegel, *Encyclopaedia Logic*, § 52, *HW* VIII, p. 137; Geraets translation, p. 100. Emphasis modified.
20. Hegel, *Encyclopaedia Logic*, Addition to § 41, *HW* VIII, p. 114; Geraets translation, p. 82.
21. As emphasised above, this is *not* to say that Hegel himself *merely* employs 'abstract' and its cognates in a negative sense; the word retains some ambivalence in his mature thought. As Osborne puts it, 'In its adjectival form "abstract" (*abstrakt*) thus remained a predominantly derogatory term in Hegel's lexicon. It denotes the one-sidedness and finitude of the concepts of the understanding … For Hegel, "bad" abstractions are the one-sided, oppositional abstractions of the understanding, considered as if they are true forms of knowledge. "Good" abstraction is the concrete abstraction of the absolute idea, containing within itself the systematic relations between the abstractions of the understanding' (Osborne, 'The Reproach of Abstraction', p. 25). It is also the case that Hegel's philosophy can be said to only incompletely ward off the 'reproach of abstraction' itself: for accounts of Hegel's unacknowledged commit-

ment to methodological 'bad' abstractions, see Lisabeth During, 'Hegel's Critique of Transcendence', *Man and World* 21 (1988), pp. 287–305 and Andrew Buchwalter, 'Hegel, Marx and the Concept of Immanent Critique', *Journal of the History of Philosophy* 29.9 (1991), pp. 260–7.
22. Immanuel Kant, 'The Jäsche Logic', *KGS* IX: 94; trans. J. Michael Young in *Lectures on Logic* (Cambridge: Cambridge University Press, 2004), p. 592.
23. Osborne, 'The Reproach of Abstraction', p. 23.
24. The clearest commitment to abstraction in the *Critiques* themselves occurs in a methodological coda to the 'Transcendental Aesthetic': 'In the transcendental aesthetic we shall, therefore, first *isolate* sensibility, by taking away from it everything which the understanding thinks through its concepts, so that nothing may be left save empirical intuition. Secondly, we shall also separate off from it everything which belongs to sensation, so that nothing may remain save pure intuition and the mere form of appearances.' Kant, *Critique of Pure Reason*, *KGS* III: 51 and IV: 31; Kemp Smith translation, p. 67 (A22/B36).
25. Immanuel Kant, 'The Blomberg Logic', *KGS* XXIV: 253; *Lectures on Logic*, p. 202.
26. Kant, 'Jäsche Logic', *KGS* IX: 95; *Lectures on Logic*, p. 593.
27. J. G. Fichte, 'An Attempt at a New Presentation of the *Wissenschaftslehre*', *FSW* I, p. 425; trans. Daniel Breazeale in *Introductions to the Wissenschaftslehre* (Indianapolis: Hackett, 1994), pp. 10–11. Emphasis modified.
28. Eschenmayer rehearses this Fichtean idea in the *Deduction of the Living Organism*: 'The theoretical philosopher must . . . raise himself above [the customary viewpoint], and this is the *higher point of reflection*. The elevation is obviously no theoretical act, but a practical one' (p. 212 below).
29. Daniel Breazeale, 'Fichte's Abstract Realism', in Daniel O. Dahlstrom and Michael Baur (eds), *The Emergence of German Idealism* (Washington, DC: Catholic University of America Press, 1999), p. 112. Emphasis modified.
30. Daniel Breazeale, 'Doing Philosophy: Fichte vs. Kant on Transcendental Method', in Breazeale and Tom Rockmore (eds), *Fichte, German Idealism, and Early Romanticism* (Amsterdam: Rodopi, 2010), p. 51. Fichte himself speaks of abstraction as an 'experiment' in 'A Comparison between Prof. Schmid's System and the *Wissenschaftslehre*', *FSW* II, p. 452; *Early Philosophical Writings*, p. 331.
31. J. G. Fichte, 'Concerning the Difference between the Spirit and the Letter within Philosophy', *FG* II, 3: 331; *Early Philosophical Writings*, p. 206.
32. Breazeale, 'Doing Philosophy', p. 51. See Martial Guéroult's discussion of this point in *L'Évolution et la structure de la doctrine de la science chez Fichte* (Paris: Belles-lettres, 1930), pp. 200–4, as well as Fichte's own presentation in 'Concerning the Concept of the *Wissenschaftslehre*', *FSW* I, pp. 72–4; *Early Philosophical Writings*, pp. 127–8.
33. Fichte, *FSW* I, p. 91; *Foundations*, p. 93. Emphasis modified.
34. Fichte, *FSW* I, p. 92; *Foundations*, p. 94.
35. Fichte, 'The Spirit and the Letter', *FG* II, 3: 329; *Early Philosophical Writings*, p. 204. Emphasis modified.
36. For Fichte, as for the early Schelling, abstraction is also a key component in the generation of valid logical propositions. Indeed, one of the basic roles of the 'abstracting reflection' (*FSW* I, p. 91; *Foundations*, p. 93) of the 1794 *Wissenschaftslehre* is to isolate the logical proposition implicit in transcendental claims. For example, Fichte writes, 'If we abstract from "I am" the specific content, namely the self, and are left with the mere form that is given with this content . . . as for purposes of logic we are compelled to do, we then obtain A = A as *the basic proposition of logic*' (*FSW* I, pp. 98–9; *Foundations*, p. 99). And he summarises at the end of Part One: 'By abstraction from the content of the material proposition *I am*, we obtained the purely formal and logical proposition "A = A". By a similar abstraction from the assertions set forth in the preceding paragraphs, we obtain the logical proposition "-A is not equal to A" . . . If now we finally abstract from the specific act of judgment, and look merely

to the form of the inference from counterposition to non-existence, we obtain *the category of negation*' (*FSW* I, p. 105; *Foundations*, p. 105). Similarly, as Schwenzfeuer has observed, in the *System of Transcendental Idealism* of 1800, Schelling also employs abstraction as a method of logical derivation. Schelling there insists, 'Logic can only arise as such by abstraction from determinable propositions' (*HKA*, 1/9, p. 51; Heath, p. 20). And he goes on to specify, in Schwenzfeuer's words, how 'abstraction removes the specific content of the proposition, in order to get at its "mere form", a logical constant'. Sebastian Schwenzfeuer, 'Logik und Transzendentalphilosophie: Schellings Interpretation des Satzes der Identität', *International Yearbook of German Idealism* 12 (2017), pp. 246–8.
37. Fichte, 'Schmid's System', p. 330.
38. Fichte, 'New Presentation', p. 39.
39. Hegel, 'Who Thinks Abstractly?', *HW* II, p. 578; Kaufmann translation, p. 463. Emphasis modified.
40. Fichte, 'Schmid's System', p. 335.
41. Fichte, 'The Spirit and the Letter', *FG* II, 3: 329; *Early Philosophical Writings*, p. 204.
42. Fichte, *FSW* I, p. 97; *Foundations*, p. 98.
43. Schelling, *On the True Concept*, p. 46 above.
44. Grant, *Philosophies of Nature after Schelling*, p. 143.
45. Schelling, *On the True Concept*, p. 51 above.
46. Schelling, *On the True Concept*, p. 48 above.
47. Schelling, *On the True Concept*, p. 49 above.
48. Schelling, *On the True Concept*, pp. 52–3 above.
49. Schelling, *On the True Concept*, p. 53 above.
50. Schelling, *On the True Concept*, p. 49 above.
51. Schelling, *On the True Concept*, p. 49 above.
52. Schelling, *On the True Concept*, p. 49 above.
53. Schelling, *On the True Concept*, p. 49 above. Schelling even considers this process of abstraction as consisting in an 'abstracting from the *Wissenschaftslehre*' itself (p. 52 above). The *Wissenschaftslehre* thus acts in *On the True Concept* as something like a *partial* abstraction from which the philosopher of nature must keep abstracting. See further Dalia Nassar, 'Intellectual Intuition and the Philosophy of Nature: An Examination of the Problem', in Johannes Haag and Markus Wild (eds), *Übergänge – diskursiv oder intuitive? Essays zu Eckhart Försters 'Die 25 Jahre der Philosophie'* (Frankfurt: Klostermann, 2013), pp. 251–2; and Lauth, *Die Enstehung*, pp. 75–81.
54. Schelling, 'Letter to Fichte, 19/11/1800', *HKA* III/2.1, p. 224; *Rupture*, pp. 44–5.
55. Schelling goes on to emphasise this further: for Fichte, 'the philosopher must from the start take up his object *as I* (i.e., a primordially already *knowing*, hence not merely objective). This is not the case in the philosophy of nature which (as the theoretical part of the system) arises through *abstraction* from the theoretical-practical *Wissenschaftslehre*' ('Letter to Fichte, 19/11/1800', *HKA* III/2.1, pp. 225–6; *Rupture*, pp. 45–6).
56. Schelling, 'Letter to Fichte, 19/11/1800', *HKA* III/2.1, p. 224; *Rupture*, p. 44.
57. Schelling, 'Letter to Fichte, 19/11/1800', *HKA* III/2.1, p. 225; *Rupture*, p. 45.
58. Nassar, *The Romantic Absolute*, p. 204.
59. Nassar, *The Romantic Absolute*, p. 211.
60. For helpful summaries of the overall argument, see Förster, *The Twenty-Five Years of Philosophy*, pp. 145, 152. Nassar, 'Intellectual Intuition and Philosophy of Nature', makes the compelling argument that Goethe and Schelling are not as methodologically distinct as Förster insists. See also the assessment of Förster's critique in Peter Fenves, 'Thankless Trouble: Ethical Contemplation of Nature', *Yearbook of Comparative Literature* 58 (2012), pp. 58–63.

61. Förster, *The Twenty-Five Years*, p. 239; emphasis modified. The quotation from *System of Transcendental Idealism* is taken from *HKA* I/9, p. 41; Heath, p. 13.
62. Förster, *The Twenty-Five Years*, pp. 248–9.
63. Nassar points this out: Förster 'agrees with Fichte's critique of Schelling's methodology' ('Intellectual Intuition and Philosophy of Nature', p. 234).
64. On this third criticism, see Nassar, 'Intellectual Intuition and Philosophy of Nature', pp. 235–8.
65. Schelling, *On the True Concept*, p. 51 above.
66. Schelling, *On the True Concept*, p. 50 above.
67. Schelling, *On the True Concept*, p. 51 above.
68. Schelling, *On the True Concept*, p. 51 above.
69. Schelling, *On the True Concept*, p. 50 above.
70. Schelling, *On the True Concept*, p. 53 above.
71. Schelling, *On the True Concept*, p. 50 above.
72. Gilles Deleuze, *The Logic of Sense*, trans. Mark Lester (London: Continuum, 1990), p. 145.
73. Fichte, 'The Spirit and the Letter', *FG* III, 3: 327; *Early Philosophical Writings*, p. 203.
74. Deleuze, *Logic of Sense*, pp. 146–7.
75. Hence, the need to abstract from the *Wissenschaftslehre* itself (see note 41 above). To put it another way, to abstract is to create a space for philosophising indifferent to positing, indifferent to self-consciousness, indeed indifferent to any thinking whatsoever. Abstraction performs absolute indifference (this is a claim we explore below). Breazeale helpfully emphasises how 'even more radical' Schelling's act of abstraction is than Fichte's in this regard ('Exhibiting the Particular', p. 93).
76. Likewise, a further component of Schelling's critique of Fichte in *On the True Concept* revolves around the extensity of the *construction* consequent on this initial act of abstraction. Once one has abstracted upwards to the highest potency, one can only construct within such high potencies; however, if one abstracts 'downwards' out of consciousness and into natural becoming, then one can construct all of reality. In other words, according to Schelling, Fichte is also ignorant of the fact that the method of *construction potentiates*; it never *de*potentiates.
77. Schelling, *On the True Concept*, p. 51 above.
78. Noticeably, Reinhold's review of Schelling's 1801 *Presentation of my System of Philosophy* focuses on precisely this problem: 'The doing away with the subjective and the objective cannot seriously be intended, because he [equally] needs both of them in order to think reason as precisely this total indifference of the objective and the subjective . . . [The *Presentation* cannot proceed] without simultaneously thinking and not thinking the objective and subjective. In this simultaneous thinking and not-thinking consists the central mystery of the new Schellingian basic principle' (quoted in Lauth, *Entstehung*, p. 161).
79. Fichte, 'Schmid's System', p. 328. Rehearsing Förster's critique, Fenves sums up this line of thought nicely: 'The elimination of the subject from intellectual intuition is itself an act of the subject and is thus self-invalidating' ('Thankless Trouble', p. 62).
80. Note, however, that it is not the *elimination* or negation of consciousness that is called for but only its suspension – a kind of nature-philosophical *epochē* of the conscious self.
81. F. W. J. Schelling, *Clara or, On Nature's Connection to the Spirit World*, *SSW* 9:77; trans. Fiona Steinkamp (Albany: SUNY Press, 2002), pp. 55–6.
82. Schelling, *Clara*, *SSW* 9:80; Steinkamp translation, p. 73.
83. Schelling, *Clara*, *SSW* 9:80; Steinkamp translation, p. 73. See Daniel Whistler, 'Silvering, or the Role of Mysticism in German Idealism', in *Glossator: Practice and Theory of the Commentary* 7, pp. 151–85.
84. Schelling, *Universal Deduction*, *HKA* I/8, p. 364.

85. Benedict Spinoza, *Treatise on the Emendation of the Intellect*, in *Collected Works*, vol. 1, ed. and trans. Edwin Curley (Princeton: Princeton University Press, 1985), p. 23.
86. Schelling, *Presentation*, *HKA* I/10, p. 125; *Rupture*, p. 151. See also Schelling's use of generative abstraction in the *Further Presentations* (*SSW* 4:256).
87. Hence, there seems to be a certain amount of confusion in Yitzhak Melamed's claim that the abstraction performed in § 1 of the *Presentation* involves positing ('Deus sive Vernunft'). Schellingian abstraction is rather an *un-positing*. It is also worth pointing out that, while the above emphasises the continuity between *On the True Concept* and the *Presentation*, the indifference of the *Presentation* is less a matter of depths and origins, in contrast to the archaeological procedure of *On the True Concept*. That is, while *On the True Concept* may roughly correspond to the Nietzschean philosophy of depths in Deleuze's Eighteenth Series invoked above, the *Presentation* approaches the Stoic philosophy of surfaces.
88. On the relation of this indifference to contemporary employments of the neuter, see Daniel Whistler, 'Abstraction and Utopia in Early German Idealism', *Russian Journal of Philosophy and Humanities* 2.2 (2017), pp. 3–22.
89. F. W. J. Schelling, *System of Philosophy in General*, *SSW* 6:142–3; Pfau translation, p. 144. See also Schelling's letter to Eschenmayer in July 1805 (*Briefe und Dokumente*, 3:222–3).

Translators' Notes to Appendix 1

1. The following is a translation of Eschenmayer and Schelling's complete extant correspondence between their first surviving letter in 1799 and July 1801, when there is a break in their communication until after the publication of Eschenmayer's *Philosophy in its Transition to Non-Philosophy* in late 1803. The text of the letters is taken from *HKA* III/1 and III/2.1. The translators' notes are for the most part based on those in the corresponding *HKA* volumes.
2. The first issue of Schelling's *Journal for Speculative Physics* appeared on 22 April 1800.
3. Saxon Reichsthaler – a currency of the Holy Roman Empire.
4. This promise was presumably made in a letter from Eschenmayer to Schelling that is no longer extant.
5. That is, Eschenmayer's *Deduction of the Living Organism*, excerpts from which are translated in Appendix 3 of the present volume.
6. Schelling had left Jena in May 1800 to spend the summer in Bamburg at the invitation of J. A. Röschlaub and Adalbert Marcus, in order to become familiar with contemporary practical medicine. Johann Andreas Röschlaub (1768–1835) (who will play an important role in this letter) was a profoundly influential physician of the time with a clinic in Bamburg. The primary German promoter of John Brown's excitability theory, Röschlaub also increasingly came under the influence of Fichtean principles in the late 1790s – and, for this reason, had already been subject to Schelling's criticism by 1799. See Nelly Tsouyopoulos, 'Andreas Röschlaub', in Olaf Breidbach and Thomas Bach (eds), *Naturphilosophie nach Schelling* (Stuttgart: Frommann-Holzboog, 2005), pp. 537–62 and Zammito, *Gestation of German Biology*, pp. 333–40.
7. Eschenmayer's letter to Schelling mentioned here is no longer extant. The 'treatise' is *Spontaneity = World Soul*, which Eschenmayer had originally planned to publish in Röschlaub's own journal, *Magazin zur Vervollkommung der theoretischen und praktischen Heilkunde* (where his *Deduction of the Living Organism* had just been published). In early 1800, Eschenmayer decided to have *Spontaneity = World Soul* transferred from Röschlaub's journal to Schelling's.
8. The French Revolutionary Wars in southern Germany had intensified in May 1800.
9. Schelling is here referring to one of the main theses of his *Universal Deduction*, published in the first two issues of volume one of his *Journal of Speculative Physics* during

1800. § 4 of this work sums up this line of thinking: 'Indeed, it has in general been shown in the author's recent writings, that *magnetism, electricity* and *the chemical process* are the *universal categories of physics*, however it is has not clearly shown how then, by means of these and only these three functions, matter may be completed. To conclude in advance, this can be shown only from the relation of these functions to space and in particular to the *dimensions* of space' (*HKA* 1/8, p. 298; trans. Iain Hamilton Grant).
10. Schelling's *System of Transcendental Idealism* had been published in mid-April 1800.
11. A reference to Schelling's own *On the True Concept of Philosophy of Nature*.
12. Both Eschenmayer's *Spontaneity = World Soul* and Schelling's *On the True Concept of Philosophy of Nature* were to appear in volume 2, issue 1 of the *Journal for Speculative Physics* in January 1801.
13. It is unclear here whether Schelling is referring to Eschenmayer's ideas in *Spontaneity = World Soul* or the now-lost letter to which this is a reply.
14. In, respectively, Part 6 and Part 4 of the *System of Transcendental Idealism*.
15. Schelling was to consider this idea more fully in § 114 of his *Presentation of my System of Philosophy*: 'The schema of the three basic forms of the dynamic processes is, as is known, the line, the angle, and the triangle, or in addition, these three processes are equated with the first three prime numbers of the arithmetic series. Just as 2 results only from the addition of 1 + 1, and 3 from the joining of 1 to 2 (so therefore these numbers are not *powers* of 1), so too, therefore, the three stages of the dynamic process [result from successive addition]. Even the chemical process arises from a triple repetition of the same 1, namely, the magnet, which in AC, AB and BC is only added to itself, and in this addition displays the first totality. Just as 1 is contained in 2, and 2 and 1 in 3, so magnetism is contained in electricity, and magnetism and electricity in the chemical process' (*HKA* I/10, pp. 186–7; *Rupture*, p. 189).
16. Schelling and Fichte's (ultimately abandoned) plans for a journal (or 'institute that would not only review single works but entire disciplines' ['Letter to Fichte, 18/08/1800', *HKA* III/2.1, p. 220; *Rupture*, p. 24]) were in a state of severe flux during autumn 1800, owing to both the fractious politics of the Jena circle and also Fichte and Schelling's growing intellectual estrangement. Nevertheless, at the end of October, Schelling had written to Fichte that the publisher Cotta had enthusiastically endorsed his version of a plan to establish such a journal with Fichte, and, Schelling adds, 'I am thinking of including in my Review everything to do with philosophy, especially natural science in all its branches, and even mathematics, history etc.' ('Letter to Fichte, 31/10/1800', *HKA* III/2.1, p. 253; *Rupture*, p. 41). For full details of the history of this project, see Kisser et al., 'Der Zeitschriftenplan', in *HKA* III/2.1, pp. 29–66 (especially pp. 62–3) and Harmut Traub's comments in *Schelling–Fichte Briefwechsel*, ed. Hartmut Traub (Neuried: ars una, 2001), pp. 243–68.
17. Eschenmayer's *Spontaneity = World Soul* was to appear two months later.
18. That is, Schelling is sending Eschenmayer the *Journal for Speculative Physics*, vol. 2, issues 1 and 2. Issue 1 contained *Spontaneity = World Soul* and *On the True Concept of Philosophy of Nature*; issue 2 contained Schelling's *Presentation of my System of Philosophy*, to which he goes on to refer in the next sentence. However, Eschenmayer must have obtained a copy of issue 1 independently of Schelling, since his review of the *First Outline* and *Introduction to the First Outline* (translated in Appendix 4), which was printed in early April 1801, already makes mention of a passage from *On the True Concept*.
19. Printed in full in Appendix 4 to the present volume.
20. Schelling had indeed made this point explicitly in the Preface to *Presentation of my System of Philosophy*: 'I have made quite frequent use besides of a general symbolic notation that was previously employed by Herr Eschenmayer in his essays on natural philosophy and the article "Deduction des lebenden Organismus" (in *Röschlaub's*

Magazine &c.). I wish all my readers would read these essays, partly for their own intrinsic interest, partly because it would put them in a more secure position to compare my system of nature-philosophy and the sort of natural philosophy produced by an idealism which, though produced quite necessarily, merely occupies the standpoint of reflection. For to grasp in its core the System of Identity which I advance here, which is wholly removed from the standpoint of reflection, it is extremely useful to become closely acquainted with the system of reflection that is its antithesis, since reflection works only from oppositions and rests on oppositions' (*HKA* I/10, p. 115; *Rupture*, p. 145).

21. Christian Wilhelm Hufeland (1762–1836) had been Professor of Medicine at the University of Jena from 1793 to 1801. In 1801, he was called to Berlin by the Prussian king. Hufeland was a particularly vehement opponent of the use of John Brown's excitability theory in medicine, a theory that Eschenmayer had been propounding in print since 1797.
22. That is, to replace the outgoing Hufeland as Professor of Medicine at the University of Jena.
23. Röschlaub was unlikely to obtain this post, presumably, at least in part, owing to his notorious championing of Brown's excitability theory. On Röschlaub, see note 6 above.
24. Eschenmayer's review of volume 1 of Hufeland's *System der praktischen Heilkunde* had been published in the *Erlanger Litteratur Zeitung* on 2 February 1801 (pp. 169–75).
25. Volume 2 of the *Journal for Speculative Physics*, which Schelling had forwarded accompanying his previous letter. The second issue of this volume includes Schelling's *Presentation of my System of Philosophy* on which Eschenmayer reflects in what follows.
26. A reference to Schelling's treatment of the law of identity in the opening propositions of the *Presentation* (particularly § 4: 'The ultimate law for the being of reason, and, since there is nothing outside reason [§ 2], for all being [because it is comprehended within reason] is the law of identity, which with respect to all being is expressed by A = A' [*HKA* I/10, p. 118; *Rupture*, p. 147]) as well as § 1 of Fichte's 1794 *Grundlage* on the 'first, absolutely unconditioned principle' ('The proposition A is A [or A = A, since that is the meaning of the logical copula] is accepted by everyone and that without a moment's thought: it is admitted to be perfectly certain and established' [*FSW* I, pp. 91–3; *Foundations*, pp. 93–4]).
27. See Fichte, *Foundations*, § 2 (on the 'second principle, conditioned as to content'): 'The proposition that "–A is not equal to A" will undoubtedly be accepted by everyone as perfectly certain and established . . . It is thus absolutely unconditioned in form, but conditioned as to matter. And with this we have also discovered the second basic principle of all human knowledge' (*FSW* I, pp. 101–4; *Foundations*, pp. 102–4).
28. Schelling, *Presentation*, § 23: '*Between subject and predicate, none other than quantitative difference is possible*' (*HKA* I/10, p. 125; *Rupture*, p. 151).
29. See Eschenmayer's claims in the *Principles of Nature-Metaphysics* (translated in Appendix 2) that the repulsive force is a positing and the attractive force a negating.
30. Schelling, *Presentation*, § 46: '*Subjectivity and objectivity can be posited as predominant only in opposite tendencies or directions* . . . *Cor.* Absolute identity's form of being can thus be universally conceived through the image of a *line*

$$\frac{^+A = B \qquad A = B^+}{A = A^0}$$

wherein the very same identity is posited in each direction, with predominant A or B in the opposite directions, while A = A itself falls at the point of equilibrium. (We

signify the predominance of one factor over the other with the + sign)' (*HKA* I/10, pp. 138–9; *Rupture*, p. 159).
31. A reference to Schelling's attempt in the previous letter to enjoin Eschenmayer to apply for Hufeland's vacated Chair of Medicine at the University of Jena. Eschenmayer would, in fact, subsequently be called to this Chair in 1811.
32. This claim would prove ironic: the correspondence ended here for three years and their next extant interaction came in response to Eschenmayer's publication of a thoroughgoing critique of Schelling (*Philosophy in its Transition to Non-Philosophy*).
33. Eschenmayer had reviewed volume 1 of Hufeland's *System der praktischen Heilkunde* in February 1801; see note 24 above.

Translators' Notes to Appendix 2

1. The following extract is translated from the opening section of A. C. A. Eschenmayer's first major German publication, *Säze aus der Natur-Metaphysik auf chemische und medicinische Gegenstände angewandt* (Tübingen, 1797) – a revised translation, often verbatim, of his Latin dissertation, *Principia quaedam disciplinae naturali, in primis Chemiae ex Metaphysica naturae substernenda* (Tübingen, 1796). Not only do the theses presented here inform the basis for the whole controversy between Eschenmayer and Schelling in 1801, but it is mainly to them that Schelling is referring in 1797 when he speaks of Eschenmayer as 'the first that I know of to attempt, in a truly philosophic spirit, to apply the principles of dynamics, as set forth by Kant, to the empirical theory of Nature, and above all to chemistry' (*HKA* I/5, p. 285; Harris and Heath, p. 249), as well as when he criticises Eschenmayer's mathematical constructions in 1799 (as discussed in Chapter 1 of the commentary).
2. On the translation of *Verhältnis*, see the Translators' Note.
3. In 1797, this is Eschenmayer's biggest departure from the Kant of the *Metaphysical Foundations of Natural Science*. For Kant, 'Chemistry can become nothing more than a systematic art or experimental doctrine, but never science proper; for the principles of chemistry are merely empirical and admit of no presentation a priori in intuition. Consequently, the principles of chemical phenomena cannot make the possibility of such phenomena in the least conceivable inasmuch as they are incapable of the application of mathematics' (*MF*, *KGS* IV, p. 471; Ellington, pp. 7–8).
4. This claim and those that follow summarise and elaborate on many of the key theses in Kant's *Metaphysical Foundations of Natural Science*, Part Two: 'Metaphysical Foundations of Dynamics'. Here, Kant argues, 'since all given matter must fill its space with a determinate degree of repulsive force in order to constitute a determinate material thing, only an original attraction in conflict with the original repulsion can make a determinate degree of the filling of space, i.e. matter, possible' (*MF*, *KGS* IV, p. 518; Ellington translation, p. 69). He also makes clear that to explain 'the dynamical concept of matter', 'one needs a law of the relation both of original attraction and of original repulsion' (*MF*, *KGS* IV, p. 517; Ellington translation, pp. 68–9).
5. Friedrich Albrecht Karl Gren (1760–98), Professor of Chemistry and Physics at the University of Halle (1788–98) and a proponent of dynamism and phlogiston chemical theory.
6. Jean-André Deluc (1727–1817), a student of Le Sage and polymath based in England who opposed Lavoisier's chemistry. He was given an Honorary Professorship of Philosophy and Geology at the University of Göttingen in 1798.
7. Johann Heinrich Voigt (1751–1823), Professor of Mathematics at the University of Jena (1789–98) and author of *Versuch einer neuen Theorie des Feuers*, referred to here.
8. Pierre Prévost (1751–1839), Professor of Philosophy and General Physics at the Academy of Geneva (1784–1809) and author of *Origine des forces magnétiques* (1788), referred to here.

9. Kant similarly writes in the *Metaphysical Foundations*: 'As concerns the procedure of natural science regarding the foremost of all its problems, namely, the explication of a possible specific variety of matters extending to infinity, one can take only two ways: the mechanical way, by the combination of the absolutely full with the absolutely empty; or a dynamical way, opposed to the foregoing, by explicating all varieties of matter through the mere variety in the combination of the original forces of repulsion and attraction. The first has, as materials for its derivation, atoms and the void' (*MF*, *KGS* IV, p. 532; Ellington translation, p. 90). He concludes, 'That mode of explication which derives the specific variety of matter . . . from the proper moving forces of attraction and repulsion originally belonging to these matters may be called the dynamical natural philosophy' (*MF*, *KGS* IV, p. 532; Ellington translation, p. 91).
10. Kant had similarly written that, on the one hand, 'matter, by its repulsive force . . . if no other moving force counteracted this repulsive one, would be held within no limits of extension, i.e., would disperse itself to infinity' (*MF*, *KGS* IV, p. 508; Ellington translation, pp. 56–7) and, on the other hand, 'without repulsive forces, all parts of matter would approach one another without hindrance and diminish the space that matter occupies' (*MF*, *KGS* IV, p. 511; Ellington translation, p. 59).
11. That is, 'A' multiplied by 'B' equals 'M'. Eschenmayer uses the dot operator to indicate multiplication throughout.
12. This is set out in detail in 'Explication 7' of Kant's 'Metaphysical Foundations of Dynamics': 'Repulsive force, by means of which matter fills a space, is a mere superficial force . . . The original attraction, which makes matter itself possible . . . is a penetrative force' (*MF*, *KGS* IV, p. 517; Ellington translation, p. 67).

Translators' Notes to Appendix 3

1. The following extracts are translated from A. C. A. Eschenmayer's *Dedukzion des lebenden Organismus*, published in Andreas Röschlaub's *Magazin zur Vervollkommnung der theoretischen und praktischen Heilkunde*, vol. 2.3 (Frankfurt, 1799), pp. 327–90 (we have also made reference to Senigaglia's recent reconstruction of the text of the essay in Eschenmayer, *Einleitung in Natur und Geschichte*, pp. 67–96). The extracts have been chosen to demonstrate Eschenmayer's conversion at this period to a post-Fichtean variant of transcendental idealism, in accordance with Schelling's remark in the correspondence printed above that it is 'the most perspicuous and penetrating' exposition of transcendental idealism in this field 'yet to exist'. They include predominantly the initial stages of the deduction of consciousness (the subsequent deduction of self-consciousness is omitted).
2. Both Eschenmayer and Schelling had made concerted efforts in 1797 to philosophically construct chemical relations. See Appendix 2 for an example.
3. In the long section omitted here, Eschenmayer goes on to analyse this imperative into two conflicting tasks corresponding to the distinction between free and necessary activity, and he does so in reference to the relation between the faculties of production and reflection in consciousness. There is the imperative of necessary activity that calls for the subject to act by producing and reflecting simultaneously, and there is the task of free activity to devote oneself in action to each of these faculties independently or successively. Combined, they constitute the overall imperative: you should act. This reasoning will become clearer in the 'Short Overview' from the text extracted below. See also Chapter 4 of the commentary.
4. In the footnote, Eschenmayer makes reference to the 'first, absolutely unconditioned principle' set out by Fichte in the 1794 *Grundlage*: 'The proposition A is A (or A = A, since that is the meaning of the logical copula) is accepted by everyone and that without a moment's thought: it is admitted to be perfectly certain and established' (*FSW* I, pp. 91–3; *Foundations*, pp. 93–4). This second, subsequent principle is that

of antithesis – that is, the positing of identity precedes any appeal to negation. See notes 26 and 27 to Appendix 1.

Translators' Notes to Appendix 4

1. What follows is a translation of A. C. A. Eschenmayer (unattributed), 'Rezension: F. W. J. Schelling, *Erster Entwurf eines Systems der Naturphilosophie* und *Einleitung zu seinem Entwurf eines Systems der Naturphilosophie*', which appeared in the Erlanger *Litteratur-Zeitung*, no. 67–8, 7–8 April 1801 (Erlangen), pp. 529–40. (The text in the review is unsigned.) As it was written by the time that Eschenmayer had managed to read a copy of Schelling's *On the True Concept* (it alludes to this essay in closing), it can be considered (along with his letter of July 1801) as one of the last words on the 1801 controversy.
2. Schelling, *Introduction to the First Outline*, § 1: 'Now if it is the task of transcendental philosophy to subordinate the real to the ideal, it is, on the other hand, the task of the philosophy of nature to explain the real by the ideal' (*HKA* I/8, pp. 29–30; Peterson, p. 194).
3. Schelling, *Introduction to the First Outline*, § 2: 'For every idealistic mode of explanation, dragged out of its own proper sphere and applied to the explanation of nature, degenerates into the most adventurous nonsense' (*HKA* I/8, p. 31; Peterson, p. 195).
4. Schelling, *Introduction to the First Outline*, § 2: 'The first maxim of all true natural science, to explain everything by the forces of Nature, is therefore accepted in its widest extent in our science' (*HKA* I/8, p. 31; Peterson, p. 195).
5. A paraphrase of Schelling, *Introduction to the First Outline*, § 4: 'It follows that in this whole we can never arrive at absolute identity, because this would bring about an absolute transition of Nature as productive into Nature as product, that is, it would produce absolute rest. Such a wavering of Nature, therefore, between productivity and product, will necessarily appear as a universal duplicity of principles, whereby Nature is maintained in continual activity, and prevented from exhausting itself in its product; and universal duality as the principle of explanation of Nature will be as necessary as the idea of Nature itself' (*HKA* I/8, p. 34; Peterson, p. 197).
6. See, for example, Schelling, *First Outline*, *HKA* I/7, pp. 85–6; Peterson, pp. 20–1.
7. This paragraph summarises Section One ('The Unconditioned in Nature') of Schelling's *First Outline*.
8. See *HKA* I/7, p. 78; Peterson, p. 14.
9. Cf. *HKA* I/7, p. 117; Peterson, p. 54, and Division II, passim.
10. The three principles presented in Schelling, *First Outline*, *HKA* I/7, p. 81; Peterson, p. 17.
11. Schelling, *First Outline*, *HKA* I/7, p. 84; Peterson, p. 19.
12. 'The original actants, however, ARE not themselves *in space*.' Schelling, *First Outline*, *HKA* I/7, p. 86; Peterson, p. 20.
13. A reference to the entire second chapter of Division One ('The Original Qualities and Actants in Nature', *HKA* I/7, pp. 84–92; Peterson, pp. 19–28), whose content Eschenmayer goes on to summarise.
14. On the translation of *Verhältnis*, see the Translators' Note to this volume.
15. Similarly, a reference to the third chapter of Division One ('Actants and their Combinations', *HKA* I/7, pp. 93–101; Peterson, pp. 28–34). Schelling specifically writes (*HKA* I/7, p. 93, Peterson, p. 29): 'All diversity of natural products can only derive from the various proportions of actants.'
16. Schelling, *First Outline*: 'Indecomposability and absolute composability must thus always coexist.' *HKA* I/7, p. 93; Peterson, p. 29.
17. Schelling, *First Outline*, *HKA* I/7, p. 101; Peterson, p. 35.
18. The proof of this thesis begins in the *First Outline* at *HKA* I/7, p. 105; Peterson, p. 39.

19. Schelling, *First Outline*, *HKA* I/7, pp. 117ff.; Peterson, pp. 53ff.
20. See *First Outline*, *HKA* I/7, p. 118; Peterson, p. 54.
21. See *First Outline*, *HKA* I/7, pp. 120–9; Peterson, pp. 57–64.
22. See *First Outline*, *HKA* I/7, pp. 136–58; Peterson, pp. 73–93. This constitutes the Second Division of the work.
23. See *First Outline*, *HKA* I/7, pp. 158–9; Peterson, p. 94.
24. Schelling, *First Outline*, *HKA* I/7, pp. 170–1; Peterson, p. 105. This marks the beginning of the Third Division of the work.
25. The 'Appendix to Chapter Three': *HKA* I/7, pp. 230–45; Peterson, pp. 158–72.
26. What follows is a paraphrase of a passage from Schelling's *On the True Concept*, p. 52 above.
27. Schelling's *Universal Deduction*, published in the first two issues of volume one of his *Journal of Speculative Physics* during 1800. For Eschenmayer and Schelling's discussion of this essay, see the correspondence in Appendix 1.
28. This thesis from the *Universal Deduction* forms a central point of discussion in the Eschenmayer–Schelling correspondence translated in Appendix 1.

Bibliography

Ackermann, Stefan. 'Franz von Baader'. In Thomas Bach and Olaf Breidbach (eds), *Naturphilosophie nach Schelling*. Stuttgart: Frommann-Holzboog, 2005. 41–60.
Alderwick, Charlotte. 'Nature's Capacities: Schelling and Contemporary Power-Based Ontologies'. *Angelaki* 21.4 (2016): 59–76.
Aristotle. *Metaphysics*. Trans. Hugh Lawson-Tancred. London: Penguin, 2004.
Asmuth, Christoph. 'Anfang und Form der Philosophie: Überlegungen zu Fichte, Schelling und Hegel'. In C. Asmuth, A. Denker and M. Vater (eds), *Schelling: Zwischen Fichte und Hegel*. Amsterdam: Rodopi, 2000. 403–17.
Bach, Thomas. *Biologie und Philosophie bei C. F. Kielmeyer und F. W. J. Schelling*. Stuttgart: Frommann-Holzboog, 2001.
Badiou, Alain. 'Mathematics and Philosophy: The Grand Style and the Little Style'. In *Theoretical Writings*, ed. and trans. Ray Brassier and Alberto Toscano. London and New York: Bloomsbury, 2004. 3–22.
Beere, Jonathan. *Doing and Being: An Interpretation of Aristotle's* Metaphysics *Theta*. Oxford: Oxford University Press, 2009.
Beiser, Frederick C. *German Idealism: The Struggle against Subjectivism, 1781–1801*. Cambridge, MA: Harvard University Press, 2002.
Beiser, Frederick C. 'Mathematical Method in Kant, Schelling, and Hegel'. In *Discourse on a New Method: Reinvigorating the Marriage of History and Philosophy of Science*, ed. Mary Domski and Michael Dickson. La Salle: Open Court, 2010. 243–57.
Berger, Benjamin. 'Schelling, Hegel, and the History of Nature'. *The Review of Metaphysics* (forthcoming).
Blumenbach, Johann Friedrich. *Über den Bildungstrieb*, 3rd edn. Göttingen: Johann Christian Dieterich, 1791.
Braekman, Anton. 'From the Work of Art to Absolute Reason: Schelling's Journey toward Absolute Idealism'. *The Review of Metaphysics* 57.3 (2004): 551–69.
Breazeale, Daniel. 'Fichte's Abstract Realism'. In Daniel O. Dahlstrom and Michael Baur (eds), *The Emergence of German Idealism*. Washington, DC: Catholic University of America Press, 1999. 99–115.
Breazeale, Daniel. 'Doing Philosophy: Fichte vs. Kant on Transcendental Method'. In Breazeale and Tom Rockmore (eds), *Fichte, German Idealism, and Early Romanticism*. Amsterdam: Rodopi, 2010. 41–62.
Breazeale, Daniel. '"Exhibiting the particular in the universal": Philosophical Construction and Intuition in Schelling's Philosophy of Identity (1801–1804)'. In Lara Ostaric

(ed.), *Interpreting Schelling: Critical Essays*. Cambridge: Cambridge University Press, 2014. 91–119.

Buchwalter, Andrew. 'Hegel, Marx and the Concept of Immanent Critique'. *Journal of the History of Philosophy* 29.9 (1991): 253–79.

Châtelet, Gilles. *Figuring Space: Philosophy, Mathematics and Physics*, trans. Robert Shore and Muriel Zagha. Dordrecht: Kluwer, 2000.

Courtine, Jean-François. *Extase de la raison: Essais sur Schelling*. Paris: Galilée, 1990.

Deleuze, Gilles. *Expressionism in Philosophy: Spinoza*, trans. Martin Joughin. New York: Zone, 1990.

Deleuze, Gilles. *The Logic of Sense*, trans. Mark Lester. London: Continuum, 1990.

Descartes, René. *Discourse on Method, Optics, Geometry, and Meteorology*, trans. Paul J. Olscamp. Indianapolis: Hackett, 2001.

Dhouib, Sarhan. 'Die Begriffe Indifferenz, quantitative Differenz und Endlichkeit in Schellings *Darstellung meines Systems der Philosophie*'. In Mildred Galland-Szymkowiak (ed.), *Das Problem der Endlichkeit in der Philosophie Schellings*. Münster: Lit-Verlag, 2011. 107–25.

Dodd, James. 'Expression in Schelling's Early Philosophy'. *Graduate Faculty Philosophy Journal* 27.2 (2006): 109–39.

Dunham, Jeremy, Iain Hamilton Grant and Sean Watson. *Idealism: The History of Philosophy*. Abingdon: Routledge, 2014.

During, Lisabeth. 'Hegel's Critique of Transcendence'. *Man and World* 21 (1988): 287–305.

Düsing, Klaus. *Schellings und Hegels erste absolute Metaphysik (1801–2)*. Cologne: Dinter, 1988.

Ellis, Brian. *The Philosophy of Nature: A Guide to the New Essentialism*. Montreal: McGill-Queen's University Press, 2002.

Engels, Friedrich. *Anti-Schelling*. In the *Collected Works of Karl Marx and Friedrich Engels, Vol. 2, Engels: 1834–42*. New York: International Publishers, 1975. 181–232.

Eschenmayer, A. C. A. *Sätze aus der Natur-Metaphysik, auf chemische und medicinische Gegenstände angewendet*. Tübingen, 1797.

Eschenmayer, A. C. A. 'Dedukzion des lebenden Organism'. In A. Röschlaub (ed.), *Magazin zur Vervollkommnung der theoretischen und praktischen Heilkunde* 2.3 (1799): 327–90.

Eschenmayer, A. C. A. 'Spontaneität = Weltseele, oder das höchste Prinzip der Naturphilosophie', In F. W. J. Schelling (ed.), *Zeitschrift für speculative Physik* 2.1 (January 1801): 3–68.

Eschenmayer, A. C. A. 'Rezension: F. W. J. Schelling, *Erster Entwurf eines Systems der Naturphilosophie* und *Einleitung zu seinem Entwurf eines Systems der Naturphilosophie*'. *Litteratur-Zeitung* 67/68 (7/8 April 1801): 529–40.

Eschenmayer, A. C. A. *Die Philosophie in ihrem Übergang zur Nichtphilosophie*. Erlangen: Walther, 1803.

Eschenmayer, A. C. A. *Psychologie in drei Theilen*. Stuttgart: Cotta, 1817.

Eschenmayer, A. C. A. *Betrachtungen über den physischen Weltbau*. Heilbronn: Scheurlen, 1852.

Eschenmayer, A. C. A. *Einleitung in Natur und Geschichte*, ed. Cristiana Senigaglia. Stuttgart: Frommann-Holzboog, 2016.

Euclid. *The Thirteen Books of the Elements, Volume 3*, trans. Thomas L. Heath. New York: Dover, 1956.

Fenves, Peter. 'Thankless Trouble: Ethical Contemplation of Nature'. *Yearbook of Comparative Literature* 58 (2012): 57–70.

Ferraguto, Federico. 'Tendency, Drive, Objectiveness: The Fichtean Doctrine and the Husserlian Perspective'. In *Fichte and the Phenomenological Tradition*, ed. Violetta L. Waibel et al. Berlin and New York: De Gruyter, 2010. 119–40.

Fichte, J. G.. *Sämmtliche Werke*. 11 vols, ed. I. H. Fichte. Berlin: Veit, 1845–6.

Fichte, J. G. 'Concerning the Nature of Animals'. In *The Science of Rights*, trans. A. E. Kroeger. London: Trübner & Co., 1889. 493–505.
Fichte, J. G. *Gesamtausgabe*. Edited by Bayerischen Akademie der Wissenschaften. Stuttgart: Frommann-Holboog, 1971–.
Fichte, J. G. 'Foundations of the Entire Science of Knowledge'. In *The Science of Knowledge*, ed. and trans. Peter Heath and John Lachs. Cambridge: Cambridge University Press, 1982. 89–287.
Fichte, J. G. *The Vocation of Man*, trans. Peter Preuss. Indianapolis: Hackett Publishing Company, 1987.
Fichte, J. G. *Early Philosophical Writings*, ed. and trans. Daniel Breazeale. Cornell: Cornell University Press, 1993.
Fichte, J. G. 'An Attempt at a New Presentation of the *Wissenschaftslehre*'. In *Introductions to the Wissenschaftslehre and Other Writings*, ed. and trans. Daniel Breazeale. Indianapolis: Hackett, 1994. 1–118.
Fichte, J. G. *System of Ethics*, trans. Daniel Breazeale and Günter Zöller. Cambridge: Cambridge University Press, 2005.
Fichte, J. G., and F. W. J. Schelling, *Schelling–Fichte Briefwechsel*, ed. Hartmut Traub. Neuried: ars una, 2001.
Fichte J. G., and F. W. J. Schelling. *The Philosophical Rupture between Fichte and Schelling*, ed. and trans. Michael G. Vater and David W. Wood. Albany: SUNY Press, 2012.
Fischbach, Franck. *Du commencement en philosophie: Étude sur Hegel et Schelling*. Paris: Vrin, 1999.
Förster, Eckhart. *The Twenty-Five Years of Philosophy: A Systematic Reconstruction*, trans. Brady Bowman. Cambridge, MA: Harvard University Press, 2012.
Forster, Michael N. *Hegel and Skepticism*. New Haven: Harvard University Press, 1989.
Forster, Michael N. 'Schelling and Skepticism'. In Lara Ostaric (ed.), *Interpreting Schelling: Critical Essays*. Cambridge: Cambridge University Press, 2014. 32–47.
Frank, Manfred. '"Identity of identity and non-identity": Schelling's Path to the "absolute system of identity"'. In Lara Ostaric (ed.), *Interpreting Schelling: Critical Essays*. Cambridge: Cambridge University Press, 2014. 120–44.
Friedman, Michael. *Kant's Construction of Nature: A Reading of the* Metaphysical Foundations of Natural Science. Cambridge: Cambridge University Press, 2013.
Gilson, Bernard. 'Présentation'. In F. W. J. Schelling, *La Liberté humaine et controverses avec Eschenmayer*, ed. and trans. Bernard Gilson. Paris: Vrin, 1988. 7–74.
Giovanelli, Marco. *Reality and Negation – Kant's Principle of Anticipations of Perception: An Investigation of its Impact on the Post-Kantian Debate*. Dordrecht: Springer, 2011.
Grant, Iain Hamilton. *Philosophies of Nature after Schelling*. London: Continuum, 2006.
Grene, Marjorie and David Depew, *The Philosophy of Biology: An Episodic History*. Cambridge: Cambridge University Press, 2004.
Guéroult, Martial. *L'Évolution et la structure de la doctrine de la science chez Fichte*. Paris: Belles-lettres, 1930.
Harris, H. S. 'The Cows in the Dark Night'. *Dialogue: Canadian Philosophical Review* 26.4 (1987): 627–44.
Heath, Thomas L. *Diophantus of Alexandria: A Study in the History of Greek Algebra*. Cambridge: Cambridge University Press, 1910.
Hegel, G. W. F. *Lectures on the History of Philosophy*, 3 vols. Trans. E. S. Haldane and Francis H. Simson. London: Routledge, 1955.
Hegel, G. W. F. 'Who Thinks Abstractly?' In *Hegel: Texts and Commentary*, ed. and trans. Walter Kaufmann. New York: Anchor, 1966. 113–18.
Hegel, G. W. F. *Science of Logic*. Trans. A. V. Miller. London: Prometheus, 1969.
Hegel, G. W. F. *Introductory Lectures on Art, Religion, and Philosophy*, ed. and trans. J. Glenn Gray. Indianapolis: Hackett, 1970.
Hegel, G. W. F. *The Difference between Fichte's and Schelling's System of Philosophy*, trans. H. S. Harris and Walter Cerf. Albany: SUNY, 1977.

Hegel, G. W. F. *Faith and Knowledge*, trans. Walter Cerf and H. S. Harris. Albany: SUNY Press, 1977.
Hegel, G. W. F. *Phenomenology of Spirit*, trans. A. V. Miller. Oxford: Oxford University Press, 1977.
Hegel, G. W. F. *Lectures on the History of Philosophy: The Lectures of 1825–1826*, 3 vols, trans. R. F. Brown and J. M. Stewart. Berkeley: University of California Press, 1990.
Hegel, G. W. F. *The Encyclopaedia Logic*, trans. T. F. Geraets et al. Indianapolis: Hackett, 1992.
Hennigfeld, Jochem. *F. W. J. Schellings 'Über das Wesen der menschlichen Freiheit'*. Darmstadt: WBG, 2001.
Høyrup, Jens. 'Dynamis, the Babylonians, and Theaetetus 147c7–148d7'. *Historia Mathematica* 17.3 (1990): 201–22.
Jahnke, Hans Niel. 'Mathematik und Romantik'. In Voker Peckhaus and Christian Thiel (eds), *Disciplinen im Kontext*. Munich: Fink, 1999. 163–98.
Jantzen, Jörg. 'Eschenmayer und Schelling. Die Philosophie in ihrem Übergang zur Nichtphilosophie'. In Walter Jaeschke (ed.), *Religionsphilosophie und spekulative Theologie: Die Streit um die Göttliche Dinge (1799–1812)*. Hamburg: Felix Meiner, 1994. 74–97.
Jantzen, Jörg. 'Adolph Karl August von Eschenmayer'. In Thomas Bach and Olaf Breidbach (eds), *Naturphilosophie nach Schelling*. Stuttgart: Frommann-Holzboog, 2005. 153–80.
Jürgensen, Sven. 'Schellings logisches Prinzip: Der Unterschied in der Identität'. In C. Asmuth, A. Denker and M. Vater (eds), *Schelling: Zwischen Fichte und Hegel*. Amsterdam: Rodopi. 113–43.
Kant, Immanuel. *Gesammelte Schriften*. 29 vols, ed. Königlich Preußische Akademie der Wissenschaften. Berlin: de Gruyter, 1900–.
Kant, Immanuel. *Critique of Pure Reason*, trans. Norman Kemp-Smith. Basingstoke: Palgrave, 1929.
Kant, Immanuel. *Lectures on Logic*, ed. and trans. J. Michael Young. Cambridge: Cambridge University Press, 2004.
Kant, Immanuel. *Metaphysical Foundations of Natural Science*. In Kant, *Philosophy of Material Nature*, trans. James W. Ellington. Indianapolis: Hackett Publishing Company, 1985. 3–134.
Katz, Victor J. and Karen Hunger Parshall. *Taming the Unknown: A History of Algebra from Antiquity to the Early Twentieth Century*. Princeton: Princeton University Press, 2014.
Kielmeyer, C. F. *Gesammelte Schriften*, ed. F. H. Holler. Berlin: Keiper, 1938.
Kosch, Michelle. *Fichte's Ethics*. Oxford: Oxford University Press, 2018.
Krings, Hermann. 'Die Konstruktion in der Philosophie: Ein Beitrag zu Schellings Logik der Natur'. In J. Stagl (ed.), *Aspekte der Kultursoziologie*. Berlin: Reiner, 1982. 341–51.
Lauer, Christopher. 'Schelling's Unfinished Dialogue: Reason and Personality in the *Letter to Eschenmayer*.' In Jason Wirth, *Schelling's Practice of the Wild: Time, Art, Imagination*. Albany: SUNY Press, 2015. 197–208.
Lauth, Reinhard. *Die Entstehung von Schellings Identitätsphilosophie in der Auseinandersetzung mit Fichtes Wissenschaftslehre (1795–1801)*. Freiburg: Karl Alber, 1975.
Leistner, Patrick. 'Anmerkungen zur Debatte zwischen Schelling und Eschenmayer in der Jahren 1803–1804'. *Contrastes: Revista Internacional de Filosofía* 19.3 (2014): 95–112.
Lequan, Mai. '1797–1799: D'une "philosophie de la chimie" au chimisme en philosophie. Les premiers écrits de Schelling sur la nature'. *Dix-huitième siècle* 42 (2010): 491–512.
Lukács, Georg. *The Destruction of Reason*, trans. Peter Palmer. London: Merlin, 1980.
Macbeth, Danielle. *Realizing Reason: A Narrative of Truth and Knowing*. Oxford: Oxford University Press, 2014.
Marchetto, Monica. 'Drive, Formative Drive, World Soul: Fichte's Reception in the Early Works of A. K. A. Eschenmayer'. *Fichte-Studien* 43 (2016): 298–314.
Marks, Ralph. *Differenz der Konzeption einer dynamischen Naturphilosophie bei Schelling und Eschenmayer*. PhD Thesis, Ludwig-Maximillians-Universität, 1983.

Marquet, Jean-François. *Liberté et existence: Étude sur la formation de la philosophie de Schelling*. Paris: Gallimard, 1973.
Massimi, Michela. 'Philosophy and the Chemical Revolution after Kant'. In Karl Ameriks (ed.), *The Cambridge Companion to German Idealism*. Cambridge: Cambridge University Press, 2017. 182–204.
Matthews, Bruce. *Schelling's Organic Form of Philosophy: Life as the Schema of Freedom*. Albany: SUNY, 2011.
Melamed, Yitzhak. '"Omnis determinatio est negatio" – Determination, Negation and Self-Negation in Spinoza, Kant, and Hegel'. In Eckart Förster and Yitzhak Melamed (eds), *Spinoza and German Idealism*. Cambridge: Cambridge University Press, 2012. 175–96.
Melamed, Yitzhak. 'Deus sive Vernunft: Schelling's Transformation of Spinoza's God'. In G. Anthony Bruno (ed.), *Freedom, Nature and Systematicity: Essays on F. W. J. Schelling*. Oxford: Oxford University Press, 2020. 84–102.
Moder, Gregor. *Hegel and Spinoza: Substance and Negativity*. Evanston: Northwestern University Press, 2018.
Moiso, Francesco. 'Die Hegelsche Theorie der Physik und der Chemie in ihrer Beziehung zu Schellings Naturphilosophie'. In R. P. Horstmann and M. J. Petry (eds), *Hegels Philosophie der Natur: Beziehungen zwischen empirischer und spekulativer Naturerkenntnis*. Stuttgart: Klett, 1986. 290–309.
Molnar, George. *Powers: A Study in Metaphysics*, ed. Stephen Mumford. Oxford: Oxford University Press, 2003.
Moore, A. W. *The Evolution of Modern Metaphysics: Making Sense of Things*. Cambridge: Cambridge University Press, 2011.
Mueller, Ian. 'Greek Arithmetic, Geometry and Harmonics: Thales to Plato.' In *Routledge History of Philosophy, Volume I: From Beginning to Plato*, ed. C. C. W. Taylor. London and New York: Routledge, 1997. 249–97.
Müller-Sievers, Helmut. *Self-Generation: Biology, Philosophy, and Literature around 1800*. Stanford: Stanford University Press, 1997.
Nassar, Dalia. 'Intellectual Intuition and the Philosophy of Nature: An Examination of the Problem'. In Johannes Haag and Markus Wild (eds), *Übergänge – diskursiv oder intuitive? Essays zu Eckhart Försters 'Die 25 Jahre der Philosophie'*. Frankfurt: Klostermann, 2013. 235–58.
Nassar, Dalia. *The Romantic Absolute: Being and Knowing in Early German Romantic Philosophy, 1794–1804*. Chicago: University of Chicago Press, 2013.
Neubauer, John. 'Zwischen Natur und mathematischer Abstraktion: der Potenzbegriff in der Frühromantik'. In Richard Brinkmann (ed.), *Romantik in Deutschland*. Stuttgart: Metzler, 1978. 175–86.
Novalis. *Schriften*, 4 vols, ed. Richard Samuel. Stuttgart: Kohlhammer, 1975.
Osborne, Peter. 'The Reproach of Abstraction'. *Radical Philosophy* 127 (2004): 21–8.
Plato, *Theaetetus*, trans. M. F. Burnyeat. In *Explorations in Ancient and Modern Philosophy: Volume 2*. Cambridge: Cambridge University Press, 2012.
Pollack-Milgate, Howard M. 'Gott ist bald $1 \cdot \infty$ – bald $1/\infty$ – bald 0: The Mathematical Infinite and the Absolute in Novalis'. *Seminar* 51.1 (2015): 50–70.
Rang, Bernhard. *Identität und Indifferenz: Eine Untersuchung zu Schellings Identitätsphilosophie*. Frankfurt am Main: Klostermann, 2000.
Redding, Paul. *Hegel's Hermeneutics*. Ithaca: Cornell University Press, 1996.
Rockmore, Tom. 'The Traction of the World, or Fichte on Practical Reason and the *Vocation of Man*'. In *Fichte's Vocation of Man: New Interpretive and Critical Essays*, ed. Daniel Breazeale and Tom Rockmore. Albany: SUNY Press, 2013. 145–54.
Roux, Alexandra. 'Introduction'. In A. C. A. Eschenmayer, *La Philosophie dans son passage à la non-philosophie*, ed. and trans. Alexandra Roux. Paris: Vrin, 2005. 11–112.
Rush, Fred. 'Schelling's Critique of Hegel'. In Lara Ostaric (ed.), *Interpreting Schelling: Critical Essays*. Cambridge: Cambridge University Press, 2014. 216–37.

Schelling, F. W. J. *Werke*, 14 vols, ed. K. F. A. Schelling. Stuttgart: Cotta, 1856–61.
Schelling, F. W. J. *Briefe und Dokumente*, 3 vols, ed. Horst Fuhrmans. Bonn: Bouvier, 1962–75.
Schelling, F. W. J. *Philosophical Inquiries into the Nature of Human Freedom*, trans. James Gutmann. La Salle: Open Court, 1936.
Schelling, F. W. J. *Die Weltalter Fragmente: In den Urfassungen von 1811 und 1813*, ed. Manfred Schröter. Munich: Biederstein und Leibniz, 1946.
Schelling, F. W. J. *On University Studies*, ed. Nobert Guterman and trans. E. S. Morgan. Athens: Ohio University Press, 1966.
Schelling, F. W. J. *Concerning the Relation of the Plastic Arts to Nature*, trans. Michael Bullock. In Herbert Read, *The True Voice of Feeling*. London: Faber & Faber, 1953. 321–64.
Schelling, F. W. J. *Historisch-Kritische Ausgabe*, 3 series, currently 24 vols, ed. the Schelling-Kommission of the Bayerischen Akademie der Wissenschaften. Stuttgart: Frommann-Holzboog, 1976–.
Schelling, F. W. J. *System of Transcendental Idealism*, trans. Peter Heath. Charlottesville: University of Virginia Press, 1978.
Schelling, F. W. J. *Bruno, or On the Natural and Divine Principle of Things*, trans. Michael G. Vater. Albany: SUNY Press, 1984.
Schelling, F. W. J. *Ideas for a Philosophy of Nature*, trans. Errol E. Harris and Peter Heath. Cambridge: Cambridge University Press, 1988.
Schelling, F. W. J. *On the History of Modern Philosophy*, trans. Andrew Bowie. Cambridge: Cambridge University Press, 1994.
Schelling, F. W. J. *System of Philosophy in General and of the Philosophy of Nature in Particular*. In *Idealism and the Endgame of Theory: Three Essays by F. W. J. Schelling*, ed. and trans. Thomas Pfau. Albany: SUNY Press, 1994. 139–94.
Schelling, F. W. J. *Stuttgart Seminars*. In *Idealism and the Endgame of Theory: Three Essays by F. W. J. Schelling*, ed. and trans. Thomas Pfau. Albany: SUNY Press, 1994. 195–238.
Schelling, F. W. J. *Clara or, On Nature's Connection to the Spirit World*, trans. Fiona Steinkamp. Albany: SUNY Press, 2002.
Schelling, F. W. J. *First Outline of the System of the Philosophy of Nature* and *Introduction to the Outline of the Philosophy of Nature*, trans. Keith R. Peterson. Albany: SUNY Press, 2004.
Schelling, F. W. J. *Philosophy and Religion*, trans. Klaus Ottmann. Putman: Spring, 2010.
Schwab, Philip. 'A = A. Zur identitätslogischen Systemgrundlegung bei Fichte, Schelling und Hegel'. *International Yearbook of German Idealism* 12 (2017): 261–89.
Schwenzfeuer, Sebastian. 'Logik und Transzendentalphilosophie: Schellings Interpretation des Satzes der Identität'. *International Yearbook of German Idealism* 12 (2017): 237–60.
Scribner, F. Scott. 'A Plea for (Fichtean) Hypothetical Idealism'. In *Fichte and Transcendental Philosophy*, ed. Tom Rockmore and Daniel Breazeale. Baskingstoke: Palgrave Macmillan, 2014. 314–30.
Senigaglia, Cristiana. 'Einleitung'. In A. C. A. Eschenmayer, *Einleitung in Natur und Geschichte*, ed. Cristiana Senigaglia. Stuttgart: Frommann-Holzboog, 2016. ix–xxxviii.
Snelders, H. A. M. 'Romanticism and *Naturphilosophie* and the Inorganic Natural Sciences, 1797–1840: An Introductory Survey'. *Studies in Romanticism* 9.3 (1970): 193–215.
Soller, Alois K. *Trieb und Reflexion in Fichtes Jenaer Philosophie*. Würzburg: Königshausen und Neumann, 1984.
Spinoza, Benedict. *Ethics*. In *Collected Works*, volume 1, ed. and trans. Edwin Curley. Princeton: Princeton University Press, 1985. 408–619.
Spinoza, Benedict. *Treatise on the Emendation of the Intellect*. In *Collected Works*, volume 1, ed. and trans. Edwin Curley. Princeton: Princeton University Press, 1985. 7–45.
Stern, Robert. '"Determination is negation": The Adventures of a Doctrine from Spinoza to Hegel to the British Idealists'. *Hegel-Bulletin* 37.1 (2016): 29–52.
Tilliette, Xavier. *Schelling: Une philosophie en devenir*, 2 vols. Paris: Vrin, 1970.

Tilliette, Xavier. *Schelling: Biographie*. Paris: Calmann, 1999.
Timmermans, Benoît. 'Novalis et la réforme des mathematiques'. In Augustin Dumont and Laurent van Eynde (eds), *Modernité romantique*. Paris: Kimé, 2011. 73–88.
Troxler, I. P. V. 'Hauptmomente aus Schellings Vortrage nach der Stunde aufgezeichnet, 1801'. In Klaus Düsing, *Schellings und Hegels erste absolute Metaphysik (1801–2)*. Cologne: Dinter, 1988. 27–62.
Tsouyopoulos, Nelly. 'Andreas Röschlaub'. In Olaf Breidbach and Thomas Bach (eds), *Naturphilosophie nach Schelling*. Stuttgart: Frommann-Holzboog, 2005. 41–60.
Uslar, Detlev von. 'Die innere Bewegung der absoluten Identität bei Schelling'. *Studium Generale* 21 (1968): 504–14.
Vater, Michael G. 'Introduction to F. W. J. Schelling, *Presentation of my System of Philosophy*'. *Philosophical Forum* 32.4 (2001): 339–43.
Vater, Michael G. 'Schelling's Philosophy of Identity and Spinoza's *Ethica more geometrico*'. In E. Förster and Y. Melamed (eds), *Spinoza and German Idealism*. Cambridge: Cambridge University Press, 2012. 156–74.
Vater, Michael G. 'Reconfiguring Identity in Schelling's *Würzburg System*'. *Schelling Studien* 2 (2014): 127–44.
Verra, Valerio. 'La "construction" dans la philosophie de Schelling'. In G. Planty-Bonjour (ed.), *Actualité de Schelling*. Paris: Vrin, 1979. 27–47.
Whistler, Daniel. 'Silvering, or the Role of Mysticism in German Idealism'. *Glossator: Practice and Theory of the Commentary* 7 (2013): 151–85.
Whistler, Daniel. 'Schelling on Individuation'. *Comparative and Continental Philosophy* 8.3 (2016): 329–44.
Whistler, Daniel. 'Abstraction and Utopia in Early German Idealism'. *Russian Journal of Philosophy and Humanities* 2.2 (2017): 3–22.
Whistler, Daniel. 'Identity Philosophy'. In Kyla Bruff and Sean McGrath (eds), *The Palgrave Handbook to Schelling*. Basingstoke: Palgrave, forthcoming.
Wiesing, Urban. *Kunst oder Wissenschaft? Konzeptionen der Medizin in der deutschen Romantik*. Stuttgart: Frommann-Holzboog, 1995.
Wirth, Jason. *Schelling's Practice of the Wild: Time, Art, Imagination*. Albany: SUNY Press, 2015.
Wood, Allen. *Fichte's Ethical Thought*. Oxford: Oxford University Press, 2016.
Wuttke, Walter. 'Materialien zu Leben und Werk Adolph Karl August von Eschenmayers'. *Sudhoffs Archiv* 56.3 (1972): 255–96.
Zammito, John H. *The Gestation of German Biology: Philosophy and Physiology from Stahl to Schelling*. Chicago: University of Chicago Press, 2018.
Zeltner, Hermann. 'Das Identitätssystem'. In Hans Michael Baumgartner (ed.), *Schelling: Einführung in seine Philosophie*. Freiburg: Alber, 1975. 75–94.
Ziche, Paul. *Mathematische und naturwissenschaftliche Modelle in der Philosophie Schellings und Hegels*. Stuttgart: Frommann-Holzboog, 1996.
Ziche, Paul. 'Die "eine Wissenschaft der Philosophie" und die "verschiedene philosophischen Wissenschaften": Wissenschafts-systematik und die Darstellung des Absoluten'. In K. Viewig (ed.), *Gegen das 'unphilosophische Unwesen': Der Kritische Journal von Schellung und Hegel*. Würzburg: Neumann, 2002. 75–94.
Zimmerli, W. C. 'Schelling in Hegel'. In Ludwig Hasler (ed.), *Schelling: Seine Bedeutung für eine Philosophie der Natur und der Geschichte*. Stuttgart: Frommann-Holzboog, 1981. 255–78.
Zimmerli, W. C. 'Potenzlehre versus Logik der Naturphilosophie'. In R. P. Horstmann and M. J. Petry (eds), *Hegels Philosophie der Natur: Beziehungen zwischen empirischer und spekulativer Naturerkenntnis*. Stuttgart: Klett, 1986. 309–29.
Zöller, Günter. *Fichte's Transcendental Philosophy: The Original Duplicity of Intelligence and Will*. Cambridge: Cambridge University Press, 1998.

Index

actant, xiii, 26–30, 55, 80–4, 89, 106, 118, 221–2
algebraic notation, 5, 95, 97, 104, 106–9, 111, 113–15, 238–9n
Aristotle, 13, 104–8, 116, 237–8n
attraction, 3, 5, 26–7, 31, 41, 43, 67–9, 71–3, 75–80, 82–4, 90, 92–4, 97–100, 103–4, 118, 147, 199–203, 222, 233n, 256–8n
attractive force *see* attraction

Baader, Franz, 10, 18, 27–8, 41–3, 60, 78, 80, 235n
Blumenbach, J. F., 146, 154, 158, 248n
Brown, John, 2, 97, 254n, 256n

chemical process *see* chemistry
chemistry, xiii–xiv, 3–4, 13, 30, 32, 40, 58, 60–1, 69–72, 74–7, 80, 86–7, 97, 99–103, 105, 108–9, 199, 201, 205, 215, 222–4, 232–3n, 236n, 247n, 254–5n, 257n

Deleuze, Gilles, 179, 244–5n, 253–4n
depotentiation, 14, 49, 97, 173–4, 176, 178, 180–1, 183, 240n, 253n
Descartes, René, 95, 107–8, 116, 154, 181, 237–8n
duplication, 99, 103, 107, 109, 115–16, 124, 132–3, 243n

electrical charge *see* electricity
electricity, 3, 5, 13, 20, 43, 58, 60–1, 74, 95, 97, 99–103, 105, 108–9, 190, 200, 220, 222–4

empiricism, 18, 20, 25, 29, 41, 47, 57, 81, 158, 160–1, 180, 189, 191, 220, 249n
epochē, 169, 253n
Euclid, 106–7
Euler, Leonhard, 33, 95, 231n

Fichte, J. G., 2–4, 11, 13, 78, 116–17, 120–1, 123–31, 134, 136–8, 143–5, 151–5, 158, 166–83, 191–3, 207–8, 211, 216, 228n, 241–2n, 244–7n, 251n, 253n, 255–6n
formalism, 13, 107, 109–12, 114–15
formative drive, 20, 97, 102, 145–6, 149, 154, 157–8, 247–8n

geometric series, 27–8, 34–7, 59, 73, 87–8, 91, 203
Goethe, J. W., 2, 10, 95–6, 105, 176, 192, 226n, 244n, 252n
gravity, 27, 39, 41–3, 68, 78, 80, 92, 98–9, 103, 105, 200, 222, 235n, 236n

Hegel, G. W. F., 13, 66, 96, 104, 110–17, 120–4, 126–8, 136, 138, 162–7, 169–71, 182, 225, 239n, 241n, 242n, 250n
Hindenburg, C. F., 94–6, 104, 108
Hufeland, C. W., 192, 197, 255–6n

intuition, 22–4, 29, 47, 50, 51, 54, 72, 75, 126, 150, 200, 202, 203, 214, 218, 220, 224
  intellectual, 51, 53, 57, 162–3, 172, 176–8, 215

irritability, 20, 97, 102, 109, 157, 222–3

Jacobi, F. H., 136

Kant, Immanuel, 2–4, 10, 13, 30, 47, 60, 66–82, 86, 92, 117, 119–20, 134, 165–7, 171, 207, 215–17, 231n, 237n, 248n
Kielmeyer, C. F., 2–3, 10, 44, 70, 105, 226n, 232n, 237n

Leibniz, G. W., 82, 95, 105, 116, 238n

magnetic line, 74, 92–3, 113, 119, 130, 137, 235–6n
magnetic polarity *see* magnetism
magnetism, 3, 13, 20, 60–1, 74, 90, 92–3, 95, 97, 99–103, 105, 108, 190, 200, 220, 223–4, 236–7, 254–5, 257
monism, 90, 93, 103, 108–9, 130, 133, 136, 141

negation, 19, 60, 68, 101, 112, 115, 120, 122, 129–30, 132, 136, 138, 148, 169–70, 181, 195, 202–3, 218, 227n, 253n, 258n
negativity, 111, 116, 169
Newton, Isaac, 33, 67, 69, 231n, 237n
Nietzsche, Friedrich, 179, 254n
Novalis, 2, 78, 95, 110, 116, 232n, 236n

ontological argument, 133–5
organism, 3–4, 24–5, 29, 31–2, 60, 101–2, 109, 140, 143–6, 149–51, 153–4, 157–8

Plato, 48, 106, 116, 179, 182, 232n, 238n
potency 0 *see* zero potency
proper science, 69, 88

rationalism, 18, 25, 29, 57, 158–61, 249n
realism, 9, 47, 50, 52, 54, 60, 155, 159, 216–17
reflection, 20–1, 32, 49, 55, 60, 96, 121, 134, 147–50, 207, 208–13, 218, 224, 258n
Reinhold, K. L., 5, 120, 253n
repulsion, 3, 5, 26, 31, 41, 43, 67–9, 71–3, 75–80, 82–4, 90, 92–5, 97–100, 103, 117–18, 147, 199–203, 222, 233
repulsive force *see* repulsion
Röschlaub, Andreas, 19, 188–90, 192, 254n, 256n

sensation, 22–4, 29, 32–3, 36–7, 51, 54, 58–9, 76, 83, 85–8, 90, 150, 173, 201, 214, 220, 230n
sensibility, 20, 97, 102, 157, 223, 237n
Spinoza, Benedict, 53, 116, 133–4, 136, 164, 176, 182, 238–9n, 244–5n, 247n
Swedenborg, Emanuel, 181

World Soul, 18, 20, 25, 41, 43, 83, 150–4, 157, 219–20

zero potency, 51, 73–4, 90, 93, 138, 174, 178, 202

EU representative:
Easy Access System Europe
Mustamäe tee 50, 10621 Tallinn, Estonia
Gpsr.requests@easproject.com

www.ingramcontent.com/pod-product-compliance
Lightning Source LLC
Chambersburg PA
CBHW050212240426
43671CB00013B/2302